# Human Factors in Cybersecurity

A field-tested framework for designing resilient, human-centered cybersecurity systems

**Nikki Robinson, DSc, PhD**
**Calvin Nobles, PhD**

<packt>

# Human Factors in Cybersecurity



**Portfolio Director:** Vijin Boricha
**Relationship Lead:** Rahul Nair
**Project Manager:** Gandhali Raut
**Content Engineer:** Akanksha Gupta
**Technical Editor:** Nithik Cheruvakodan
**Copy Editor:** Safis Editing
**Indexer:** Pratik Shirodkar
**Proofreader:** Akanksha Gupta
**Production Designer:** Jyoti Kadam
**Growth Lead**: Ankita Thakur
First published: March 2026
Production reference: 1250326
Published by Packt Publishing Ltd.
Grosvenor House
11 St Paul's Square
Birmingham
B3 1RB, UK.
ISBN 978-1-80611-833-5
www.packtpub.com

# Foreword

*That sounds like a Layer 8 issue.*

If you've spent any meaningful time in cybersecurity, you've heard some version of this OSI model joke. I've been hearing it for over two decades. It's the knowing laugh shared between engineers when an incident, mistake, or malfunction traces back not to a misconfigured firewall or an unpatched vulnerability, but to a person, a click, a shortcut, or a moment of fatigue. The punchline has always been the same: the human is the problem.

In the beginning, I laughed along. But somewhere in those two decades, the joke stopped being funny, not because it wasn't true, but because it perpetuated a culture that was not conducive to security.

In 2019, I started a podcast with a close friend called Hacker Valley Studio. What most people don't know is that we almost called it *Layer 8*. We chose that working title because we recognized something that this industry has been slow to fully embrace: while uninformed human action is one of the greatest vulnerabilities in any security program, human beings are also the greatest asset. The people behind the keyboards, the analysts triaging alerts at 3 a.m., the security leaders making impossible decisions with imperfect information, they aren't weaknesses or a joke. They *are* the answer to our plight.

That conviction is exactly why this book matters so deeply to me.

*Nikki Robinson* is one of those rare leaders in cybersecurity who communicates not through hype or headline, but through her work and her sustained contribution to this community. She doesn't seek the spotlight; she builds the stage that others stand on. Alongside her co-author *Calvin Nobles*, she has produced something that goes far beyond the usual cybersecurity awareness literature, the well-meaning but ultimately squishy books that tell us to *foster a security culture* without ever showing us how.

What Nikki and Calvin have done here is different. This is a true methodology. A rigorous, field-tested framework for understanding how human beings actually think, decide, and fail under pressure, and for designing systems that work *with* that reality instead of against it. They draw from Human Factors Engineering, a discipline born in the crucible of aviation safety during World War II, and they apply it to cybersecurity with the kind of precision and operational empathy that only comes from people who have lived this work. That surely speaks to the Marine Veteran in me. The *3 U's* framework—*User, Usage, Usability*—is deceptively simple and profoundly actionable. The adaptation of the HFACS model to cyber incidents reframes how we investigate failures, pushing us past the lazy conclusion of *user error* and into the systemic conditions that made the error inevitable. The honest examination of SOC analyst burnout, cognitive overload, and alert fatigue is a mirror held up to every security operations center in the world.

I am an optimistic person by nature. Anyone who knows me will tell you that. But there is one soapbox I stand on that carries a warning tone, and I will not step down from it: we are in the calm before the storm.

We are standing at the dawn of autonomous attacks. Artificial intelligence has become a tool that scales human innovation and motivation in extraordinary ways, but it scales attacks in kind. The adversary no longer needs a team of skilled operators to find and exploit your weaknesses. They need an agent. And soon, they will have countless agents probing for targets of opportunity at a speed and scale that no purely technical defense can match.

This is the reality we are walking into. And it demands that we not only get our own houses in order and strengthen the foundations of our cybersecurity programs, but that we learn to leverage AI in that fight. Most importantly, and this is the part I need you to hear, we *must* learn to leverage human nature itself. Our intuition. Our creativity. Our ability to adapt, to collaborate, to recognize when something simply doesn't feel right. They are capabilities to be cultivated and championed.

That is what this book teaches you to do.

The best part is that it could not arrive at a more critical moment. As the threat landscape accelerates beyond what any single tool or platform can contain, the organizations that will endure are the ones that understand a fundamental truth: resilience is not about surviving a threat. It is about designing systems, cultures, and teams where people can think clearly, act decisively, and recover stronger than before. Nikki and Calvin don't just argue this point and send you off to figure out a way forward, they hand you the blueprint to use today.

If you are a CISO trying to make the case for investing in your people as seriously as you invest in your tools, this book is your evidence. If you are a SOC leader watching your analysts burn out under a flood of false positives, this book is your intervention plan. If you are an architect designing the next generation of security systems, this book will change how you think about every interface, every alert, and every workflow you build.

This is the book we need right now. I'm grateful Nikki and Calvin wrote it, and I'm honored to welcome you into its pages.

Read it. Apply it. Share it. The storm is coming, and our people are how we weather it.

**Chris Cochran, Field CISO and VP of AI Security, SANS Institute.**

# Contributors

## About the authors

**Nikki Robinson** is a Senior Technical Staff Member, an Adjunct Professor, inventor and frequent speaker in the Cybersecurity space. She holds a DSc in Cybersecurity and a PhD in Human Factors. She is an award-winning, best-selling author of two previous titles, *Mind the Tech Gap* and *Effective Vulnerability Management*. She has over 18 years' experience across IT and cybersecurity operations, holding multiple industry certifications.

*I could not be more grateful for the opportunity to write this book; a culmination of my experience and research career all living in one book. First and always, to my daughters, who have cheered me on every step of the way, thank you. I am so proud of you both and honored to be your mother. Remember, anything is possible with hard work. Now go brush your teeth!*

*To my co-author, Calvin, thank you for your time, collaborative spirit, and brilliant insights. This book would not have been possible without you. When are we getting lunch?*

*To the brilliant team at Packt, thank you for your support, professionalism, and guidance along this journey. Major thank you to Rahul for reaching out to me, here's to many more fruitful collaborations. We did it!*

**Dr. Calvin Nobles**, a native of Mount Vernon, Georgia, is the Portfolio Vice President and Dean of the School of Cybersecurity and Information Technology at the University of Maryland Global Campus (UMGC). Dr. Nobles holds four doctoral degrees; a Ph.D. in Management and Engineering Technology, a Ph.D. in Human Factors, a Ph.D. in Offensive Cyber Engineering, and Doctor of Business Administration. With more than three decades of distinguished leadership spanning cybersecurity, the financial sector, academia, and military service, Dr. Nobles is widely regarded as a visionary leader dedicated to advancing STEM education through experiential learning. A retired U.S. Navy Commander, he has served as a Cybersecurity Policy Fellow at Harvard University and a Cybersecurity Fellow at the New America Think Tank in Washington, D.C. and is recognized as one of the nation's leading researchers in human factors engineering for cybersecurity.

*This book represents the culmination of sustained reflection, research, and commitment, and I am deeply grateful for the opportunity to write on human factors in cybersecurity, a topic I have championed for more than a decade. Writing a book is never a solitary endeavor, and this work has been shaped by the encouragement, insight, generosity, and unwavering support of many people along the way. I am profoundly thankful for my village, whose love, uplift, and belief in me sustained this journey in meaningful ways. I am especially indebted to my family for their enduring love, patience, encouragement, and steadfast confidence in me throughout the writing process. Their support provided both the foundation and the motivation to continue this work across many demanding seasons. Above all, I give thanks to God for the strength, wisdom, grace, and perseverance to bring this project to completion.*

I also extend my sincere appreciation to my colleagues, mentors, friends, and professional peers whose insights, feedback, and scholarly engagement helped sharpen the ideas presented in this volume. Their willingness to challenge my thinking and offer thoughtful perspectives significantly strengthened the quality of this work. I am equally grateful to the students, practitioners, and leaders whose experiences continue to inform my understanding of the field and reinforce the importance of this scholarship. Finally, I offer special thanks to Dr. Nikki Robinson, as well as the publisher and editorial team, for their guidance, professionalism, encouragement, and commitment to bringing this project to fruition.

# About the reviewer

**Josiah Dykstra**, Ph.D., is a cybersecurity researcher, consultant, and author with more than 20 years of experience in cybersecurity, human factors, and applied research. He is the owner of Designer Security and serves as a Principal Cyber/AI Research Portfolio Lead at a leading advanced research and development organization. Previously, he spent 19 years at the National Security Agency and held a strategy role at Trail of Bits. Dr. Dykstra holds a Ph.D. in computer science from UMBC, has authored more than 50 peer-reviewed papers and three books, and has been recognized with the Presidential Early Career Award for Scientists and Engineers (PECASE).

# Table of Contents

## Chapter 8: Cyberpsychology in Cybersecurity 177

# Preface

Cybersecurity is not only a technical problem; it is a human one.

Every alert that appears in a security operations center must be interpreted by a person. Even with AI coming to the forefront to analyze and summarize alerts, a human must remain in the loop for cybersecurity alerts and incidents. Missing something could spell disaster for any organization. Every vulnerability must be prioritized by someone making a judgment call. Every incident response requires teams of humans communicating under pressure. Security tools may generate the signals, but people make the decisions. When those systems are poorly designed for human use, the results are predictable: overload, missed signals, cognitive bias, fatigue, and ultimately failure.

For decades, industries such as aviation, healthcare, nuclear power, and industrial safety have studied how people interact with complex systems. They have learned that performance is not simply about individual skill or effort. Instead, it is shaped by environment, workflow, interface design, cognitive limits, organizational culture, and decision-making under uncertainty. When systems are designed with human capabilities and limitations in mind, safety and performance improve dramatically.

Cybersecurity is only just beginning to fully adopt these lessons.

In many organizations, analysts are expected to process thousands of alerts per day while navigating multiple tools with inconsistent interfaces. Detection engineers must translate threat intelligence into meaningful detections while balancing false positives and operational cost. Vulnerability management teams face overwhelming volumes of findings without clear prioritization frameworks. Incident responders must coordinate across teams in high-stress situations where time and clarity are critical.

These are not purely technical challenges. They are human factors challenges.

This book explores how principles from human factors engineering can be applied to cybersecurity operations. Rather than focusing solely on technology, it examines the interaction between people, tools, processes, and the technical solutions they rely on to perform their job functions. It looks at how cognitive load affects analysts, how interface design influences decision-making, how bias shapes investigation outcomes, and how motivation and organizational culture influence security performance.

## Who this book is for

This book is written for cybersecurity professionals who work at the intersection of technology and human decision-making. It is intended for security operations analysts, detection engineers, incident responders, vulnerability management teams, security leaders, and anyone responsible for designing or operating cybersecurity programs. It will also be valuable to researchers, human factors practitioners, and technology leaders interested in understanding how cognitive science, behavioral insights, and system design influence cybersecurity outcomes.

## What this book covers

*Chapter 1, The Human Element and Cybersecurity*, explores the historical, conceptual, and practical aspects of human factors engineering (HFE) in cybersecurity.

*Chapter 2, Current Challenges in Cybersecurity*, focuses on the current challenges for cyber professionals, including modern technology and complexities, security fatigue, mental workloads, and the technological impact on burnout.

*Chapter 3, Rethinking Incident Response through the lens of Human Factors*, covers the basics of incident response from a human factors perspective, not focusing solely on the tools and techniques that an IR analyst may use.

*Chapter 4, Human Factors in Security Operations*, covers modern challenges that any Security Operations or SOC team may face, including overloaded dashboards, complex tooling, and alert fatigue.

*Chapter 5, Human Factors in Vulnerability Management*, explains how adding human factors in vulnerability management will lead to better remediation practices, faster time to remediation, ultimately focusing on the vulnerabilities that matter, and reducing the extra noise.

*Chapter 6, Human Factors Engineering-as-a-Service*, explains how Human Factors Engineering as a Service can help organizations reduce risk more effectively by intentionally designing security systems to align with real human capabilities and limitations.

*Chapter 7, Addressing Stress, Fatigue, and Burnout in Cybersecurity*, covers the pathway to burnout, cybersecurity environments and unique stressors, theoretical frameworks, and burnout mitigation strategies.

*Chapter 8, Cyberpsychology in Cybersecurity*, studies the relationship between human behavior, cognition, and digital settings, which have become known as cyberpsychology.

*Chapter 9, Benefits of Human Factors Analysis and Classification System in Cybersecurity*, provides a comprehensive framework review for applying HFACS to cybersecurity operations, including its definition, scope, origin, and theoretical foundations.

*Chapter 10, Identification and Technology Strategies of Human Factors in Cybersecurity*, explains to cybersecurity leaders and practitioners how to identify human factors in cybersecurity, integrate technology strategies for HFE, and provide a strategic roadmap for HFE.

*Chapter 11, Implementation Path for Human Factors in Cybersecurity*, bridges theory and execution by transforming the psychological, cultural, and technical principles discussed throughout the book into a structured roadmap for cybersecurity leaders, managers, and practitioners.

# To get the most out of this book

The concepts discussed in this book are most valuable when they are applied to real operational environments. As you read, consider how each idea relates to the systems, workflows, and teams within your own organization.

Throughout cybersecurity operations, individuals are constantly making decisions under pressure. Alerts must be triaged quickly, vulnerabilities must be prioritized, and incidents must be investigated with incomplete information. The goal of this book is to help you better understand how human cognition, system design, and organizational structures influence those decisions.

As you move through the chapters, reflect on questions such as the following:

- Where do analysts in your environment experience overload?
- Which tools create friction instead of clarity?
- Where might cognitive bias influence investigation outcomes?
- Which processes depend on heroic effort rather than well-designed systems?

Readers in different roles may find certain chapters particularly relevant to their work.

- Security operations analysts may focus on topics such as alert fatigue, attention management, and decision-making under uncertainty.
- Detection engineers may benefit from discussions around alert design, signal clarity, and automation.
- Vulnerability management teams may find value in chapters related to prioritization, motivation, and reducing decision bias.
- Security leaders and program architects may use the material to rethink how systems, workflows, and incentives are designed across their organizations.

Many of the ideas in this book are best explored collaboratively. Consider discussing these concepts with your team, using them to evaluate existing processes, or identifying opportunities to experiment with small improvements. Human factors improvements do not always require large technological investments; often, they begin with a better understanding of how people interact with the systems we build.

## Download the color images

We also provide a PDF file that has color images of the screenshots and diagrams used in this book. You can download it here:`https://packt.link/gbp/9781806118335`.

## Conventions used

There are a number of text conventions used throughout this book.

**Bold**: Indicates a new term, an important word, or words that you see on the screen. For instance, words in menus or dialog boxes appear in the text like this. For example: **Incident Response (IR)** is the area within cybersecurity where IR analysts respond to potential security threats or act in real time to a cyberattack.

> **Note**
>
> Warnings or important notes appear like this

> **Tip**
>
> Tips and tricks appear like this

# Get in touch

Feedback from our readers is always welcome.

**General feedback**: If you have questions about any aspect of this book or have any general feedback, please email us at `customercare@packt.com` and mention the book's title in the subject of your message.

**Errata**: Although we have taken every care to ensure the accuracy of our content, mistakes do happen. If you have found a mistake in this book, we would be grateful if you reported it to us. Please visit `http://www.packt.com/submit-errata`, click **Submit Errata**, and fill in the form.

**Piracy**: If you come across any illegal copies of our works in any form on the internet, we would be grateful if you would provide us with the location address or website name. Please contact us at `copyright@packt.com` with a link to the material.

**If you are interested in becoming an author**: If there is a topic that you have expertise in and you are interested in either writing or contributing to a book, please visit `http://authors.packt.com/`.

# Free benefits with your book

This book comes with free benefits to support your learning. Activate them now for instant access (see the "*How to Unlock*" section for instructions).

Here's a quick overview of what you can instantly unlock with your purchase:

**DRM-Free PDF Version**

Download DRM-free PDF and ePub copies of this book.

**7-Day Packt Library Access**

Get 7-day unlimited access to 8,000+ books and videos. No credit card required.

Available for first-time Packt+ trial users only.

**Next-Gen Reader Access**

Read this book on Packt Reader with progress sync, dark mode and note-taking.

## How to Unlock

Scan the QR code (or go to `packtpub.com/unlock`). Search for this book by name, confirm the edition, and then follow the steps on the page.

UNLOCK NOW

*Note: Keep your invoice handy. Purchases made directly from Packt don't require one*

## Share your thoughts

Once you've read *Human Factors in Cybersecurity*, we'd love to hear your thoughts! Scan the QR code below to go straight to the Amazon review page for this book and share your feedback.

*https://packt.link/r/1806118335*

Your review is important to us and the tech community and will help us make sure we're delivering excellent quality content.

# 1

# The Human Element and Cybersecurity

Cybersecurity fails not because technology is weak but because people make mistakes. One click on a phishing email, one reused password, or one ignored warning can open the door to catastrophic breaches. Malicious threat actors know this, and they exploit it relentlessly. The truth is clear: human behavior is the greatest vulnerability in any security system. Ignoring human factors is like locking every door while leaving the windows wide open. The solution is not more complexity; it is smarter design. By understanding how people think and act, we can create security that feels natural, training that sticks, and policies that people actually follow. Organizations that invest in human factors do more than reduce risk. They build a culture where every employee becomes a defender, not a liability. In today's threat landscape, technology alone cannot win. The strongest cybersecurity strategy is one that turns human weakness into human strength. The real question is not whether you can afford to do this but whether you can afford the cost of not doing it.

Despite decades of technical advancement, the most persistent vulnerability in cybersecurity is not technological; it is human. The 2025 Verizon Data Breach Investigations Report found that nearly 60% of security breaches stem from human error, a figure that has remained consistent over the years (Verizon, 2025). Further reinforcing this trend, Proofpoint's 2024 Voice of the CISO reported that 74% of **Chief Information Security Officers** (**CISOs**) identified human error as the most pressing cybersecurity risk, up from 60% in 2023 and 56% in 2022. A report by Proofpoint (2024) highlights that 80% of CISOs highlighted broader human challenges and friction, including negligence, distraction, and unintentional actions, as among the most significant threats to organizational security over the next two years.

One of the most consequential cybersecurity risks to organizations is human error. **Human factors engineering** (**HFE**) offers a scientific and disciplined means to mitigate a substantial portion of this risk by designing socio-technical systems that explicitly account for human limitations and predictable vulnerabilities in perception, attention, memory, and decision-making. Rather than presuming perfect vigilance, flawless recall, or consistent policy compliance, HFE aligns security technologies, interfaces, and workflows with how people actually process information, allocate attention, make judgments under uncertainty, and execute tasks under time pressure, interruptions, and cognitive load.

When security controls are engineered to reduce unnecessary complexity, clarify cues and feedback, and fit user roles and contexts, the probability of common failures decreases, including misconfigurations, unsafe workarounds, and inadvertent disclosure. In this framing, human error is not treated primarily as an individual shortcoming to be corrected through admonition or training. Human errors are indirectly targeted and reduced through intentional design choices that anticipate normal performance variability and build resilience into the system. For example, confirmation prompts and "undo" functionality for destructive actions (such as deleting a document or revoking access) introduce a deliberate pause and recovery pathway, thereby preventing a routine slip from becoming an irreversible error.

Securing the human element in cybersecurity is a complex challenge, and progress is frequently impeded by nonscientific approaches and superficial solutions that mask the true science of HFE. This includes slogans and blame narratives, one-size-fits-all awareness campaigns, compliance checklists disconnected from daily work, and security controls that add friction without improving usability. Science and evidence-based methodologies must remain at the forefront because they translate into practical, testable mitigations grounded in how people actually work, decide, and perform under real constraints. Advancing human-centered cybersecurity through HFE, therefore, depends on reducing reliance on these surface-level interventions and collaborating on solutions that fit real roles, real workflows, and real decision-making contexts. In this effort, human factors engineers and human systems engineers, working in concert with psychologists, cognitive scientists, neuroscientists, and behavioral scientists, are essential to shaping and designing cybersecurity systems that anticipate human limitations, reduce unnecessary burden, and enable secure behavior by design.

This chapter explores the historical, conceptual, and practical aspects of HFE in cybersecurity. In this chapter, *human factors* refers to the scientific study of how people perceive, decide, and perform within socio-technical systems, while HFE is the applied engineering discipline that translates that science into requirements, designs, and evaluations that shape safer and more effective human-system interaction. **Human-centered design (HCD)** is a complementary approach that applies these insights through iterative, user-informed design and testing so that technologies and workflows align with actual user needs, contexts, and constraints. Drawing on psychology, cognitive science, and systems engineering, HFE provides a rigorous, evidence-based methodology for understanding and strengthening human-system interaction. HCD supplies a practical process for implementing those findings in usable, resilient solutions. By reframing the human element from a liability into a design opportunity, cybersecurity can evolve toward more usable, resilient, and adaptive systems. This chapter introduces the human element in cybersecurity, defines key concepts, and presents practical principles; it then applies lessons from aviation, articulates the strategic value of HFE, advances the rationale for human-centered cybersecurity, addresses the role of organizational culture, and concludes with exploring how human factors engineering can be integrated into organizational culture through example scenarios. This is aimed at enhancing cybersecurity resilience through HFE-informed HCD.

In this chapter, you will learn about the following topics:

- Understanding the human element in cybersecurity
- Exploring the historical origins of human factors engineering
- Defining human factors in cybersecurity
- Applying human factors lessons from aviation to cybersecurity
- Using human factors to achieve human-centered cybersecurity
- Integrating organizational culture with human factors engineering
- Synthesizing HFE as a strategy for cybersecurity resilience

> Note
>
> **Your purchase includes a free PDF copy + exclusive extras**
>
> Your purchase includes a DRM-free PDF copy of this book, 7-day trial to the Packt+ library (no credit card required), and additional exclusive extras. See the *Free benefits with your book* section in the *Preface* to unlock them instantly and maximize your learning.

# Understanding the human element in cybersecurity

Cybersecurity breaches are not just technical failures; they are human ones. Sophisticated malware and zero-day exploits may make headlines, but many successful attacks still hinge on exploiting predictable user behavior. Social engineering, phishing, and capitalizing on poor security hygiene remain among the most frequently used methods of exploiting weaknesses. As long as organizations continue to pursue technological solutions with little regard for the human element, these practices will yield the same ineffective results. For example, an employee who is rushing between meetings may approve a multifactor authentication prompt without noticing that it was triggered by an attacker, or a staff member may bypass a secure file-sharing process because it is slower than emailing an attachment. Social engineering remains especially effective when an email appears to come from a senior leader requesting an urgent wire transfer, or when a convincing "IT support" message pressures a user to reset a password through a counterfeit portal. Even routine security hygiene failures often emerge from design and workflow friction, such as complex password rules that encourage reuse, or unclear access request processes that lead teams to share accounts "temporarily" and never revisit the risk. As long as organizations continue to deploy technological controls without accounting for the human element, these same patterns will persist, and security investments will continue to yield inconsistent, avoidable outcomes.

Numerous studies support this reality. The *Chartered Institute of Ergonomics and Human Factors (2022)* concluded that nearly 90% of breaches are attributable to human error. These findings underscore the need for a shift in cybersecurity strategy, from fortifying technological perimeters to designing systems that drive the human behavior and performance that organizations need. A key element is designing for the desired human behavior and performance, which reduces organizational risk. Other socio-technical fields, such as aviation, healthcare, nuclear power, and space operations, demonstrate that designing and accounting for human weaknesses and limitations leads to optimal performance and lower risk.

Adversaries increasingly exploit predictable psychological triggers, including urgency, fear, curiosity, authority, and social obligation, because these cues reliably compress deliberation and increase the likelihood of rapid, unverified action. In practice, attacks are often engineered to create a narrow decision window: a "payment overdue" notice designed to provoke anxiety, a "security alert" intended to trigger immediate compliance, or an "executive request" crafted to leverage hierarchy and perceived accountability. Under these conditions, the user is not simply making a choice; they are making a choice while distracted, time-constrained, and cognitively loaded. This is why the user interface becomes a frontline control surface. The interface is where critical decisions are made, including whether to trust an email, approve a multifactor authentication prompt, download an attachment, grant application permissions, or share access to a file. If those interactions are ambiguous, noisy, or poorly timed, the system effectively transfers risk to the user at the precise moment when adversaries are attempting to manipulate attention and decision-making.

Adversaries increasingly target psychological triggers, such as urgency, fear, or curiosity, to gain access to secure systems. In this context, the user interface becomes the new frontline. Without integrated HFE, even the most advanced cybersecurity tools can become operationally fragile because poor usability, excessive friction, unclear cues, and unmanageable alert volume lead to predictable behaviors such as habituation, workarounds, and erroneous confirmations (Ncubukezi, 2022). For example, frequent noncritical warnings condition users to click through prompts without reading them, and complex access procedures can incentivize shortcuts such as password sharing or the use of unsanctioned tools to complete work. HFE addresses these failure modes by aligning security controls with real workflows, reducing cognitive burden at decision points, designing warnings and confirmations that are specific and actionable, and ensuring that secure choices are the easiest choices to execute correctly.

# Exploring the historical origins of human factors engineering

HFE emerged as a formal discipline during World War II in response to unacceptable rates of aviation accidents. Seminal work by Fitts and Jones (1947) demonstrated that many "pilot error" events were better explained as design-induced failures: cockpit layouts, controls, and displays that conflicted with human perceptual limits, attention constraints, and decision-making demands. That evidence catalyzed a durable shift in safety-critical domains away from a deficit model of "fixing the human" and toward a systems model of "fixing the system." As the field matured across cognitive psychology, ergonomics, physiology, and systems engineering, HFE established a practical premise: predictable human limitations are not aberrations to be trained away but design constraints to be engineered around (Chapanis, 1999 Rogers & McGlynn, 2018).

This history matters for cybersecurity because modern security failures mirror the same attribution error that aviation learned to correct. Cyber incidents are frequently described as "user mistakes" (clicking a link, reusing a password, or approving a prompt), and many organizational responses still prioritize admonition, awareness campaigns, and compliance policing. The aviation lesson is that persistent "human error" signals a design problem in the broader system, not merely a training gap in the operator. In cybersecurity, the equivalents of poorly designed cockpits include ambiguous authentication prompts, overly complex access workflows, noisy alerts in security operations centers, confusing administrative consoles, and policies that conflict with how work is actually executed.

Early HFE research provides direct guidance for human-centered cybersecurity design and decision-making today: conduct task and workflow analysis before adding controls; minimize cognitive load at decision points; design warnings and confirmations to be specific, timely, and actionable; build forcing functions and recovery pathways (for example, phishing-resistant authentication, contextual MFA, and reversible destructive actions); evaluate controls in realistic simulations that replicate time pressure, interruptions, and competing priorities. Framed in this way, the historical overview is not a standalone narrative. It establishes the chapter's central argument that cybersecurity resilience increases when security is treated as a socio-technical systems problem and engineered to be robust to normal human performance variability rather than dependent on idealized human behavior.

Unfortunately, in cybersecurity, HFE has not yet been recognized as a distinct engineering discipline. The constant, repeated episodes of human behavior as a central causal factor in cybersecurity incidents are telling. Many organizations are building enormous cybersecurity ecosystems with little regard for human vulnerabilities and limitations.

# Defining human factors in cybersecurity

Human factors, also known as ergonomics, is the scientific discipline that examines the interactions between people and other elements within a system. Its purpose is to use evidence from research and real-world observation to shape design decisions so that systems fit human capabilities and limitations, rather than forcing people to adapt to poorly designed processes. In practice, human factors reduce avoidable complexity, anticipate predictable mistakes, and support dependable performance when people are under time pressure, interrupted, or managing high workloads. By systematically analyzing and evaluating how work is actually done, human factors strengthen safety, protection, and comfort while also enhancing system outcomes such as efficiency, effectiveness, and operational resilience.

Cybersecurity professionals are often expected to design systems that work for people, but many have never been formally introduced to the science that helps achieve this goal. There is a widespread misunderstanding of what "human factors" really means. In both industry and academic circles, the term is frequently lumped in with general user behavior, missing its true identity as a well-established scientific discipline focused on optimizing how humans interact with systems.

A recent review of over 100 academic articles that use the term "human factors" in their titles found that fewer than 10% defined it in line with widely accepted standards (Nobles & Burrell, 2024). This inconsistency creates more than a scholarly oversight. It produces practical confusion with real consequences. When the field does not clearly define human factors as a scientific discipline and professional practice grounded in evidence-based methods, organizations are more likely to reduce it to generic "user behavior" or to awareness training, making it far harder to incorporate human factors into cybersecurity strategy in a rigorous and effective manner.

Understanding human factors in the right light means seeing it as a design-driven approach. It is about shaping systems that support how people think, behave, and make decisions, particularly in high-pressure environments such as cybersecurity. Instead of focusing on fixing user errors after the fact, HFE is about designing technology that reduces the likelihood of those errors in the first place. It is a shift from a reactive to a proactive approach, and from blaming the user to building more innovative and resilient systems that help account for human limitations and weaknesses.

Think of a cybersecurity plan that not only addresses problems when they occur but also anticipates them and designs systems that work in harmony with people, rather than against them. Integrating human factors into cybersecurity represents a paradigm shift in fundamental beliefs, realigning the human element as the central aspect in cybersecurity. It demonstrates a shift in attitude, moving away from blaming users and intentionally designing for the behaviors and performance desired.

Cybersecurity has long focused on what individuals do wrong, such as clicking on suspicious links, disobeying rules, and making poor choices under stress. That point of view is not entirely erroneous, but it is incomplete and often misleading. Organizations significantly influence individual behavior; thus, inadequate consideration of both unintentional and deliberate actions imposes responsibility on the organization itself. It presents a limited view of human behavior as a problem rather than a benefit. The real opportunity lies in understanding how people use systems and then optimizing those systems to work better for them by accounting for people's strengths and weaknesses.

This is where the field of HFE comes into play. This field is not just about making fewer mistakes; it is about getting the best results. It asks, "*How can we make technology and settings that help people do well, even when things are stressful and dangerous?*" When used in cybersecurity, the results could be powerful and innovative, transforming traditional cybersecurity practices and defense mechanisms.

Why not create security solutions that are easy to use, responsive, and help people make informed decisions, rather than requiring repeated education to navigate complicated, inflexible systems? Why not address the core causes of those behaviors—overload, misunderstanding, and burnout—rather than punishing people who fail to follow the rules? Unfortunately, this proactive strategy has not gained widespread adoption in the cybersecurity community. One significant reason is that people often do not fully understand what "human factors" entail. In many companies, the term still refers to mistakes made by users or breaking the rules. That narrow description misses the field's bigger design-driven possibilities. It is like attempting to improve flying by simply examining what pilots do wrong, rather than considering how the cockpit is designed, how communication works, or how air traffic control operates.

There is also a lack of knowledge. Most cybersecurity teams lack knowledge of psychology, cognitive science, and ergonomics, all of which are essential components of human factors. Because of this, technical security solutions come first, and people come second. This imbalance creates instruments that are safe in theory but annoying in practice, which ultimately weakens the defenses they were intended to reinforce.

Organizations need a more precise and comprehensive understanding of human factors to address this issue. This new definition should focus on system design, human performance, and ensuring that people's behavior aligns with security goals. With that foundation, cybersecurity teams can utilize HCD to create systems that are not only safer but also easier to use, more intuitive, and more resilient.

This change extends beyond the classroom. The effects in the real world are tremendous. Systems that fail to account for how people think and work can lead to problems, including cognitive overload, security fatigue, poor automation utilization, and decision paralysis. Organizations can start to solve these problems with insight and purpose by viewing human factors as a solution space, rather than merely a list of problems.

Cybersecurity is not just a concern with technology. It is not easy to manage in a digitally and technologically advanced society. To fix it, you need more than firewalls and protocols. You need to understand how people work under pressure and have great respect for them. When businesses adopt this point of view, they do not merely lower risk. They create systems and cultures that are inherently safe.

## Identifying and utilizing human factors principles

This section outlines several human factors principles that provide a framework for designing systems that account for the human element and human performance. It is important to note that, in HFE, a system comprises a group of people, processes, procedures, tools, resources, and environments. In cybersecurity, the system could be the end-to-end security ecosystem that surrounds a business function, including the users who perform the work, the security policies and procedures they are expected to follow, the identity and access management tools they interact with, the devices and applications they use daily, the security operations workflows that monitor and respond to threats, the training and support resources available to them, and the organizational and physical environments in which all of these activities occur.

*Table 1.1* outlines essential principles applicable to cybersecurity. It does not encompass all possible human factors principles; however, it lists some critical factors. The human factors principles listed here are indicative of proven practices developed by other socio-technical domains:

| **Principle** | **Description** | **Reference** |
|---|---|---|
| **User-centered design** | Involve users throughout the design process to align systems with their needs and limitations | Norman (2013) |
| **Minimizing cognitive load** | Simplify tasks and organize information to reduce mental strain | Wickens et al. (2004) |
| **Consistency and predictability** | Ensure system behavior is intuitive and consistent | Wickens et al. (2004) |

| **Accessibility and inclusivity** | Design for diverse populations, including those with disabilities | Sanders & McCormick (1993) |
|---|---|---|
| **Error prevention and recovery** | Use intuitive controls and provide clear error recovery pathways | Shneiderman & Plaisant (2010) |
| **Simplicity and clarity** | Avoid unnecessary complexity in the interface and workflow | Norman (2013) |
| **Feedback** | Provide immediate, understandable responses to user actions | Sanders & McCormick (1993) |
| **Psychosocial considerations** | Account for job demands, autonomy, and well-being | Neumann et al. (2021) |

*Table 1.1: Human factors principles (Nobles, 2025)*

Again, these principles are not exhaustive but offer a foundation for integrating HFE into cybersecurity systems and policies. Let us look at them in some detail:

- **User-centered design**: User-centered design requires involving intended users throughout requirements definition, prototyping, testing, and iteration so that security controls fit real tasks, constraints, and decision points rather than idealized behavior (Norman, 2013). In cybersecurity, user-centered design means observing how employees authenticate, share files, handle exceptions, and respond to alerts, then shaping workflows so secure actions are natural, efficient, and sustainable. User-centered design also treats "workarounds" as diagnostic signals that the system is misaligned with the realities of work, and it uses that insight to redesign the control rather than blaming the user.
- **Minimizing cognitive load**: Minimizing cognitive load simplifies tasks and structures information so users can make accurate decisions under time pressure, interruptions, and competing demands (Wickens et al., 2004). In cybersecurity, minimizing cognitive load means reducing the number of steps to complete secure actions, presenting only the information needed at the moment of choice, and eliminating unnecessary mental translation, such as forcing users to interpret ambiguous warnings or memorize complex rules. Minimizing cognitive load also supports faster and more reliable incident response by prioritizing alerts with actionable context, which reduces fatigue-driven errors and missed signals.

- **Consistency and predictability**: Consistency and predictability ensure that system behavior, terminology, and interaction patterns remain stable across tools and situations so that users can form accurate mental models and execute actions with confidence (Wickens et al., 2004). In cybersecurity, consistency and predictability reduce errors that arise when different systems use different labels for the same concept, present the same risk with different visual cues, or require different steps for equivalent tasks. Consistency and predictability also enhance operational coordination in security teams by standardizing how alerts, severity ratings, and response actions are presented, thereby decreasing handoff friction and decision delay.
- **Accessibility and inclusivity**: Accessibility and inclusivity ensure that security technologies and workflows support diverse users, including those with disabilities and varying levels of experience, so that secure behavior is achievable for the entire workforce (Sanders & McCormick, 1993). In cybersecurity, accessibility and inclusivity require interfaces that work with assistive technologies, authentication experiences that do not rely on a single sensory modality, and communications that are readable and unambiguous. Accessibility and inclusivity reduce insecure workarounds that emerge when legitimate users cannot effectively use the approved security pathway, which strengthens both compliance and resilience.
- **Error prevention and recovery**: Error prevention and recovery anticipate predictable slips and mistakes and build safeguards and recovery pathways so that routine human error does not become irreversible harm (Shneiderman & Plaisant, 2010). In cybersecurity, error prevention and recovery include confirmations for destructive actions, context-rich prompts that reduce accidental approvals, and "undo" mechanisms such as reversible permission changes and rapid account recovery procedures. Error prevention and recovery also include designing workflows that make it difficult to commit high-impact errors silently, while making it straightforward to detect, correct, and learn from mistakes when they occur.
- **Simplicity and clarity**: Simplicity and clarity remove unnecessary complexity from interfaces and workflows so that users can understand what is happening, what action is required, and why it matters (Norman, 2013). In cybersecurity, simplicity and clarity mean plainly described security actions, streamlined access requests, and a visual hierarchy that highlights the most important cues at decision points, such as distinguishing legitimate login prompts from suspicious ones. Simplicity and clarity increase the likelihood that users will follow secure processes because the secure path is understandable, quick to execute, and less error-prone than improvisation.
- **Feedback**: Feedback provides immediate, understandable responses to user actions so that users can confirm outcomes, detect issues early, and adjust behavior appropriately

(Sanders & McCormick, 1993). In cybersecurity, feedback includes clear confirmation messages after password changes, access approvals, or file-sharing actions, as well as alerts that explain what happened, what risk is present, and what the user should do next. Feedback strengthens learning and trust because users can see the consequence of an action and verify that the system recorded it correctly, which is especially important during incident response when uncertainty can drive hesitation or incorrect action.

- **Psychosocial considerations**: Psychosocial considerations account for job demands, autonomy, stress, and well-being because human performance and decision quality are shaped by workload, organizational climate, and sustained pressure (Neumann et al., 2021). In cybersecurity, psychosocial considerations include designing security operations center (SOC) operations to reduce chronic alert overload; clarifying roles and escalation pathways; and ensuring adequate recovery time, staffing, and psychological safety for reporting near misses. Psychosocial considerations reduce burnout-driven errors and turnover-related fragility by making secure performance sustainable, which strengthens the reliability and continuity of cybersecurity operations over time.

Together, these principles provide a practical foundation for integrating HFE into cybersecurity systems and policies by treating human limitations as design inputs, aligning controls with real work, and engineering environments in which secure behavior is the default and error is containable rather than catastrophic.

# Applying human factors lessons from aviation to cybersecurity

Aviation offers a mature, evidence-driven model for managing risk in complex socio-technical systems, and cybersecurity can directly adopt many of its human factors practices rather than inventing new approaches in isolation. Both domains rely on tightly coupled technologies, standardized procedures, and human operators who must make rapid decisions under uncertainty, time pressure, and information overload. Aviation's safety gains were not achieved by demanding perfect performance from pilots and maintainers; they were achieved by redesigning systems, training teams for predictable breakdowns, and building learning mechanisms that treat human error as a signal of system vulnerability. Cybersecurity can use the same orientation by shifting from a primary focus on "fixing users" through awareness campaigns toward "fixing the system" through usable security design, workload-aware operations, and engineered recovery pathways. The practical implication is that security controls, interfaces, and workflows should be treated as safety-critical design artifacts that must be tested, standardized, and continuously refined around real human capabilities and limitations.

The first transferable practice is aviation's emphasis on team-based performance and coordination through **crew resource management (CRM)** and **single-pilot resource management (SRM)**. CRM and SRM formalize behaviors that reduce errors, including structured communication, shared situational awareness, task prioritization, cross-checking, and disciplined decision-making. In cybersecurity operations, the analog is the security operations center and incident response ecosystem, where analysts, engineers, and business stakeholders must coordinate quickly with incomplete information. Applying CRM/SRM concepts in cybersecurity means establishing standard briefings and handoffs, using shared mental models for incident severity and risk, implementing explicit "challenge-and-verify" norms before high-impact actions (for example, firewall changes or account lockouts), and designing escalation protocols that reduce ambiguity during crises. These practices transform incident response from an ad hoc, personality-driven activity into a repeatable operational discipline that reduces errors, limits rework, and improves response quality under pressure.

A second aviation practice that cybersecurity can adopt is the systematic identification of human-error precursors, exemplified by the "Dirty Dozen" framework (for example, fatigue, complacency, inadequate communication, and lack of resources). The value of such a framework lies not in the list itself but in the disciplined habit of treating performance variability as predictable and manageable. In cybersecurity, a comparable approach would be treating conditions such as alert overload, excessive context switching, unclear ownership, ambiguous interfaces, and chronic time pressure as measurable risk factors that can be engineered down. This perspective supports targeted interventions such as alert rationalization, decision-support redesign, staffing models aligned to demand, and simplified workflows that reduce error likelihood. Instead of asking why an analyst "missed" a signal, the organization examines whether the system produced too many low-value alerts, insufficient context, or conflicting procedures that made the miss predictable.

A third aviation-derived practice is the establishment of strong reporting cultures supported by safeguards that encourage honest disclosure of mistakes and near misses. Aviation's safety privilege concepts and programs, such as voluntary reporting systems, illustrate how learning accelerates when people can report hazards without automatic punitive consequences. Cybersecurity can benefit from a similar "learning-first" model by implementing protected internal reporting channels for misconfigurations, near-miss phishing events, procedural breakdowns, and control failures, paired with rapid learning loops that translate reports into design and policy changes. This approach aligns with the logic of a just culture: inadvertent errors and system-induced mistakes are treated as opportunities for system improvement, while reckless or malicious behavior remains subject to accountability. The outcome is more complete event reporting, earlier detection of latent vulnerabilities, and faster mitigation before adversaries exploit recurring patterns.

Implementing aviation-like safety privilege in cybersecurity requires careful alignment with legal and regulatory obligations, because cybersecurity incidents can trigger mandatory external reporting under sectoral rules, privacy regulations, and state breach-notification laws. The practical lesson from aviation is that protections and transparency can coexist when the boundaries are clearly defined: privileged internal learning channels can be designed to promote reporting and analysis, while separate processes handle legally required external notifications. Cybersecurity organizations can pilot hybrid models that combine confidentiality protections, anonymized or de-identified reporting where appropriate, and tiered accountability standards that distinguish human error from negligence or intentional misconduct. Over time, these pilots can generate evidence about what increases reporting, what reduces repeat errors, and what governance structures maintain trust without undermining compliance.

Overall, the aviation case demonstrates that sustainable risk reduction emerges from systems thinking, disciplined operational practices, and engineered learning mechanisms, not from exhortations to "be more careful." Cybersecurity can apply these human factors lessons by designing security controls that are usable in real working conditions, training teams in coordinated decision-making and cross-checking, measuring and reducing error precursors such as workload and ambiguity, and building non-punitive reporting cultures that convert near misses into concrete improvements. In this sense, aviation's human factors history serves as a practical blueprint: it shows how a high-stakes domain moved from blaming individuals to engineering resilient systems, and it provides a tested set of practices that can strengthen cybersecurity performance, reliability, and organizational learning.

## The strategic value of human factors engineering

HFE carries strategic value in cybersecurity because it reduces **organizational risk** at the point where most security controls succeed or fail: human interaction with security technologies, policies, and operational workflows. Here, "strategic value" denotes quantifiable enterprise outcomes associated with risk management, including reductions in incident likelihood and incident impact, improved operational continuity, improved decision quality during high-tempo events, stronger regulatory and audit performance, and preservation of stakeholder trust. Strategic value, in this framing, also includes measurable improvements in control effectiveness, because control effectiveness depends on reliable human execution under real conditions of time pressure, interruption, workload, and ambiguity. HFE advances risk reduction by treating human limitations and predictable weaknesses as design constraints and then engineering socio-technical systems so that secure actions remain comprehensible, efficient, and resilient under normal performance variability.

Cybersecurity strategies often focus investment on technical capabilities such as encryption, endpoint protection, and threat detection, yet organizational exposure persists because human-system interaction remains underdesigned. Authentication prompts, access provisioning, configuration interfaces, alert queues, incident workflows, and policy enforcement mechanisms collectively form a risk-bearing surface where errors, workarounds, and delays become predictable. HFE connects directly to cybersecurity strategy by translating evidence about human cognition and behavior into concrete design requirements and governance decisions that reduce failure probability across the surface. Examples include reducing cognitive load at decision points, increasing the clarity and specificity of warnings and confirmations, improving signal-to-noise in security operations tooling, standardizing terminology and interaction patterns across platforms, and embedding recovery pathways that limit the blast radius when mistakes occur. Each design choice serves as risk control because it alters the probability distribution of error and the time-to-detection and time-to-recovery profiles that determine impact.

A human-centered cybersecurity strategy requires more than general system design language; a human-centered cybersecurity strategy requires an explicit integration of HFE into risk governance, operating models, and performance measurement. HFE-informed strategy links security requirements to task demands and operational constraints, aligns security policies with real workflows, and structures accountability around system design decisions rather than solely around individual compliance. A mature strategic posture, therefore, treats usability, workflow fit, and decision support as core components of security architecture, alongside technical safeguards. Under such a posture, organizational risk reduction becomes traceable to specific interventions, such as fewer misconfigurations, fewer unsafe access practices, fewer erroneous approvals, reduced alert fatigue, improved incident coordination, and improved recovery outcomes.

## Using human factors to achieve human-centered cybersecurity

Technical defenses such as firewalls, encryption protocols, and access control systems anchor many cybersecurity programs, but these controls address only part of the risk. As threats grow more sophisticated and connectivity expands, organizational outcomes increasingly depend on how people interpret prompts, follow workflows, and make decisions under pressure. Human-centered cybersecurity treats the human element as a strategic lever rather than a residual vulnerability by designing security around human behavior, interaction patterns, and cognition. For example, an organization can deploy strong multifactor authentication, yet a poorly designed approval prompt can still lead employees to approve fraudulent "push" requests during busy work periods, enabling account takeover.

Cybersecurity, therefore, functions as a behavioral and organizational challenge as much as a technical one. Every control ultimately depends on human action: a manager approves access, an analyst triages alerts, a developer configures permissions, and an employee decides whether to click a link or report a suspicious message. Users bring different experiences, cultural norms, and cognitive styles, and those differences shape how users perceive risk and respond to security guidance. When organizations ignore these realities, they often create systems that users resist, misunderstand, or bypass. For example, when a secure file-sharing tool requires too many steps, teams frequently revert to emailing attachments or using unsanctioned platforms to meet deadlines, thereby increasing exposure even when the "approved" tool is available.

Grobler et al. (2024) offer a practical way to structure human-centered cybersecurity through the "3U's" framework: **user, usage, and usability**. The framework helps leaders and designers ask three complementary questions: who must make security decisions, how does the organization expect security to function in day-to-day work, and how easy does the system make it to behave securely? The following paragraphs explain each "U" and illustrate how each appears in real cybersecurity contexts. Refer to *Figure 1.1*:

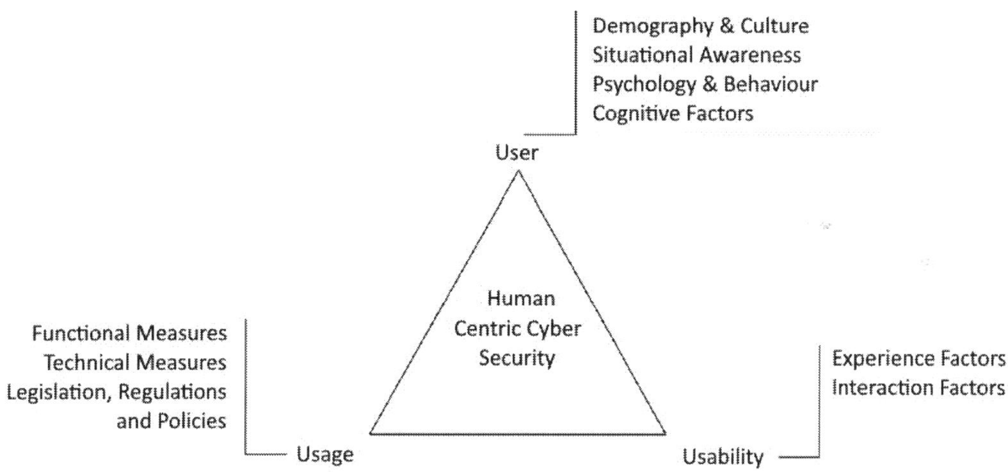


*Figure 1.1: The 3U's of human-centric cybersecurity (Grobler et al., 2024)*

**User** refers to the people who interact with security controls, including employees, administrators, developers, vendors, and security operators. Users differ in role, experience, authority, stress levels, and familiarity with threats, and these differences shape how users interpret risk cues and act on instructions. For example, a finance employee who processes invoices all day can become a prime target for invoice fraud, while a new hire may not recognize subtle signs of a credential-harvesting email. Human-centered cybersecurity designs with these differences in mind by tailoring friction, guidance, and safeguards to role-specific tasks. For instance, the organization can require stronger verification steps for wire transfers or privilege escalation than for low-risk actions, and it can provide in-context prompts that teach users what to check at the moment of decision rather than relying only on annual training.

**Usage** describes how people actually use security controls within real workflows, including authentication, access requests, secure sharing, patching, incident reporting, and compliance activities. Usage focuses on the operational reality of security: whether controls integrate into daily work or collide with it. For example, a complex access request process can push teams to share accounts "temporarily," and unclear remote access steps can lead staff to adopt unmanaged tools for speed and convenience. Human-centered cybersecurity designs for sustainable usage by embedding security into normal routines and reducing unnecessary steps. For instance, the organization can automate device updates during low-disruption windows, integrate least-privilege access requests into a familiar ticketing workflow, and use just-in-time access with clear expiration and renewal prompts to reduce permanent overprovisioning.

**Usability** evaluates the user experience of security controls, including clarity, effort, feedback, and confidence. It addresses whether users can understand what the system asks them to do, complete actions efficiently, and recognize when something goes wrong. Poor usability increases error rates, habituation, and workarounds. For example, frequent non-actionable warnings train users to click through dialogs without reading them, and confusing administrative consoles increase the likelihood of misconfiguration that exposes data. Human-centered cybersecurity improves usability by reducing cognitive load, presenting actionable information, and providing clear feedback. For instance, number-matching MFA can reduce accidental approvals, phishing warnings can explain the specific risk signal detected, and configuration interfaces can include guardrails, safe defaults, and reversible changes to prevent a single mistake from becoming a major incident.

Together, user, usage, and usability provide a practical foundation for designing cybersecurity that reduces organizational risk and strengthens resilience. User considerations ensure that security aligns with role-based decision-making and real human variability. Usage considerations ensure that controls fit operational workflows and remain sustainable under productivity demands. Usability considerations ensure that interfaces and processes make secure actions understandable and straightforward, especially when time pressure and distraction increase error likelihood. When organizations integrate all three, cybersecurity shifts from a reactive function that depends on vigilance to a proactive system that guides secure behavior by design.

By applying the 3U's framework, organizations can operationalize the chapter's broader human-centered cybersecurity argument: security outcomes depend on engineered human-system interaction, not only on technical capability. This approach supports measurable organizational outcomes, including fewer policy violations and workarounds, fewer successful social engineering events, lower misconfiguration rates, faster incident response, and stronger trust in security processes. In an environment where threats evolve quickly, organizations gain a durable advantage when they design security systems that empower users to make correct decisions in the flow of work rather than expecting users to compensate for poor design.

# Integrating organizational culture with human factors engineering

Security behavior is inseparable from organizational culture because culture shapes how employees perceive risk, interpret policies, respond to authority, and decide whether security requirements feel legitimate or burdensome. A human-centered cybersecurity strategy, therefore, treats culture as a risk variable, not as background context. When leaders align security expectations with how work actually happens, employees adopt secure behaviors more consistently; when leaders ignore cultural realities, employees often respond with disengagement or informal workarounds that undermine otherwise-sound technical controls.

Culture influences security outcomes through three practical mechanisms: **users**, **usage environment**, and **usability**. Users vary in norms around deference, collaboration, and communication, which affects how they interpret security messages and escalation guidance. The usage environment includes local workflow pressures, team expectations, and implicit "how we do things here" rules that determine whether secure steps get followed or bypassed. Usability determines whether tools and processes support secure action in the flow of work or create friction that employees circumvent. For example, during an executive-impersonation phishing campaign requesting an "urgent document review," employees in a highly hierarchical workplace may comply immediately to avoid appearing unresponsive, while employees in a consensus-driven environment may first confirm the request in a team chat; a human-centered approach addresses both contexts by implementing a required secondary verification step for high-risk requests, publishing a clear "verify-before-comply" workflow, and routing verification through the communication channels that each group actually uses.

Organizations strengthen resilience when their cultures encourage reporting, learning, and shared accountability rather than blame. Employees report suspicious messages, near misses, and process breakdowns more frequently when leaders reinforce psychological safety and treat reports as inputs for system improvement instead of occasions for punishment. A practical example is an organization that rewards early reporting of suspected phishing and uses that feedback to tune email filters and update prompts; the organization reduces repeat incidents because the culture accelerates learning, and the tooling improves based on real user experience. In this way, culture becomes a strategic asset that amplifies HFE's impact by increasing adoption, reducing resistance, and turning everyday behavior into an active component of organizational risk reduction.

# Synthesizing HFE as a strategy for cybersecurity resilience

Across today's digital environment, organizations face cyber threats that continue to grow in sophistication, speed, and scale. Many programs respond by adding technical controls and expanding training, yet breaches persist because failure often occurs at the point of human interaction with those controls. HFE strengthens cybersecurity by reducing organizational risk through design. HFE aligns security tools, workflows, and communications with how people actually perceive information, allocate attention, and make decisions under time pressure. Rather than asking employees to compensate for confusing systems, HFE reduces error likelihood, improves decision quality, and builds operational resilience through usable interfaces, manageable cognitive demands, and feedback-driven improvement.

HFE advances human-centered cybersecurity through three mutually reinforcing levers. First, HFE improves **user interaction** by streamlining workflows, clarifying prompts, and providing immediate, actionable feedback so that the secure path is the easiest path to follow. Second, HFE reduces **cognitive overload** by organizing information around the decision at hand, limiting unnecessary complexity, and presenting guidance in formats that users can execute quickly, even during interruptions and high workload. Third, HFE strengthens **organizational performance** by shaping training and communication around real tasks and by establishing feedback loops that continuously refine controls based on frontline experience, rather than relying on static policies and one-way awareness messaging. Together, these levers shift cybersecurity from a compliance-driven model to an engineered, learning-oriented system that supports secure behavior in daily operations.

Let's consider a scenario of SOC alert overload and missed escalation. A security operations team receives thousands of daily alerts, many of which lack context and require analysts to pivot across multiple tools to determine the severity. Under this cognitive load, analysts begin triaging by habit, close "routine" alerts quickly, and miss a true-positive signal that indicates lateral movement. An HFE-informed redesign changes outcomes by reducing noise and improving decision support: the SOC consolidates alert views, standardizes severity labels, suppresses low-value alerts, and presents key context at the first point of review (asset criticality, user activity, known threat pattern, and recommended next step). The team also implements a structured handoff checklist and a clear escalation trigger so that analysts do not rely on memory or intuition when fatigue increases. The result is not simply a better interface; it is lower risk because the system reduces the probability of omission errors and shortens the time to detection when a real incident occurs.

Let's now consider another scenario, around access provisioning friction and insecure workarounds. An organization requires employees to request access through a complex approval process that takes days, uses unclear forms, and provides little status feedback. Teams under delivery pressure share credentials or grant broad access "temporarily" and forget to revoke it, creating persistent overprivileged accounts. An HFE-informed approach redesigns the workflow to fit real operational constraints: role-based access templates reduce decision complexity, requests route through a familiar ticketing interface with clear status updates, and time-bound access expires automatically unless reapproved. The system adds simple, contextual guidance that explains why a request requires additional approval and what alternatives exist. This redesign reduces workarounds by lowering friction, while also reducing organizational exposure by limiting excessive permissions and making secure behavior the most efficient option.

These scenarios illustrate the central point of this section: cybersecurity resilience improves when organizations engineer security around human performance rather than expecting perfect compliance. HFE enables that shift by improving usability where decisions occur, reducing cognitive burden where errors concentrate, and embedding communication and learning mechanisms that keep controls aligned with evolving work practices and threats. When leaders integrate HFE into their cybersecurity strategy, organizations reduce avoidable incidents, improve response reliability, and create a culture in which secure behavior becomes a supported capability rather than a constant struggle against poorly designed systems.

# Summary

This chapter argued that cybersecurity's most persistent weakness is human behavior, with major industry reports indicating that many breaches arise from human error amplified by poor usability and misaligned security workflows. The chapter contended that technical controls remain necessary but insufficient unless the cybersecurity strategy incorporates human cognition, context, and real-world work practices.

The chapter positioned HFE as the evidence-based discipline for reducing these risks, drawing lessons from aviation's shift toward designing systems that anticipate human limitations. It clarified HFE's definition, introducing core principles (for example, user-centered design, reduced cognitive load, accessibility, and a just culture) and applying frameworks such as the 3U's (user, usage, and usability) to align security with actual behavior.

Finally, the chapter emphasized organizational culture as a determinant of security behavior and recommended culturally aware design, feedback loops, and participatory methods to move beyond compliance toward resilient, intuitive security ecosystems that reduce risk and strengthen trust.

The next chapter, *Chapter 2, Current Challenges in Cybersecurity*, will delve deeper into the modern threat landscape.

# References


- Chapanis, A. (1999). *The Chapanis Chronicles: 50 years of human factors research, education, and design.* Santa Barbara, CA.
- Chartered Institute of Ergonomics & Human Factors (CIEHF). (2022, March 16). "The role of human factors in delivering cyber security: An overview for cybersecurity decision-makers" (White Paper). .
- Fitts, P. M., & Jones, R. E. (1947). "Psychological aspects of instrument display: Analysis of 270" pilot error" experiences in reading and interpreting aircraft instruments" (No. TSEAA-694-12A). *Dayton, OH: Aeromedical Laboratory, Air Material Command.*
- Grobler, M., Gaire, R., & Nepal, S. (2021). "User, usage, and usability: Redefining human-centric cyber security". *Frontiers in Big Data*, 4, 583723.
- Ncubukezi, T. (2022, March). "Human errors: A cybersecurity concern and the weakest link to small businesses". *In Proceedings of the 17th International Conference on Information Warfare and Security* (p. 395).
- Nobles, C., & Burrell, D. (2024). "Exploring the variability of human factors definitions in cybersecurity literature." *MWAIS 2024 Proceedings*, 28.
- Nobles, C. (2025). "Human factors engineering in explainable AI: Putting people first". *Proceedings of the 20th International Conference on Cyber Warfare and Security*, ICCWS 2025, USA, 313-322.
- Proofpoint. (2024). *2024 Voice of the CISO: Global insights into CISO challenges, expectations, and priorities.* `https://www.proofpoint.com/us/resources/white-papers/voice-of-the-ciso-report`.
- Rogers, W. A., & McGlynn, S. A. (2018). "Human factors and ergonomics: History, scope, and potential." In *Human Factors and Ergonomics for the Gulf Cooperation Council* (pp. 1-20). CRC Press.
- Verizon. (2025). *2025 Data Breach Investigations Report.* Verizon Communications Inc. `https://www.verizon.com/business/resources/reports/dbir/`.

## Get this book's PDF version and more

Scan the QR code (or go to `packtpub.com/unlock`). Search for this book by name, confirm the edition, and then follow the steps on the page.

UNLOCK NOW

*Note: Keep your invoice handy. Purchases made directly from Packt don't require an invoice.*

# 2

# Current Challenges in Cybersecurity

Cybersecurity professionals, whether analysts, engineers, or architects, are managing increasingly complex and challenging technical ecosystems, not to mention emerging and highly sophisticated threats. Cyber teams are under immense pressure to make rapid and accurate decisions to protect their organization. This pressure comes from both boards and regulators due to the risk of data breaches and full organizational compromise. As adversaries gain ground with more technology and easier-to-exploit vulnerabilities, the demand on cyber teams continues to grow.

This chapter focuses on the current challenges for cyber professionals, including modern technology and complexities, security fatigue, mental workloads, and burnout. Cybersecurity challenges are not simply technical but also have a psychological and cognitive factor. The intersection of human cognition and technical infrastructure is where the newest challenges facing cybersecurity teams will be seen.

In this chapter, we will cover the following topics:

- Modern challenges in cybersecurity
- Social engineering
- Mental workloads and cognition
- Insider threats deep dive
- Tool sprawl and linkage to burnout

## Modern challenges in cybersecurity

Before diving into exactly why it is so pertinent to integrate human factors research into cybersecurity, let us first examine the current landscape of cybersecurity. With the rise in ransomware, phishing, and targeted spear phishing campaigns to carry out credential theft, account compromise, and vulnerability exploitation, it is becoming easier to infiltrate systems.

With the use of advanced attack techniques and the inherent complexity of systems, attackers have an advantage when trying to access networks or steal credentials. In most areas, organizations implement technical and process-based controls to combat those types of attacks. But if the technical factors alone were stopping the threats, there would be fewer data breaches and successful ransomware attacks.

### Updated statistics

In the 2025 *Proofpoint Threat Report*, we see a marked uptick in social engineering attacks via email fraud and phishing, denoting a continued increase in psychological techniques to trick users. Each year, we see a rise in the number of successful attacks on large organizations, showing the need to continue to grow our cybersecurity posture and maturity level as attackers gain sophistication.

Along the same lines, the *IBM X-Force Threat Intelligence Index* report from 2025 highlighted that phishing was the initial access vector in 41% of the attacks that the group studied. In the same X-Force Threat Intelligence report, **business email compromise** (**BEC**) was identified as one of the fastest-growing threats, although that type of attack has been used for many years.

*BEC attacks* target **chief executive officers** (**CEOs**) or other high-level executives at organizations by compromising their email accounts and monitoring them for months, or sometimes years. The individual who compromised the account will learn the patterns, behaviors, and frequency of the emails exchanged to understand the executive's language and email style. Once ready, they will send an email to the **chief financial officer** (**CFO**) requesting funds or a wire transfer to be sent to an account owned by the attacker. But this is just one example; BEC attacks can target anyone to deceive employees, customers, or vendors into transferring money or disclosing data.

### Most common attack vector

Given those statistics, it is no surprise that phishing continues to be the most common attack vector for conducting a multitude of attacks. Phishing refers to email-based attacks that use a variety of techniques to encourage users to click on links, download documents, or give away their usernames and passwords.

Phishing attacks have a variety of goals, including the following:

- Encouraging users to click on a malicious link that will download malware or ransomware
- Providing a Word document or PDF that contains malware or ransomware, encouraging the user to open or download the document
- With targeted phishing, or spear phishing, attacks, focusing on specific individuals to either request them to send money to offshore bank accounts or provide confidential data to a spoofed account
- Conducting spam-bombing attacks to distract users, using known good domains and links, from noticing other types of phishing attacks

Phishing emails have become so sophisticated that it can be very difficult for users to identify that emails are from spoofed domains or contain malicious links. Scammers will use familiar-looking sender names, urgent language, or fake login pages to attempt to gain information from the user.

One of the reasons this continues to be the most common attack vector is because of the low cost and potential high reward for successful phishing campaigns. It costs very little to craft one email or smishing (text-based phishing) message and send it to thousands or tens of thousands of users.

It remains relatively easy to bypass common security controls, for example, accounts that do not use **multi-factor authentication** (**MFA**). Even with technical controls in place, such as **endpoint detection and response** (**EDR**) and firewalls, attackers can exploit the human layer of any organization. This common attack vector alone highlights the need to understand users, the tools they use, and how security impacts the business.

## Most common exploits

There are numerous vulnerabilities and misconfigurations exploited regularly, and based on data from 2023 and 2024, we will continue to see similar exploit patterns. Exploitable vulnerabilities such as Log4j use remote code execution, server-side request forgeries with email servers, and privilege escalation. These types of attacks are seen again and again across a variety of vendors and products.

Other common exploitable vulnerabilities include SQL injection from external-facing systems and memory corruption, which can be implemented through phishing attacks. An example that the industry continues to use year over year is the Equifax breach from 2017, where an Apache Struts vulnerability remained unpatched and was exploited, allowing the attackers to steal over 147 million records. This breach is a cautionary tale to patch systems that have known exploited vulnerabilities and typically show up in the **cybersecurity and infrastructure security agencies** (**CISA**) **known exploited vulnerabilities** (**KEV**) catalog.

As shown in the following figure, there are multiple avenues that bad actors will use to exploit vulnerabilities, each leading to consequences such as credential theft, malware, or cloud account compromise. These threat vectors provide an example of how one may exploit vulnerabilities to gain access to data or compromise credentials:

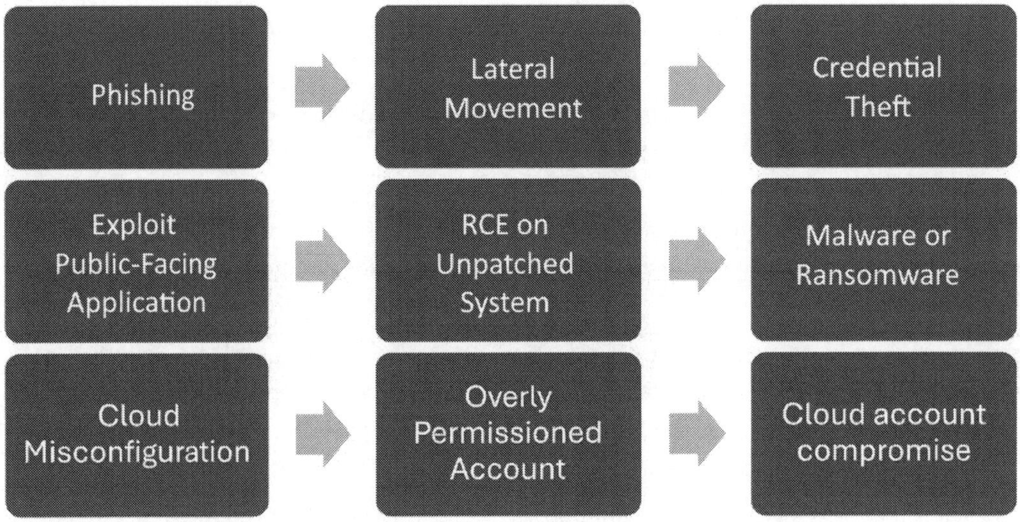


*Figure 2.1: Common attack patterns for highly exploitable vulnerabilities*

For commonly exploited misconfigurations, cloud environments continue to give attackers a foot in the door, for example, open S3 buckets in an **Amazon Web Services** (**AWS**) environment, default credentials across any account or system, and overly permissive **identity and access management** (**IAM**) roles. There has also been a rise in the misconfiguration of assets being externally facing that should be internal only, as well as exposed administrative interfaces or web applications that could give access to data that should only be accessed with administrative permissions.

## Most common attack patterns

One of the most common tools in our cybersecurity toolbelt is the MITRE ATT&CK framework. It provides a comprehensive view of how attackers enter networks and the common patterns they follow as they conduct a variety of different techniques. The primary attack patterns that are used give us an indication of why human factors is the missing link in preventing complex cyberattacks.

The following figure shows several different techniques used to conduct multiple attacks. For example, an insider threat could result in a number of consequences, just as credential stuffing could be used to take over an API or a user account. Each type of attack vector, as shown in the MITRE ATT&CK framework, results in numerous challenges, whether exploiting a vulnerability or choosing to steal credentials. Based on current trends, credential theft continues to be one of the main motivations for cyberattacks.

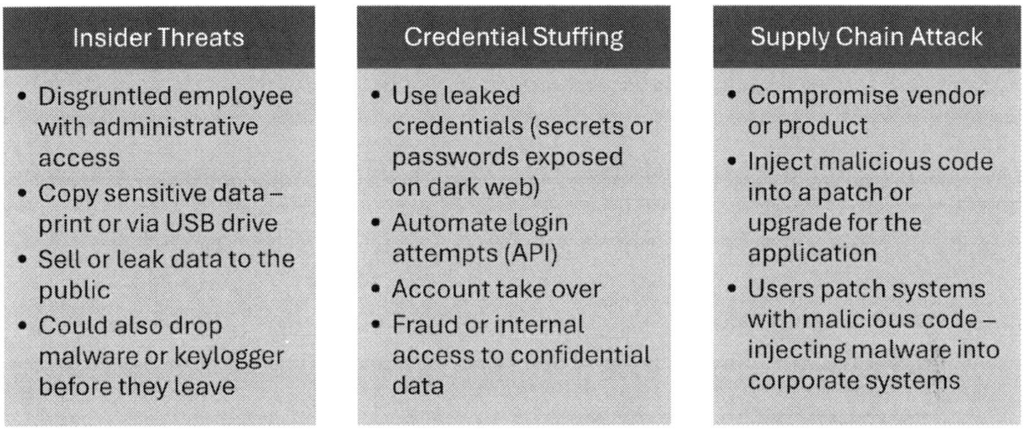


*Figure 2.2: Examples of attack vectors and consequences for systems/accounts*

Some of the common attack patterns described here include insider threats, credential stuffing, and supply chain attacks. Insider threats are a very well-known example of a cyber threat with a human factor, being the result of an employee with administrative access leaking business or proprietary secrets. Each of these threats has been conducted against a multitude of organizations, some being highly successful. For example, credential stuffing was used in the Zoom data breach in 2020, which leveraged previously leaked credentials, resulting in thousands of accounts being taken over.

Supply chain attacks have risen since 2020, including multiple high-profile examples such as Log4j and Kaseya VSA in 2021. In the Kaseya VSA example, the Revil group compromised remote management software that the company used, leaving over 1,000 companies susceptible to ransomware. This impacted multiple supermarket chains and caused outages worldwide, showing the linkage and impact of misconfigured software on our access to food and supplies. This impacted over 50 different **Internet Service Providers** (**ISPs**) and over 800 businesses, with some reports indicating that as many as 1,500 businesses may have been impacted by the ransomware attack.

# Social engineering

Given the extensive list of exploitable vulnerabilities and misconfigurations, understanding the full attack picture is essential. As an example, if default credentials are used in a web application, it could be possible for an attacker to leverage those credentials to conduct privilege escalation and gain access to internal systems.

But the examples of credential theft and privilege escalation primarily show technical controls and vulnerabilities that are exploited; they don't address the psychological aspects of how these attacks are conducted. Social engineering is the practice of bad actors leveraging psychological techniques to understand users and the way they operate. They are commonly carried out due to the simplicity and scalability of these techniques, as well as the attacker's ability to abuse and exploit people's trust.

In this section, we will explore the use of social engineering in a number of ways and where the human factors discipline becomes important. As technology becomes inherently more complex, primarily due to the interconnectedness of systems and infrastructure, so does the need to understand people through the human factors lens. Our cloud environments and mobile devices now provide a number of entry points into organizations, and not just access points, but paths directly into business-critical systems.

## The prevalence of social engineering

There are numerous forms of phishing used today, and they each have their own specific use case or form of contact:

- **Phishing**: Mass emails that may look like they are from a social media or gaming company or a bank or credit union
- **Spear phishing**: Targeted phishing to an individual or group of individuals at an organization, for example, a **Human Resources** (**HR**) team
- **Whaling**: Similar to BEC, targeting high-level executives
- **Vishing**: Phishing through voice, which is now more common with deepfake technology that can mimic individuals
- **Smishing**: Phishing through text, either to have people click on malicious links or prompt MFA to induce MFA fatigue in users
- **Clone phishing**: Duplicating real emails, which replace legitimate URLs with malicious ones

Phishing and targeted attacks such as whaling and spear phishing continue to be relatively easy for attackers to carry out. Phishing requires very little cost, and even targeted attacks, while they take much more time to conduct, are still low-cost. While URL spoofing techniques already exist, AI-generated visuals can make phishing pages and emails appear more legitimate, increasing the likelihood that users will trust malicious links. But AI isn't just used in image and video generation; it is now prevalent in formatting emails, leading to fake websites that appear very much like the real websites that they are spoofing. It is increasingly more difficult for humans to distinguish between AI images and true content.

## Smishing – a rising tide

Smishing, a text-based form of phishing, has grown exponentially due to the widespread use of texting. SMS-based technologies also lack additional spam filters like the ones in the email services that are commonly used in organizations, leaving individuals open to text-based attacks. While mobile carriers do provide their own phishing and scam protection, most organizations need to add additional layers of defense to protect users from scams and fraud. Smishing attempts are also harder to detect while being just as simple to conduct as traditional phishing with emails.

According to Proofpoint's Threat Report from 2023, smishing and text-based attacks increased by almost 330% in that year. According to the FCC, almost 70% of mobile device users have received suspicious or malicious text in the past year. But the most common smishing scenarios leverage the same attack techniques as phishing, leaving users with another technical mechanism to steal information or credentials.

Some of the most common smishing scenarios from 2024 include package delivery scams, banking or tax scams, MFA or 2FA bypass, and employment scams. Account lockouts for streaming services and shopping sites are also a common technique used in both smishing and phishing. Attackers will pretend to be a representative from a bank or government entity, urging users to act quickly by either filling out a form with personal information or verifying login credentials on fake websites.

## Vishing and why it is successful

Like smishing, vishing uses scams and notifications to attempt to steal information from users. Unlike phishing and smishing, though, vishing can be highly sophisticated and leverage several psychological and social engineering components to trick users. There are three main reasons why bad actors like to use vishing: to either steal sensitive information such as **social security numbers** (**SSNs**) or MFA codes, to transfer money, or to provide remote access to laptops or other systems.

Vishing can be highly successful due to the prevalence of hybrid work cultures, AI voice cloning, and **Voice over IP** (**VoIP**) spoofing. AI voice cloning now allows bad actors to use AI-generated deepfakes to mimic executives or someone of authority in the workplace to fool users. VoIP spoofing allows individuals to impersonate banks, government officials, and IT departments, for example, a helpdesk support technician asking for a password or credential rotation.

According to IBM's X-Force report in 2023, vishing attacks have increased by over 50%. Due to the combination of vishing and BEC-style attacks, the FBI's IC3 report from 2024 estimated that businesses lost over $2.4 billion. Because vishing and AI-based deepfakes now allow attackers to mimic executives or even loved ones, it is even more critical for defenders and users to understand psychological and engineering practices.

## Examples of successful social engineering attacks

Phishing, smishing, and vishing continue to provide a source of strain for cybersecurity teams and users. There are multiple ways that technology can help prevent them, including implementing MFA, strong networking, and IAM best practices. But without proper implementation, attackers can continue to gain access to systems or exploit vulnerabilities.

Technical controls are not the only components essential to helping our cyber teams. To explore this topic in more depth, we will investigate some examples of cyber breaches where human factors engineering may have helped detect or prevent them before they caused too much damage.

### Fake employees

While there are numerous recent examples of fake employees either being offered full-time positions at companies or pretending to be employees, there are three notes that highlight the sophistication of these attacks.

To start, there is the example of AI voice-cloning calls against a UK energy firm in 2023, where the CEO's voice was cloned using publicly available recordings from speeches and other engagements. The voice that the attacker used was able to convince a financial director to send over 200,000 pounds to a foreign bank. Using AI voice cloning is the modern equivalent of the traditional BEC attacks using emails.

Another example of a successful social engineering attack is the use of IT helpdesk calls that stole MFA codes from users during the MGM Resort breach in 2023. The attackers pretended to be IT staff while on calls with employees and HR, claiming that there was an account issue. The attackers then either installed remote access tools or requested that the MFA codes sent to phones be read off by the unsuspecting employees. The attackers were able to convince users to reset MFA, which allowed them entry to systems to conduct a ransomware attack.

There are multiple companies that have reported fake job candidates who used deepfake videos during interviews or some type of voice manipulation. In 2022, the FBI issued a statement alerting individuals to the way that attackers are applying to remote IT jobs. Through publicly available data, the attackers seem most interested in roles where elevated permissions would be required, such as developer or administrative positions.

In some of these attacks, common technical controls such as MFA were in place, but they were easily bypassed by attackers using psychological and social engineering techniques. But designing systems that minimize reliance on trust-based communication could be a positive step to combat these types of attacks. This is where human factors engineering principles can help us to design more effective systems.

## Missing technical controls and misconfigurations

While multiple examples of missing technical controls have been mentioned, there is one in particular that highlights how easily technical aspects can be bypassed. The cyberattack against Microsoft Power Apps in 2021 used a combination of discovering open cloud storage, pulling sensitive or confidential data, and potentially selling or ransoming the data.

During this breach, there was a default misconfiguration in an application that exposed over 38 million records. This was a common application used by governments, healthcare organizations, and private companies. There was over 1,000 applications created using Power Apps that ultimately exposed the data across multiple sectors.

The availability of this application gave users access to privileged accounts to create applications that could result in misconfigurations and introduce data security risks. Because of this, a large amount of data was left unsecured and available for the taking. Even with the implementation of a common application, users were still able to introduce misconfigurations, which ultimately led to significant data loss.

# Mental workloads and cognition

There is an eternal struggle between IT and cybersecurity teams, explored in the book *Mind the Tech Gap: Addressing the Conflicts between IT and Security Teams* by *Nikki Robinson (2021)*, around usability versus security. Technical and security teams can be combative or disagree on technical controls or implementation based on user requirements, business needs, or even security initiatives.

In a classical sense, organizations feel as though they will sacrifice usability for their user population if they implement security enhancements. But this simply is not true. Adding security at the right layer will enable product usability and design, without adding burden to the users. In this section, we will cover the common areas where products and applications struggle to identify the benefits of security over usability and functionality.

## Cognitive bias in systems design

Cognitive bias, the first human factors concern in designing systems, is how specific applications or tools favor information that confirms beliefs from the user. One example is when users have settings enabled for their history and other preferences, a search engine will rank content higher that aligns with their preferences. For example, a user may see an article that suggests that there are fewer ransomware attacks these days, so they may not consider it a threat. There are also AI-based diagnostic tools that rely very heavily on historical data, which may reinforce stereotypes or misinformation.

Another case of cognitive bias is availability heuristics, which is the tendency to overestimate the importance of specific or recent events over factual information. For instance, a threat detection system might overreact, or isolate systems based on the most recent type of data breach, versus up-to-date threat intelligence information. A system may also use a type of feedback mechanism to elevate or focus on the opinions from users with the highest comment or interaction rate.

Anchoring bias, a parallel notion in cognitive bias, is relying too much on the first piece of information received, versus using additional resources or research to back up findings. In a system designed for shopping experiences, a pricing tool might rely on the first quote, which may add bias to additional or subsequent results. A more specific example is in a hiring application, the first applicant's scores might alter or skew the results of other candidates.

A particularly interesting case, when it comes to the increase in automation for manual or repetitive tasks, called automation bias, is the ability for decisions or AI outputs to be overly trusted by users. For example, doctors use AI diagnostic tools without researching them more heavily or validating the findings with additional resources. A more cybersecurity-centric example is **Security Operations Center** (**SOC**) analysts who accept a finding stating that no threat was detected and don't carry out any additional investigation to validate those findings.

## Perception and cognition

It is critical to cover the high-level concepts before understanding the impact across the cybersecurity space. The discipline of human factors introduces both psychological and engineering practices into cybersecurity, offering an understanding of humans in combination with the technology we consume.

SOC analysts and security engineers monitor large volumes of data, including logs, dashboards, and alerts, from multiple consoles. To determine a true positive versus a false positive, analysts depend on visual perception to direct their attention, cognitive load to understand how much data can be processed at once, and pattern recognition to find anomalies in detections. A SOC analyst requires high-risk indicators with perceptual clues, heuristic reduction to understand why an alert is important, and recognition over recall, which reduces the risk of focusing on the history and memorization of tasks.

Cybersecurity teams are under a lot of pressure to make quick, high-impact decisions, such as isolating a machine or rotating someone's credentials automatically. Because cyber analysts, engineers, and architects are only humans, they are also potentially influenced by cognitive biases, stress, incomplete information, or time constraints to make the best decision for risky situations.

A final note on perception and cognition, though they will be explored in more depth in future chapters: security professionals typically manage multiple applications and consoles, adapt to constantly changing industry trends, and use custom scripts or automation to manage their workloads. This provides a potential avenue for misconfigurations in systems, missed updates, or mishandling of credentials, secrets, or API keys, leading to account compromise and privilege escalation.

## Poor interfaces

When the **user interface** (**UI**) or **user experience** (**UX**) is poorly designed across applications, it can lead to poor user decisions, which could impact risk management activities in the organization. UI is about the look, feel, and layout of an application; this includes the buttons, colors, and icons that a user will interact with. UX refers to the overall journey and emotion a user has while interacting with it, which is more about how easy, efficient, and satisfying it is to interact with said application. Similar to cognitive bias, a decision can be affected by how the choices are presented in an application.

Specific to application design, a user may see the wording "confirm deletion" for files and select it, choosing to remove their files without understanding the impact. But if a system shows "You will remove your work forever if you delete from the recycle bin," it will alert the user to the serious implications of removing those files forever. It provides the user with a warning and the consequences of taking an action, versus confirmation of an action.

## Password and MFA policies

Most individuals maintain dozens or hundreds of passwords for work, entertainment, banking applications, shopping, and healthcare. Because we live in an app-centric world, users must create logins, passwords, and some sort of MFA implementation across each application. This creates several security challenges:

- Passwords are reused in personal and corporate applications, leaving business accounts susceptible to account compromises
- The use of password lockers or vaults to maintain numerous accounts and logins mean leaving users' most valuable credentials in a third-party application, which could be breached
- Users will look for workarounds that compromise security because of the cognitive overload of trying to remember the various password strengths and complexities across multiple applications

Platforms will have unique and sometimes conflicting password requirements. Some applications will require a symbol, while others will not let you enter the password if a symbol exists. Other systems will require a forced password reset after 30 days, while others will request a token challenge through an authenticator application or an SMS token for the MFA component.

Another complexity for users is that password advice continues to change year to year. For years, users were told to change passwords often, use complex combinations, not reuse passwords, and not write any passwords down. But based on the most recent password requirements from NIST, users shouldn't have to reset passwords unless there is evidence of compromise and passphrases are better than a complex string of symbols.

Unfortunately, humans are relatively predictable when it comes to password logic. Users commonly swap letters with numbers, for example, using a "3" instead of an "e," or use memorable numbers, such as the current year or their birth year, at the end of a password. Since most of these patterns are expected, attackers will build scripts and automation to predict passwords and use them in brute-force or credential-stuffing attacks.

## Lack of human-centered design

Just as with password management, a lack of human-centered design can cause users to compromise security in favor of "ease of use." Because of the multitude of MFA solutions present today across applications, including SMS, email validation, authentication apps, biometrics, and hardware tokens, users are forced to learn and maintain a variety of options. For example, some applications may only work with one provider's authenticator app, while another only works with a competitor's, meaning that for only two submissions, the user must use two different authenticator applications.

Along with the multitude of MFA solutions, users must also deal with the various states and maturity levels of the authentication options. Some MFA systems will time out quickly (within 30 seconds), while others have poor accessibility or require application switching for copy and paste options. Several mobile devices have altered their OS-based controls to allow automatic copying of SMS-based codes for application submission.

Another example of poor design is non-intuitive security dashboards for administrators that lack clear prioritization of alerts or notifications. It is also possible for critical alerts to be missed in the console without context or understanding of their impact on the environment. Administrators can suffer from alert fatigue, leading to them disabling monitoring or tuning out alerts because of constant interruptions and noise.

A final example of making security overcomplicated in applications is when security prompts use language that is confusing for users. Prompts are typically used to help users understand why an action may be taken by an application, an interaction the user must decide to conduct, or maybe an organization-wide policy that applies to all users. If the language is vague or confusing, a user may, with all good intentions, select an option that they believe is secure but in actuality is not.

The following are two examples of prompts that could confuse users:

- "Your session may have been compromised. Would you like to reset your password or generate a new token?"
- "Please choose an option: 1. Regenerate Key 2. Delete Session 3. Cancel"
  This is an example of a prompt without context of what each action will do

Users might not understand the threat, leaving them to choose the option that sounds least impactful, potentially opening them up to security risk if their account is compromised. Ideally, the user's credentials should be automatically rotated, forcing a reset rather than relying on the user to choose the appropriate action.

# Insider threats deep dive

Insider threats continue to grow in sophistication, as demonstrated by the technique of a fake candidate applying for a job at an organization so that they can acquire insider information. Other examples are a disgruntled employee or someone who was fired or laid off, who has access to confidential information that could harm the organization if leaked. Insiders could also have access to business-critical systems that they could take down or disrupt.

## Malicious versus negligent

Common mechanisms for insiders to act in a company include unintentional, negligent, and malicious behaviors. For the purpose of implementing human factors principles into cybersecurity, we will focus on negligent and malicious behavior. Negligent behavior refers to a user bypassing common security controls due to poor UX, a misunderstanding of policies, or even frustration with the constant security measures that impact their efficiency. Malicious behavior refers more to an individual motivated to steal data to gain something in return.

Some examples of negligent behavior related to attempting to bypass security measures are sharing logons, using personal devices for work because enterprise applications are too slow to support workloads, or copying files offline because access to tooling is not available. Each of these violations could have a serious impact on the organization, from data exfiltration to account compromise, even if the user is simply trying to perform their tasks.

Either of these behaviors can be influenced by internal or external factors. Negligent actions could be the result of constantly changing security policies, overly restrictive administrative environments that require multiple logins and slow access management processes, or even the pressure to succeed from executives or customers. Malicious behavior could also be derived from numerous sources, including extortion, bribery, beliefs that are misaligned with the organization, or even social pressures or experiences.

## Behavioral warnings

Behavioral analysis can be a useful tool in understanding users and possible insider threats. Insider threat behavior can be determined by identifying user access to sensitive or unusual information, logins at hours outside of their normal scope, or downloads of an extraordinary number of files in a short amount of time.

Outside of the technical warnings for insider threat behavior, it is important to notice when individuals feel mistreated or disengaged from their work activities. It is possible they feel a lack of trust or unclear motivation for their work, leading to stress and frustration. An employee who feels frustrated may not act out in a malicious fashion; they could simply be looking for an easier way to conduct their work that meets deadlines and expectations from leadership.

## Organizational influence on cybersecurity

A lot of research has been carried out over many years that focuses on the organizational culture around cybersecurity and the benefits of a positive security culture. Having shared values and beliefs encourages individuals to align with security policies, understand and report risks, and prioritize security over risky behaviors. Security does not have to be a blocker; it can be an enabler for the business and have a positive impact on systems and users when implemented using human factors ideals.

Security policies are critical to any organization; they provide guidance and focus on what risks are acceptable versus what is unacceptable. However, overly strict, confusing, or irrelevant policies could lead users to skirt policies or disregard them altogether. Human-centered policies address the cognitive load and context of complex tasking, which aligns with how their employees perform their individual job functions.

There is a common misconception in the cybersecurity and technical community that human factors in cybersecurity mean security awareness training. While that does become a subset of the discipline, the focus is more on psychology and how we can build better tools and applications for humans. Providing feedback loops for users can positively impact behavior reinforcement; humans learn better when feedback is available for positive or corrective actions. An example is a user who is reporting a phishing email but getting no response, never learning whether that phishing email was in fact malicious or whether it was a routine communication.

# Tool sprawl and the linkage to burnout

The term **shadow IT** has been around for some years, and with the advent of AI systems, we now see shadow AI as part of our terminology and understanding of where unknown systems and applications may exist in the technological landscape. For example, an administrator may need to work on a development server before pushing to production. They may deem it unnecessary to include inventory systems or install EDR on the server, because it is ephemeral and only holds development data. This server may inadvertently expose vulnerabilities or misconfigurations externally, leaving the capability for a bad actor to move from the development system into production.

## System and API sprawl

System sprawl continues to evolve with multi-cloud, hybrid cloud, including combinations of on-premises data centers and cloud or containerized applications. Businesses have adapted their technology stacks for scalability, resiliency, and speed for development to production. This means the interconnectivity between systems continues to grow more and more complex, allowing multiple avenues for entry by bad actors.

**API sprawl** is seen due to the ease of use and accessibility of APIs for developers and administrators, which streamlines access to data. Unfortunately, unlike servers and containers, APIs do not always have proper authentication mechanisms in place, may lack logging or monitoring, and may inadvertently allow enhanced privileges. There may also be limited insight and oversight into API connections, because they are not traditionally tracked in an inventory system.

With technology sprawl, there are a number of human factors challenges that start with the interconnectivity of systems. Administrators may experience task fragmentation due to switching between systems, as well as tool fatigue with the need to look at multiple log sources to track API usage. If systems come online quickly, teams may miss documentation or ownership, including **role-based access control** (**RBAC**), which could protect those API endpoints.

System and API sprawl are not solely technical debt with negative implications; they are cognitive issues. Each tool, endpoint, key, credential, and secret opens an avenue for vulnerabilities and misconfigurations to occur. The more tools, systems, applications, and infrastructure that we maintain, the more time we spend making decisions on the security of that technology.

## DevOps and leaking secrets

**DevOps** and **DevSecOps** have both been used in large development teams, aiming to move away from the traditional waterfall style of waiting until the end of development activities to implement testing and security. DevSecOps introduces security practices into DevOps pipelines, but depending on the nature of the implementation, it could be a small team that is now responsible for development, operations, and security activities.

While this movement has encouraged development teams to implement security on the frontend of product development, security could still be pushed aside in favor of speed. Designing guardrails that help to encourage security by default could be seen as a detriment to speed, although more commonly, **continuous integration/continuous deployment** (**CI/CD**) pipelines automate security practices within testing and scanning processes.

Automation aids in implementing security in development pipelines; for example, **static application security testing** (**SAST**) and **dynamic application security testing** (**DAST**) can automate security analysis and simulate attacks while the application is running. But without proper documentation or understanding of what automation is occurring, it could produce quite a bit of noise for developers, who may in turn tune out those alerts.

# Summary

Cybersecurity is no longer defined by solely technical components such as firewalls, EDR solutions, and encryption protocols. It is much more than that; it is about the mental workloads, the cognitive implications, as well as the burnout and stress that affect cybersecurity effectiveness. Technical debt, API sprawl, misconfigurations, poor UI/UX design, and many more aspects are just the start of the cybersecurity challenges. What is most clear, after evaluating the technical aspects of cybersecurity attacks and impact, is that the human factor is more important than ever.

As organizations continue to grow in both technology and complexity, the solutions designed for the users who rely on them must evolve as well. Cybersecurity attacks, threat vectors, and an increased threat landscape require more than technical solutions; they require an understanding of the humans who use said technology. Without expanding our knowledge and reach into the way we build, manage, and design systems and applications for our users, we will continue to see ransomware, phishing, insider threats, and technical debt.

In the next chapter, the focus shifts to a specific group within cybersecurity teams, the SOC. With an abundant amount of research and data around how security analysts experience stress, burnout, and fatigue, it is an area rich to explore how cognition and perception impact analysts within the SOC. Because the SOC is the first line of defense for any organization, it is crucial to understand the cognitive load, interface design implications, and team dynamics that, whether positively or negatively, impact performance.

# References


- *The Human Factor – Vol. 1: Social Engineering* | Proofpoint US. `https://www.proofpoint.com/us/resources/threat-reports/human-factor-social-engineering`

- IBM X-Force 2025 Threat Intelligence Index | IBM. `https://www.ibm.com/thought-leadership/institute-business-value/report/2025-threat-intelligence-index`
- *Business Email Compromise: The $55 Billion Scam* | Internet Crime Complaint Center (IC3), `https://www.ic3.gov/PSA/2024/PSA240911`
- *OWASP API Security Project* | OWASP Foundation, `https://owasp.org/www-project-api-security/`
- 2023 Mainframe Infrastructure Benchmarks, Global | Forrester, `https://www.forrester.com/report/The-Human-Cost-Of-Toolchain-Complexity/RES177842`


# Get this book's PDF version and more

Scan the QR code (or go to `packtpub.com/unlock`). Search for this book by name, confirm the edition, and then follow the steps on the page.

UNLOCK NOW

*Note: Keep your invoice handy. Purchases made directly from Packt don't require an invoice.*

# 3

# Rethinking Incident Response through the Lens of Human Factors

**Incident Response (IR)** is the area within cybersecurity where IR analysts respond to potential security threats or act in real time to a cyberattack. IR is the act of protecting data, systems, and operations by detecting, containing, eradicating, and recovering from security incidents. IR is like firefighting; there is always a new incident, alert, or investigation that requires quick decision-making, fast action, and efficient resolution. Even with advancements in technology, several IR responsibilities and actions are manual or require human intervention. An IR analyst will have a wide range of skills and abilities, including carrying out malware analysis, leveraging multiple investigative tools, and understanding how and when to respond to a cyberattack.

This chapter will cover the basics of IR from a human factors perspective, rather than focusing solely on the tools and techniques that an IR analyst may use. A data breach or cyberattack is a technical event, but our analysts and responders are human. We will first dive into the individual components of IR, providing an introduction for each area of human factors.

In this chapter, we will cover the following topics:

- The incident response life cycle
- Limits of perception and cognition
- Human factors intervention
- Building learning and system resilience
- A case (or two) for human factors

## The incident response life cycle

There are standard frameworks for IR. NIST has defined an IR life cycle, which serves as an important reference for building an IR team and process. IR is not a singular technical activity or process; instead, it is a set of complex decisions and forensic investigations that must occur to determine the severity, breadth, and overall impact of a cyberattack. In the following figure, you can see the comprehensive steps in a modern IR program, spanning from preparation all the way back to iterating processes and improving workflows for the next incident:

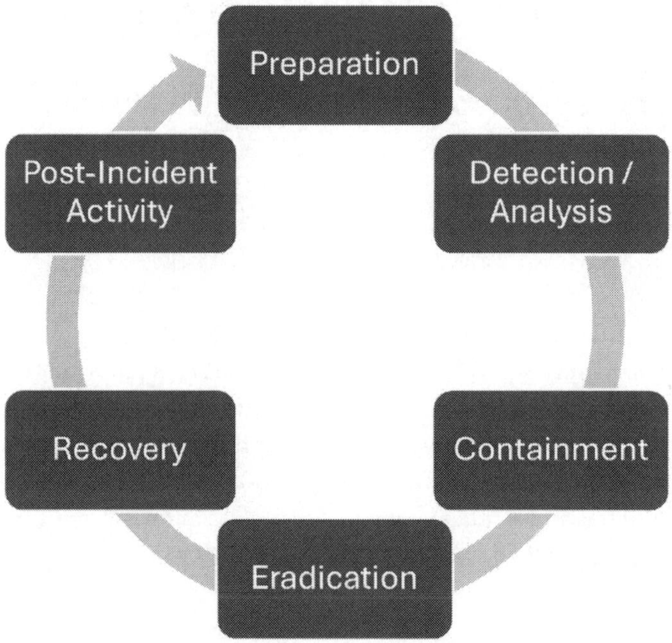


*Figure 3.1: IR life cycle*

The first step, preparation, includes defining roles and responsibilities, along with the appropriate communication channels, in the event that an incident occurs. The second step, detection and analysis, is where IR teams, in conjunction with the security operations center (SOC), **Threat Intelligence** (**TI**), and **Detection Engineering** (**DE**) teams, identify potential threats and prioritize them based on relevance and severity.

The NIST guidelines group containment, eradication, and recovery together as one step, where cyber teams will actively reduce damage, remove malware, and bring systems back online if they are impacted by a cyberattack. The last step, post-incident activity, is the feedback loop that carries **After-Action Reports** (**AARs**) back into the preparation step, constantly honing and evolving IR processes and procedures.

Each of these steps blends perfectly into the next; however, in typical IR processes, the focus is on the technology or processes. There are many mentions of communications plans, but not always the information that lends itself to IR teams adding to or complementing their programs with human factors and psychological information. For example, consider the containment step. The goal is to stop an incident by whatever technical means necessary. But these guides don't typically talk about the pressure on the team during this step; what if teams accidentally isolate the wrong asset, leading to business or revenue impact? Another example is, during the recovery step, what types of mental workloads do teams need to balance to ensure systems are operational quickly, with enhanced security, and to ensure the incident never occurs again? There will likely be multiple mental workloads, with decisions that impact the business and the security of the organization, as well as ensuring teams interact optimally for a mutually beneficial outcome.

Without understanding human factors, IR guidance could potentially lead teams to miss improving practices or detecting gaps in tooling or even fail to identify where the problems lie in their own programs. Crafting a powerful problem statement is the best way to identify the real issues or concerns, rather than focusing solely on the technological aspects.

Problem statements help teams understand (in the simplest context) what is going wrong, possible symptoms or indicators, the impact or consequences, as well as the audience of the issue. A clear and concise problem statement can be the difference between successfully solving a problem and choosing a solution before understanding where the real issues are. If teams and leaders continue to believe that the problem is technology-driven, instead of looking at the people who manage that technology, their problem statements will continue to miss the mark.

During incidents, analysts operate under extreme cognitive load, increasing the likelihood of missed indicators and decision errors. Poorly designed security tools and interfaces create friction that slows investigations and contributes to fatigue. Communication failures between responders, leadership, and supporting teams further complicate coordination when remediation is critical. IR playbooks that do not account for real human behavior often fail under stress, fatigue, and multitasking. Over time, these pressures lead to burnout and high turnover, weakening organizational response capabilities and leaving systems more vulnerable to attack.

## Preparation, policies, and roles

In every phase of the IR life cycle, there are policies and processes that must be followed. For example, if supporting or working for the federal government, there may be policies that state that an incident must be reported within a two-hour window. Or an organization may have internal processes that outline a robust reporting and communication chain leading to the executives, based on the severity of the incident.

During IR procedure planning, it is essential to define who will act during an incident. Typically, this may include establishing an IR leader, a communication coordinator, and, depending on the scope of the incident, an individual responsible for client communication. These roles are essential to ensuring proper messaging between teams, establishing a process for resolving an incident quickly, and limiting the "blast radius" of a cyberattack.

This type of coordination requires quick decision-making, highly effective communication, and technical expertise for a variety of incident use cases. Throughout the IR life cycle, human factors could provide a mature and enhanced response to any type of incident. Without a solid engineering and psychological framework, incidents could lead to finger-pointing, blame, frustration, and stress across teams.

## Detection and analysis

The second step, detection and analysis, requires coordination across several technical tools and teams. IR teams may have automation in place to monitor logs, intrusion detection systems (IDSs), firewalls, networking devices, and endpoint detection and response (EDR). During this step, analysts will triage alerts for malware, unauthorized access to systems, or phishing with malicious links to determine **Indicators of Compromise** (**IOCs**).

But with so many tools, techniques, processes, configurations, and alerts to monitor and update, alert fatigue could set in for SOC analysts and incident responders. Alert fatigue can lead to missed alerts, false positives or false negatives, or delayed processing in detecting an incident. So, human factors comprehension becomes an integral part of setting up a proper detection and analysis workflow.

Depending on the size of the organization, tools may be fragmented, making the decision-making process for responders and analysts more complex. For example, a larger security organization will use multiple EDR solutions, network monitoring applications, and dashboards displaying alerts from multiple sources. Each of these panels may provide disparate information that an analyst needs to parse and understand quickly. Decisions for incident responders must be quick; they are typically acting after the alert of a cyber incident.

With information overload and cognitive workloads, analysts may struggle with effective triage and focusing on what matters most. For example, an incident responder may be handling multiple incidents at one time that include different system owners, alternating customer requirements, and possible legal or global restrictions on how to respond to that incident. Juggling all this information can be challenging to ensure that each incident is responded to within a specific timeline and without feeling the additional pressure of missing a containment action, leading to a larger breach.

IR requires pattern recognition to identify true positives, but with multiple layers of bias, both in the tooling and in humans, errors in detection and analysis will occur. While bias can exist from the responder's perspective, it can also exist in the tooling, for example, if it determines that an incident is a false positive versus a true positive. Many IR tools rank alerts using predefined scoring systems. If those scoring models are poorly tuned, responders may focus on high-scoring alerts while ignoring lower-scoring ones that are actually critical.

## Containment, eradication, and recovery

As the third step in the NIST IR life cycle, containment, eradication, and recovery are compiled together into one component. This step is focused on *limiting the blast radius and stopping the bleeding*. IR teams isolate affected systems and work to contain the damage by shutting down ports, blocking malicious domains, and removing malware or other harmful files to restore system integrity. They also collaborate closely with system and application owners to ensure that systems are brought back online in a clean, secure, and fully operational state.

Incident responders will use a variety of tools to isolate hosts, remove unauthorized access to systems, rotate credentials, and ultimately monitor systems at a heightened state to ensure there is no reinfection. One example is ransomware, where ransomware reinfection rates can be high, due to its ability to hide in integral system components. For environments affected by ransomware, watching for possible malware or IOCs of bad actors attempting to gain access is a critical step.

But during these activities, responders and analysts must make critical decisions under time pressure and maybe even uncertainty around the type of attack. It can take precious time to understand the impact, and without higher levels of approval, there could be doubt when executing actions. There is a need for fast and effective communication from the security team to system owners, the legal team, and leadership. Any miscommunication could lead to delays in action and possible worsening of the impact across the environment.

## The value of after-action reports

Once the dust has settled from an incident, threats have been eradicated, and systems are stable, it is common for IR teams to run an AAR to identify what worked, what did not, and how to change processes and playbooks for more effective and faster responses. Teams may choose to update IR plans and communications paths, share findings with leadership or even externally (where appropriate), and tune detections or notifications.

But if incidents are poorly handled, teams may resort to a blame-focused AAR instead of a constructive feedback-oriented approach. AAR should not focus on individual faults or blame teams for missing security controls but should leverage a systems thinking and engineering approach instead. Also, teams should leverage institutional knowledge to document, transfer knowledge, and ultimately learn from the situation. A culture focused on education and improvement will foster open and honest communication, which could help with detecting and preventing similar instances in the future.

## Playbooks and action

Most IR teams operate with a set of playbooks that either automate processes and communication or provide a list of instructions to follow in order, depending on the situation. **Security Orchestration, Automation, and Response** (**SOAR**) may be used to automate processes that are recorded in playbooks. An example is auto isolating a server if malware is detected.

Playbooks include many factors that come from human experience or IR best practices, including the following:

- Decision points – what, where, when, and why
- Roles and responsibilities – who and what
- Communication processes – who, when, and what
- Tools and techniques – what and when
- Containment and recovery protocols – dependent on the situation

IR playbooks must be designed with human usability in mind, not just technical completeness or dashboard metrics. During an active incident, responders are often operating under extreme time pressure, cognitive overload, and stress, which significantly affects their ability to process complex instructions. Playbooks that are overly dense, poorly organized, or filled with jargon can slow decision-making and increase the likelihood of errors. Instead, effective playbooks should prioritize clear structure, concise steps, visual hierarchy, and easily accessible decision points, so responders can quickly understand what actions to take next.

Although the playbooks are created using tools and automation, without a human factors engineering approach, they may be overly complex, lack appropriate timing, or lead to the wrong action being taken during an event. Another form of bias, action bias, refers to the human tendency to favor taking immediate action rather than pausing to analyze a situation, even when gathering more information before deciding would be optimal. Incident response playbooks are intended to counteract this tendency by providing structured guidance that encourages verification and analysis before response actions are taken. However, if playbooks contain unclear instructions, oversimplified workflows, or are not informed by real-world operational experience, they may inadvertently reinforce action bias by pushing responders toward immediate actions without adequate context or analysis. Any automation used by an IR team should provide visual coordination tools, shared views, and a common language for all engaged teams, while also supporting external cognitive scaffolding by allowing systems to track information and automate routine decisions rather than relying on human memory.

## The dangers of tools and techniques

As mentioned in all steps of the IR life cycle, responders may be using a multitude of tools to determine the cause, impact, and IOCs. *Figure 3.2* references the various tools and data sources that an IR team may need to utilize during an incident:

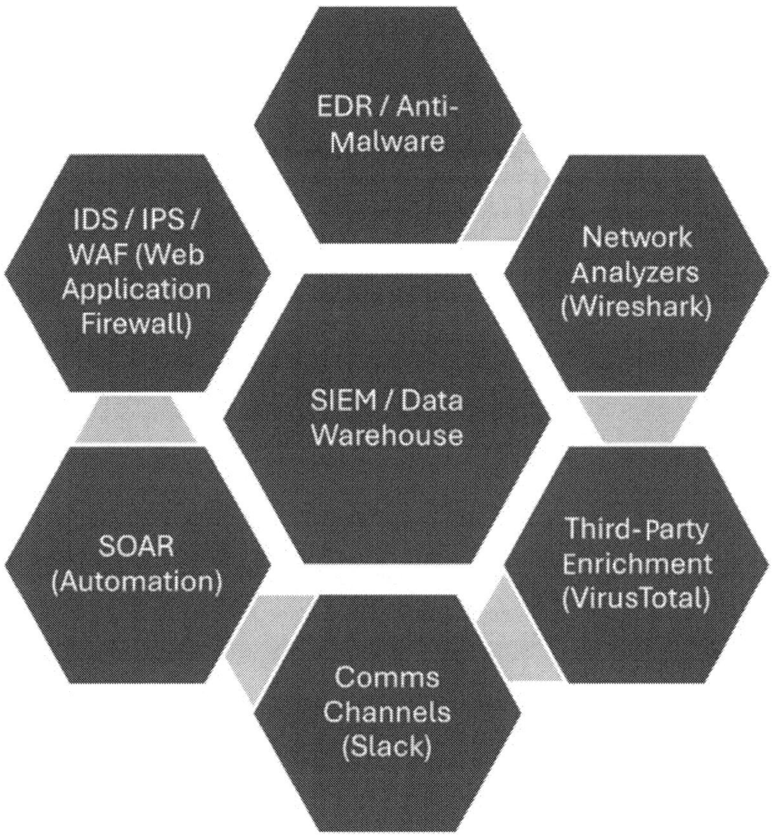


*Figure 3.2: Tools required by an IR team*

IR teams rely on a multitude of tools to provide support before, during, and after an incident. Responders must review all aspects of telemetry to determine the impact, exposure, and criticality of the incident. Tools and automation in IR are not only technical in nature but can also incorporate human factors principles that improve IR tooling by reducing confusion, response delays, and errors.

As shown in the preceding figure, IR teams use tools for detection, monitoring, network analysis, TI, forensics, and endpoint management. But so many tools will potentially provide too much data, which can make it difficult to prioritize data sources or correlate information across multiple systems.

Overwhelming interfaces make it difficult for responders to focus, leading to a reduction in situational awareness. Our attention spans are minimal, with some recent studies suggesting that our attention spans are only eight seconds when interacting with online content (`https://sambarecovery.com/rehab-blog/average-human-attention-span-statistics`). This means that every new dashboard, application, incident, and communication has the potential of distracting us from tasks. When dealing with a high-pressure situation such as data breach, incident responders must retain as much focus as possible.

Task switching can lead to mental fatigue or an increased error rate, which prevents a positive cognitive flow for responders. For example, when dealing with very sophisticated attacks, incident responders need to follow forensic evidence, document findings, and communicate with stakeholders, all while tracing the behavior of possible attackers. Any break in this logical flow could lead to missed indicators, lag time in remediation, or communication failures while context switching between tasks.

# Limits of perception and cognition

Cybersecurity as a domain is often discussed as defenders and attackers at war against exploits, patches, and proper defenses. We focus on the technical aspects of IR but lack the inclusion of human factors, such as attention, perception, and our own judgment and experience. We cannot solely focus on the networks and endpoints in an environment; we must also understand and integrate the minds, experience, and intellect of our cyber-defenders.

Human cognition has its limits. Our brains can only process so much data at once, our focus and attention can be split in multiple directions, and our memory is far shorter than that of a computer. Our decision-making, especially in an IR context, is full of biases, blind spots, and limited knowledge or awareness, even with years of experience. In IR, responders are asked to triage multiple alerts in real time, correlate information from multiple tools with different datasets, and interpret signals in a short amount of time.

In some cases, humans can hold only five to nine items in their working memory. This means that if responders have to look at 10 different tools at a time, without automation or excessive notetaking, data points may be lost. When we are under stress, we may experience the phenomena of attention narrowing or decision fatigue, leading to increased time to make decisions or making the wrong call, leading to a larger incident. This does not mean that the human mind is weak or incapable but understanding how our brains work will make sure that we create the best possible tooling and processes to support cognition and perception.

## Limits of automation

Without automation, we are left to sort through piles of data, which could mean losing precious time and delays in reacting to an incident. But with too much automation, we may miss true-positive alerts, leading to a serious cyber incident or data exfiltration. Security analysts and incident responders rely heavily on processing massive amounts of data quickly to detect and respond to alerts. However, too much automation could lead to automation bias, that is, the overreliance on automated decisions even when they conflict with our own judgment or we have evidence to the contrary.

Automation bias can reduce attentional vigilance, according to Parasuraman & Riley (1997), specifically in highly complex domains such as IR and cybersecurity at large. Almost 30 years later, in a 2024 paper titled *Artificial Intelligence (AI) Safety and Automation Bias*, automation bias is mentioned as a critical component of AI deployment and readiness. It could lead responders to ignore anomalies because "the system did not alert," even if it could be a true positive. The automation story is not all bad, though. If automation is built with transparency, responders can use their own judgment and knowledge of the environment to validate the findings.

## Siloed knowledge bases

Another human factors challenge facing IR teams is the presence of siloed knowledge bases and fragmented information spread across multiple tools, documents, and teams, as well as varying skill levels. Because technology gives us the data, but not the comprehension of that data, teams may keep their knowledge siloed or maintain a close hold on their processes. In the technical fields, in general, there can be a feeling of wanting to hold on to knowledge to be a **Subject Matter Expert** (**SME**).

Tools may keep detections, logs, and TI reports siloed unless there is a large data warehouse that collects and stores all this information together. In larger teams, this may be the case, although there may be larger siloed teams that maintain their own data and use it based on their skillsets and objectives. For example, a TI team may keep their techniques siloed because of their own objective of leveraging **Open Source Threat Intelligence** (**OSINT**) data to identify specific IOCs or targeted areas of the business.

Researchers have introduced the distributed cognition theory, which explains shared information structures such as dashboards, playbooks, and incident timelines improve team performance rather than focusing solely on the expertise of a single individual. Without awareness across the IR team, there may be missed handoffs of data or details for an investigation, possible duplication of efforts, or delays in escalating a critical event to the next team. An initial component to help with using a shared vision is to use a collective dashboard or a visual timeline for all team members, providing cross-role visibility into tasks, actions, and case work.

## Stress and time pressure

For many responders, action is the most critical component of an investigation, not necessarily thinking about policies or procedures during a critical event. Responders may need to juggle time and case work with the forensic investigation, communicate with technical teams and executives, as well as handling any other legal or regulatory compliance components that they must adhere to. All these technical and psychological challenges can be stressful, with pressure to complete tasks quickly, leading to higher levels of anxiety.

Responders may experience a variety of human factors components, including reduced memory capacity based on cognitive workload, attention narrowing, as mentioned earlier in the chapter, and increased reliance on heuristics, increasing bias. Stress can have a major impact on our cognition, including our memory retrieval and executive functioning, as well as causing challenges with making decisions, leading to decision paralysis or decision inertia.

Each dashboard, tool, alert, communication channel, and investigation will be unique, some with higher levels of stress. But in each case or cyberattack, responders must act efficiently and with excellent decision-making skills. With the proper tools and processes in place and human factors engineering awareness, teams will be able to handle heavy caseloads with reduced stress.

## Cognitive workload

For many analysts and responders, their cognitive workload is constantly stretched and pushed, sometimes during an active attack or just by the sheer volume of alerts and technical details that must be reviewed constantly. Cognitive workload is the amount of mental effort that it takes our brains to process information, make decisions, and complete tasks. Even in smaller environments, the amount of data may be so large that it is difficult to automate or act on it all. Tools have their own built-in scoring or risk mechanisms that may not always align, for example, the **Common Vulnerability Scoring System** (**CVSS**) for vulnerabilities versus a vendor's specific risk score within their tool.

Even evaluating those types of risk requires inherent knowledge, decision-making, and the skill of responders to understand the context for each alert. With multiple false positives or limited context around alerts, responders will need to triage and investigate across multiple systems and disparate risk-scoring mechanisms. Without intelligence alert grouping, baselined risk scores, or appropriate tags for systems, IR teams may struggle with cognitive or information overload. Alert fatigue, which will be discussed in future chapters in more depth, is the desensitization to events based on too many signals or false positives.

## Human factors intervention

But it's not all bad news. IR teams can leverage a multitude of human factors skills and techniques to improve and refine their practices and processes. Before diving into solutions, IR teams should ask themselves some critical questions to gauge how effectively their systems leverage an understanding of human cognition and decision-making abilities:

- How can responders make accurate decisions when stress levels are high during a cyberattack?
- How can our IR teams understand the impact of perception on responding to and investigating alerts?
- How can our tools or processes be aligned to reduce mental load without compromising sustained awareness during an incident?

Human cognition and perception are not signs of weakness; they are measurable functions of how our brains process large quantities of data. As humans, we are susceptible to automation bias, confirmation bias, and cognitive overload. These functions can be tracked and measured to reduce mistakes in highly complex environments.

## Critical stages of decision-making

First, the basic decision of "is this a real alert, false positive, or potential noise or interruption" can keep a team from seeing a true positive. The technical inputs at this stage may come from EDR or a SIEM event, pattern matching and analysis, or TI or hunting activities. The specific human factors risks at this stage include possible alert fatigue, confirmation bias, or limited context of risk scores or vulnerabilities. To resolve this with a human factors engineering (HFE) approach, IR teams should use summarized or automated threat context within their tool stack, use confidence levels based on user or system activity (present and historical), and provide decision support with the use of playbook triggers.

A second and vital moment of decision-making is asking: does this need to be escalated to senior levels, executives, or our customers? At what point during containment or eradication do IR teams need to communicate with senior leadership based on their findings and actions? Most of the inputs at this stage are based on predefined severity levels, the scope of the incident, and business impact, either on internal systems or on clients. To combat potential issues at this stage, HFE principles would interject risk scoring with specific visual indicators, such as red/green flags, threshold-based prompts based on pattern matching, and clearly defined roles and responsibilities for escalation.

A third important area to focus on is remediation. This is the moment where decisions could impact how quickly systems are brought online to support the business or potentially put online before they are completely free of malware or ransomware, with an opportunity for reinfection. Teams are looking for the root cause of the infection or event and focus on eliminating the threat(s). IR groups look at malware analysis tools, logs, vulnerability data, and misconfigurations at either the host, application, or network layer. Potential psychological impacts include *satisficing* or deciding that a solution is "good enough"; overreliance on prior incidents or data points; and not having a full understanding of how the attacker was able to enter the network. But IR processes could include remediation checklists, artifacts from prior events, and notifications of dependency risks in systems.

Finally, a post-incident review or AAR is carried out after a cyberattack has occurred. IR teams will look at the timeline of the incident, the communication workflow and outputs, as well as any lessons learned from both positive and negative perspectives. A few of the human factors considerations are a culture that focuses on blame rather than a retrospective, memory decay if waiting too long after an event to review and document, and failure to follow up on recommendations and outcomes. But teams can use visual representations for decisions and impact within a graphical interface, provide prompts for AARs, and share revisions with broader teams, encouraging feedback and enhancements for better decision-making.

## Cognitive-ready IR

Bringing IR teams away from solely focusing on technical reviews means adapting mental models to handle complex and dynamic situations. This can also elevate individual contributors and managers to hone their skills, make better decisions, and handle stress under pressure. Technical teams can learn to focus on situational awareness, pattern recognition, coordination, and mental modeling to improve decision-making.

For example, when looking at an incident, have an IR team take a step back and evaluate what they're looking at before diving into remediation. Many times, an analyst or engineer will delete logs or pertinent information before ever getting to forensics, thereby potentially erasing helpful evidence. Train IR teams to examine each step thoughtfully. While we can process high volumes of data quickly, to ensure we make the right decision, it's best to discuss it with teammates or even take a five-minute break to reset our thought process.

IR teams can use technology to their advantage by creating comprehensive, not overwhelming or distracting, dashboards that only show the top three or five most important bits of information. Alerts should be correlated and handled automatically with proper summaries. However, those summaries should be available in real or near-real time, with role-specific or team-specific data. As an example, do not have tools that simply list alerts; use automation to group similar alerts, reduce false positives, and ultimately tune out noise so that teams won't even see them. Reducing the amount of information coming into an analyst's feed will help them focus on the problems that matter. This provides a shared understanding across the team, whether team members are newer to the role or organization or have been with the team for some time.

A common theme among any cyber team will be training focused on adaptability and flexibility, instead of running through a list or merely treating it as a checkbox exercise. Teams should train with tabletop exercises that go off script and maybe deal with unique or uncommon scenarios. As an example, have your team start with a common scenario, such as a relatively simple data exfiltration incident with one known exploited vulnerability. Then, add some IOCs from an **Advanced Persistent Threat** (**APT**) group, which becomes a zero-day attack. Allow the ramp-up of stress and pressure on the team to push them to act quickly, tossing in unexpected events. It's not meant to stress the team out, but to prepare them to think and act quickly during unexpected events. But be sure to allow teams the opportunity to discuss and relax after the scenario and talk about the stress, the pressure, and any frustration, as well as how they handled it.

Powerful communication comes in many forms, but just like with alerts and notifications, IR teams will want their communication methods to be high-fidelity and trustworthy. Without a consistent and effective communication channel, teams will start to tune out potentially vital information because of alert fatigue. Any time incidents or data are passed between teams is a critical time to make sure there is structure and it is role-based and timely. IR teams can use mental models or taxonomies such as those from NIST or MITRE to add a more human factors approach to their IR playbooks and communication strategies.

## Scenario-based exercises

Chaos is not something that would typically be recommended for IR teams during a tabletop exercise. However, there is power in testing and working through a chaotic situation as a team, especially when the stakes are lower and the situation is not as stressful. Tabletop exercises can even be fun and bring the team together, while also identifying possible gaps in playbooks or even how teams make decisions for escalation paths. To explore this further, let's cover a few example scenarios that may be fun for IR teams to test.

In IR tabletop exercises, the terms *cold state* and *hot state* describe the level of pressure and realism experienced by participants—in this case, our incident responders. A cold-state exercise occurs in a low-stress environment where participants calmly discuss how they would respond to an incident. A hot-state exercise simulates more closely the operational conditions of an actual security incident. From a human factors perspective, cold-state exercises focus on procedural understanding, while hot-state exercises test decision-making, cognitive workload, and team coordination under stress.

Tabletop exercises can be ineffective as they frequently fail to replicate the real cognitive, operational, and environmental pressures responders experience during actual incidents.

Many exercises are overly scripted, allowing participants to follow expected answers rather than actively analyze evolving and complex situations. This can create a false sense of preparedness because responders are not practicing navigating incomplete information, conflicting data, or time pressure.

The first scenario for a tabletop exercise is considering a credential-stuffing account on a third-party vendor that has administrative access to internal systems and datasets. The primary goal would be to test the response to external authentication compromise or account takeover events. Teams should determine the best time and event to escalate to an incident, what identity and MFA techniques are implemented, how and when users are notified, and whether there are any laws or regulations that teams must follow. A fun twist on the exercise could be that the attacker is using spoofed IP addresses that look like customer domain logins.

Another very relevant scenario for a tabletop exercise could be a zero-day exploit in a third-party library or application in a business-critical system. This event focuses on software supply chain security and involves a number of teams, including engineering, security, and procurement or legal teams, depending on the chosen scenario. IR teams will want to determine what inventory solution would provide those application details, what approvals would be required for patching, and the potential impact on production, as well as any legal or notification communications that should be integrated. To add an extra element, teams could find that the application is not catalogued in their application inventory and is internet-facing.

For a bit of variety, another type of scenario that teams could focus on as a tabletop exercise is a phishing attack that led to a **Business Email Compromise** (**BEC**). IR teams can focus on the social engineering implications that led to a spear-phishing campaign, as well as any subsequent financial motivation impacting HR and finance teams. They will need to determine how quickly they can detect email or account compromise and email tampering, identify wire transfers and processes, and notify both internal and external teams. As an unexpected twist, teams could have to adjust for an attacker who has already spoofed the CEO's email address and sent payment requirements to the CFO.

Adding some variety to tabletop exercises can prepare teams mentally for numerous attack vectors and scenarios and processes for remediation and recovery. To make any tabletop exercise exciting and memorable for participants, consider having a facilitator who acts as a social engineering proponent, adding conflicting decision points to test playbooks, as well as a delay to communications. These activities will lead the team to find inconsistencies in processes, understand gaps in communication, and identify areas where roles or responsibilities should be better defined.

## Psychological safety and a culture of openness

Another area for IR teams to implement human factors components is addressing the challenge of making mistakes and errors, which could lead to a poor perception of the IR team or processes. Incidents are considered to be issues with technical alerting or notification, but they could be greatly improved with a culture of acceptance and understanding of human error. Teams may choose to skip a process or fail to report an issue because of fear of repercussion or the perception that an individual, rather than the tools or technology, failed.

Blame culture can lead IR teams or even leadership to fear punishment or embarrassment, and it could even lead to the underreporting of potentially serious issues. IR teams may lack psychological safety, meaning they worry about misrepresenting data, misleading stakeholders, or even the blame that may be placed on them or other teams. To combat blame culture, IR teams should emulate an SRE culture that focuses on open communication for fixing systems instead of punishing teams for technical issues.

In an IR context, adopting SRE practices means treating incidents as opportunities to improve systems and processes, rather than assigning blame to individuals. This encourages psychological safety, allowing responders to report mistakes, near misses, and failures without fear of punishment. SRE culture also prioritizes clear runbooks, automation to reduce repetitive cognitive workload, and structured post-incident reviews that focus on systemic issues rather than human error alone. Another issue around human error that IR teams face is confusion between three facets of the response process: error, adaptation, and allowing for innovation. Crafting a proper problem statement allows the teams to focus on deviations as workarounds or even possible improvements to systems, rather than a mistake or an issue. Framing and scope are essential for errors, making sure that real errors are categorized as such, rather than something that was a technical control or configuration.

## Confirmation bias

Confirmation bias, as described previously, is the way that we search for, interpret, and even choose information based on our perception or assumptions. This means that we could be missing or misinterpreting valid data because our own bias contradicts the evidence in front of us. Specific to IR teams, this could mean focusing on one explanation of an event rather than exploring other options, dismissing evidence that conflicts with someone's interpretation, or seeing new data only through a biased lens based on what they found or discovered previously.

IR teams must act quickly, making decisions around an alert, event, or incident that could have a major impact, but this could lead to confirmation bias. An example of confirmation bias in an IR situation is evaluating a phishing alert and determining that it looks similar to prior events. This is considered a **cognitive trap**, where teams may miss a spear-phishing or BEC event because it looked benign based on prior experience and patterns. The ticket or incident could be closed without a more thorough analysis, simply based on past harmless events that looked similar, even though there may be indicators of something else occurring.

As another example, IR teams may see a malware alert and determine it to be a false positive because the team saw something similar in their lab or test environment. This is another cognitive trap because a common alert could be hiding the initial stage of a ransomware attack. For example, the team may see a PowerShell script attempting to run with administrative privileges and reach out to the system owner, who may consider that normal behavior. But in fact, there was something else occurring, and the team missed it as they were solely thinking of their previous experience.

For our final example, consider an incident that begins with data exfiltration that is much larger than typical cases. A responder considers this the beginning stage of an APT attack and overlooks a possible insider threat scenario. A cognitive trap in a different direction, this one considers a more complex explanation over a simpler one that would track more closely with the behavior of the data exfiltration alert. The responder may miss warning signs, such as recent resignations, disgruntled employees, or accounts being misused, that would indicate a possible insider event rather than an external threat.

# Building learning and system resilience

Within the IR space, our cybersecurity teams are typically measured on how quickly a threat is detected and eradicated, focusing on quantifiable metrics for **Mean Time to Remediation** (**MTTR**) or **Mean Time to Detection** (**MTTD**). But the technical aspects are not the only important parts of a resilient IR process or the systems that back them up. A resilient IR process is structured to continue functioning even when conditions change quickly, information is incomplete, or systems behave unexpectedly due to a breach. It emphasizes flexibility, clear decision-making structures, and the ability for responders to adjust actions, containment, or eradication based on real-time conditions. Effective IR teams are also measured by how quickly and effectively they learn from incidents, events, alerts, and possible missed detections.

Creating a cybersecurity training and process loop encourages teams to find gaps in systems, assumptions, and, very specifically, communication processes, which could mean the difference between a successful and unsuccessful ransomware attempt. But there are two key areas where IR teams can build human factors into their processes: the ability to adapt after an incident and sharing insights that build upon the institutional knowledge shared between teams. IR teams are responsible not only for detecting and containing incidents but also for absorbing disruption, adapting to new data, and recovering operations while focusing on investigative insights. With intention and collaboration, responders and their leaders can design resilient systems and a feedback learning process for continuous improvement.

The integration of human factors principles can help reduce fear-based responses toward reporting errors, allowing us to design systems that support our cognitive workloads and memory functions and prepare mental models based on experience. Human-centered design can ensure that learning is not a byproduct of an incident but a built-in mechanism for responders and cybersecurity team members. *Building resilience* in systems is not just about bouncing back; it is about truly improving all areas of the IR life cycle to futureproof the team.

# Foundations of trust

To build **resilient systems**, IR teams must have trust—in themselves, their teams, and their reporting structure. The core IR team must be based on interpersonal trust, and not just between the people on the teams but with their tools and leadership as well. In an IR team with deep trust and focus, analysts and responders can speak up about errors or issues without concern about retribution. This leads them to report possible issues or incidents early, escalate when necessary, and positively impact AARs with honest feedback.

Similar to psychological safety, *Edmondson (2004)* discusses how teams can more quickly adapt and improve performance so that individuals feel safe. The original study was done for hospitals and in the aviation industry, where human lives are at stake, but the principles remain the same. Translating psychological safety to IR, processes, and tools should allow teams to escalate issues quickly, provide honest feedback even when it can be difficult to hear, and allow individuals to acknowledge mistakes or errors.

A real-world example involves responders who failed to escalate an incident after ransomware was discovered on critical systems. In this case, the responders were nervous about telling their leadership that ransomware was spreading due to the possibility of being fired or removed from their jobs. Instead, ransomware spread to critical systems such as databases, encrypting and locking out the backbone of the environment, delaying development work, and impacting customers, ultimately leading to revenue loss. If the team was supported or felt encouraged to share information quickly, they may have contained or even eradicated the ransomware before it spread too far within the network.

# Communications handoffs and automation

Automation is all about balance. If automation is in place but it takes too long, is inaccurate, or ends up performing actions incorrectly, it can be a detriment to the IR teams that need trustworthy automation. If the automation fails to support the decisions of the IR analysts or responders, systems are considered to be more fragile than resilient. If the tools or automation lack transparency, have poor integration with other tools, or conduct work in silo, IR teams will not reap the benefits of a robust and trustworthy automation implementation.

For example, if alerts are lacking context or there is no explanation behind the actions, IR teams may lose trust or faith, reverting to manual or error-prone tasks instead. Hutchins, way back in 1995, discussed distributed cognition theory, where teams operate as cognitive systems that rely on representations. Even then, psychological studies have shown that individuals perform better when they can review a representation of data, as we do now with alerts, dashboards, and visualizations.

Using these types of **distributed systems** and information can help share an understanding of the IR process and teams. One of the best ways to use automation and communication tools is to adopt explainable automation that uses traceability and rationale for decisions around alerts and tasks. Using chat platforms where teams can collaborate quickly will allow the distribution of decisions across different groups, such as IR, to executives. A final recommendation: use user-centered flows that build automation to support reflection and even uncertainty in decisions, which encourages a focus on resiliency and reliability, versus the speed of carrying out tasks and resolution.

## Feedback loops in tooling and procedures

Feedback loops are the bread and butter of any IR team to balance and improve communications, tooling, and processes. Given the ever-evolving landscape of cybersecurity threats, techniques, emerging technologies, and laws and regulations, IR teams must continuously improve to keep up. As mentioned previously, when a healthy platform of trust exists within an IR team, individuals can use reflection to turn an incident into an actionable insight.

During an incident, analysts and responders are focused on the event or restoring systems to production. But the incredible value of an incident is that once the incident is resolved, teams have the opportunity to evaluate it. If feedback loops do not exist in tooling or processes, organizations and IR teams specifically will be doomed to miss patterns of repeated alerts, as well as potential blind spots in detections or tooling, as well as lacking effective tooling or automation potential. Organizations must continue to expand their capacity to improve, or else they may be stuck repeating the same mistakes again.

A real-world example of this is an IR team that conducts a retrospective after a particularly devastating incident. In this scenario, the team missed a detection, which led to a massive data exfiltration of crown jewel data or **Intellectual Property** (**IP**). During the retrospective, the team focuses on blaming each other for the lack of detections, misconfigurations of alerts, and, ultimately, not focusing enough on the data, leading to mistakes across the team. This exercise leaves the IR team frustrated, angry, and pointing fingers at each other, instead of sharing true and actionable data.

Teams should instead focus on implementing some best practices to build robust feedback loops. First, teams should use **structured AARs** with scripted prompts around how decisions are made, how teams handle uncertainty, and the various paths for coordination and collaboration that were used. Structured AARs evaluate how the response was conducted, identify what worked well, determine what failed, and capture lessons learned to improve future responses.

Next, teams should integrate those lessons learned into everyday practices, such as alert tuning and building proper logic and transparency into automation and scripting. Finally, IR teams should keep a well-documented **decision library** that helps them learn, iterate, and detect trends in decisions that are either working or not working and require improvement.

# Resilient learning systems

The focus behind improving IR teams through human factors is to turn an incident into a cycle of growth and development. Each incident, alert, detection, or event is an opportunity to learn, adapt, and build more resiliency in IR processes and tooling. As many academic and technical resources claim, it is not a matter of *if* an organization gets breached, but *when*. This means that we can either continue to repeat the errors or mistakes from the past or open a path to evolution.

Resilient systems for learning and education are built when both technology and humans work and grow together. Specifically, to an IR team, playbooks will be updated and adapted, tools will be updated and able to mold around user behavior, and past events will inform and update decision-making processes for the future. IR teams can pull from resilience engineering and the four capabilities that make up the process:

1. Anticipate possible disruptions or interruptions to systems and tools.
2. Monitor emerging threats and system or network health for anomalies.
3. Respond to real-time events that may be ambiguous or challenging.
4. Learn and respond to events or incidents from both failure and success, never fearing failure.

The following figure illustrates a five-level maturity model that describes how IR practices evolve within an organization. It shows the progression from a reactive state, where incidents are handled in an ad hoc manner, to a resilient, learning-driven culture in which feedback, training, and continuous improvement strengthen the organization's ability to manage cybersecurity incidents:

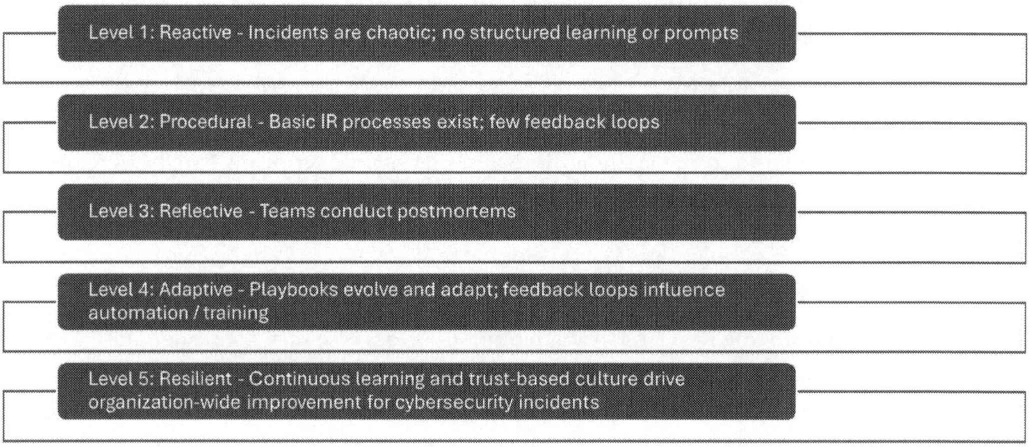


*Figure 3.3: Resilience maturity model*

Incidents are not the result of solely mistakes or poor decisions, but also when systems are poorly designed or ignore adaptive reasoning from mistakes or errors. Teams should consider a resiliency maturity model to improve system design and allocate time to continuously iterate and build more mature IR programs. Using the preceding figure, teams can start from level 1, a reactive mindset, and progress to level 5, a more resilient and robust IR model. Every security and IR team will be at a different level of maturity; the idea is to determine where the team fits based on current processes and efficiency, then build human factors capability in a way that is sustainable.

# A case (or two) for human factors

There are multiple considerations for integrating human factors into IR teams, but let's put it all into practice. We will look at two example cases: the Capital One Breach in 2019 and the Maersk incident in 2017. These examples have been provided due to the nature and size of these incidents, not to cast blame or victim-shame. On the contrary, these events are not simply about missed detections or misconfigurations in systems but evaluating the human factors and psychological aspects.

## The Capital One breach

To summarize this well-known breach, a former AWS employee exploited a misconfigured **web application firewall** (**WAF**) to gain access to systems. The actor was able to exfiltrate data from over 100 million user accounts. One of the unique aspects of the attacker in this situation was that they leaked a lot of the details of the data breach themselves in public forums, highlighting legacy data and **poor patch management** in the environment.

Ultimately, though, there were several factors that led to this event. First, alert fatigue was identified in the indictment from the **United States (US) Department of Justice (DoJ)**. Another aspect was that the SOC experienced **normalization of deviance**, meaning critical alerts were missed because of the volume of noise in alerts. Finally, misconfigurations were undocumented and left unremediated, with a lack of communication between the cloud teams and IR and SecOps.

This case highlights the multiple recommendations that we have discussed and how they may have either prevented this event or provided early detection that something was amiss:

- Reduce any friction between teams and improve communication
- Tune and tailor alerts based on feedback loops
- Provide open and honest collaboration on legacy vulnerabilities or misconfigurations —reduce blame or shame around patching

## Maersk and NotPetya

A final example to highlight the importance of human factors in IR teams is the Maersk environment that was brought down by the **NotPetya worm** in 2017. This worm was able to infect a Ukrainian accounting system that was left unpatched, bringing down their global network. Laptops on the helpdesk started displaying strange notes about either files being encrypted or repairing the filesystem without prompting.

This event had multiple areas where human factors principles could have positively impacted the organization. First, there was a **lack of segmentation** of systems; the laptops and computers were impacted quickly because of their interconnectivity. There was an over-reliance on centralized systems, leading to a single issue impacting their network on a global scale. Finally, the recovery of the environment was due to the team finding an offline domain controller, a fortuitous find rather than a sign of resilience in their architecture.

With the addition of a few human factors components, this cyberattack may have had less impact or been detected faster. First, if there was a comprehensive and mature focus on organizational memory, processes and system data could have been catalogued and a robust response procedure created. Redundancy awareness or building resilient systems that are able to withstand outages or cyberattacks, would have provided a robust recovery plan.

# Summary

IR is often framed as a purely technical process, but human factors ultimately determine its success or failure. Success is defined as the efficient resolution of an incident, while failure is the inability to resolve incidents efficiently. Cognitive biases, stress, workload distribution, and communication dynamics all play critical roles in how responders perceive, analyze, and act during an incident.

Poorly designed alerts, unclear roles, and fatigue (of all varieties) can slow containment and lead to mistakes. But with the assistance of well-structured processes, psychological safety, and effective collaboration, recovery can be accelerated and the overall impact reduced.

This chapter highlighted the importance of recognizing cognitive limitations, such as decision paralysis, and implementing strategies that offset them using scenario-based exercises and error reporting. Designing tools that align with natural cognitive processes and fostering trust within cross-functional teams are essential steps to strengthening resilience.

Transitioning to the next chapter, we will expand these ideas into the day-to-day reality of security analysts, the constant monitoring of high-volume data streams, the unique stressors of shift work in critical positions, and the systemic challenges of balancing automation with human judgment.

# References


- CISA. *Tabletop Exercise Packages.* Cybersecurity and Infrastructure Security Agency.
- Edmondson, A. (1999). *Psychological Safety and Learning Behavior in Work Teams.* Administrative Science Quarterly.
- Endsley, M. R. (1995). *Toward a Theory of Situation Awareness in Dynamic Systems.* Human Factors.
- Georgetown Center for Security and Emerging Technology (CSET). *AI Safety and Automation Bias.* `https://cset.georgetown.edu/publication/ai-safety-and-automation-bias/`
- Google. *Site Reliability Engineering: How Google Runs Production Systems.* O'Reilly Media.
- Hollnagel, E. *Safety-I and Safety-II: The Past and Future of Safety Management.*
- Hollnagel, E. *Cognitive Workload Technical Brief.* Office of the Chief Human Capital Officer.
- Hutchins, E. (1995). *Cognition in the Wild.* MIT Press.
- National Institute of Standards and Technology (NIST). *SP 800-61 Rev. 3: Incident Response Recommendations and Considerations for Cybersecurity Risk Management – A CSF 2.0 Community Profile.* Computer Security Resource Center (CSRC).
- RSAC Conference. *Incident Response Documentation: Building for Resilience, Not Just Recovery.* `https://www.rsaconference.com`
- Sunstein, C. R., et al. *Opinion Dynamics with Confirmation Bias.* PMC.

# Get this book's PDF version and more

Scan the QR code (or go to `packtpub.com/unlock`). Search for this book by name, confirm the edition, and then follow the steps on the page.

**UNLOCK NOW**

*Note: Keep your invoice handy. Purchases made directly from Packt don't require an invoice.*

# 4

# Human Factors in Security Operations

**Human Factors Engineering** (**HFE**) has implications across many cybersecurity disciplines, but the backbone of any cybersecurity team is the **security operations center** (**SOC**). A SOC could be comprised of many different skillsets, tools, techniques, and processes. Whether supporting a government agency, a healthcare organization, or a manufacturing company, the SOC is the first line of defense against threats.

But like **incident response** (**IR**) teams, SOC teams commonly face challenges because of the sheer volume of alerts, notifications, tools, and the constant sophistication of attackers and threats. IR teams typically become involved after an incident has occurred, where a SOC team is considered the first line of defense for detection and prevention. To begin, let's cover the structure and organization of a SOC while addressing the possible pressure and stress of working in a security operations environment. HFE can provide insight into where gaps may exist and how to address them with a human-centric and engineering approach.

In this chapter, you will learn about the practical applications of integrating human factors in SecOps teams. We will cover some of the modern challenges, such as overloaded dashboards, complex tooling, and alert fatigue, that a SecOps team faces. Then, we will cover some of the easier and more practical ways to resolve these challenges, including color coding, using automation properly within tooling, and balancing structure and **standard operating procedures** (**SOPs**) with operational activities. Finally, you will learn how to integrate human factors into SecOps teams, including adaptive decision-making, incorporating human-centered analysis, and integrating human cognition limits into tasking.

In this chapter, you will cover the following topics:

- Defining security operations
- Key human factors challenging in security operations
- Cognitive demands on a modern SOC
- Beyond alert fatigue
- Role of explainability
- Interface and system design for analyst success
- SOPs and the pitfalls of structure and rigidity
- Incorporating human factors for SecOps teams

# Defining security operations

A SOC's group of analysts is responsible for maintaining an organization's security posture. While SOC teams have evolved over the last few years, the mission remains the same: protecting the organization from ongoing cyber threats with early identification and investigation. SOC teams, depending on the size of the organization, may operate several different functions:

- **Threat monitoring**: EDR, SIEM, XDR, and other tooling
- **Triage for alerts**: Analysis of alerts to determine TP versus FP
- **Threat hunting**: Depending on team size, may look for threats based on intelligence, including **indicators of compromise** (**IOCs**), anomalous behavior in logs, and misconfigurations or exploitable vulnerabilities
- **Incident escalation**: Once a threat is validated, an incident will be created and passed to a separate IR team
- **Tuning and rules**: Update detections to improve accuracy

Typically, a SOC team interfaces with the other aspects of a cybersecurity program, including the IR team, the threat intelligence or threat hunting teams, vulnerability management, as well as any IT or cloud operations teams. An SOC team may be internal to the organization or an external third-party entity, but its mission remains the same, provide 24/7 support to protect the organization. These security analysts can have a wide variety of skills, from data science backgrounds to development or IT operations experience.

## Running a 24/7 operation

Most SOC operations are 24/7 or use a *follow-the-sun* model, having teams across the globe to support multiple geographies. In smaller organizations, SOC teams could operate in one or two time zones, but larger teams are most likely global; it all depends on the organization's needs and size. Regardless of team structure, most teams will still experience a shift handoff. In smaller teams, SOC analysts will most likely experience sleep disruption during high-alert times or even if there is certain expertise required on specific events.

Some of the other challenges of a 24/7 operation are analyst burnout, desensitization, team cohesion, or challenges in handing off alerts during shift changes. This is common for any 24/7 team, but in SOC, decision-making on possible critical alerts could have serious implications. Missed detections, lack of escalation, or critical alerts could all compound the stress and fatigue that analysts experience. SOC teams must monitor any number of tools, dashboards, events, and alerts, and use a combination of on-premise and third-party open source tools to conduct a comprehensive investigation.

Analysts experience a high volume of alerts, pressure to investigate events quickly, and limited closure on those alerts. Communication is a critical component of any SOC, and with the high volume of information, it can be important to use a standardized mechanism for sharing details. Without that, teams will experience frustration with limited information or even lack any kind of common communication channels. When teams have to collaborate in a consistently high-stress environment, it could lead to alert fatigue, cognitive overload, or even challenges in handing off details to the next group.

# Key human factors challenges in security operations

SOC teams can benefit greatly from integrating HFE practices due to burnout, high-stress environments, and disparate tools leading to cognitive overload and alert fatigue. Including additional factors such as desensitization to critical alerts, SOC team members and leadership can identify gaps and solve them with the understanding of HFE and psychological principles. Instead of focusing on technology and tooling, teams can address decision-making and configurations with a focus on the individual and team structure instead.

Human factors challenges and implications include cognitive overload, alert fatigue, desensitization to cyber threats, and tool complexity within SecOps environments. These demands on SecOps teams can lead to attention management issues, missed detections, and high false positive rates, which can lead to memory workload issues.

## Cognitive overload

Cognitive overload can occur for two main reasons within a SecOps team: either data is siloed, making it difficult to identify patterns, or dashboards and tools are fragmented, forcing analysts to log into too many different systems with unique interfaces and user experiences. This is where SecOps teams can benefit from building better visualizations or leveraging design teams to discuss possible improvements. HFE is not solely about the psychological implications of tool design, but also the engineering practices behind it and the visualizations that work better for humans. Without a full understanding of engineering practices, tools may be misconfigured, leading to missed detections, high false-positive rates, and ultimately leading to other cognitive overload challenges, such as attention management and fatigue.

For example, if a SecOps team is flooded with false-positive alerts day after day, individuals may start to feel like they are drowning in a sea of alerts. It can feel like an impossible mountain to climb, never reaching the peak. This impacts morale and the desire to continue working to close tickets. If one feels like they cannot ever have a positive impact, they may burn out, feel frustrated, and ultimately not see a point in continuing to do their work.

Understanding our cognitive limitations and functions can help identify gaps in technology or tooling. For example, a SOC group may use tools with different color schemes. Imagine a tool that uses red, yellow, and green to indicate a critical, medium, or low alert, and another tool that uses a heat map to indicate a possible critical event. For something that may sound simple, our brains must adjust and adapt every time we switch to that tool, leading to possible stress or frustration during context switching.

## Alert fatigue and desensitization

Alert fatigue is a well-studied and documented event across multiple cybersecurity teams, but especially in a SecOps environment. The entirety of the mission focuses on automation and the manual review of alerts across the organization. But when the alert volume is high and the fidelity is low, it can lead to frustration or stress from seeing so many alerts that are not relevant. Not only that, but teams may feel defeated by the sheer volume of events; it can feel like climbing a mountain and never reaching its peak.

A great example of alert fatigue is a SOC analyst sitting at their desk for eight to ten hours a day, staring at multiple screens and tools, all showing alerts and notifications for potential cybersecurity events. Imagine that 95% of those events are false positives, meaning that the majority of their day is spent watching alerts that are due to operational activity, expected behavior, or benign administrative tasks. Repetitive and mundane tasks lead to burnout, frustration, and overall dissatisfaction with their job, feeling like climbing a mountain that has no peak. Without any engaging or innovative projects, an individual will start to feel bored, possibly miss alerts, and eventually leave their job, seeking projects and tasks with more complexity or that are far more fulfilling.

This section will simply outline the common challenges around alert fatigue and why it exists, but in later sections, we will cover how to combat fatigue with a variety of methods. Desensitization to alerts could happen for several reasons. It may be that there are far too many alerts coming into the teams; maybe there are multiple dashboards that display network, email, mobile device, and identity alerts. Looking at hundreds or thousands of alerts a day for eight to ten hours straight could make anyone become complacent.

Tuning and tailoring alerts is an essential tool to combat desensitization, and to help reduce the common events that may be false positives, or even if they are true positives, they may not be relevant given a pattern of operational behavior. For example, imagine a flood of alerts because a systems administrator is performing testing on their server. This may generate a ton of alerts for the SOC, requiring resources to spend time on reaching out to the system owner, understanding the behavior, and ultimately refining the alerts. This is only one type of alert that must be monitored; at scale, it can be challenging to review, remediate, and understand each alert while also running the operations center.

## Tool complexity handoffs

Tools, applications, dashboards, and bears, oh my! Any operations team works with a variety of tools, but SecOps teams must use a variety of sources to gain insights into whether an alert is a TP or an FP. The larger and more complex the technical environment, the more tools that will be required. For example, an organization running in an AWS cloud environment may only opt to use some of the in-house tooling to manage SIEM and inventory. However, an organization that uses a multi-cloud approach may want to use a third-party SaaS product or even use multiple cloud platforms' unique tool offerings.

This tool complexity means analysts look at data streams from multiple platforms, often in different contexts and using a variety of fields. For example, one tool may use a risk calculation of low, medium, critical, and high, with a numerical value of 1-10, while another risk-scoring mechanism for the same data uses 1-100. Something simple, such as numerical scores require additional cognitive processing to determine the impact or criticality of the alert. To show just a sample of how SOC tooling meets cognition, *Figure 4.1* displays an example of SOC tools, some of the cognitive concepts while analysts review alerts, and the communications, process, and documentation outputs expected during an alert review:

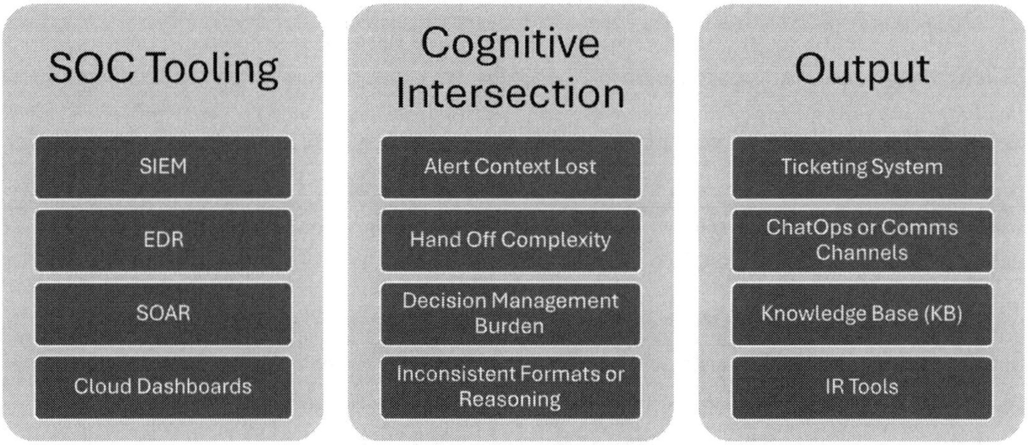


*Figure 4.1 – Where cognition meets tooling*

For example, take a SIEM, the center for logging and a trigger point to create alerts that may identify malicious behavior or patterns. Those logs must be parsed, reviewed, and contain some automation to provide a detection that funnels to the SOC. From there, an analyst must use playbooks, their own inherent knowledge and skills, and understand what each alert means, both in isolation and as a possible pattern or trend. Multiple forms of communication come from each alert, possibly a ticket that is closed or escalated to the IR team, communications channels for quick investigations, as well as possibly tuning for alerts or additional updates to **Knowledge Base** (**KB**) articles or playbooks. Another layer of complexity on top of tooling is the shift changes that occur between time zones or analysts who finish their day and hand off tasking to the next group. During this time, open cases may be re-assigned, whether context is provided or detailed notes, and another analyst must take the case and determine a path forward. In some cases, more analysis will be required, or the case may be closed, but without a proper and detailed description of the event, TP alerts may be missed.

# Cognitive demands of a modern SOC

Modern SecOps teams rely on a variety of automation techniques to build detections, comb through mountains of data, and combat the stress and pressure that comes with a highly critical business function. There are many new findings in the academic and research communities that highlight opportunities to implement human factors understanding into building a high-performance SOC team.

Alert fatigue has been discussed, but this is just one of the many levels of fatigue that a SOC analyst or SecOps team may face. An article from *Swimlane* in 2022 highlighted that analysts receive thousands of alerts per day, sometimes spending hours performing an initial analysis, and can miss critical events. In the survey conducted, there were over 60% of analysts who reported fatigue as a possible indicator of missed detections. Another academic *research paper* from 2025 on alert fatigue in SOC teams remains a challenge, highlighting the need to evaluate other areas of human factors opportunities for analysts.

## Attention management

Our cognitive functions only stretch so far, and with a finite number of cognitive resources available, analysts must research threats, document and present findings, and monitor tools and a variety of alerts. Paying attention to all these different factors while under constant stress makes it difficult for humans to pay close attention to every detail and aspect. Without an understanding of how our focus and attention work as part of our cognitive reasoning and decision-making for complex problem sets, we may miss a possible opportunity to bridge those gaps.

Specifically, attention management in a SecOps team could be impacted by interrupt-driven alerts or communications, context switching, a high level of vigilance during shifts, and inconsistent interfaces across a variety of tools. When analysts are constantly moving between signals, chat interfaces, and constant escalations, it can be difficult to maintain focus on a specific case or item. That, combined with the context switching between six to ten different tools, leads to ineffective focus.

There are multiple techniques that SOC teams can utilize to address attention management for SOC analysts in several practical ways. Most importantly, attention is something that we all struggle with, so some of these strategies may be useful across teams and disciplines. First, prioritize and filter alerts so that analysts are only presented with the most relevant and high-risk events, which will also help in reducing noise and preventing constant context switching. Second, design tools and dashboards that group related alerts and highlight key signals, which are critical components in both attention and burnout. Third, implement structured workflows and protected focus time, ensuring analysts can complete investigations without continuous interruptions from new alerts or messages.

## Working memory limits

Working memory is where we hold the latest and most important information in short-term storage in our brains. In the cognitive psychology world, working memory can only retain about 4+1 chunks of data at a time. The original designation for understanding working memory was seven items, plus or minus two. This limit becomes incredibly relevant in a high-paced and multi-faceted environment such as SOC. Analysts must retain IP addresses, user information, business context, alert data, and signals, and develop hypotheses based on this data, simultaneously.

Modern cognitive science research suggests that the true capacity of working memory is closer to about four meaningful items, not seven. When people remember more, they usually rely on chunking strategies, prior knowledge, or external components and tools rather than pure working memory capacity. For example, remembering a familiar phrase or pattern counts as a single "chunk," even though it contains multiple elements. Because of this, modern human factors and interface design guidance have shifted away from the 7 ± 2 rule. Systems that present analysts with many simultaneous alerts, indicators, or decision points can easily exceed realistic cognitive limits, which, based on how current SOC teams operate, could be a huge detriment to the success of the team.

A few areas where working memory is challenged are in cross-tool overload, context loss, and interruptions for analysts based on escalations, because individuals must move between suspicious IPs, user logs, ticket details and descriptions, EDR or malware alerts, and network analysis. Context loss can happen because of the sheer volume of data that must be reviewed, as well as moving from one alert to another in a short time, which could lead to missing or losing key details for each case. In any security operations team, having to escalate alerts or investigations during a triage stage could mean losing context or understanding while juggling multiple investigations.

There are psychological studies from 2010 (`https://pmc.ncbi.nlm.nih.gov/articles/PMC2864034/`) that show memory becomes error-prone when our brains try to hold onto multiple unrelated items, especially in a disruption-based environment such as a SOC. Information must be retained in our working memory, and when pieces of data start to leak out, analysts may misremember IPs, misinterpret logs, or make incorrect correlations based on bad data or the components that we put together out of order.

# Cognitive overload and decision-making

SOC analysts must maintain and utilize multiple interfaces, for example, a SIEM for log events and an EDR dashboard or alerts from servers and systems. Cognitive overload is the phenomenon where an individual exceeds their working memory, described previously, and this can cause slowdowns, errors in documents or decision-making, and even lead to higher stress. When there are higher mental demands placed on a SOC analyst, the first line of defense of any cybersecurity team, it can be a driver to overanalyze critical alerts, experience burnout or frustration, and ultimately lead to missed signals or detections.

But cognitive overload can come from a variety of sources, including the need to enter data in multiple areas, mentally shuffling context, and inflexibility when it comes to checklists or processes. When analysts must enter the same information into a ticketing system, a **security orchestration and automation and response** (**SOAR**) platform, and maybe emails or notes to leadership, they can suffer from mental friction due to an overload of working memory demands. Experiencing inflexibility when it comes to checklists or playbooks can lead to *checklist bias,* where analysts follow a prescriptive process versus using adaptive reasoning to resolve incidents.

People have noticed that *continuous partial attention* to tasks can seriously impact and reduce task-switch resilience. Even in recent ACM studies and workshops, the result of multidisciplinary research, like we are doing here with human factors in cybersecurity, can provide meaningful solutions to cognitive-load and mental resiliency for high-stress and multi-tasking environments. Without understanding how analysts and operators experience psychological or mental workloads, organizations may struggle to identify and resolve common issues in a SecOps environment.

# Beyond alert fatigue

Alert fatigue and mental workloads are one component of what a SecOps team experiences, but what about the other cognitive factors? Analysts and operators may suffer from other factors, such as a massive flood of *noise* or alerts, a barrage of false positives to sift through, and psychological aspects such as *learned helplessness* or confirmation bias. Some areas of human factors engineering are seen across cybersecurity disciplines, but they each have unique aspects that can erode our ability to make clear and quality decisions.

## Signal to noise

SecOps teams must wade through a sea of alerts, hundreds or thousands of alerts and signals that diminish one's ability to determine a true threat versus noise, or irrelevant alerts. In human factors research, there can be a decline in *perceptual sensitivity* when an individual is experiencing cognitive fatigue, meaning that analysts and operators could start to lean more conservative (escalate everything) or more erratic (wild swings between true positives and false positives) in their reporting.

Vigilance decrement is when the attention of the analyst can deteriorate within 15 minutes of starting a task that requires incredible focus. This phenomenon can be a challenge when a SOC analyst may be on a shift for eight to ten hours, requiring vigilance on alerts for most of that time. Even if analysts take breaks every couple of hours or have a long break in between those hours, they may need to focus for several hours at a time. With an average of *4,500 alerts a day* and false-positive rates anywhere between 67% and 99%, requiring focus for an entire shift through the noise would be difficult for anyone.

Wading through the constant barrage of alerts and signals can lead to decision fatigue. Imagine reviewing thousands of signals a day, only to have one or two that are meaningful or may lead to an incident. An analyst may go through an entire shift and never escalate an incident to the IR team. Individuals may be prone to taking shortcuts, ignoring complex or nuanced alerts, or reverting to defaults instead of providing a cohesive picture of an event.

Decision fatigue could be the result of several human factors, but an onslaught of noise makes decision-making the primary duty of any SOC analyst.

## False positives

False positives, false alarms, or looking at alerts in the wrong direction can make alerts and investigations take up to almost *40% longer* without boosting detection rates for true positives. That statistic was based on a controlled experiment to determine, when false positive alerts are at a higher rate, how analysts in a SOC role perform. Essentially, the researchers found that analysts performed lower on handling false positive events because of the reduction in discerning true signals. This study alone highlights the need to provide an accurate picture of alerts and signals to analysts; otherwise, stress, burnout, and decreased performance could all occur.

Outside of alert fatigue and stress or burnout, analysts may also experience a loss of trust in the data and decreased morale for their overall job and duties. When analysts are constantly looking at false alarms, they are more prone to be skeptical or believe alerts are *noise*, rather than providing a true investigation. Not only does a high rate of false positives reduce confidence in the tooling and automation around alerts, but it can also make analysts feel a lack of purpose or that their work is not as impactful (which is simply not true).

SOC analysts are the unsung heroes of cybersecurity teams, but without the proper alerting, automation, and tooling in place, they may suffer from risk passivity, skepticism, and low morale. There are several possible human factors areas to improve the experience for analysts, including providing automation that makes sense, providing adaptive alert management, as well as training and workflows that reduce the burden and false positives.

Effective automation should handle repetitive and low-value tasks such as data enrichment, log aggregation, and basic triage so analysts can focus on higher-level analysis for more complex cases. When automation is transparent and predictable, analysts are more likely to trust and effectively use it, reducing cognitive load and improving overall efficiency. Bad automation will not be used and could even cause mistrust in the future for any subsequent development activities.

Adaptive alert management helps SOC analysts manage the volume and complexity of alerts by dynamically prioritizing and organizing them based on context, risk, and analyst feedback. Give the power back to the analysts, encouraging them to help tune, tailor, and refine alerts. Instead of presenting every alert with equal urgency, adaptive systems can group related alerts, adjust severity levels, and highlight the most relevant information.

Clear procedures for triage, investigation, and escalation reduce uncertainty and ensure analysts spend less time navigating ambiguous processes. Well-designed training programs and structured workflows can help analysts quickly understand how to evaluate alerts and determine appropriate responses. Empowering analysts to work independently requires robust documentation and process workflow to support their work. Provide them with background information and allow them the creativity and confidence to triage, react, and make good decisions.

## Learned helplessness

Learned helplessness is a common psychological phenomenon where repeated exposure to frustration or stress can lead individuals to stop changing their position or situation, even when a possible solution is available or even right in front of them. This phenomenon goes way back to 1972 but was studied as recently as 2022 in organizational and cybersecurity contexts. What this means to SOC analysts is that when they face constant alerts that are either low priority or low fidelity, it means there are very rarely positive outcomes. Tickets are either deemed false positives, low risk, or irrelevant for the user behavior, marking analysts to either dismiss or escalate issues, with little room in the middle.

With the constant shift in priorities from threat actors or executives, skilled analysts may perceive that there is no reward or meaning to react to an alert. If there is a consistent event to respond to low-fidelity alerts and either no action is taken or it is deemed a non-incident repeatedly, individuals may disengage or feel as if their work is not meaningful. SecOps personnel could experience alert apathy, reduced initiative, or even burnout because of the previous two phenomena.

To remedy learned helplessness, cybersecurity teams can implement a few techniques to provide individuals with the tools to reduce it. Provide analysts with the authority to investigate, escalate, and remediate issues within defined boundaries. When analysts see that their actions directly affect outcomes, they regain a sense of control and effectiveness. Show analysts how their investigations contributed to stopping threats, improving detections, or strengthening defenses. Regular incident reviews and recognition reinforce that their efforts matter and lead to tangible improvements.

## Perception and confirmation bias

Perception and confirmation bias are two related psychological functions that may overlap or have an impact when combined within a SecOps environment. Perception bias is when an individual evaluates data based on their own experience, which may impact how they understand a situation. Whereas confirmation bias is when an individual factors data based on their beliefs, even discounting evidence that contradicts their own beliefs.

When SOC analysts must handle ambiguous threats or alerts, they may unconsciously rely on their beliefs to filter data that they expect, or do not expect, to exist. This could manifest in a few ways; as an example, an analyst sees a familiar IP address that they know is a benign address, ignoring other indicators that could mean a system compromise. Or, another example, an analyst sees behavior for a user that seems like it's always a false positive when other indicators combined could mean an account takeover or full system compromise.

The cost of any form of bias within a SecOps setting could lead to misidentified alerts, reinforcement loops using past decisions or assumptions, and putting too much trust in tooling. When any team trusts in a tool too much, it could miss misconfigurations, have either too many or too few alerts, or give itself a narrow mental model. Threats change quickly, and overreliance on tooling without updating strategies and configurations could lead to missed detections or real threats.

To combat perception and confirmation bias, SOC teams can implement a few strategies to ensure clear communication and action on events. Leadership should provide analysts with standardized investigation steps that require checking multiple possible causes before reaching a conclusion. Structured workflows help prevent analysts from jumping to the first explanation from the first dataset. Incorporate training and procedures that encourage analysts to actively look for evidence that contradicts their initial hypothesis. This practice helps counter confirmation bias and ensures analysts evaluate alerts based on objective evidence rather than expectations.

# Role of explainability

Digging further into the human factors aspects of any SecOps teams, the role of **explainability** focuses more on *why* a system or alert is triggered for analysis. A few components from the **user interface** (**UI**) and **user experience** (**UX**) side of tooling are feature attribution, confidence scoring, and logic paths, such as the MITRE ATT&CK framework. This is where cognition meets the analyst and the tooling they used to be successful in their work.

Feature attribution is the cue for an analyst to see an alert flagged for very specific anomalous behavior, for example, some network traffic identified as odd because it is outside of normal business hours. Using a confidence scoring mechanism allows a SecOps team to determine anomalous behavior within a certain degree of confidence. In combination with attack pathing or mapping, these techniques create a cohesive picture for analysts that shifts security tooling from a passive picture to a more collaborative system.

## Automation bias versus automation distrust

Automation is a powerful component to reduce manual tasks, burnout, and frustration across teams. However, when automation is used incorrectly, SecOps teams could miss true positive alerts, be overwhelmed with false positives, and ultimately lose trust and faith in technology. Since SOC analysts rely on SIEM and logging solutions, SOAR, ML-based threat detection, and even **user and entity behavior analytics** (**UEBA**), these tools must operate at maximum efficacy. Without a trustworthy and reliable system, teams may experience automation bias or automation distrust.

Automation bias occurs when a team relies too heavily on automation or even AI outputs, whether they are fully complete or missing context. An example would be using an ML-based security tool that provides part of a picture, creating alerts that determine a TP versus FP without context. The analyst must trust the tool configuration to perform their work, but this trust could lead to accepting potentially false information. On the other side, automation distrust is the rejection of AI or ML-based tool decisions because of a lack of transparency in the decision-making process.

For a specific example, consider a SOC team that has been inundated with alerts, but has a smaller team of five analysts for a mid-sized organization. The team must automate initial detection and response as much as possible, which requires them to trust the outcome of alerts. The team initially started quite skeptically, but they soon learned how helpful it was and allowed them to work on more complex cases. But automation drift occurred, meaning that the AI tooling started to lean more towards identifying false positives, even when there were indications that an APT group may be targeting their systems. The team trusted the automation too much, ignoring possible indicators, leading to a large-scale ransomware attack. While this may seem like a dramatic escalation, relying too heavily on automation could lead to missed detections or incorrect assumptions about telemetry.

There are multiple human factors areas within automation bias and distrust, including cognitive load, uncertainty, and decision logic that seems confusing or opaque. This mistrust or bias is not just based on one analyst or individual, but rather a systematic problem when it comes to security tooling and configuration. As an example, a burnt-out or frustrated SOC team may overly rely on tooling decisions from an AI-based response simply because they don't have the time, energy, or support to work through any misconfigurations.

## Explainability in concrete examples

Without explainability, security tools can become opaque (heavy with noise), untrusted, and ultimately reinforce bias, which, in the last section, we noted was a serious detriment to running a successful SecOps team. The first example where explainability is essential is in the tool procurement or transition phase. When a security analyst team is choosing a new SOAR solution, without a fully comprehensive decision matrix on which tools work and which ones don't, analysts could feel that they are left out of critical tooling decisions.

Another example where explainability could mean the difference to an effective SOC team is using training and teaching mechanisms for decision-making and automation trust. Providing the technical background and transparency around why a tool operates gives confidence to the analysts who use it. For example, if a tool simply states that an alert is "not significant" without any description or analysis, it could be easy to dismiss the selection entirely or trust it far too easily.

Consider a SOC team that manages five different dashboards, two EDR consoles, one SIEM, one ticketing system, and one consolidated interface. Depending on the type of alert, an analyst may need to look at any combination of the tooling to make a determination on how to proceed. While looking at five different tools is daunting enough, random combinations of telemetry without any set pattern can be frustrating or even confusing.

But SOC teams can use a variety of techniques to ensure explainability is part of their tool stack. First, teams should inquire about transparency in tooling during procurement, or even as part of technical support calls or engagements. Teams can also train and run learning sessions on how to use automation appropriately, whether that is from the development team or the SecOps team perspective. Ideally, SecOps teams will have some engagement and choices when it comes to selecting tools, choosing automation that works for them, and ultimately being part of the procurement process.

## Dashboard overload

Another important human factors engineering challenge for SecOps teams is dashboard overload. This occurs when SOC analysts are utilizing multiple tools, applications, web interfaces, and usually a combination of dashboards. Multiple dashboards present a number of challenges, including a lack of context, disorganized or scattered information, and excessive data represented in multiple views. As mentioned previously, SOC analysts have between six and ten different dashboards or tools to monitor, and in larger organizations, this could be even more.

From a psychological perspective, cognition is impacted by multiple dashboards in the form of information blindness, context switching, and attention tunneling, which may result in slowness in response to detections. Information blindness is when analysts have trouble finding and understanding detections because of the sheer volume of data. Context switching is a well-known issue for any individual who must work back and forth between disparate tools and siloed data. Attention tunneling can also happen to anyone who must swap between tools, where one focuses solely on one screen, missing other alerts or detections in other applications.

There are some very real-world impacts to dashboard overload, the first being a possible delay in escalation for high or critical alerts. One well-studied consequence is the high turnover of analysts who are frustrated, overwhelmed, and tired of dealing with multiple tools. Even though this phenomenon has been well researched, teams continue to struggle with tool and dashboard overload, leading to a constant revolving door of training new personnel, analysts leaving due to frustration, and training again. With this constant rotation of new personnel, it could be increasingly difficult to identify more sophisticated attacks using lateral movement within the environment.

# Interface and system design for analyst success

There are options to reduce the possibility of dashboard overload, the various forms of bias and trust, and other limitations that we experience. The technical tools and applications we use are highly customizable, or we can build controls around them to make them more usable for analysts. But even with integrated dashboards, user-centered design, and adaptive interfaces, these do not get to the core of tool design. By digging into some true examples of interfaces and color specifics, we will explore opportunities to create comprehensive interfaces for security analysts.

## Poor UX in SIEM

Poor UX does not exist simply in the design of the interface, but can be present because of the configuration, or lack of configuration, done by the implementation team. For example, a SecOps team starts to see a flood of alerts that all have the same weight (all highs) or have no context for the alert. This flood of alerts may indicate ransomware or some other sophisticated attack, but if alert floods happen regularly with the same pattern, this may appear more like a false-positive flood. Alert floods could certainly be an attacker trying to gain access to systems, or it could be done as a technique to hide malicious behavior in a constant stream of noise.

Let's look at a real-world example of how poor design and inconsistent navigation affect the team when they are constantly switching between tools or dashboards. For example, a separate set of tools will each have different colors, fonts, pages, and locations for alerts, event logs, profiles, and even historical context for threat intelligence. This can cause cognitive friction, meaning the sheer amount of effort required for a user to understand and interact with a product. For a security analyst, this could mean frustration, leading to errors from the extra mental energy to complete tasks, close tickets, react to alerts, or even respond quickly.

Errors and frustration could also arise from the lack of visual correlation between events and alerts, either within one tool or across multiple dashboards. As an example, a SIEM may fail to link events together that span time, systems, or users and system accounts. This means that analysts may have to piece together information and timelines with siloed information, potentially delaying the response to a critical event. On top of that, if the tool has poor search capabilities, it could take even more time to query logs or filter alerts with regex or SQL queries. With a high turnover of analysts who may or may not be proficient in the development of complex queries, this could create bottlenecks or other areas of frustration. This would only compound the turnover rate.

## Visual and cognitive aspects

In cybersecurity roles, and SecOps specifically, teams review and interpret complex information about threats, detections, alerts, and communications. There are many SIEM solutions that do not consider cognitive psychology or the intricacies of visual ergonomics, relying solely on data and query languages to build patterns and understanding around massive piles of information. But more specifically, there are visual aspects to consider when selecting a tool or configuration for SecOps teams:

- Use priority-based color schemes – red, yellow, green (where appropriate)
- Adaptive grouping – tagging for environments and systems
- Heatmaps – for threat intelligence, modeling, detections, and alerts
- Timeline views and graphics – for overall security tool interfaces and alerts
- MITRE ATT&CK framework overlays – tactics, techniques, and protocols against detections
- Threats escalated visually – up arrows or red versus green

The preceding examples help to resolve potential visual cues that could turn a pile of incomprehensible data into a gold mine of coordinated streaming alerts. If SOC interfaces rely too much on red, yellow, and green, they could also miss using heat maps or other types of visual effects to give context to the colors. Without the proper hierarchical structure or sizing of data, vulnerability or threat scans may take additional time, again, slowing the analysts from being able to find true positive alerts.

Teams should be aware of progressive disclosures, affordances, temporal visualizations, and context versus causality. Progressive disclosure helps SOC analysts view summary-level indicators at a high-level, allowing the individual to choose when they want more details. As an example, a SIEM alert initially displays only the alert type, severity, affected host, and timestamp. When the analyst clicks on the alert, the interface expands to show process trees, network connections, and grouped alerts. Further expansion provides raw logs and packet data, including headers. This prevents the analyst from being overwhelmed with large volumes of data immediately while still allowing deeper investigation when the analyst chooses.

Affordances refer to design elements that indicate how a user should interact with a tool or interface. A SOC-relevant example would be a dashboard that displays a large **Isolate Host** button next to a compromised endpoint. The button is clearly labeled and placed near the host details, signaling to responders that containment can be initiated directly from that location. Design elements like this help to reduce the cognitive burden on analysts and reduce the amount of time searching for functionality.

Temporal visualizations are related to heatmaps or the timelines mentioned previously, giving teams specific views and pattern matching for change over time. A practical example of temporal visualization in a dashboard is a timeline including a phishing email received at 9:02 AM, with the malicious attachment executed at 9:04 AM, detailing credential access at 9:06 AM, and lateral movement began at 9:12 AM. This sequential timeline offers an analyst a different view of events to determine where containment should occur.

Context versus causality; when reviewed incorrectly, analysts could draw conclusions about a true positive versus a false positive, or read indicators incorrectly, leading to missed events or time wasted on non-events. Context refers to events occurring around the same time, while causality means one event directly causes another. Say an analyst notices that a server reboot occurred shortly after a malware alert. The timeline might suggest the malware caused the reboot, but further investigation reveals that the reboot was scheduled maintenance.

## Color coding

Color coding is the most common mechanism for individuals to determine which alerts are most critical, versus others that can be ignored or maybe glossed over in favor of more severe detections that require investigations. One of the major challenges, however, is that most tooling uses a red, yellow, green system to indicate where and when to look at the alerts. A number of studies address the visual load of tools on cognitive load, including an article by *Design Studio* (`https://www.designstudiouiux.com/blog/what-is-cognitive-load-in-ux/`).

Prior research has found that when color coding is done incorrectly, it can lead to alert fatigue or misinterpretation of data, especially in a high-paced environment such as a SOC.

Some of the common challenges with color coding in a security environment are the overuse of red or yellow, leading to desensitization, a lack of keys or guidance, and showing only color indicators and lacking icons or any label for the data displayed. Simply because SOC analysts must look at many tools, there may be inconsistent use of color across modules or dashboards. For example, some SOAR tools may show red indicators for critical alerts, while others may show a heat map with colors that bleed from yellow, orange, and red depending on the location of the threat, not the threat itself.

With the race for security tooling in the market, some tools overly rely on animations or blinking, swirling colors to indicate data moving between a system and a SIEM. Some of these animations might be challenging for SOC analysts or distract from the true data and severity of the alerts. Any additional visual components could add to the stress or frustration of an analyst during an event or incident. But security tools that stick to three to five primary colors and use accessible color palettes and consistent mappings across views can help to ensure color coding does not cause unwarranted cognitive load.

## Alert grouping

Alerts for a SOC team come from many sources, including log events, EDR alerts, network traffic and mappings, telemetry from threat intelligence sources, and even more. But when the data comes in either inconsistently or comes from independent and isolated sources, analysts may lack the connection between those data points. If alerts remain unstructured or uncoordinated, SecOps teams will have to manually correlate logs with behaviors, anomalies, and IOCs. Alert grouping is essential to SecOps teams to cluster related alerts into either one incident or one cyber event stream for analysis.

Without grouping alerts into proper sections or streams, analysts may be looking into the same incident or the same telemetry, but for different reasons. High or critical alerts may be misclassified or missed entirely simply because of the large volume of data coming in from multiple sources. As an example, consider a multi-cloud environment with two different event types coming in with the same EDR data across both. The alert and decision fatigue mentioned previously are exactly the cognitive implications that could happen without proper alert grouping.

Proper alert grouping, even across security tools, helps to reduce the overall volume of alerts and can even provide a reduction in duplicative efforts. Analysts can focus their attention on the alerts that matter, which provides them with the proper time to triage alerts more quickly and focus on high-fidelity patterns. Any tool or automation that lacks the ability to correlate a high volume of alerts will continue to be a stream of disparate information that analysts will have to review manually.

## Interaction latency

A last comment on the design challenges of security tooling for SecOps teams: interaction latency. This is when there is a delay between a user input and when the system responds or provides an output back to the user. An example would be running either simple or complex queries against a SIEM to investigate single or grouped alerts. Because SOC teams must act swiftly on alerts, any latency in data response could reduce trust in the tools, increase frustration, or even break an analyst's mental flow during heightened investigation.

Some of the most common areas in tools where individuals may experience latency are when opening an alert panel, loading data between or across tools, running custom and complex queries, and switching sites or views. Each action could lead to delays in making decisions on whether to investigate an alert further or not, adding seconds or minutes to each detection. Each of these latency components could lead to a partial or even abandoned investigation, simply because analysts must move from detection to detection. But if teams implement a couple of strategic tooling configurations, they may be able to combat latency issues. Running caching for local alerts could provide quick reviews and loading data asynchronously in between investigations and optimizing load times for specific datasets are opportunities to build human factors into cybersecurity tooling.

# SOPs and the pitfalls of structure and rigidity

On the process side of security operations teams, the tools, interfaces, and design of the technology that analysts and engineers use are not the only human factors considerations. **SOPs**, playbooks, runbooks, and policies help to support consistency and compliance requirements. But threats and detections don't always follow the standards and procedures that are outlined by either corporate policy or laws and regulations. More often, cyber events are unpredictable, constantly evolving, and while actors may use the same types of techniques, they may come at different times and use unique signals.

## Standardization and uncertainty

In the world of cybersecurity, IOCs are constantly changing, threats evolve and leverage new techniques, and security tooling provides a backbone for consistency and support to SecOps teams. However, there is a balance between rigid policies and oversight, and the ability to be flexible and adapt to the changing technology and threat landscape. If policies and processes are too standardized, teams may suffer from missing situational context or using their experience and expertise to investigate alerts.

Analysts may be required to follow a set of playbooks or incident response procedures, leading them to make conclusions that may be inappropriate or blend threats and alerts together, missing the most important context of a situation. For example, if a SOC analyst must escalate an incident to an incident response team only when a true system compromise is noted, they may miss a possible system compromise that could be a precursor to a more sophisticated attack. Ransomware attacks are typically a set of innocuous and long-form steps before the system encryption scripts are ever dropped. Analysts may miss those signs if they only escalate when a true-positive occurs.

There is a common misconception about security in general being a "check box" exercise, especially when it comes to compliance. But other areas of cybersecurity groups could be required to follow steps in such a rigid manner that they may skip using their expert opinion or judgment in a cyber incident. If SecOps teams are forced to comply with SOPs or policies, they may delay responding to incidents that seem out of the norm or escalate when it is not necessary.

As with excessive or misplaced automation, SecOps teams could suffer from learned helplessness or even "checklist fatigue," constantly going through the motions of running through steps instead of using their expertise. If playbooks and runbooks are designed for older threats and not updated with the emerging threats and IOCs, analysts may respond in classic ways to threats, rather than evolving their processes to align with current and emerging threat trends. Automation can either assist or compound the challenges with process workflow, including relying too heavily on automation decisions, devaluing human insight and expertise, and relying on playbooks when threat actors may be able to subvert or avoid them.

# Incorporating human factors for SecOps teams

Even with common challenges such as alert fatigue, dashboard overload, and cognitive workloads, human factors engineering design and principles can help detect the real problem areas for SecOps teams. It is not just the tools that we use, but how we use them in a cybersecurity context. The world of cyber threats and the techniques that are being used require us to be flexible, adaptive, and innovative in our approach. Consistency must be balanced with the ability to move quickly and pivot when threat actors change tactics and techniques.

## Adaptive decision-making

If teams can adopt a more adaptive decision-making framework, security analysts will be able to dynamically review and respond when in highly stressful situations. Individuals will be given the autonomy to focus more on context using their expertise and collaboration with others, instead of following strict rules or processes. To support this, leadership must encourage innovation and deductive reasoning for decision-making, allowing a culture of growth and support before and during incidents.

For an adaptive mindset to be applied across the team, a few principles must be *staked in the ground* for this to be successful. Leadership should encourage teams to interpret signals and detections based on context clues or experience, provide elastic and flexible workflows or a process to update SOPs and policies in an iterative fashion, and encourage SOC teams to discuss and rethink playbooks as new threats emerge. A culture of collaboration can bring a SecOps team to an even higher level of maturity. This can also reduce burnout and turnover for analysts, giving them a voice and decision when it comes to how best to respond and build playbooks.

## Human-centered analysis

Creating a human-centered analysis of the SecOps team comprises the alignment of processes, tools, and cognition. With a deep focus on cognitive strengths and limitations, reduction of fatigue in both decision-making and mental workloads, and a collaborative culture, analysts will be given opportunities to contribute and grow their skills within their team. Human factors engineering principles are not just focused on design and UX, it is more about building cognitive reasoning and understanding into an operational environment. A SecOps team's ability to prioritize tasking and make decisions quickly could be the difference between a small, contained incident and a much larger cyber event.

SecOps leadership should incorporate alignment of how humans process and connect data streams using context-based solutions and grouping of information. Flexibility is the means to success across tooling and processes, allowing updates and adaptability to changing threats and the explosion of AI and ML-based tools that threat actors are using today. The SOC is the first line of defense against attacks, and if we shift our focus from detections to human cognitive experience, teams may be more prepared to handle sophisticated and well-coordinated attacks that may evade common detection techniques.

With the integration and understanding of human cognition, the SecOps team moves from a reactive environment to a knowledge-based and resilient environment. Decision-making is the cornerstone of any successful integration of human factors engineering into SecOps teams, technology, and processes.

# Summary

Inside every SecOps team, a quiet battle unfolds each day. Analysts stare at glowing dashboards filled with alerts, logs, and dashboards across multiple tools, trying to separate real threats from the routine ones and false positives. Every beep, color, and flashing indicator demands attention, but this can distract security analysts from the real cyber threats. This chapter looked beyond technology and into the minds of those behind the monitors, our front lines of defense, the SecOps team – the people who consistently and deftly navigate chaos, fatigue, and the constant hum of threat data. Here, human factors take center stage in solving some of our more complex cybersecurity operations challenges, including cognitive overload, bias, and balancing memory workloads. When a tool design or interface confuses rather than clarifies, detections or real threats can be missed, increasing risk.

Beyond the technical landscape, this chapter underscored the critical importance of culture, collaboration, and resilience within SecOps teams, regardless of the size of the organization. Psychological safety, communication dynamics, and shared situational awareness all influence how teams coordinate and recover from high-stress events. Through human factors engineering principles, organizations can design operations that reduce cognitive friction and encourage adaptive decision-making. Ultimately, the chapter argued that the future of SecOps lies not only in smarter tools but in systems intentionally engineered for the humans who defend them. In our next chapter, we will cover how vulnerability management teams and activities can be enhanced with human factors principles.

# References


- Swimlane. *The Top SOC Analyst Challenges (+ Infographic)*. `https://swimlane.com/blog/top-soc-analyst-challenges/`.
- ACM Digital Library. *Research article (DOI: 10.1145/3723158)*. `https://dl.acm.org/doi/10.1145/3723158`
- BusinessWeek (archived). *Continuous Partial Attention*. `https://web.archive.org/web/20090127061147/http:/www.businessweek.com/business_at_work/time_management/archives/2008/07/continuous_part.html`
- Frontiers in Psychology. *Research Article (2020)*. `https://www.frontiersin.org/journals/psychology/articles/10.3389/fpsyg.2020.579188/full`
- arXiv. *Research paper (arXiv:2505.23397v2)*. `https://arxiv.org/html/2505.23397v2`
- arXiv. *Research paper (arXiv:2307.07023)*. `https://arxiv.org/abs/2307.07023`

# 5

# Human Factors in Vulnerability Management

Unlike SecOps and incident response teams, vulnerability management is a skill that most technical teams require. SecOps teams focus on triaging alerts and determining true positive events, while incident responders take over when an incident has possibly occurred and requires further investigation. SecOps teams are at the core of any cybersecurity program; the firefighters and initial decision makers protecting an organization.

While vulnerability management is a core cybersecurity function, the tasking and remediation portions could be handled by system owners, developers, cyber engineers, or IT operators. Since vulnerabilities are released consistently across all levels of the technology stack, including the **operating system** (**OS**) layer, network equipment and devices, applications and tools, browsers, **software as a service** (**SaaS**) applications, and more, responsibility for addressing them often extends beyond a single role. Vulnerabilities could be considered on a wide-ranging scale, from low risk to zero days, with no patch or configuration available to remediate, leaving systems open to exploitation.

Since vulnerability management activities are handled across multiple teams, human factors engineering is a valuable component to add to all aspects of the **Vulnerability Management (VM)** lifecycle. To understand where cognition, bias, design, and risk scoring can be aligned to resolve complex vulnerability challenges, this chapter will cover the full VM lifecycle, what a typical VM analyst or engineer experiences, as well as the prioritization and remediation challenges experienced in VM activities. Understanding human factors in vulnerability management will lead to better remediation practices, faster time to remediation, and ultimately to focusing on the vulnerabilities that matter and reducing the extra noise.

In this chapter, you will cover the following topics:

- VM lifecycle
- A day in the life of a VM analyst
- Vulnerability detection and mitigation
- Cognitive demands on VM teams
- Cybersecurity versus IT – friction
- Prioritization and bias
- Human-centered vulnerability management

# VM lifecycle

The VM lifecycle is critical to all teams that perform patch management, secure configuration, **continuous integration/continuous delivery (CI/CD)**, and risk management when it comes to what technology to update, decommission, or uplift. The VM lifecycle aids cybersecurity teams in starting with a framework from the identification of vulnerabilities all the way through remediation. Since each aspect of technology includes some type of VM activity, the VM lifecycle gives a comprehensive framework to follow to identify, assess, prioritize, remediate, and monitor vulnerabilities. Using the lifecycle offers teams a proactive vulnerability discovery approach, aligning resources strategically, and a more consistent and repeatable process for VM remediation. There are many iterations of the VM lifecycle, but this chapter follows the lifecycle shown in *Figure 5.1*:

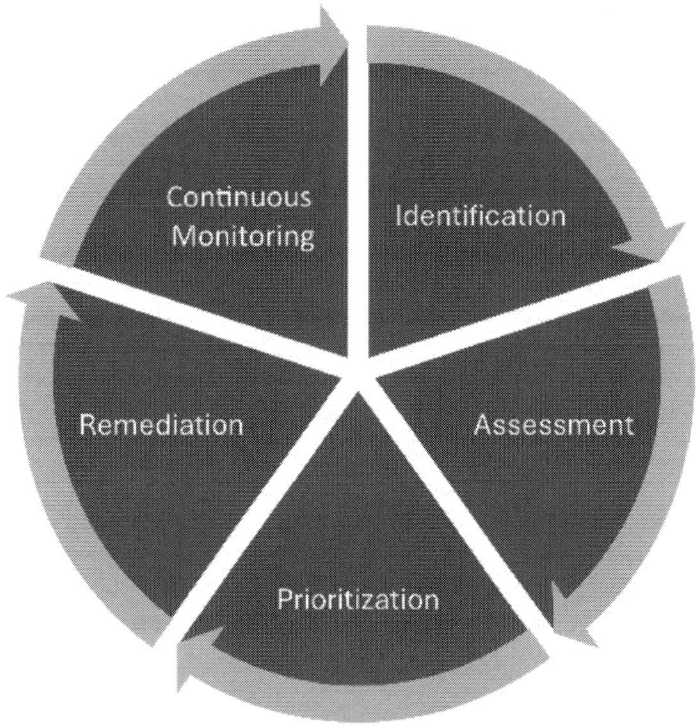


*Figure 5.1: VM lifecycle*

Unfortunately, vulnerabilities are released at such a high rate that it can be difficult for any team to catch up and remediate everything. Using the lifecycle and with an eye on human factors, teams can understand exploitable vulnerabilities, pinpoint the most critical or exploited vulnerabilities, and automate workflows around remediation. For example, teams can leverage automation for patch management and discovery of rogue assets to cut down on the mountain of vulnerabilities and focus on the ones that matter the most.

Leveraging human factors within the VM lifecycle will help engineers select the vulnerabilities of the most importance with the benefit of context. For example, teams may be so overloaded with thousands or tens of thousands of vulnerabilities that it is impossible to remediate them all. With a more scientific approach, teams can build a repeatable process and reduce the noise of low-impact or no-exploit vulnerabilities. This reduces the risk profile of the network while also helping teams eliminate the possibility of burnout and spending too many hours solely on remediation activities that do not move the security needle. Exploring each step of the VM lifecycle will help to address the current state of vulnerability activities and how human factors can impact and mature each step.

## Identification

Identification and keeping a robust inventory of assets, tools, applications, and third-party SaaS products is the first step to any VM process. Identification is the process of using either an inventory or vulnerability scanning tool, maybe even EDR tooling, to determine what assets exist on the network. Many teams struggle with this first step because of shadow AI, shadow IT, and other ephemeral assets, such as containers or serverless architecture, that require a variety of different discovery mechanisms. Shadow AI is the use of AI tools, LLMs, or other implementations without inventory or proper monitoring in place. Shadow IT is any IT system, network device, application, or tool that is implemented but not catalogued and monitored through regular inventory or detection capabilities. Because assets may change IP addresses, be brought online and offline at will, and engineers may be working on multiple environments without cataloguing assets, it can be very difficult to get a full and complete inventory picture of the environment.

To learn about vulnerabilities in far more depth, there are numerous resources available, including books titled *Effective Vulnerability Management* by Chris Hughes and Nikki Robinson, as well as *Practical Vulnerability Management* by Andrew Magnusson. To be able to assess and prioritize assets, there must be a clear picture of what assets are online versus offline, discovery of rogue assets or shadow IT, and any cloud accounts that are managed throughout an organization.

Asset discovery is the first step to ensure that as ephemeral assets (such as containers) come online, they are scanned, catalogued, and documented to understand possible risk. As an example, most system owners will suggest scanning only the image for a container, versus the container itself, so that they can resolve any issues with the image, which will be propagated to all the containers.

## Assessment

After all assets have been catalogued, the assessment step includes running automated vulnerability scans, hopefully daily or every other day, if necessary. Assessment is the critical step to understanding what assets, vulnerabilities, and configurations matter the most to an organization. This step will look different at almost every organization because of varying security frameworks, regulations, or legal implications for data retention. Vulnerability scans are used to help understand the vulnerabilities, configurations, and compliance of all assets available for scanning. It is essential to run these scans consistently and automatically to find vulnerabilities quickly and to be able to move to the next step, prioritization, as vulnerabilities are released. These scans can be done by either on-premises or SaaS products, both cloud-based by the platform (examples: AWS Inspector) or purchased as a separate product (examples: Tenable, Wiz, or Qualys).

Vulnerabilities are not just **common vulnerabilities and exposures** (**CVE**) IDs hosted in the **national vulnerability database** (**NVD**), but they are also configuration issues, IAM settings, or overly permissioned accounts, as well as network settings such as open ports or external-facing assets. Building a comprehensive picture of assets means understanding which ones are most vulnerable, what they are connected to, and the overall risk to the environment. The more connected the systems, the higher the risk, and the larger the radius for exploitability across the network.

## Prioritization

While every step of the VM lifecycle is important, prioritization can mean the difference between keeping up with vulnerabilities and potentially missing something that could lead to ransomware or other types of malware. Not every vulnerability is built the same, for example, a SQL injection vulnerability could mean direct access from an attacker to the SQL database. Whereas an overly permissioned AWS account could mean full account compromise if the account has been subjected to an **account take over** (**ATO**).

Prioritization means context – not simply understanding the **common vulnerability scoring system** (**CVSS**) score or the **exploit predictability scoring system** (**EPSS**), but what that system means to the business or the organization. For example, to prioritize effectively, teams need to understand the criticality of the system, business context, whether it is internal or external-facing, what applications are installed, and many other technical factors. As far as compliance, teams will also need to know what benchmarks they must meet, if they need to adhere to any federal or national regulations, and any specific technical controls required.

An internal-facing application server that only two or three people have access to will not rank high on the priority scale. However, an internet-facing application with business-critical data that has multiple critical, highly exploited vulnerabilities would be the top priority for remediation. Each decision when it comes to prioritizing vulnerabilities reduces risk, allows teams to focus on what matters, and ultimately encourages automation for the systems that can withstand updates.

## Remediation

Remediation is the final step for fixing vulnerabilities. That could mean patching, resolving a misconfiguration, or moving an application behind a firewall, but full remediation is not always possible. At times, security engineers must get creative to protect assets if patching cannot be conducted. For example, there may be a legacy application for which no modern replacement exists, meaning that system must be protected with clever network segmentation and zero trust principles for account management. Even if a full fix is not available when a vulnerability is found, organizations can take action to protect assets while a patch or configuration is being created.

Remediation encompasses a wide variety of activities, including patching, configuration updates, segmentation of networks or applications, and even automation. For example, remediation for one system might mean actually applying a patch, but on another, it may be removing any external-facing access until the system can be fully patched, to avoid impacting business operations. Remediation is not just about adhering to whatever guidance is provided by a vendor, but may require creative solutions or compensating controls versus specific remediation steps.

With the massive increase in vulnerabilities that are found and remediated every day, organizations must focus on the vulnerabilities that matter the most. The previous step, prioritization, and remediation work hand in hand to ensure organizations focus on the protections that matter most. The first step for remediation is to automate wherever possible. Even if production systems cannot be patched automatically, dev and test environments should be patched automatically within a standard maintenance window. Setting expectations for users during maintenance windows, such as patching and configuration resolution, is just as important as the remediation itself. Without proper communication about downtimes or maintenance, users may be resistant to change or concerned about impacts, which could ultimately lead to change fatigue if too many changes are made at random times.

## Continuous Monitoring (ConMon)

The ConMon step is the final piece of the VM lifecycle, and it also loops back to the first step, identification. ConMon can mean a lot of different tasks, processes, or tools that identify newly discovered assets, vulnerabilities, misconfigurations, servers, and applications, or cloud accounts that are not categorized or monitored by the vulnerability scanning process. But ConMon activities span across cybersecurity teams and are put directly in the hands of the IT, development, or engineering groups for remediation. ConMon is the act of continuously monitoring systems for vulnerabilities, configuration drift, or new security issues. ConMon activities are typically performed using vulnerability scanners, EDR tooling, and other operations tools for observability or configuration management (e.g., ServiceNow).

ConMon could be the action of scanning new vulnerabilities daily across the environment, or it could be the validation that patches and secure configurations remain in place. For example, setting up robust IAM processes initially in a cloud account does not mean they will stay in a secure manner for long. It is possible that processes break down, individuals are added to groups with heightened permissions, or account owners do not automatically remove users after a certain amount of time or when they are offboarded. Another common ConMon area is the consistent identification of rogue assets or shadow IT. Dynamic asset discovery should be done frequently, even hourly, to identify new assets as they come online to ensure they are hardened, contain a secure baseline, and have vulnerability monitoring tools installed, for example, EDR or Tenable agents.

# A day in the life of a VM analyst

A VM analyst doesn't simply follow the VM lifecycle to the letter; it lays a solid foundation, but zero-day vulnerabilities, emerging technology, and threats, as well as advanced sophistication around **tactics, techniques, and procedures** (**TTPs**), require anyone who handles VM to be flexible and adaptable. As seen in the previous chapter, rigid processes and frameworks don't always align with a mature and resilient cybersecurity team. To understand some of the complexities in a VM program, let's dig deeper into the daily life of someone who manages VMs, whether that's an analyst, engineer, SRE, cloud expert, or developer. Alerts and reporting are essential to a VM analyst's workload to help prioritize, remediate, or identify new risks that require additional analysis.

Human factors impact a wide range of what occurs daily for anyone dealing with vulnerability management activities. For example, risk perception influences how analysts interpret vulnerability severity, sometimes leading them to underestimate or overestimate the real-world impact of a vulnerability. Decision-making and prioritization are critical human factors areas because vulnerability management programs often produce large volumes of findings that require analysts to determine what should be addressed first. Cognitive load and information overload can occur when analysts must review thousands of vulnerabilities, which can lead to missed issues or delayed remediation. Tool usability and interface design affect how easily analysts can interpret vulnerability scan results, understand context, and identify remediation steps.

## Vulnerability alerts and reports

The bane of any vulnerability management team is reports. Whether for audit purposes, tracking remediation, or prioritizing vulnerabilities, reports must be created and analyzed. Depending on the organization, some VM teams will create and customize reports for IT and development teams. Reports could also be required for audits and assessments (internal or external), to fulfil technical control for either ConMon or inventory management requirements.

But the sheer volume of vulnerabilities could result in massive spreadsheets, reports, and metrics with little context. Solely looking at a list of vulnerabilities lacks context and only shows the number of vulnerabilities and their score or risk, not the potential impact on the environment. For example, an organization with 100,000 vulnerabilities across two cloud environments would be an incomprehensible list to review manually. Fortunately, with the advent of multiple open source and available **large language models** (**LLMs**), vulnerability reports can be reviewed quickly, and prioritization can be given based on a number of factors.

For example, an organization could build autonomous AI agents that inspect vulnerabilities, match them against inventories, and provide feedback as if they were a VM analyst to provide remediation actions, or even take actions themselves. Technologically speaking, organizations are on the verge of consuming and prioritizing vulnerabilities at far larger numbers at higher speeds, making those massive reports much easier to digest. But this is still a future state; currently, teams are still struggling with mountains of vulnerabilities and reports to prioritize remediation actions.

Alerts for vulnerabilities fall very much in the same category as what SOC analysts deal with, although VM analysts focus more on the remediation of the vulnerabilities than the attack patterns and TTP's associated with them. That is not an *all-or-nothing* statement; however, depending on the maturity of the VM program, they may use **threat intelligence** (**TI**) or OSINT to prioritize and focus on the vulnerabilities that matter the most. For example, healthcare organizations have been classically targeted by ransomware, so based on intelligence, they may choose to remediate exploited vulnerabilities associated with ransomware groups or **threat actors** (**TAs**).

# Workflows

The backbone of any VM practice is its workflows. Workflows could be set up for several reasons, such as automatically sending reports to cloud engineering teams or submitting a ticket for a vulnerability found through a change management tool such as ServiceNow, to track remediation. Each grouping of automated tasks allows for a faster flow of information and up-to-date vulnerability remediation guidelines, and encourages speed when it comes to identification and prioritization. Getting vulnerability data to the right people quickly can help reduce the possible exploitability window. For example, there are usually very small windows of opportunity once vulnerabilities are publicly disclosed to remediate before TAs leverage those exploits to gain access to systems.

A few example workflows that may be seen across vulnerability management activities are sequential, state machine, rule-based, and parallel workflows. A sequential workflow is done in a linear order, one step at a time, which is the way vulnerability scans are done sequentially throughout systems, servers, and applications. A state machine workflow transitions between different states, just like when vulnerabilities are handled from discovery to closure, including states such as **Open** or **Resolved**. A rule-based workflow would be automated based on predefined rules, such as when vulnerabilities are prioritized based on CVSS scoring or specific conditions. Parallel workflows are when multiple tasks can be done at the same time, such as when multiple development teams need to work together on a series of vulnerabilities.

# Regulatory or legal compliance

One of the other large factors in the prioritization and remediation of vulnerabilities includes any regulatory or compliance aspects. Some organizations may face federal cyber regulations, while others may need to comply with a specific framework to do business in a specific area.

Each of these frameworks have their own technical controls, requirements, and expectations for everything from encryption mechanisms to data retention.

Whether organizations are complying with the **payment card industry data security standard** (**PCI-DSS**) for credit card transactions, the **health insurance portability and accountability act** (**HIPAA**) for healthcare data, or the **general data protection regulation** (**GDPR**) for the personal data of individuals who reside in the EU, there are sometimes unique and custom technical configurations that must be applied to be compliant. For example, for federal organizations or contractors following **national institute of standards and technology** (**NIST**) guidelines, they must follow the NIST 800-53r5 for patch management standards. Each of these regulations requires technological controls that must be validated during audits or assessments, and vulnerability management is common across all of them.

Human factors fit into the regulatory and compliance area of VM within policy interpretation, communication of compliance efforts, coordination between teams, and audit readiness. While many researchers and organizations consider security and compliance as different areas, they make parallel efforts to support the organization. Because of the vast array of policies and regulations, understanding and interpreting these controls quickly and correctly is essential to operational actions and remediation timelines. Communication and coordination between teams, whether with structured reports or to provide status, directly impact the risk posture of the organization and compliance with laws and regulations. And finally, audit readiness requires all components of VM to be aligned with logs, ticket trails, and record-keeping across all technical teams.

## Timelines to remediate

Remediation is the benchmark for the success of a VM program, including human factors components such as expertise, behavior, and measurement to build better detections and ultimately make the best decisions based on risk. Most **service-level agreements** (**SLAs**) for VM frameworks require *critical vulnerabilities* to be remediated within 2-3 days, *high vulnerabilities* within seven days, and *medium* to *low* vulnerabilities within 30 days or more. Some of the most common metrics within remediation are **mean time to remediate** (**MTTR**), average **time to action** (**ToA**), vulnerability recurrence rate, and patch compliance. While these are not the only metrics that matter, these are some of the most interesting ones to follow for VM program health in a cybersecurity program.

MTTR is the amount of time to fix a vulnerability or exposure, where human factors concerns such as cognitive workload, delays with coordination between teams, and the qualitative quality of tickets and vulnerability details can impact the ability to resolve risks quickly. The time between the discovery of a vulnerability and assigning or determining the owner responsible for action could lead to alert fatigue and miscommunication between groups, potentially causing friction.

The amount of time between the public disclosure of a vulnerability and final remediation or mitigation could be delayed due to unclear ownership of assets or applications. Patch compliance, an important metric for a number of regulations, is the number of assets patched within an SLA, where it can feel like climbing a mountain that one can never reach the peak. All of those compounding factors could lead any individual (whether on the cybersecurity side or in development/IT) to frustration, misaligned goals, and possibly negatively impact risk scores. However, with better detection and mitigation strategies that include human factors engineering principles, organizations can work towards a more mature VM lifecycle.

# Vulnerability detection and mitigation

Detecting vulnerabilities relies heavily on the prior steps of identification and assessment to be successful, and even then, detecting vulnerabilities is a moving target. Vulnerabilities may be upgraded in CVSS score, severity, or determined to be exploitable after they have been identified, sometimes weeks or even years later. Once detected, a strategy must be determined for remediation or mitigation – how to ultimately remove or reduce the risk of said vulnerabilities. Mitigation could mean many different activities, leading to additional data points, time required for analysis, and ultimately the decision to remediate or provide compensating controls.

Detection and mitigation activities are some of the most complex components within the VM lifecycle. Teams must be able to find all systems and applications, understand their risk posture, and determine what remediation is possible given a complex technology landscape. Whether it is **infrastructure as code** (**IaC**), multi-cloud environments, or a combination of on-premises and cloud infrastructure, developers and engineers could be juggling a lot of vulnerabilities. For example, developers may be responsible for container patching, OS-level (Linux or Windows) configurations, as well as networking within a cloud environment (either network devices or security groups within the account). To combat some of the complexities within detection and mitigation, cybersecurity teams can implement some understanding of cognition and design into their VM strategies. Cognition in this context is the amount that any one individual would need to understand about vulnerabilities, including the depth of knowledge required for remediation activities such as scoring, context, mitigation, or compensating control implementation.

A practical way to integrate human factors into this process is to design vulnerability dashboards that present information in a clear, prioritized format aligned with how we process information. For example, an organization might implement a dashboard that highlights vulnerabilities affecting critical systems using simple visual indicators, contextual risk explanations, and clear remediation steps rather than long lists of CVE entries. By reducing cognitive load and making prioritization easier to understand while juggling multiple priorities, analysts can more quickly identify the vulnerabilities that require immediate mitigation and coordinate with system owners to address them.

## CVSS and EPSS scoring

CVSS is the common score given to vulnerabilities with a CVE ID hosted in the NVD. Over years of both academic and technical research, it has received some criticism for the lack of context that users see when they use it in their own tech stack. However, this should be considered a base score, something to start with. Otherwise, teams may be chasing an endless number of vulnerabilities and never feel like they are accomplishing risk reduction on any kind of large scale. CVSS is not intended to be used alone; it is an opportunity for teams to start with a number of pre-calculated metrics to help them focus on what matters.

For example, if teams solely focus on high and critical vulnerabilities, they may miss lower-scoring vulnerabilities that have a serious impact or could be used in chained vulnerability attacks, but without context, the vulnerability scoring could leave developers, engineers, and analysts stressed out, cognitively overloaded, and experiencing multiple levels of security fatigue. Since vulnerabilities come out at a rate of roughly 130 a day, according to Maze (`https://mazehq.com/blog/2025-wrapped-the-year-vulnerabilities-broke-every-record`), if teams must fix every vulnerability, it could become a full-time job, leading to the same burnout that SOC analysts feel with an overwhelming amount of tickets.

The EPSS offers a prioritization of exploitable vulnerabilities based on the likelihood or predictability that a vulnerability will be exploited, but even with this and the CISA **known exploited vulnerability** (**KEV**) catalog, teams may still feel underwater with vulnerabilities. If a team must comply with federal regulations to patch *every* vulnerability within a predefined window, teams will need to identify, resolve, and catalog every aspect of remediation. For full-time developers or cloud engineers who have other development or operational activities, without automation or an alternative way to remediate items quickly, they may be stuck with end-of-life or legacy tools and applications, piling onto their already full workloads.

## Vulnerability scanning and dashboards

Scanning for vulnerabilities is the backbone of discovery and categorization, leading to prioritization and remediation steps in the VM lifecycle. While there are many scanning products on the market, this section will focus on human factors challenges of dashboards and scan results that could lead to cognitive overload and security fatigue. Without a good interface to interact with vulnerability data, teams may be stuck with massive spreadsheets without context or information to help prioritize remediation activities.

For example, an environment with over 20,000 vulnerabilities is required to comply with NIST controls in an environment with federal data. All vulnerabilities must be remediated within a thirty-day window or require a waiver or exemption while remediation is ongoing. If there are critical vulnerabilities that are related to legacy applications, the team must identify a way to either update or remove that software from the systems. If the application itself cannot be updated because of an **End-of-Life (EoL) operating system**, teams may be stuck in a loop of legacy applications until they can upgrade the OS. The amount of time spent on understanding, planning, and ultimately resolving those vulnerabilities means additional time *not* spent on the other 20,000 risks that sit open.

Dashboards, as seen in the two previous sections, can either be incredibly helpful or a massive burden on analysts and engineers. If a VM analyst solely works from a dashboard, the design and visualizations need to support the risk-based approach and remediation work the team is conducting. For example, if teams do not remove vulnerabilities using "exclusions," they may continue to see the same type of *noise* that a SOC analyst will see when triaging alerts. If the dashboard is cluttered with multiple tables, diagrams, and graphs, any analyst or engineer may find it difficult to parse through the vulnerabilities that matter.

A team should consider views that are either "Top Five" or "Top Ten" vulnerabilities as mattering the most. For example, a "Top Five Most Exploited Vulnerabilities" dashboard will help teams prioritize the vulnerabilities that could have a serious impact on their network. Another consideration is that teams may want to use urgency-driven hierarchical views, using font size and color to show which vulnerabilities are overdue. Context-aware filters are critical, showing the likelihood of exploitation, assets, and owners, whether external-facing or business criticality, to avoid multiple facets of fatigue and bias. A final important note, role-sensitive views offer a deeper level of context filtering, showing the data that matters to the individual roles or groups that the team cares about, reducing noise and distracting data.

## Volume of vulnerabilities

According to a recent article (`https://www.sentinelone.com/cybersecurity-101/cybersecurity/vulnerability-management-metrics/`) by SentinelOne in 2025, almost 38,000 vulnerabilities were disclosed in 2024, with 2025 trending to be even higher. Since VM activities take place across an organization at a continuous, high-paced rate, teams must work together to identify who owns, responds to, and ultimately remediates vulnerabilities. Some of the challenges associated with that sheer number of vulnerabilities are that tools can vary dramatically, depending on what scoring they use, maybe leveraging their own proprietary risk scoring. In some cases, the scoring metrics are shared, helping teams understand the meaning, but in others, the scoring mechanism could lead to confusion or misconception around what vulnerabilities matter the most.

Some of the most common vulnerabilities, according to the 2025 Verizon DBIR Report (`https://www.verizon.com/business/resources/reports/dbir/`), are buffer overflows, overly permissioned accounts, **cross-site scripting (XSS)**, SQL or command injections, and improper input validation. To compound these common weaknesses in systems, misconfigurations (such as an exposed network port) and unpatched **EoL** or legacy applications are the most common attack vectors. There is a wide range of vulnerabilities used to gain access to systems, and even if they are exploited in the wild, system owners really have minutes or hours to patch before they could possibly be exploited. This means, regardless of operational activities, workload, or project deadlines, all of these tasks must be dropped to patch or resolve critical zero-day vulnerabilities.

A common challenge for security teams is the sheer volume of vulnerabilities, either because of limited staffing, inconsistent tools or scores across products, or lack of context for the vulnerabilities that matter the most. VM teams may miss critical issues, miscalculate or misclassify vulnerabilities and risks, or delay remediation because of misunderstanding simply because of the volume of vulnerability details. A subject that the co-author of this book, *Nikki Robinson*, has written about extensively is that teams may ignore or overlook vulnerabilities scored as *low* or *medium* simply because of their score, even if they are exploited in the wild. With a heightened focus on *high* and *critical* vulnerabilities because of regulations or guidance, teams may miss the vulnerabilities that are on internet-facing or exposed systems that contain business-critical data.

To integrate human factors techniques directly into the compounding list of overwhelming data, consider grouping vulnerabilities by affected system, exploit availability, and business impact, and the dashboard may highlight the "Top 10 remediation actions this week" rather than thousands of individual findings. This reduces cognitive load and helps teams focus on manageable tasks. One real-world example is organizations that integrate vulnerability scanners with asset criticality and threat intelligence to automatically reduce thousands of findings into a few dozen high-risk remediation tickets for patch teams.

# Cognitive demands on VM teams

Overwhelmed with piles of vulnerabilities, strict remediation guidance, and small technical teams to conduct manual activities, it's no stretch that VM teams are feeling the stress. VM teams experience heavy demand on their cognitive functions due to working memory load, automation bias, decision fatigue, and potential impacts on morale and motivation to resolve *all the vulnerabilities*. One example of automation bias in the context of VM teams is whether patching for production systems should be automated. Yes, automated patching would reduce the amount of manual inputs and mental workload, but it could have a serious business impact if patches are corrupted or cause undesired outages or availability issues.

With these aspects in mind, human factors engineering principles may drive to the root of the problem. VM teams are under cognitive and psychological burden to identify, prioritize, and remediate vulnerabilities and misconfigurations quickly.

Some interesting vulnerability metrics that are compounding the challenges internally for cybersecurity teams include the average amount of vulnerabilities seen *per asset* in an enterprise, at around six (*Peer Benchmarking Dashboard, 2025,* `https://source.whitehatsec.com/help/sentinel/secops/dashboards-peer-benchmarking.html#:~:text=Across%20all%20industries%2C%20the%20average,this%20customer%20a%20fruitful%20target`). The number of critical vulnerabilities that were exploited within the last month after a patch was released, as of 2023 data available, was over 40% (Mandiant 2024 Report, `https://services.google.com/fh/files/misc/m-trends-2024.pdf`). Just with these two statistics, VM teams could be struggling to constantly patch and resolve vulnerabilities solely to protect them from exploitation, not even addressing the other hundreds or thousands of vulnerabilities that could be leveraged in a vulnerability chaining attack. The 2023 report from the Ponemon Institute found that the average length of time to patch critical vulnerabilities could range from 60 to 120 days, meaning that teams are struggling with either technical or organizational challenges to remediate vulnerabilities.

## Blame culture

Blame culture was addressed in previous sections, such as with the IR teams who may build a blame-focused **after-action report** (**AAR**) versus focusing on the impacts on the organization and what can be done to fix them in the future. However, the impacts of blame culture on vulnerability management are more on the possible impact to production systems with patching or configuration changes, the reduction or lack of reduction of risk in the environment, or who conducts remediation activities. For example, a VM team may spend time trying to identify system or application owners, who point the finger at others for remediation activities, leading to possible blame on the VM team for ineffective remediation.

The same can occur in VM teams, where a missed vulnerability during a scheduled scan or an unresolved patch could result in negative actions taken by leadership. For example, if a team is subject to federal regulations and fails to patch systems within the remediation window, they could be at risk of losing a contract, where leadership may provide disciplinary actions, including **performance improvement plans** (**PIPs**), writing an individual up, or even termination if it impacts the contract. If teams are subjected to a *blame culture* versus an organization that aims to gain an understanding of the complex VM landscape, engineers and analysts may suppress reporting, react with risk avoidance, and ultimately lose trust in either their cybersecurity teams or individuals who are responsible for VM actions.

Individuals may fail to report vulnerabilities or even misconfigurations that are overdue because of punishment, being written up, being put on a PIP, or embarrassment related to other team members. Risk aversion could occur when team members avoid making updates or changes because of possibly introducing new vulnerabilities, facing operational issues or downtime, or additional technical debt being discovered during the process of vulnerability identification. Ultimately, when teams lose trust in either the procedures or their teammates, they may continue to hide vulnerabilities or even refuse to work with others and share information, leading to hidden risks and exposures.

But building a comprehensive engineering discipline and complementary design solution for VM analysts can help to avoid a blame culture. For example, after an incident or during an investigation into how a vulnerability was missed, teams should ask questions such as "What technical or procedural controls led to a possible missed vulnerability?" Investigations should focus on problem statement creation, building on where the challenges exist, whether process-based, budget, resource management, or possibly because of conflicting guidance. If teams must *remediate everything* but also manage operational and functional components of systems, they may have competing goals to make sure the systems are online following an SLA uptime, versus improving the security of their systems.

## Psychological safety

Psychological safety is another human factors component that traverses multiple groups within cybersecurity, including VM teams. But safety looks different depending on the role, processes, and tools that individuals use. For example, VM teams are under different types of pressure for the remediation of vulnerabilities quickly across IT and engineering teams based on regulations, while SOC analysts are hyper-focused on triaging and resolving alerts and detections, such as isolating systems with malware installed. From a VM analysis perspective, if individuals fear reporting missed vulnerabilities, re-prioritizing remediation activities, or sharing potential gaps in knowledge, teams could be prone to higher amounts of errors or missed findings.

The definition of psychological safety in this context is that teams can feel confident that they will not be punished or publicly shamed. For a VM team, that is a foundational component to identify vulnerabilities, share their findings, and ultimately make the best decisions to reduce risk. For example, say a junior VM analyst is nervous to share findings about a vulnerability that may not match the classic criteria for a *high* or *critical* exploitable risk, even if they feel it is the right thing to do based on their experience. If evidence is not shared of *high* or *critical* vulnerabilities, and remediation is delayed, if the vulnerability is exploited, that team will be directly responsible for the outcomes, whether full system compromise or a data breach. It is also possible that cross-functional teams that work together to reduce risk may not share findings because of prior disagreements or dealing with a blame culture, leading to unremediated vulnerabilities and increased risk.

To avoid potential psychological safety issues, organizations can implement a number of strategies across teams. The first is to normalize uncertainty; there should be no expectation that every technical individual is an expert in vulnerability management in depth. Security teams can help to support technical teams by prioritizing the vulnerabilities that matter the most, providing context, and ultimately helping make decisions for mitigation or remediation. Retrospectives should be open and honest, removing the blame and finger-pointing, focusing solely on what happened, not to punish or shame individuals. Finally, rewarding the practice of asking thoughtful and insightful questions, whether they agree or disagree with each other, allows for open discussion. Psychological safety is a critical component of the VM lifecycle, but without understanding how individuals are motivated, we are only solving a part of the human factors challenge.

## Motivation theory

Not commonly explored within cybersecurity topics, motivation theory is the understanding of what motivates individuals to drive certain behaviors. Unfortunately, it can be easy to slip into mandates or procedures that force remediation or use fear-based incentives, such as being fined or fired, to force a specific action. Some of these tactics may provide a short-term motivator, but ultimately can lead to all the issues listed previously in *Psychological safety*, such as the use of a blame culture.

For VM teams to be successful, motivation is an inherent and important function to understand. Because of the massive piles of vulnerabilities, it can be increasingly easy for individuals to ignore or even delay patching and other remediation activities. To provide a more specific example, **self-determination theory** (**SDT**) provides a comprehensive framework for understanding what motivates individuals based on three drivers that could be leveraged across VM activities (developers, IT teams, and cybersecurity groups).

Instead of framing remediation purely as compliance work, leadership can introduce positive reinforcement mechanisms such as team recognition, internal leaderboards, or performance metrics tied to remediation goals. Consider a practical scenario where a company integrated vulnerability remediation metrics into engineering performance dashboards and highlighted teams that achieved rapid patch turnaround on critical vulnerabilities. This created a sense of ownership and competition that increased engagement with the vulnerability management process. Teams that are rewarded for tasks that may otherwise be repetitive and mundane can help encourage remediation activities as a positive action, versus a compliance checkbox activity.

# Cybersecurity versus IT – friction

The areas of responsibility can sometimes be muddy for remediation activities; therefore, IT and cybersecurity teams tend to be at odds, which can often cause friction. This friction leads to missed deadlines for remediation, disagreements on the path to resolution, and ultimately a lack of cohesion between teams. One of the most pivotal areas of divergence between technical teams is their main mission. A cybersecurity team cares about the amount of risk on systems and, ultimately, about reducing that risk. A development team is focused on speed, meeting customer requirements, and building products and applications that work well for their systems, and IT teams, whether networking, cloud engineering, or SRE-focused, are dedicated to the uptime and operations of those systems.

These goals can be conflicting, leading to frustration, confusion, and misaligned priorities. For example, a cybersecurity team that requires four days to resolve critical vulnerabilities may find themselves at odds with IT teams who have once-a-week maintenance windows, meaning they will always be behind on vulnerabilities, leading to tension. These teams may end up arguing, not trusting each other, or getting frustrated with the constant communication on delays and missed vulnerability remediation dates, but human factors can help to understand the root of the issue. These teams have individual priorities, incentive structures, and goals that may be misaligned. To understand both teams more in depth, we will cover how both IT and cybersecurity teams, in a general sense, experience vulnerability management activities, including roles, responsibilities, and mission.

## Information technology view

Whether running large multi-cloud environments, performing IAM, network engineering, infrastructure, or operations activities, IT teams are typically juggling multiple environments, levels of software, applications, and technology stacks. IT professionals are measured on availability, stability, and the most common metric, uptime. Usually, uptime is dictated in an SLA, such as 99% or 99.999%, within a contract to ensure that systems remain online and expectations are set for the consumers or customers. IT teams' focus will be on enhancing resiliency, building new systems for projects or architectural changes, and reducing operational or manual tasks.

The largest difference between teams is how they define and describe *risk*. A major risk to IT teams is if systems go down because of patching, upgrades, or any other disruption to service or operations. An unplanned outage could mean loss of trust in the team, possible disciplinary action, or even the loss of a contract if it continues to happen frequently. A change or a patch without testing thoroughly could mean a major liability for the team. The infrastructure or **area of responsibility** (**AOR**) for the technical stack means that any patches or upgrades will need to be done in a development environment and tested thoroughly, adding time to remediation for any patches or vulnerabilities.

## Developer view

In our modern world, development is the bread and butter of most organizations that are building or shipping products. Given the speed at which teams are developing and pushing code to production, vulnerability management is one of the most important components of their work. Shipping a product that has inherent vulnerabilities or has not been scanned could put an organization at serious risk. Developers may or may not also manage the infrastructure that hosts their tools and applications, meaning they may be DevOps or DevSecOps teams, operating and maintaining a number of different containers, OS levels, and applications.

Developers are inherently focused on their pipelines, repositories, processes, and ultimately the requirements for whatever product or application they are tasked with. They may have short deadlines, multiple open source libraries and tools, as well as infrastructure to manage if they are part of a DevOps team. Depending on the team structure, developers may not only be responsible for patching and managing their applications, but also the containers or cloud environment as part of the infrastructure. The concept of DevOps encourages collaboration between software developers and the IT teams that manage operating systems, containers, and cloud services, but that may not always be the case. If the teams are small, developers may end up holding responsibility for all components, meaning they must patch and manage from the infrastructure through the applications.

In contrast to IT teams, developers view **risk** as any slowness or impediment to their timelines, development work, or security tasking. If teams must bake security into their applications or use a DevSecOps approach, they could perceive this as a negative impact on the timelines of the project. For example, teams who are working on building AI or agentic approaches would need to build in guardrails for prompt injection before they can push to production. Security tools such as vulnerability scanners, whether **static application security testing** (**SAST**) or **dynamic application security testing** (**DAST**), could mean delays in development because they must focus on remediation instead of quickly building and deploying.

## Cybersecurity view

Finally, let us discuss cybersecurity and cybersecurity teams' unique perspective. Whether on a red team or blue team, managing **threat intelligence** (**TI**) or **threat hunting** (**TH**) missions, or defending networks against misconfigurations and vulnerabilities, cybersecurity teams have a very different view on risk. Risk to a cybersecurity team means gaps or holes in the walls that protect the organization. Sometimes, technical teams consider cybersecurity teams impediments or blockers for productivity, but cybersecurity professionals simply want to protect the organization. If systems are down, applications or accounts are compromised. Cybersecurity teams are just as concerned with the availability of systems as they are with integrity and confidentiality (the common CIA triad).

Risk is everywhere that a cybersecurity analyst looks, from unpatched systems to misconfigured APIs, and insecure code being pushed to production applications. But security tools, blocks, network segmentation, patches, and other applications of controls could be seen as conflicting with IT and development efforts. That can lead to tension, friction, and frustration when attempting to implement those controls across environments. Even using a user-centered design within security tooling will not resolve the tension or disagreements between teams; this one is purely psychological and requires some innovative thinking.

Human factors is composed of engineering, design, and psychology principles. As part of the *design* part of HFE, design thinking can provide a meaningful vehicle for open discussion and creative problem-solving for tough cybersecurity challenges.

When bridging the variety of missions, roles, and responsibilities, as well as the different technologies and drives of IT, developers, and security teams, it's easy to see how human factors can integrate to resolve common vulnerability challenges. Even if each team is driven by very different motivations, there are many mechanisms to help teams collaborate, understand each other's priorities, and focus on the prioritization of vulnerabilities.

# Prioritization and bias

Vulnerability management may seem relatively straightforward: find a vulnerability and patch or apply the proper configuration. However, due to the overwhelming flood of new vulnerabilities, reliance on old or legacy technologies, and overly complicated cloud and development environments, it isn't quite that simple. Finding, assessing, and resolving vulnerabilities becomes more challenging when teams must add business context, competing goals, and project deadlines, as well as limitations in tools and automation. Outside of the technical challenges, human factors can get to the root of the issues, including prioritization and various types of bias.

Cognitive load, availability bias, anchoring, and groupthink are all common human factors components that can impact VM actions. With increased cognitive load, teams may look for shortcuts or overly rely on CVSS scores or automation versus using contextual risk scores. Availability bias could make recent or critical vulnerabilities look more urgent, even if the systems are behind firewalls, not externally facing, or maybe even only apply to one specific version of a product. Anchoring is when severity rankings from various scanners and VM tools influence decisions, whether context exists in the scoring or not, and groupthink, an issue that occurs when teams are stressed and under serious pressure to remediate vulnerabilities, and make poor decisions by leaving in legacy applications instead of ripping them out and replacing them with new infrastructure.

To integrate human factors into regular VM activities, they can start by implementing structured prioritization frameworks that combine vulnerability severity with asset criticality, exploit availability, and business impact. This reduces reliance on individual judgment and prevents analysts from focusing only on familiar systems or high-profile vulnerabilities. Next, organizations can use standardized triage workflows and checklists that guide analysts through consistent evaluation steps, helping to reduce inconsistent decision-making across teams. Third, training programs should focus on cognitive bias awareness to aid analysts in recognizing common biases, such as anchoring on CVSS scores or recent incidents, and encourage more balanced decision-making.

## Risk fatigue

Like alert fatigue with security analysts in a SOC, risk fatigue means feeling overwhelmed and conditioned to think that every risk is not really a risk, meaning that nothing is urgent or important. The difference with risk fatigue is that it is not simply a cybersecurity problem; it could impact *any* team that has to deal with VM assessments, prioritization, and remediation. Teams that are exposed to *critical* and *highly exploitable* vulnerabilities repeatedly lead individuals to experience desensitization and burnout. If everything is critical, nothing is critical. Since vulnerabilities come out at such a high rate, analysts and engineers may feel that they are constantly firefighting with no real perceived benefit or progress.

Risk fatigue can also lead to decision paralysis. When there are far too many competing priorities and risks, teams may be stuck in deciding the best course of action for prioritizing vulnerability remediation. For example, using tools that only say *critical*, *high*, *medium*, or *low*, leveraging language that is tiered or hierarchical, including user impact, likelihood of exploitation, and a countdown for remediation timelines, could help reduce risk fatigue. Without a feedback loop of information, teams may not realize the impact of their actions on the environment. For example, if teams continue patching their systems every month without any indication that they are reducing risk, they may feel as though their actions are futile. One consideration would be to show vulnerability reports as "patches applied" versus "vulnerabilities remaining." Shifting the visualization from a negative to a positive can help teams see the impact they're having on risk reduction efforts.

## Fear-based response

Fear is a common and natural human reaction, but in a cybersecurity context, it can impact judgment and decision-making. If IT, development, and security teams are concerned about being blamed for missed patches, being in the news for a data breach, or regulatory compliance fees and impacts, they may make decisions that hide potential risks. Decisions made for the short-term perception of remediation could lead to higher risk overall, and actually lead to a data breach, making those worst fears come true. But the fear of technical teams could be shown via multiple avenues, displayed in fear of failure, blame, or living in a culture where it is not tolerated to make mistakes.

Fear of failure could lead security teams to push overly restrictive controls or force systems online for a perceived risk, versus validating that the risk exists. Fear of blame could be a developer not vocalizing EoL or **end of support** (**EoS**) concerns, leading to possible exploitation of vulnerabilities or even loss of a customer when they find massive security vulnerabilities. Finally, when a culture of fear takes over a team or organization, people may hide old technology (shadow IT) rather than discuss and fix legacy applications. This culture of fear could have other impacts that ultimately lead to system compromise, credential theft, or a data breach. Implementing blameless postmortems and psychological safety practices could be the first step to combating fear.

## Contextual risk scoring

Scoring systems such as CVSS and EPSS were created to help prioritize the remediation of vulnerabilities, misconfigurations, and other risks due to possible threats and exploitation. Those scores attempt to quantify risk as a baseline, but more often, technical teams use them as the backbone for prioritization, missing business context, interpretation of risk, and limitations within the environment. Risk scores are subject to a number of human factors concerns, including poor decision-making and misaligned priorities across teams, leading to the tension and friction mentioned previously. Scoring systems can suffer from a static view of risk, a lack of context, and over-reliance on the same scores, possibly missing the real risks in the environment.

For example, if teams only focus on a CVSS score, they may miss lower-scoring vulnerabilities on systems even though they are internet-facing and could be exploitable or lead to vulnerability chaining attacks. If cybersecurity and technical teams do not question the score or add threat context from threat intelligence, teams may not see the most important risks. As another example, healthcare systems have classically been associated with a higher threat of ransomware, so those cybersecurity teams should not solely focus on the *critical* and *high* vulnerabilities but also follow the MITRE ATT&CK framework to see which attack chains are associated with **advanced persistent threat** (**APT**) groups to determine which risks are most critical.

Static vulnerability and risk scores could come with other human factors complications, such as anchoring bias, misalignment of mental models, and leveraging automation in incorrect ways. Anchoring bias is when individuals rely too heavily on the first piece of information presented to them, meaning that technical professionals could see a vulnerability score from a security tool and use that as the basis of remediation without context. When IT, development, and cybersecurity teams have various goals and perspectives, they leverage different mental models that could be misaligned easily. Finally, when teams use too much automation solely based on CVSS or EPSS, teams could miss blind spots in risks that are considered *low*, without understanding their impact on systems. For example, a SQL injection vulnerability may be considered a *low* for a variety of metrics within a risk score, but it could be *critical* for a web application that is internet-facing, and the backend SQL database contains other vulnerabilities.

# Human-centered vulnerability management

So, how can vulnerability management teams experience a more contextual-based prioritization and remediation VM program? Through a clear understanding of context and organizational risk, an understanding of psychological safety and motivation, as well as the empathy to understand that each team is focused on the same thing, the success and security of the organization. When security teams are struggling with data quality, security tool overload, and issues with fear-based responses and trust, teams can leverage human factors insights to determine the root cause of scoring, risk, and threat concerns.

## Human input and automation

The topic of automation will continue to be an important component of cybersecurity teams and the intersection of human factors: a delicate balance between automating manual tasks for reduced human error and burnout, but too much, and it could set individuals into a desensitized loop. Automation should not be considered a singular activity, to automate patching for a development environment, for example. When automated patching is enabled, a continuous monitoring process should be put in place to evaluate that the automation is working as intended, that it continues to meet the initial requirements, and that it does not need to be tuned or enhanced over time.

If a development environment is patched automatically at the OS layer, but never for applications, tools, or libraries, this could still lead to manual intervention and the same types of frustration. Automation should be leveraged in a maturity model, adding more automation in patching when systems are tested and validated to be resilient. But that is not the only continuous monitoring step for automation; does it still need to be automated? Could the team instead remove unused or outdated libraries? Automation should not be a static *yes* or *no*, but an evaluation of why it is needed, what it is used for, and ultimately, whether there is another, simpler option that would improve security.

## Cross-team feedback loops

The importance of collaboration between teams cannot be overstated. The ability to share honest comments within a trusted feedback loop between teams can mean the overall success or failure of a VM mission. When developers can share the stress or frustration of security controls, and security teams can be open-minded to find creative solutions, it is possible to find a resolution quickly and efficiently. On the other side, if security teams can be trusted partners for IT and engineering teams, they can reduce risk and be an ally when challenging technical problems occur.

## Role-based dashboards

Specifically for vulnerability scanning and reporting, dashboards are not a one-size-fits-all solution for IT, operations, developers, and security professionals. Developers should be able to see vulnerabilities specific to their repositories and code, *clear* remediation paths that include secure code options, integration into their own tooling, and secure baseline support from trusted code bases. IT and operations teams need something different, a dashboard that shows exposure and impact, dependencies, or impact, such as rebooting a system to apply a patch, and trends over time for risk reduction. The view means everything; it could mean looking at patches applied to improve morale, versus looking at a massive pile of unremediated vulnerabilities.

However, cybersecurity teams also need a specialized view. Simply looking at misconfigured systems or insecure code will not give them the holistic security view they require. Cybersecurity professionals will want to see TI feeds, continuous monitoring reports, attack paths, and impact, as well as possible exploitable vulnerabilities. Teams will need to be able to see the organizational assets and risks across the enterprise, while balancing business context and where to focus the most. Simply viewing 20,000 vulnerabilities will not aid remediation efforts, but a dashboard with the most critical risks, the most valuable assets, and overdue vulnerabilities will be a helpful start. Human-centered vulnerability management focuses on aligning teams and focusing on collaboration, visibility, and empathy for how other teams operate, and aligning automation and tooling.

For example, a large enterprise using a vulnerability scanning platform may generate 40,000–60,000 findings each week. Instead of presenting the full dataset to all users, the organization can create separate dashboards for vulnerability analysts, patch management teams, and leadership. The vulnerability analyst dashboard would focus on triage and investigation, displaying a limited amount of data based on exploit availability, asset criticality, and external exposure. The interface might highlight "Top Critical Vulnerabilities Requiring Analyst Validation" with visual indicators and provide quick access to exploit intelligence, affected assets, and recommended remediation guidance. The patch management dashboard would instead show grouped remediation tasks such as "Windows Servers-Critical Patch Required on 12 Systems," allowing administrators to focus on actionable patching work rather than vulnerability scoring. Security leaders would only see the information most pertinent to them: their business unit, organization, or section of the business.

# Vulnerability validation

Validation of vulnerabilities focuses on the deep understanding that VM is about reducing risk, not just fixing every vulnerability. With the increased number of vulnerabilities released daily, it is important to focus on the vulnerabilities that have the most impact. If teams continue to try to remediate everything, they will be plagued by false positive detections, a lack of context, and noise from detections that could lead to wasted time and effort. But with human factors insights, teams can build a trustworthy and repeatable process to identify, assess, and remediate vulnerabilities quickly. Any team responsible for VM may experience knowledge silos, cognitive load, and a lack of trust of both tooling and teammates.

However, with this awareness, VM teams can focus on exploitable vulnerabilities, validation playbooks, and automation to build step-by-step automatic remediation and workflows that operate between teams. Validation playbooks help teams to ensure they are focused on the right vulnerabilities, workflows provide automation from identification to remediation, and team collaboration hinges on highly effective communication channels. Removing siloes between teams will build better trust and relationships, which will ultimately lead to lower risk and faster remediation.

## Summary

In this chapter, we explored how vulnerability management is as much a human system as it is a technical one. We started with the reality that security teams are flooded with vulnerabilities and misconfigurations, and yet the real challenge cyber professionals face is how people perceive, prioritize, and act on that information. We reviewed the cognitive load placed on analysts who must constantly triage noisy data, the impact of bias on decision-making, such as over-prioritizing "shiny" critical CVEs or recent high-profile vulnerabilities over lower-profile or medium-profile vulnerabilities, which may be highly exploitable. When roles, workflows, incentives, and communication paths are misaligned with the actual risk landscape, exposures and threats continue to grow.

We then examined how to redesign vulnerability management to be human-centered instead of tool-centered. That included building clearer mental models for teams, including helping people understand not just *what is vulnerable*, but *what happens if this is exploited in our environment*. We discussed making risk more tangible and contextual through better visualization, language, and storytelling: translating raw scan outputs into narratives that matter to system owners and executives and using dashboards that support decision-making instead of overwhelming it. The chapter also covered how to create healthier workflows between security, IT, and business stakeholders, from more thoughtful ticketing and escalation paths to feedback loops that prevent the same issues from being overlooked or missed.

# Get this book's PDF version and more

Scan the QR code (or go to `packtpub.com/unlock`). Search for this book by name, confirm the edition, and then follow the steps on the page.

**UNLOCK NOW**

*Note: Keep your invoice handy. Purchases made directly from Packt don't require an invoice.*

# 6

# Human Factors Engineering-as-a-Service

**Human Factors Engineering-as-a-Service (HFEaaS)** in cybersecurity provides an innovative and scalable mechanism for integrating human factors engineering and human-centered design expertise to address persistent human-element challenges such as burnout, fatigue, human error, and alert fatigue. A central premise of HFEaaS is that organizations reduce risk more effectively when leaders intentionally design security systems to align with real human capabilities and limitations. This alignment reduces predictable errors and friction while enhancing safety, performance, and resilience. HFEaaS operationalizes this premise by embedding usability, cognition, and behavioral considerations into security tooling and workflows, thereby reducing vulnerabilities created by decision fatigue, security fatigue, and human–system misalignment. Through on-demand access to human factors engineers, organizations can incorporate human factors principles, cognitive science insights, and user-centered methods into system development lifecycles without maintaining a dedicated in-house HFE team. This approach is especially salient in high-stakes domains such as cybersecurity, healthcare, and artificial intelligence, where the gap between system complexity and human cognitive or physical capacity can quickly translate into operational failure. HFEaaS further relies on iterative design and evaluation to minimize human-centered friction, strengthen trust in security controls, and enhance operational resilience.

Despite HFE's relevance to cybersecurity risk reduction, implementation has lagged behind the field's technical investments. **Human Factors Engineering (HFE)**, originating in the 1940s and grounded in experimental psychology, is therefore essential in cybersecurity to reduce human-driven risk, empower people as active defenders, and deliberately design cyber environments that align with human constraints, cognitive functions, and behavioral tendencies in ways that enhance end-user performance and secure behavior (Nobles, 2019). When organizations deploy non-intuitive security technologies or restrictive controls that do not fit real work, friction increases between users and security mechanisms (for example, authentication, access requests, and secure-sharing workflows). As a result, compliance with required policies declines (such as MFA use, least-privilege access, and data-handling procedures), and users adopt workarounds (for example, password reuse, credential sharing, bypassing approved tools, or shifting work into unsanctioned applications) that undermine security objectives. Human error arising from poor interface design, cognitive stress, and insufficient training remains a major driver of breaches and disruptions, with some estimates attributing roughly 90% of incidents to human-related factors (Hill, 2020).

HFEaaS addresses this gap by supplying a structured, interdisciplinary capability that many security teams lack, particularly given limited exposure to HFE principles and the scarcity of human factors specialists, psychologists, and cognitive scientists within cybersecurity functions (Nobles & Robinson, 2024). In addition, because conventional awareness efforts often yield limited durable behavior change (Coffey, 2017), HFEaaS positions expert consultation, modeling, and evaluation as a practical pathway to embed human behavior and decision-making into system design, training, and operational processes. Although HFEaaS remains a novel, emergent model, it offers organizations a practical mechanism to access human factors practitioners and specialized expertise without having to build and sustain that capability internally. By enabling systematic integration of human factors expertise into cyber operations, HFEaaS supports the engineering of security environments that protect people by design rather than relying on end users to compensate for flawed or misaligned controls.

In this chapter, the following four topic areas will be covered:

- Scope and impact of the HFE talent shortage
- What is as-a-service?
- What is HFEaaS?
- The differentiation of HFEaaS
- The positive and negative aspects of HFEaaS
- The business imperatives of HFEaaS
- Use cases for HFEaaS in cybersecurity
- Driving behavioral change through HFEaaS

- HFEaaS in artificial intelligence in cybersecurity
- The distant future of HFEaaS

## Scope and impact of the HFE talent shortage

The cybersecurity sector faces a pronounced imbalance between the demand for specialists in human factors, psychology, behavioral sciences, cognitive ergonomics, task design, usability testing, and human error analysis, and the available talent pool, resulting in critical operational shortcomings and increased organizational risk. While human factors practitioners, psychologists, behavioral analysts, industrial engineers, and cognitive scientists are distinct professions, we will refer to this group collectively as human factors practitioners to highlight the talent gap in cybersecurity. Not only is the lack of human factors practitioners working in cybersecurity concerning, but the omission of human factors expertise also exacerbates the issues surrounding human-related challenges and friction.

The lack of HFE expertise often leads organizations to overly rely on security tools and controls that introduce excessive complexity, create non-intuitive workflows, and erode user trust, thereby compromising usability and increasing risk exposure. The following examples show how these issues manifest in real-world cybersecurity contexts:

- **Excessive complexity**:
    - **Authentication burden**: Users must manage multiple logins, frequent MFA prompts, and short session timeouts across different systems, which encourages password reuse, approval fatigue, and delayed updates to reduce interruptions. HFE would have prevented this by designing authentication around real task flow and cognitive load, consolidating sign-on where feasible, tuning re-authentication to risk, and using humane session management that preserves security without imposing constant attentional switching.
    - **Overengineered security steps**: Secure file transfer requires several approvals and manual classification steps for routine sharing, prompting staff to send attachments via email or use unsanctioned cloud tools to meet deadlines. HFE would have prevented this by mapping routine sharing workflows, reducing unnecessary steps, automating low-risk classifications, and designing a "secure-by-default" transfer experience that meets deadlines without pushing users toward workarounds.
- **Non-intuitive workflows**:
    - **Access provisioning friction**: The access-request process requires navigating unfamiliar forms with unclear terminology and no status visibility, leading teams to share credentials "temporarily" or request overly broad permissions to avoid

repeated delays. HFE would have prevented this by applying user-centered form design, plain-language permissions, guided requests, transparent status tracking, and progressive access that aligns with least privilege while minimizing repeat requests.

  - **Incident reporting confusion**: Employees cannot easily determine how to report a suspicious email or device behavior, so they forward messages to colleagues instead of using the reporting mechanism, delaying containment and reducing visibility. HFE would have prevented this by embedding reporting into the primary work surface (for example, a one-click "report" in email), providing clear prompts and feedback, and using recognition-based cues that reduce ambiguity at the moment of action.

- **Diminished user trust**:
  - **Alert and warning habituation**: Frequent low-value security pop-ups and generic "suspicious activity" warnings train users to dismiss prompts without reading them, increasing the likelihood of approving a fraudulent request. HFE would have prevented this by designing for signal quality and attention management, reducing false alarms, prioritizing alerts by severity, and presenting actionable, specific messages that support correct decisions rather than conditioning dismissal.
  - **False-positive fatigue in operations**: Analysts repeatedly investigate benign alerts with limited context, leading to skepticism toward alerting systems and slower response when a true positive appears. HFE would have prevented this by improving alert usability and decision support, enriching alerts with context, establishing triage-oriented interfaces, and calibrating detection thresholds so that the analyst's time and trust are protected as scarce operational resources.

Security tools designed without incorporating human factors principles often generate adverse implications that compromise both usability and security resilience. In such systems, the cognitive demands placed on users are often misaligned with their actual capabilities, resulting in increased error rates, task fatigue, and diminished situational awareness. Rather than addressing these root causes through thoughtful design, many organizations adopt a reactive posture, prioritizing compliance enforcement and user training after errors occur, rather than proactively engineering systems that account for human strengths and limitations (Bada & Sasse, 2015 IBM Security, 2020). This approach not only fails to prevent recurrence but often exacerbates user frustration and disengagement.

Moreover, security mechanisms that are unintuitive or inconsistent with user mental models tend to be circumvented through informal workarounds or outright policy violations. Such behaviors are not mere indicators of negligence or organizationally induced; they reflect a systemic design failure in which security defenses, policies, processes, procedures, or tools obstruct rather than support secure behavior. These adverse outcomes are further intensified by a critical shortfall in human factors expertise within cybersecurity operations. Without human factors specialists capable of evaluating cognitive load, usability constraints, and behavioral feedback, organizations struggle to implement user-centered design principles that are foundational to robust security architectures. Consequently, the absence of human factors integration not only perpetuates technical vulnerability but also erodes user trust and operational effectiveness across the cybersecurity landscape.

Without embedded human factors expertise, security teams often struggle to understand how cognitive processes, behavioral tendencies, and human factors principles influence interactions between users and technical controls, rendering defensive architectures brittle and prone to human-induced failures. HFEaaS could bridge this talent gap by providing on-demand access to specialized practitioners, such as psychologists, cognitive scientists, HFEs, and usability experts, who conduct cognitive workload analyses; cognitive, physical, and ergonomic assessments; and task-based usability testing. This approach enables organizations to shift from reactive error management to proactive human-centered design interventions. Furthermore, HFEaaS is based on bringing expertise and a scientific approach to drive an iterative methodology grounded in evidence-based human factors principles throughout all phases of cybersecurity operations, thereby reducing friction and organizational risk and vulnerabilities.

# What is as-a-service?

The "as-a-service" model has become a popular approach for organizations looking to reduce upfront costs and simplify access to technology and expertise. Instead of making significant capital investments in infrastructure or in-house capabilities, businesses can pay for services as needed. This allows them to focus on their core operations while leveraging advanced tools and support from external providers. While this model encourages innovation and flexibility, it also presents challenges, including data privacy concerns, regulatory compliance, and the risk of becoming overly dependent on a single vendor. These issues require careful planning and clear strategies to address.

One emerging application of this model is HFEaaS, which gives organizations access to specialized human factors expertise without the need to hire full-time staff. HFEaaS can help design systems and processes that account for how people think and behave, reducing mistakes and improving performance. It offers a way to strengthen cybersecurity programs by making them more user-friendly and resilient to human limitations. Until human factors professionals become a standard part of cybersecurity teams, HFEaaS offers a practical and scalable solution for organizations seeking to address the human aspect of cybersecurity risk.

## What is HFEaaS?

HFEaaS is an emerging concept that provides organizations with access to human factors practitioners to help enhance institutions' cybersecurity operations. HFEaaS is a strategic approach that provides on-demand, scalable access to human factors experts, integrating ergonomic assessments, cognitive workload analyses, and user-centered methodologies into cybersecurity workflows without the need for permanent in-house teams. Embedding HFE as a core design principle enables the anticipation of human limitations, the reduction of system vulnerabilities, and the transition from reactive to proactive cybersecurity strategies in an increasingly complex threat landscape. Rather than treating human error as an unpredictable risk, HFEaaS enables organizations to proactively monitor, analyze, and optimize human-system interaction across the enterprise.

As a new conceptual framework, HFEaaS aims to integrate human-centered design and human factors principles into the overall cybersecurity ecosystem, encompassing policy guidance, data-driven decision-making, technology decisions, human performance (including fatigue, stress, and burnout), automation, and employee experience, among others. HFEaaS operationalizes the integration of human factors knowledge and concepts into high-stakes situations through systematic, scalable, and purposeful methods by utilizing approaches from cognitive psychology, behavioral science, and usability engineering. This method reframes human interaction as a crucial and flexible layer of system resilience rather than just as a source of mistakes. Usability tests, interface redesigns, cognitive burden improvements, and iterative feedback systems that support corporate objectives are all standard features of HFEaaS solutions. HFEaaS offers a proactive approach to overcoming human limitations and weaknesses through scientific human factors methods, as cyber threats increasingly exploit human vulnerabilities.

## The differentiation of HFEaaS

People who are familiar with IaaS, SaaS, and PaaS often expect on-demand access, scalability, pay-as-you-go pricing, and self-service. HFEaaS can be on-demand and modular, but it is typically not self-service because human factors outcomes depend on practitioner-led methods and interpretation rather than a purely automated interface. HFEaaS should also not be framed as eliminating the need for skilled staff, since organizations still need capable teams to implement and operationalize changes; instead, it provides scalable access to specialized HFE expertise and repeatable methods that internal teams can apply across the system lifecycle.

HFEaaS presents an integrative framework that centers on empirical, scientific evaluation of human–system interaction, differentiating it from conventional **as-a-Service (aaS)** models that emphasize system health through operational performance indicators such as error logs, uptime metrics, and aggregate usage statistics. HFEaaS prioritizes human factors evidence, such as task complexity, workload demands, performance variability, and recurrent cognitive error patterns, to diagnose how design features, workflow constraints, and environmental conditions shape security-relevant behavior and decision-making. By foregrounding this data, HFEaaS enables behaviorally informed and context-specific interventions, including the redesign of interfaces and workflows, modifications to decision support, and adjustments to procedural controls to reduce predictable error pathways. This methodological shift reframes human input not as a primary source of system instability but as a modifiable and supportable component of socio-technical resilience, thereby establishing human performance as an engineered capability that can be strengthened through deliberate design, targeted training, and continuous operational feedback.

HFEaaS creates operational environments that prevent propagation mistakes and maximize user engagement under pressure by integrating behavioral science, based on cognitive load theory, decision heuristics, and stress-performance relationships, directly into technical workflows. Organizations can reframe human capability as a flexible yet crucial asset to reliability thanks to its emphasis on iterative usability engineering, ergonomic system design, and dynamic feedback loops. This is especially true in high-stakes, complex domains such as cybersecurity, aviation, and critical infrastructure. In doing so, HFEaaS systematizes the improvement of human performance as a foundation for risk mitigation, security, adaptability, and strategic value in sociotechnical ecosystems, broadening the scope of conventional service delivery.

*Table 6.1* illustrates the differences between the new HFEaaS paradigm and established "as-a-service" models, such as Software-as-a-Service, Infrastructure-as-a-Service, and Artificial Intelligence-as-a-Service. By directly integrating human factors principles into cybersecurity operations, HFEaaS focuses on optimizing human-system interaction, whereas standard "as-a-service" models concentrate on delivering technological functionality through tools, platforms, and scalable infrastructure. HFEaaS focuses on decision-makers, analysts, and operators who are responsible for performance in high-stakes situations, rather than just end users and technical teams:

| Feature | Traditional aaS (e.g., SaaS, IaaS, AIaaS) | HFEaaS |
| --- | --- | --- |

| Primary Focus | Technology delivery and functionality | Human factors principles are integrated into cybersecurity operations to optimize the human fit, aligning with and achieving desired behaviors |
|---|---|---|
| Service Output | Tools, platforms, infrastructure | Human factors expertise to reduce friction around the human element in cybersecurity, cognitive workload analysis, design recommendations, and training |
| Target Beneficiaries | End users and technical teams | Organizational executives, cybersecurity professionals, analysts, operators, and decision-makers in high-stakes systems |
| Error Mitigation Strategy | Automation, redundancy, and scalability | Intentional design, behavioral adaptation, cognitive load reduction, and UI/UX rework |
| Data Use | Logs, usage metrics, performance benchmarks | Human factors risk assessment, human factors data, cybersecurity reporting data, help desk data, etc. |
| Operational Domains | IT, DevOps, Software Development | Cybersecurity and IT domains |
| Customization Approach | API integrations, configuration options | Tailored human-centered interventions based on organizational context |

*Table 6.1: HFEaaS versus traditional as-a-service models*

HFEaaS uses deliberate system design, cognitive load management, behavioral adaptation, and UI/UX refinement to address vulnerabilities in human behavior, rather than the traditional emphasis on automation and redundancy for error mitigation. Data consumption also differs: HFEaaS includes contextualized user interaction data, such as help desk records and behavioral indicators, as well as human factors risk assessments, whereas traditional models prioritize performance metrics and logs. From an operational perspective, HFEaaS encompasses not only software development and IT but also cybersecurity, aviation, and other fields where human performance is essential to resilience and safety. Crucially, unlike the generic application programming interface settings typical of traditional "as-a-service" offerings, its customization approach emphasizes customized, human-centered interventions that correspond with the particular demands and behavioral dynamics of the business.

# The positive and negative aspects of HFEaaS

HFEaaS has both positive and negative aspects because it functions as a socio-technical capability that can reduce risk when implemented rigorously, yet it can also introduce new dependencies, costs, and governance challenges if adopted superficially or without integration into cybersecurity operations. On the positive side, HFEaaS can enhance organizational resilience by providing on-demand expertise to redesign high-friction security workflows, reduce cognitive overload and alert fatigue, strengthen secure-by-default interactions, and improve training transfer through task- and context-relevant interventions.

On the negative side, HFEaaS may create implementation complexity through stakeholder coordination and change management, introduce vendor and data-handling risks, increase short-term operational friction during redesign and rollout, and produce limited benefits if leaders treat it as a stand-alone service rather than embedding it into governance, engineering lifecycles, and performance measurement. You need to understand this balance because it clarifies what HFEaaS includes, such as task and workflow analysis, usability evaluation, cognitive load assessment, interface and alert redesign, human-centered policy and training design, and continuous feedback mechanisms. You also need to understand this balance because it establishes the conditions under which HFEaaS reduces risk versus when it may shift risk or fail to scale. The subsections that follow define the HFEaaS concept and service components, describe implementation models and integration points across cybersecurity and development lifecycles, examine governance and measurement approaches, and conclude with practical considerations for sustaining value amid evolving threats, technologies, and organizational constraints.

## The positive aspects of HFEaaS

HFEaaS provides human factors capability that enables organizations to embed human-centered design and evaluation into cybersecurity initiatives without maintaining dedicated in-house specialist teams. By simplifying interfaces and workflows at key decision points, HFEaaS reduces operational friction, strengthens usability, and lowers predictable human error while increasing system adoption and adherence to required security policies. HFEaaS also supports sustained secure behavior by addressing cognitive overload and burnout through alert rationalization, workload-aligned processes, and training and feedback mechanisms that reinforce secure actions within everyday work.

The subsections that follow describe the positive aspects of HFEaaS across four dimensions. Specifically, they address how HFEaaS provides scalable expertise without full-time staffing, enhances usability to reduce human error, supports secure behavior change through human-centered design of training and policy, and improves overall system adoption and policy compliance by aligning security mechanisms with user needs and organizational workflows.

## Scalable expertise without full-time staffing

HFEaaS offers a scalable and flexible alternative to traditional staffing models, providing specialized expertise in HFE without requiring organizations to maintain in-house professionals. HFEaaS is essential due to the high cost of recruiting and retaining full-time staff with expertise in cognitive ergonomics, behavioral science, and usability engineering, which can be prohibitive, especially for small and medium-sized enterprises. HFEaaS offers a solution by making expert consultation and implementation support available on demand, thus enhancing organizational agility and responsiveness to emergent usability or security challenges. HFEaaS relies on a dedicated team of HFE consultants who provide expert support to the organization whenever needs arise. HFEaaS enables the cost-effective integration of human-centered principles into cybersecurity operations, eliminating the long-term financial commitments associated with full-time employment.

## Enhanced usability and reduced human error

A primary strength of HFEaaS lies in its ability to enhance system usability and mitigate human error through the application of human-centered design and cognitive ergonomics. For example, enhanced usability in SOC operations occurs when a SIEM alert screen includes essential context and an obvious next step. For example, the alert view shows asset criticality, the user involved, a brief correlated timeline, and a one-click link to the correct playbook action, which reduces tool switching, speeds triage, and lowers missed true positives. Many cybersecurity breaches originate from human-system interaction failures, such as misconfigurations, weak authentication practices, and accidental data exposure. By embedding usability principles into system architecture, such as intuitive interface layouts, error-tolerant workflows, and user-friendly authentication processes, organizations can implement context-rich MFA, such as number-matching prompts that display the application, device, and location, to reduce accidental approvals. Organizations can streamline access by using role-based request bundles with automatic expiration to limit overprovisioning and reduce delays. Organizations can strengthen email defenses by adding phishing banners that identify the specific risk signal and provide a one-click option to report the message. HFEaaS reduces friction between users and security technologies. This alignment minimizes the cognitive burden on users, promoting smoother task execution and reducing the likelihood of security-compromising mistakes. The result is a more resilient cybersecurity posture built upon human-system compatibility, rather than reliance solely on technological countermeasures.

## Support for secure behavior change

HFEaaS contributes significantly to promoting secure user behavior by incorporating psychological and behavioral insights into training and awareness programs. Traditional security training often fails to account for individual cognitive differences or learning preferences, resulting in limited behavioral change. In contrast, HFEaaS employs evidence-based methods, including microlearning, adaptive content delivery, and behavioral nudging, to facilitate informed decision-making. These interventions are designed to align with users' mental models and real-world contexts, thereby increasing both engagement and retention. By aligning training with how people process information and make decisions under stress or time constraints, HFEaaS improves the translation of knowledge into consistent, secure behavior, thereby strengthening the human layer of defense in cybersecurity ecosystems.

## Improved system adoption and policy compliance

Systems and policies that reflect human-centered design principles are inherently more likely to be embraced by users. HFEaaS facilitates the creation of security solutions ranging from software interfaces to procedural guidelines that are intuitive, context-aware, and compatible with users' workflows. When users find systems easier to use and more relevant to their operational context, resistance to adoption decreases, and policy compliance increases. Moreover, well-designed systems reduce the temptation to circumvent security measures, which often occurs when controls are perceived as burdensome or obstructive. Thus, HFEaaS not only enhances the user experience but also reinforces compliance with organizational security protocols, resulting in more robust and sustainable cybersecurity outcomes.

## Mitigation of cognitive overload and burnout

In high-intensity environments such as **security operations centers** (**SOCs**), analysts are frequently exposed to continuous alerts, rapid decision-making demands, and high cognitive workloads. HFEaaS addresses these challenges by introducing ergonomic solutions and cognitive support tools that help manage mental strain. HFEaaS addresses these challenges by introducing ergonomic solutions, such as optimized workstation layouts, adjustable displays, and fatigue-reducing shift and break design, and cognitive support tools, such as context-rich alerts, decision checklists, standardized incident playbooks, and just-in-time prompts that guide secure actions and reduce mental strain. Techniques such as interface simplification, intelligent task prioritization, and automation of routine operations enable analysts to maintain situational awareness without becoming overwhelmed. These enhancements reduce fatigue, decision fatigue, and burnout, which can compromise vigilance and increase the likelihood of errors. By optimizing the human-technology interaction in SOCs, HFEaaS fosters operational resilience and supports long-term workforce sustainability in cybersecurity functions.

HFEaaS offers several positive attributes that strengthen cybersecurity performance by reducing human-centered risk and improving how security systems function in real operational conditions:

- **Reduced human-centered friction**: HFEaaS decreases cognitive, behavioral, and procedural barriers, enabling users and security teams to complete secure tasks with less confusion, delay, and unnecessary effort.
- **Stronger secure behavior**: HFEaaS increases adherence to required security practices by aligning controls and workflows with real decision-making patterns, reinforcing secure habits through design rather than relying primarily on reminders or enforcement.
- **Lower error rates and greater resilience**: HFEaaS improves reliability through clearer interfaces, improved task structure, and contextual decision support that prevents predictable mistakes and enables safe recovery when errors occur.
- **Expanded human factors capability**: HFEaaS extends specialized expertise to organizations without dedicated internal HFE staffing, accelerating progress on persistent human-element risk drivers such as alert fatigue, misconfiguration, and unsafe workarounds.
- **Better sociotechnical fit**: HFEaaS integrates technical controls with human compatibility, strengthening cross-functional collaboration and ensuring that security tools and processes perform effectively within everyday work environments.

## Challenges with HFEaaS

HFEaaS adoption often stalls because many cybersecurity leaders prioritize technology-centric defenses and underestimate the role of HFE in reducing organizational risk, thereby limiting budget allocation and executive sponsorship. Integration can also prove difficult because HFEaaS requires cross-functional coordination to redesign workflows and embed human-centered practices into development lifecycles and security operations. Finally, organizations must manage privacy and governance risks associated with collecting user interaction data and relying on external providers, while also addressing the challenge of demonstrating return on investment with metrics that credibly link usability and behavior improvements to reduced incidents and lower operational disruption.

## Limited awareness and organizational buy-in

HFEaaS continues to face notable barriers to organizational adoption, particularly within cybersecurity contexts that prioritize technology-centric defenses. Many decision-makers remain unaware of the strategic contributions HFE can offer in mitigating security risks. As a result, budget allocations often favor traditional safeguards such as network monitoring, encryption, and access control, while human-centric strategies are underfunded or overlooked. The limited awareness contributes to a narrow perception of cybersecurity that overlooks the underlying behavioral and cognitive vulnerabilities frequently exploited by adversaries. Building awareness through case studies, executive education, and empirical demonstrations of HFEaaS effectiveness is essential for advancing adoption across industries.

## Integration complexity

Integrating HFEaaS into established cybersecurity operations requires cross-functional collaboration that is often difficult to achieve in practice. Coordination among departments such as information technology, human resources, compliance, and cybersecurity is necessary to embed HFE into secure system design and operational workflows. In organizations where silos are entrenched or communication pathways are underdeveloped, HFEaaS integration efforts may be fragmented or misaligned. Additionally, the absence of standardized integration protocols or governance frameworks can hinder the seamless implementation of HFEaaS principles into the software development lifecycle or risk management processes. Overcoming these challenges demands strategic alignment, leadership support, and a systems-thinking approach to change management.

## Data sensitivity and privacy concerns

The application of HFEaaS often involves collecting sensitive data, including behavioral metrics, cognitive load indicators, and user interaction patterns. While such data enables more effective customization of cybersecurity interventions, it also raises serious ethical and legal considerations. Without appropriate safeguards, the collection and use of personal or biometric data can violate user privacy, lead to compliance violations, or erode trust among stakeholders. Ensuring transparency, informed consent, and adherence to regulatory standards such as the General Data Protection Regulation is crucial. Organizations must establish ethical data governance frameworks that balance innovation and individual rights, and clearly define how user data is handled, stored, and used in HFEaaS deployments.

## Dependence on external providers

Reliance on third-party vendors to deliver HFEaaS introduces potential risks related to quality control, contextual relevance, and organizational continuity. Not all vendors possess the necessary cybersecurity domain expertise or an understanding of industry-specific regulatory environments. Misalignment between the service provider's approach and the organization's operational realities can lead to suboptimal outcomes. Furthermore, dependence on proprietary tools or frameworks may create vendor lock-in, limiting organizational flexibility and innovation. To mitigate these risks, organizations should establish transparent service-level agreements, invest in knowledge transfer, and prioritize partnerships with providers that offer adaptable and evidence-based HFEaaS solutions.

### Underdeveloped metrics for return on investment

Quantifying the value of HFEaaS remains a persistent challenge due to the qualitative nature of many of its outcomes. While traditional cybersecurity investments can be measured by metrics such as threat detection rates or reduced response times, HFEaaS often yields improvements in areas such as user experience, cognitive efficiency, and behavioral compliance. These benefits are inherently more challenging to capture with standard performance indicators. The lack of widely accepted evaluation frameworks for human-centered interventions complicates efforts to justify long-term investments in them. To address this gap, future research should focus on developing validated metrics that correlate HFEaaS implementation with measurable improvements in cybersecurity posture, workforce performance, and organizational resilience.

HFEaaS offers clear organizational advantages, including reduced human-centered friction, fewer predictable errors and workarounds, improved adoption of security controls, and more sustainable performance in high-tempo environments through lower cognitive overload and burnout. At the same time, HFEaaS introduces practical challenges that leaders must manage, including integration complexity across functions, privacy and data-governance obligations, dependence on external providers, and the need to demonstrate return on investment with credible metrics that connect human-centered outcomes to reduced risk. Recognizing both the benefits and constraints positions HFEaaS as a business-relevant capability rather than a discretionary enhancement: it directly supports core imperatives such as enterprise risk reduction, operational continuity, regulatory readiness, workforce retention, and protection of customer and stakeholder trust. When organizations govern HFEaaS rigorously and embed it into cybersecurity and development lifecycles, they can convert the human element from a recurring source of incidents into a managed source of resilience that strengthens long-term business performance.

## The business imperatives of HFEaaS

The adaptability of the HFEaaS model is a crucial feature that enables businesses to scale human factors interventions according to project requirements. To respond quickly to emerging challenges such as zero-day cybersecurity threats, urgent regulatory changes, and shifting user requirements, providers maintain interdisciplinary teams that can be rapidly redeployed across concurrent engagements. This operational agility facilitates iterative design and ongoing user feedback loops, where prototype testing and real-time behavioral analytics inform system improvements well in advance of full deployment. End-to-end development cycles thus become more effective and robust against usability problems that might otherwise materialize as expensive post-launch fixes.

In terms of finances, HFEaaS transforms the conventional capital-intensive investment in human factors knowledge into a variable operational expense model that lowers organizational risk and improves budget predictability. Organizations use HFEaaS suppliers on a use basis instead of hiring, training, and maintaining a permanent staff of usability engineers, cognitive psychologists, and ergonomists. Before investing more resources, this approach enables small-scale pilot studies of human-centered treatments, such as task analysis workshops or heuristic evaluations, to confirm their efficacy.

Another essential component of the HFEaaS value proposition is the ability to adapt designs rapidly. HFEaaS suppliers ensure that usability tests and UI changes occur within accelerated delivery cycles by coordinating human factors procedures with lean and agile development approaches. Teams can identify problems early in system prototypes by continuously integrating task performance data, behavior tracking, and user input. Targeted interventions, such as streamlining intricate operations, enhancing alert displays, or eliminating unnecessary cognitive steps in incident response playbooks, are informed by these insights. This kind of responsiveness enhances user satisfaction, strengthens the security posture, and improves operational efficiency.

HFEaaS's organized implementation approach usually consists of four stages, each supported by iterative improvement and the acquisition of empirical data. To identify performance bottlenecks and error-prone interactions, the evaluation phase employs methods such as process mapping, cognitive task analysis, and usability audits. Through adaptive interface design, security-by-design feature specification, and focused training modules, solutions are customized to fit the corporate context. To facilitate user acceptance, deployment incorporates these interventions into real-world settings, utilizing seamless security safeguards and ergonomic improvements. Successful methods are subsequently extended across units through scaling and iteration, which include continuous feedback loops and are driven by analytics to promote continuous improvements and the cultural acceptance of human-centered design concepts.

Applications of HFEaaS across various industries demonstrate its strategic value. By creating error-tolerant interfaces and cognitive support systems that prioritize important alerts, weed out unnecessary messages, and simplify job switching for analysts, HFEaaS improves incident response workflows in cybersecurity operations centers. By optimizing data entry workflows, reducing alert fatigue, and minimizing cognitive overload in high-stress clinical scenarios, service-based human factors interventions in electronic health record systems have significantly improved patient safety and clinician efficiency in the healthcare industry. Similar to this, ergonomic improvements and cockpit automation assessments aided by HFEaaS have enhanced pilot situational awareness, reduced workload during critical flight phases, and helped to lower the number of human error events in aviation quantifiably.

Additionally, HFEaaS provides a tactical advantage when navigating complex ethical and regulatory environments. Organizations can comply with strict usability criteria, as required by regulatory bodies for medical devices or for information systems under data protection frameworks, by incorporating systematic user feedback methods and iterative design processes. To avoid costly non-compliance penalties and strengthen company credibility, HFEaaS suppliers assist clients with recording human factors assessments, creating verifiable user testing records, and demonstrating conformance with industry standards.

Other advantages of implementing HFEaaS include improved customer satisfaction and competitive differentiation. By providing straightforward, dependable, and accessible experiences, human-centered design enhances stakeholder trust, reduces user frustration, and fosters user loyalty. Usability improvements have been linked in human factors research to increased market responsiveness, higher-quality results, and enhanced productivity across various industries. Businesses that adopt HFEaaS establish a culture of excellence in human-system integration and continuous development, establishing themselves as pioneers in operational resilience and user experience.

# Use cases for HFEaaS in cybersecurity

This section presents a concise set of cybersecurity use cases that illustrate how HFEaaS reduces organizational risk by improving human–system interaction. Each use case briefly defines the operational problem, explains how HFEaaS is applied, and describes the resulting impact on security outcomes. The intent is to provide original, practical examples that demonstrate how HFEaaS strengthens human-centered cybersecurity and complements technical controls.

## Use case 1: SOC operations and incident response

SOCs often struggle with alert overload, fragmented tooling, and high cognitive demand, which increases triage errors and slows response during time-sensitive events. HFEaaS applies task analysis, cognitive workload assessment, and interface redesign to prioritize actionable alerts, standardize escalation cues, and reduce tool switching by placing essential context and next steps at the point of decision. This improves analyst accuracy, shortens time-to-detect and time-to-respond, reduces alert fatigue, and lowers the likelihood that high-severity threats go unnoticed or uncontained.

## Use case 2: usability of security tools and controls

Many identity, endpoint, and compliance tools deliver strong technical capability but impose non-intuitive workflows that users bypass when deadlines and friction collide. HFEaaS applies usability testing and heuristic evaluation across the lifecycle to simplify high-frequency interactions such as authentication, access requests, secure sharing, and policy acknowledgements, while introducing error-tolerant pathways such as clear confirmations, reversible actions, and context-rich prompts. The outcome is reduced workarounds, fewer user-driven misconfigurations, higher adoption of key controls, and improved adherence to required security procedures because secure actions become easier to execute correctly.

## Use case 3: cybersecurity training and secure behavior

Many awareness programs increase exposure to content yet fail to produce durable behavior change because training is generic, detached from real tasks, and delivered without reinforcement in the flow of work. HFEaaS redesigns training around role-specific scenarios and decision points, using microlearning, realistic simulations, and just-in-time nudges to reinforce correct actions during routine workflows such as email handling, data sharing, and authentication. This approach increases retention and improves due to predictable decision errors.

## Use case 4: secure software development lifecycle

Security vulnerabilities often persist because teams discover usability-driven failure points late, after deployment, when redesign becomes costly, and adoption becomes more difficult. HFEaaS embeds human-centered practices into secure design by participating in requirements definition, design sprints, prototyping, and iterative usability evaluation to identify where users will predictably misunderstand controls, misuse features, or create unsafe workarounds. This reduces post-deployment vulnerabilities, improves the usability of secure features, and strengthens resilience by ensuring that security requirements align with actual workflows and user cognition.

## Use case 5: human performance, fatigue, and workforce sustainability

Cybersecurity teams frequently operate under sustained high workload, frequent interruptions, and high-consequence decision-making, which increases fatigue, burnout, and error risk, particularly during major incidents. HFEaaS applies workload assessment and operational ergonomics to support scheduling design, role clarity, handoff structure, and cognitive support tools such as checklists, decision aids, and standardized runbooks. These interventions reduce cognitive overload, improve reliability under stress, decrease turnover risk, and sustain operational readiness during prolonged threat activity.

### Use case 6: human-centered root cause analysis

Incident investigations often focus on technical indicators and individual mistakes while missing the underlying human–system conditions that made failure likely, such as confusing interfaces, unclear policies, weak feedback, or ambiguous ownership. HFEaaS adds a structured human factors lens to post-incident review through error causality mapping, workflow reconstruction, and identification of latent conditions that shaped decisions before and during the event. This produces higher-quality corrective actions that address root causes, reduce recurrence, and improve organizational learning by converting "human error" into specific design and process changes.

### Use case 7: human oversight in AI-enabled security automation

Security organizations increasingly deploy automation and AI for detection, triage, and response, but poorly designed human oversight can create overreliance, missed failures, and delayed intervention when automation behaves unexpectedly. HFEaaS applies human-in-the-loop design principles to define clear intervention points, transparency cues, and operator controls that support calibrated trust and rapid recovery when models misclassify or drift. The impact is improved decision quality, reduced automation surprise, stronger accountability, and more reliable outcomes from AI-enabled security operations.

### Non-cyber domains and HFE

Healthcare, aviation, nuclear operations, and industrial safety have long used HFE to reduce error in high-risk environments by designing systems that anticipate human limitations and support reliable performance. Cybersecurity shares characteristics of complexity, time pressure, and consequences, which make these domains instructive. The core implication for this chapter is that cybersecurity can adopt comparable human-centered practices through HFEaaS to strengthen resilience and reduce organizational risk, while remaining focused on cybersecurity-specific workflows and controls.

## Driving behavioral change through HFEaaS

Behavioral change is a foundational element in the pursuit of cybersecurity resilience because everyday human decisions and actions frequently create the conditions that adversaries exploit. HFEaaS offers a structured, human-centered approach to promoting secure behavior by embedding HFE principles into the design of security controls and the workflows in which those controls operate. Rather than relying primarily on training or policy reminders, HFEaaS reduces predictable error pathways by aligning systems with how people actually perceive risk, allocate attention, and make decisions under time pressure, interruption, and competing priorities.

In practice, HFEaaS shifts cybersecurity from a reactive, technology-centric posture to proactive risk reduction by designing secure behavior into routine work. For example, HFEaaS can redesign authentication and access approval experiences to reduce accidental approvals and rushed decisions through clearer prompts, context-rich verification, and error-tolerant steps that slow only the highest-risk actions. HFEaaS can also reduce cognitive overload in security operations by prioritizing actionable alerts, presenting essential context at the point of triage, and standardizing escalation cues so that analysts do not rely on memory or informal heuristics during fatigue. In end-user contexts, HFEaaS can strengthen resistance to phishing and social engineering by pairing scenario-based microlearning with just-in-time nudges, such as one-click reporting, specific risk explanations in email banners, and feedback loops that reinforce correct actions when they occur. These interventions convert "behavior change" from a training objective into an engineered outcome by making secure actions easier to execute correctly, harder to bypass, and more consistent across diverse roles and work environments.

A core aspect of fostering secure behavior involves addressing cognitive biases that impair users' ability to detect and respond to cyber threats. Biases such as inattentional blindness, decision fatigue, and overconfidence can diminish situational awareness and lead to risky choices. HFEaaS mitigates these risks through cognitive task analysis and user-centered interface design, simplifying interactions and reducing mental workload. Practical implementations include more intuitive authentication processes, visual threat indicators, and real-time guidance during security-critical tasks. These design improvements enhance user focus and decision-making, reducing the likelihood of errors and bolstering cybersecurity posture.

Training and education, though essential to behavioral change, often fall short when delivered through generic, static methods. HFEaaS introduces personalized, experiential learning environments that promote deeper engagement and knowledge retention. Interactive simulations, scenario-based exercises, and gamified modules are tailored to individual learning styles, helping users build practical skills in identifying phishing attempts, managing credentials, and responding to social engineering attacks. These immersive experiences reinforce secure behavior through active participation and positive reinforcement, leading to more durable and consistent cybersecurity habits across an organization.

Behavioral change in cybersecurity is gaining momentum, but what is surprising is that most organizations do not seek expertise in behavioral science to assist with such efforts. When it comes to changing behavior in cybersecurity, it should be intentional, scientific, customizable, and effective. One such model is the **Capability, Opportunity, Motivation – Behavior (COM-B)** model, which provides a simple perspective on behavior change, as shown in *Figure 6.1*.

The COM-B model provides a fundamental framework for comprehending behavior as a resultant attribute of three interrelated constructs: (a) capability, (b) opportunity, and (c) motivation (Willmott et al., 2021). This paradigm can be implemented through HFEaaS by human factors engineers to enhance behavioral interventions by systematically aligning system design with human limitations and traits, thereby optimizing engagement, adherence, performance, and outcomes. Refer to the following figure:

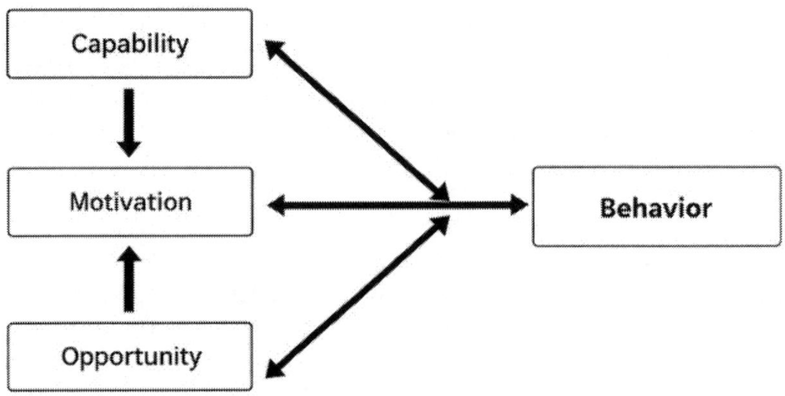


*Figure 6.1: Basic COM-B model*

Capability, characterized as the physical and psychological ability to execute an activity (Willmott et al., 2021), can be enhanced by HFEaaS by integrating cognitive support tools, task simplification techniques, and adaptable interfaces. HFEaaS solutions frequently address skill deficiencies, decision-making limitations, and attentional limitations through focused human factors design, thereby enhancing user preparedness and confidence in executing essential tasks.

Opportunity, which encompasses external physical and social facilitators of behavior (Willmott et al., 2021), is enhanced by HFE through the reconfiguration of the environment, both physical and digital, to reduce friction, eliminate contextual obstacles, and promote accessibility. HFEaaS establishes supportive environments that facilitate the attainment of desirable behaviors through ergonomic assessments, workflow analysis, and inclusive design strategies.

Motivation, encompassing reflective processes (such as goal-setting and planning) and automatic drivers (including emotional and habitual responses) (Willmott et al., 2021), can be shaped by HFEaaS via the implementation of behavioral nudges, persuasive design, and feedback mechanisms. By mitigating cognitive load, enhancing emotional engagement, and leveraging intrinsic reward processes, HFEaaS cultivates enduring motivation that aligns with company objectives or user intentions.

In this integrated approach, behavior is perceived not solely as an individual decision but as a systemic consequence influenced by the interaction of interventions informed by human factors. In practical fields such as cybersecurity, healthcare, and workplace safety, HFEaaS can implement the COM-B paradigm by integrating behavioral insights into tools, processes, and technologies, thereby enabling quantifiable enhancements in user behavior and system resilience.

The COM-B model can be integrated into HFE frameworks to assess how engineered improvements in capacity, opportunity, and incentive affect behavior, especially within intricate sociotechnical systems. HFE initiatives aim to enhance individual behavioral drivers and provide synergistic effects by intentionally manipulating motivational processes. Comprehending these dynamics is essential for creating adaptive, human-centered systems that correspond with strategic goals while reducing human error.

Social engineering remains one of the most challenging forms of cyberattacks to defend against, as it relies on human manipulation rather than system vulnerabilities. HFEaaS counters this threat by integrating principles from social psychology into training programs and system architecture. Techniques such as role-playing, phishing simulations, and contextual alerts empower users to recognize manipulation tactics and respond appropriately. By embedding social engineering defenses into daily workflows, HFEaaS enables a shift from reactive risk mitigation to proactive, user-informed cyber defense.

Sustained behavioral change requires an iterative design process supported by continuous feedback. Human factors engineers facilitate this by collecting behavioral data, identifying friction points in user interactions, and informing ongoing system enhancements. Security protocols, user interfaces, and feedback mechanisms are refined based on real-world usage patterns and user input. This dynamic process ensures that security systems evolve in tandem with user needs and emerging threats, creating a continuously improving alignment between human behavior and system performance.

Ultimately, the success of behavioral change initiatives depends on cultivating a culture of human-centered cybersecurity and placing humans as the central point and intentionally designing for them. This paradigm moves beyond technical compliance to embrace users as the essential participants, operators, and defenders in the cybersecurity ecosystem. HFEaaS operationalizes this shift by integrating behavioral science, system usability, and human-centered design into every layer of cybersecurity strategy. In doing so, it redefines resilience not only as a matter of technical capability but as the outcome of intentional, secure, and empowered human behavior.

## HFEaaS in artificial intelligence in cybersecurity

HFEaaS is crucial for enhancing **artificial intelligence (AI)** in cybersecurity by integrating human-centered design into the development and operation of intelligent security systems. As AI becomes increasingly essential to cybersecurity tasks such as threat identification, behavioral analytics, and autonomous response, collaboration between human analysts and AI-driven solutions emerges as a crucial element in operational efficacy. HFEaaS provides organized, scalable access to human factors knowledge, ensuring that AI systems are designed with consideration for cognitive workload, situational awareness, and human interpretability. By customizing AI interfaces to align with the cognitive and behavioral characteristics of security professionals, HFEaaS enhances the quality of decision-making, mitigates alert fatigue, and accelerates incident response times.

Furthermore, HFEaaS enhances AI-driven cybersecurity by facilitating the development of explainable AI and reliable systems. Confidence in AI is crucial in high-stakes settings, such as SOCs, where human operators must swiftly evaluate and respond to AI-generated insights. HFEaaS employs heuristic evaluations, task analysis, and user feedback loops to guarantee that AI models deliver transparent, contextually rich outputs that correspond with human reasoning processes. This is especially crucial in addressing insider threats or intricate, multifaceted attacks because excessive dependence on obscure AI choices may result in overlooking or misinterpreting them. According to Galaits et al. (2022), the effective incorporation of AI into cybersecurity relies not only on the efficacy of the model but also on users' comprehension and trust in AI-generated recommendations.

Ultimately, HFEaaS promotes ongoing human-AI collaboration in cybersecurity settings by enabling adaptive system architecture and operational robustness. As cyber threats progress, the tools and methods utilized by defenders must also adapt. HFEaaS facilitates the iterative evaluation and reconfiguration of AI-cybersecurity interfaces, guaranteeing conformity with the evolving requirements of analysts and the changing strategies of adversaries. This dynamic flexibility improves the long-term sustainability of AI implementations by integrating feedback from practical applications into subsequent versions. Moreover, by mitigating human limits such as fatigue, attention span, and perceptual bias, HFEaaS facilitates the development of technologies that enhance human strengths rather than exacerbate vulnerabilities. The incorporation of human factors into AI-driven cybersecurity operations is not merely a technical requirement but a strategic asset for safeguarding digital infrastructure.

## The distant future of HFEaaS

In an ideal scenario, the cybersecurity sector would acknowledge the significance of HFE and integrate it as a fundamental component of its defense strategy. However, in reality, HFE continues to progress slowly as a corporate cybersecurity priority. This is attributable not to irrelevance but to a deficiency in awareness. Cybersecurity has consistently faced a singular, enduring challenge: human behavior. At the convergence of humans and technology, HFEaaS emerges as a potent and timely solution.

The primary objective of HFEaaS is to avoid fostering long-term dependency. Instead, it serves as a strategic initiative to integrate essential human factors expertise into cybersecurity operations until the sector develops a sustainable and adequately qualified workforce of human factors specialists. Until the pipeline is built, the necessity for HFEaaS is both pressing and persuasive. It must address the persistent and frequently overwhelming challenges faced daily by end users, security analysts, and leadership teams. This friction results in inaccuracies, exhaustion, and heightened security vulnerabilities.

By integrating HFE principles and methodologies into cybersecurity frameworks, HFEaaS facilitates the development of systems that prioritize human needs rather than undermine them. It enables enterprises to develop behavioral frameworks that promote optimal user engagement, reduce cognitive load, and facilitate secure decision-making. HFEaaS facilitates the optimization of incident response systems, improves alert prioritizing, and creates more user-friendly security solutions, thereby fostering behaviors that correspond with security objectives and human capabilities.

The complete potential of HFEaaS in cybersecurity remains uncertain due to its recent emergence; however, its significance can be deduced by analyzing its effects in other high-risk sectors. HFE has consistently demonstrated its effectiveness in various domains, including healthcare, aviation, nuclear power, and industrial safety. These disciplines have long recognized the imperative to design in accordance with human capabilities and limits. Their efforts in HFE have led to enhanced operational safety, increased system resilience, and a substantial decrease in mistake rates.

Cybersecurity has the potential to achieve analogous advantages. HFEaaS is not merely a service; it is a conduit to a future in which security solutions are both technologically sophisticated and human-centric. It advocates for a paradigm shift in perception, recognizing individuals not as liabilities to be controlled, but as resources to be cultivated. By implementing HFEaaS, enterprises make a significant advancement in developing cybersecurity solutions that are both efficient and sustainable.

# Summary

As the cybersecurity landscape becomes increasingly intricate and adversaries become more adaptable, the human element remains both the foremost vulnerability and the most underutilized advantage. HFEaaS is a revolutionary approach to realigning cybersecurity with human skills, behaviors, and requirements. It is neither a transient solution nor a superficial improvement. HFEaaS signifies a fundamental transformation in how businesses can implement human-centered design at scale, particularly in contexts where talent deficits, cognitive strain, and usability issues jeopardize both resilience and performance.

HFEaaS addresses a significant deficiency in cybersecurity strategy by providing an accessible, scalable, and systematic method for incorporating human factors knowledge in essential areas. It recognizes the pressing necessity to tackle the human-technology interface and presents a service-oriented approach that integrates empirical insights into the daily operations of security teams, developers, and decision-makers. HFEaaS establishes the foundation for more intuitive, safe, and efficient systems through focused interventions, continuous feedback loops, and rigorous user-centered analysis.

In conclusion, HFEaaS is not merely a service; it is a strategic necessity for any organization dedicated to developing cybersecurity technologies that complement rather than hinder user interaction. Investing in HFEaaS today enables firms to transition from reactive problem-solving to proactive performance design, changing the human element from a risk factor into a fundamental component of cyber resilience.

The next chapter, on addressing stress, fatigue, and burnout in cybersecurity, is essential because sustained cognitive overload and high-consequence decision-making degrade attention, judgment, and response reliability, thereby increasing organizational risk. Human-centered interventions, such as workload-aware staffing and scheduling, alert rationalization, clearer handoffs, and ergonomic decision supports, sustain performance during prolonged operations while improving retention and long-term resilience.

## References


- Amershi, S., Cakmak, M., Knox, W. B., & Kulesza, T. (2014). Power to the people: The role of humans in interactive machine learning. *AI Magazine*, 35(4), 105–120. DOI: 10.1609/aimag.v35i4.2513
- Bada, M., Sasse, A. M., & Nurse, J. R. C. (2019). Cyber security awareness campaigns: Why do they fail to change behaviour? In Proceedings of the International Conference on Cyber Security for Sustainable Society (pp. 118–130).
- Bonneau, J., Herley, C., Van Oorschot, P. C., & Stajano, F. (2012). The quest to replace passwords: A framework for comparative evaluation of web authentication schemes. *2012 IEEE Symposium on Security and Privacy*, 553–567. DOI: 10.1109/SP.2012.44
- Carayon, P., Schoofs Hundt, A., Karsh, B. T., Gurses, A. P., Alvarado, C. J., Smith, M., & Flatley Brennan, P. (2006). Work system design for patient safety: The SEIPS model. *Quality & Safety in Health Care*, 15(Suppl 1), i50–i58. DOI: 10.1136/qshc.2005.015842 PMID: 17142610

- Carayon, P., Wust, K., Hose, B. Z., & Salwei, M. E. (2021). Human factors and ergonomics in health care. *Handbook of human factors and ergonomics*, 1417-1437.
- Coffey, J. W. (2017). Ameliorating sources of human error in cybersecurity: technological and human-centered approaches. *In The 8th International Multi-Conference on Complexity, Informatics, and Cybernetics*, Pensacola (pp. 85- 88).
- Dekker, S. (2016). Drift into failure: From hunting broken components to understanding complex systems. CRC Press. DOI: 10.1201/9781315257396
- Galaitsi, S., Trump, B. D., Keisler, J. M., Linkov, I., & Kott, A. (2022). Cybertrust: From Explainable to Actionable and Interpretable AI (AI2).
- Grobler, M., Gaire, R., & Nepal, S. (2021). User, usage, and usability: Redefining human-centric cyber security. *Frontiers in Big Data, 4, 583723.*
- Hill, M. (2020, February 6). 90% of UK data breaches due to human error in 2019. *Infosecurity Magazine*: `https://www.infosecurity-magazine.com/news/90-data-breaches-human-error/`
- IBM Security. (2020). *Cost of a data breach report 2020.* IBM. Retrieved from `https://www.ibm.com/security/digital-assets/cost-data-breach-report/1Cost%20of%20a%20Data%20Breach%20Report%202020.pdf`
- (ISC)² Cybersecurity Workforce Study, 2023: `www.isc2.org/Research/Workforce-Study`
- Leveson, N. G. (2011). The use of safety cases in certification and regulation. MIT:
- Li, K., Guo, J., Zeng, S., & Che, H. (2024). Reliability assessment of man-machine systems subject to probabilistic common cause errors. *Quality and Reliability Engineering International*, 40(5), 2399–2422. DOI: 10.1002/qre.3544
- Nobles, C. (2019). Establishing human factors programs to mitigate blind spots in cybersecurity. MWAIS 2019 Proceedings, 22: `https://aisel.aisnet.org/mwais2019/22`
- Nobles, C., & Robinson, N. (2024). The benefits of human factors engineering in cybersecurity. Cybersecurity Risk Management: Enhancing Leadership and Expertise, 53.
- Nobles, C., & Burrell, D. (2024). Exploring the variability of human factors definitions in cybersecurity literature. *MWAIS 2024 Proceedings*, 28: `https://aisel.aisnet.org/mwais2024/28`

- Nobles, C., Rangarajan, A., & Burrell, D. (2025). Human factors engineering- as-a-service in cybersecurity. *IGI Global Scientific Publishing*, 29: `https://doi.org/DOI: 10.4018/979-8-3693-6437-6.ch014`
- Parsons, K., McCormac, A., Pattinson, M., Butavicius, M., & Jerram, C. (2017). A study of information security awareness in Australian government organisations. *Information Management & Computer Security*, 23(4), 360–379.
- Rajivan, P., Aharonov-Majar, E., & Gonzalez, C. (2020). Update now or later? Effects of experience, cost, and risk preference on update decisions. *Journal of Cybersecurity, 6*(1), tyaa002.
- Russ, A. L., Fairbanks, R. J., Karsh, B. T., Militello, L. G., Saleem, J. J., & Wears, R. L. (2013). The science of human factors: Separating fact from fiction. *BMJ Quality & Safety*, 22(10), 802–808. DOI: 10.1136/bmjqs- 2012- 001450 PMID: 23592760
- Shaw, E. D., Ruby, K. G., & Post, J. M. (1998). The insider threat to information systems: The psychology of the dangerous insider. *Security Awareness Bulletin*, 98(2), 1–10.
- Thomas, M. J. (2017). Training and assessing non-technical skills: A practical guide. CRC Press.
- Wickens, C. D., & Hollands, J. G. (2000). Signal detection, information theory, and absolute judgment. *Engineering psychology and human performance, 2*, 24-73.
- Wickens, C. D., Helton, W. S., Hollands, J. G., & Banbury, S. (2021). *Engineering Psychology and Human Performance*. Routledge. DOI: 10.4324/9781003177616
- Willmott, T. J., Pang, B., & Rundle-Thiele, S. (2021). Capability, opportunity, and motivation: an across contexts empirical examination of the COM-B model. *BMC Public Health, 21*(1), 1014.

## Get this book's PDF version and more

Scan the QR code (or go to `packtpub.com/unlock`). Search for this book by name, confirm the edition, and then follow the steps on the page.

UNLOCK NOW

*Note: Keep your invoice handy. Purchases made directly from Packt don't require an invoice.*

# 7

# Addressing Stress, Fatigue, and Burnout in Cybersecurity

Stress, fatigue, and burnout are wreaking havoc on organizations, especially when it comes to cybersecurity. While these physiological conditions are not new, the prevalence rates of stress, fatigue, and exhaustion in cybersecurity professionals are alarming. Recent studies indicate that approximately 66% of IT security personnel report experiencing significant stress, while around 50% report symptoms consistent with fatigue and burnout (Rangarajan et al., 2025). These statistics underscore the pressing need to investigate not only the causes and effects of these conditions but also effective mitigation strategies to promote healthier work environments.

In the context of cybersecurity professionals, stress can arise from various factors, including rapid technological changes, the high stakes associated with data breaches, and the overwhelming demand for constant vigilance (Casper & Sonnentag, 2020). As cybersecurity professionals, you are frequently responsible for protecting critical systems and sensitive information against increasingly sophisticated cyber threats. Fatigue, which is a prolonged state of exhaustion resulting from physical or mental effort, is particularly relevant due to the long working hours and intensive demands of cybersecurity roles. Professional exhaustion is a more severe manifestation of chronic stress, characterized by emotional exhaustion, depersonalization, and a reduced sense of personal accomplishment (Maslach & Leiter, 2016). Collectively, these conditions present significant challenges for cybersecurity practitioners, affecting both their well-being and efficiency in an environment already marked by high stress. Research indicates these factors contribute to decreased productivity, increased absenteeism, and higher turnover rates, further exacerbating the skills gap within the cybersecurity workforce (NASEM, 2025). Consequently, promoting awareness and implementing mental health support systems are crucial not only for individual professionals but also for the resilience and integrity of cybersecurity organizations.

Through this chapter, we will examine the interrelation between stress, fatigue, and professional exhaustion among cybersecurity professionals. Although these concepts are distinct, they are interconnected within a complex dynamic that affects both personal well-being and organizational efficiency. High levels of stress can lead to fatigue, which, in turn, contributes to professional exhaustion. Conversely, the experience of professional exhaustion can exacerbate stress levels, creating a harmful cycle that undermines professional performance and mental health. Understanding this interconnection is essential for developing targeted interventions to mitigate potential risks.

In this chapter, we will discuss the following key topics:

- Pathway to burnout
- Cybersecurity environment and its unique stressors
- Theoretical frameworks for understanding stress and fatigue
- Assessment and measurement
- Organizational-level contributors to stress, fatigue, and burnout
- Prevention and intervention strategies

# Pathway to burnout

The transition from stress to burnout follows a methodical and rising path that is well-documented in occupational health and human factors research. **Stress** manifests in the preliminary phase, often triggered by increased job demands, time constraints, task intensity, or life stressors. Moderate stress can sometimes enhance performance, but prolonged exposure to stressors without effective coping strategies leads to an imbalance between demands and resources. Burnout emerges when sustained job demands chronically exceed available job resources, producing cumulative exhaustion and disengagement, because demands are the persistent physical, cognitive, emotional, and organizational requirements of work (for example, workload, time pressure, role ambiguity, emotional labor, and high-stakes accountability), whereas resources are the enabling support that reduce strain and sustain performance (for example, autonomy, staffing, supervisory support, clear priorities, recovery time, usable tools, training, and recognition). This mismatch undermines psychological and physiological stability, exposing you to the risk of cumulative tiredness. **Fatigue** arises when rest and recuperation fail to counterbalance continuous stress, resulting in chronic exhaustion, interrupted sleep patterns, and reduced ability to maintain focus. As this condition persists, you will experience physical exhaustion and cognitive impairments, which diminish productivity and decision-making ability. *Figure 7.1* depicts this progression from stress to burnout.

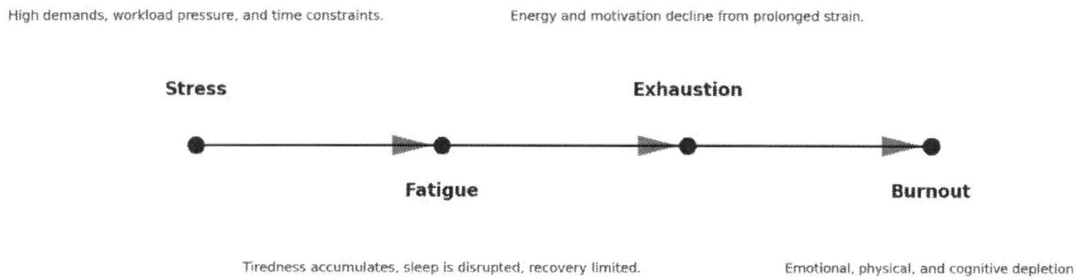


*Figure 7.1: Timeline progression to burnout*

Over time, unresolved weariness evolves into exhaustion, indicating a more profound level of strain characterized by depleted energy reserves, reduced motivation, and increased vulnerability to errors and disengagement from your tasks. If this trajectory is not addressed, it leads to **burnout**, a complex condition characterized by emotional tiredness, depersonalization or cynicism, and diminished professional efficacy (Maslach & Leiter, 2016). At this stage, you might experience significant deficits in well-being and job performance. This can induce feelings of helplessness if you are unable to prevent security breaches or effectively mitigate their consequences. Burnout can potentially lead to turnover, absenteeism, and reduced organizational resilience. The timeline emphasizes the importance of taking early actions during the stress and fatigue phases to prevent the subsequent consequences that can lead to burnout.

Events or circumstances that upset your psychological balance and call for adaptive coping are known as **life stressors**. Examples of life stressors include the death of a close family member, health issues, job loss or sudden financial strain, divorce or major relationship conflict, serious illness or injury, and forced relocation or housing instability. Stressors are usually categorized by frequency and duration. According to the **American Psychological Association** (**APA**), stress can be broadly divided into three categories:

- **Episodic acute stress**: These are repeated episodes of acute stress without sufficient recovery time
- **Chronic stress**: This results from continuous, persistent stressors such as financial hardship, pressure at work, or health problems
- **Acute stress**: This is brief and usually occurs in response to immediate challenges or threats (Nwobodo, 2023)

Reeves et al. (2024) identify predictive factors for exhaustion and poor sleep quality among cybersecurity professionals, including excessive workloads, lack of control over work processes, and insufficient social support. Poor sleep quality amplifies the effects of exhaustion by degrading cognitive function, emotional regulation, and resilience. Chronic stressors such as long working hours, high-stakes responsibilities, and the need for constant vigilance can lead to cumulative fatigue, which in turn increases the likelihood of burnout. Singh et al. (2023) note that prolonged exposure to such stressors can impair cognitive performance and emotional resilience, further compromising your ability to respond effectively to evolving cyber threats. While the onset of stress can stem from a multitude of issues, our key objective is to reduce stress to prevent it from becoming chronic.

Addressing stress, fatigue, and exhaustion in cybersecurity requires systemic organizational change. Gupta et al. (2024) and Rangarajan et al. (2025) stress the importance of restructuring work environments to support employee mental health and promote sustained engagement. Organizations should implement effective interventions such as establishing regular rest schedules, promoting work-life balance, and providing access to mental health resources (Arora & Hastings, 2024). Tailored programs, including mindfulness training and stress management workshops, can also reduce the prevalence of exhaustion. By fostering a culture that prioritizes mental well-being, organizations can improve employee resilience, job satisfaction, and overall performance. By integrating supportive practices into organizational culture, the cybersecurity profession can better safeguard the well-being of its workforce while enhancing effectiveness in combating evolving threats.

# Cybersecurity environment and its unique stressors

In a cybersecurity environment, organizational leaders, incident responders, and security analysts must evaluate conflicting information, sort through a high volume of machine-generated warnings, and adapt to adversaries that continually evolve their strategies, tactics, and processes. Conflicting information in cybersecurity refers to situations in which practitioners receive incompatible, ambiguous, or rapidly changing signals about what is happening, what to prioritize, or what action is correct, across tools, teams, policies, or leadership direction. It contributes to burnout by increasing cognitive load, uncertainty, and perceived loss of control, which drives sustained stress and emotional exhaustion.

Organizational cultures that may unintentionally increase stress through regulatory constraints, skewed incentives, and communication gaps between technical and business stakeholders further exacerbate these operational needs. The human factors that influence this environment are increasingly being documented in peer-reviewed literature. These factors include alert fatigue, high-stakes decision-making under time pressure, the difficulties of a rapidly changing threat landscape, and the impact of organizational culture on stress levels (Patterson et al., 2023 Nobles, 2022 Tariq et al., 2025). The cybersecurity industry imposes a unique stress profile that necessitates coordinated interventions across technology, procedures, and culture, according to an integrated analysis of these aspects.

## High-stakes decision-making under time pressure

In cyber operations, crucial decisions such as when to initiate confinement, isolate assets, or initiate external communication often need to be made under extreme time pressure. According to Nobles (2022), one of the main causes of stress and burnout among cybersecurity workers is time constraints and high-stakes decision-making situations. This highlights cyber-specific circumstances, such as ongoing high-intensity operations and increased executive visibility during incidents, quickly changing adversary strategies, and competing demands related to service continuity, technical remediation, legal requirements, and reputational issues (Patterson et al., 2023). In such situations, cybersecurity professionals frequently employ cognitive heuristics, which expedite decision-making but increase the risk of mistakes, especially when these mental shortcuts tend to focus on certain details rather than doing thorough assessments of the issue. Some examples of cognitive heuristics in cybersecurity include the availability heuristic, which leads analysts to overprioritize threats that are recent or highly publicized; anchoring, which causes fixation on the first alert or initial hypothesis despite new evidence; and automation bias, which drives overreliance on SIEM/EDR outputs even when contradictory indicators appear. These circumstances can result in two problems: either teams take containment measures too quickly, which unintentionally warns attackers and makes the response harder, or act too slowly and give adversaries more time to expand their access (Van der Kleij et al., 2017). These dynamics underscore how the severe time constraints of cyber disasters significantly impact decision-making processes and outcomes.

Research on the efficacy of **computer security incident response teams** (**CSIRTs**) indicates that coordination, role clarity, and the cognitive burden of multi-stakeholder decision-making during emergencies are ongoing performance issues. Pre-negotiated decision rights, cross-functional simulation exercises, and post-incident reviews that convert unwritten experience into codified guidelines are suggested methods to lessen these effects (Patterson et al., 2023 Van der Kleij et al., 2017). Predefined decision authority can be documented in a short escalation and approval guide that specifies what the incident commander is empowered to do immediately (such as isolating network segments or revoking keys) once agreed-upon triggers occur, while routing business-impact decisions to executives with a clearly defined decision-time expectation.

Cross-functional simulations can be run as short tabletop drills with timed injects (legal, communications, operations) that force real-time use of escalation paths and message templates, followed by a post-incident review that converts the decision log into updated runbooks, thresholds, and a small set of measurable improvements (for example, time-to-triage, time-to-containment). Decision-support automation, well-defined escalation criteria, and organized operational cycles that preserve analyst focus during acute events are evidence-based strategies for overcoming these difficulties.

## Alert overload and signal-to-noise challenges

**Security operations centers** (**SOCs**) operate on both human judgment and automated tools. Detection systems often generate numerous warnings and alerts, which you must quickly classify, correlate, and prioritize. According to peer-reviewed studies on alert fatigue in SOCs, operators' confidence in security tools is damaged, their vigilance is reduced, and they are more likely to miss important incidents because of high alert volumes, poor precision, and a lack of contextual information (Tariq et al., 2025). Three main mechanisms cause alert weariness:

- Cybersecurity detection models may generate excessive false positives, miss true attacks, or fail to recognize new threats because benign activity heavily outweighs malicious examples in training data (class imbalance) and because adversaries change tactics over time, causing model drift
- Analysts must manually piece together the context due to the fragmented nature of telemetry across different data sources, which slows inquiry timeframes and adds to cognitive strain
- Analysts' attention is diverted from truly high-priority concerns by low-value and repeated ticketing procedures (Kearney, 2023)

There are quantifiable effects of alert overload on employee well-being and organizational results. Long-term alert overload can cause increased turnover intentions among SOC analysts, lower detection performance, and higher error rates (Nobles, 2022). Threat hunting has shifted from simply reacting to alerts to proactively investigating based on hypotheses, helping to enhance overall signal quality (Mahboubi et al., 2024).

Mitigation strategies include using machine learning models to learn from analysts' adjudications to improve accuracy, combining related alerts into single incident records through hierarchical triage processes, and fine-tuning detection systems to reduce unnecessary alerts and improve precision. The alert and signal-to-noise challenges may be resolved through organizational measures, such as incorporating analyst input into detection rule updates, setting aside specific time for rule maintenance, and implementing secure-by-design vendor criteria to reduce unnecessary alarms (CISA, 2023).

> **Note**
>
> Alert and signal-to-noise issues can be reduced by treating detections as maintained products through three practical measures: Analysts tag recurring false positives during triage; a weekly review turns the top patterns into rule refinements; a protected twice-

> weekly maintenance block is used to tune noisy rules after environment changes (for example, cloud migration drift); procurement applies secure-by-design vendor criteria, requiring pilots that demonstrate low-noise defaults, explainable detections, and actionable alert content before purchase.

## Rapidly evolving threat landscape

The rapidly evolving cybersecurity landscape functions as a chronic stressor because continuously shifting threats, technologies, and requirements force professionals to maintain constant vigilance, repeatedly re-learn tools and tactics, and make high-stakes decisions under uncertainty and time pressure. Because of the commercialization of attack tools, new technologies and ways to exploit new vulnerabilities are emerging, and adversary strategies and attack surfaces are continually evolving. Due to this dynamic environment, defenders face what Choo (2011) refers to as a *"moving target"* dilemma, where defensive playbooks must be revised frequently, and knowledge quickly becomes outdated. According to peer-reviewed research, there are two main approaches to addressing this difficulty.

- Acceleration of **observe–orient–decide–act (OODA)** cycles of defenders using **cyber threat intelligence (CTI)**. Context-rich, behavior-oriented intelligence that combines proactive threat hunting and detection engineering has replaced indicator-based feeds in CTI (Santos et al., 2025). For example, a behavior-based example is a cyber threat intelligence report that describes a ransomware actor using exposed virtual private network credentials, then adding a new administrator account, deleting backups, and initiating rapid file encryption; threat hunters search logs for that sequence, and detection engineers turn it into detection rules and automated containment actions instead of relying on static internet protocol addresses or file hashes.
- Structured threat hunting, a tactic that proactively detects unusual behaviors before they escalate into events by utilizing analytical frameworks, adversary emulation, and iterative scoping (Mahboubi et al., 2024).

The dynamic nature of the threat landscape also makes collaboration across various organizational boundaries more difficult. Supply chain dependencies, cloud-native systems, and third-party services create distributed responsibility. According to Ahmad et al. (2021), gathering and sharing ideas across these barriers is essential for successful organizational learning from occurrences. This can be done by creating repeatable cross-boundary learning routines that move incident knowledge across internal teams, cloud providers, and suppliers (Patterson et al., 2023). For example, run a quarterly cross-organizational tabletop that includes security, information technology operations, legal, and the managed service provider to rehearse decision rights and communications, implement a standardized "two-page incident packet" that is shared with vendors and internal stakeholders to align on root cause and required control changes, and establish a supplier vulnerability disclosure and patch-cadence process that requires third parties to provide timelines, compensating controls, and verification evidence after remediation.

Recurring vulnerabilities and misconfigurations reappear in new forms, often due to the teams' lack of formal learning procedures to learn from past issues, thereby sustaining crisis cycles. A formal learning procedure refers to a repeatable, documented workflow that captures lessons from incidents and near-misses, translates those lessons into concrete control and process changes, and verifies that changes were implemented and are effective, rather than relying on informal memory or ad hoc fixes; such procedures increase flexibility and resilience by enabling teams to adapt quickly to recurring vulnerability patterns and attacker-driven variation without reverting to crisis-driven improvisation (Patterson et al., 2023). In practice, "treating detection content as code" means storing detection rules, correlation logic, and response playbooks in version control with peer review, testing, and traceable change history; for example, a noisy cloud authentication rule is updated through a pull request that includes test cases and acceptance criteria (reduced false positives without loss of true positives), then deployed via a controlled pipeline and monitored for performance. Incorporating incident reviews into change management means that each incident produces a structured after-action record and a required set of change tickets that flow through the normal governance path (for example, a change advisory board) with deadlines, owners, and verification evidence; for example, a misconfiguration incident triggers a change request to enforce infrastructure-as-code guardrails, a second change to add automated configuration drift alerts, and a third change to update the hardening standard, with completion validated in a follow-up review cycle (Cybersecurity and Infrastructure Security Agency, 2023).

Affected populations can reduce stress from a constantly evolving threat landscape by shifting from "always catching up" to a managed operating model:

- **Stabilize priorities with a threat-informed focus**: Select a small set of high-likelihood/high-impact threats and align controls, detections, and training to those patterns rather than chasing every headline
- **Time-box continuous learning**: Reserve a fixed weekly block (for example, 60–90 minutes) for structured learning and retire the expectation of ad hoc, after-hours catching up
- **Productize detections and runbooks**: Maintain a backlog for noisy alerts, update rules on a cadence, and convert incident lessons into simple decision trees to reduce uncertainty during response
- **Pre-negotiate decision rights**: Define who can isolate systems, rotate keys, or shut down services at each severity level so decisions are not renegotiated under pressure

- **Automate low-value work safely**: Automate enrichment, deduplication, and ticket routing to reduce cognitive load while keeping human judgment for high-impact actions
- **Use cross-functional drills**: Short tabletop exercises build shared mental models, reduce blame, and speed coordination when real incidents occur
- **Protect recovery and boundaries**: On-call rotations, handoffs, and minimum rest periods reduce chronic fatigue and prevent stress accumulation

## Organizational and cultural pressures

Workplace cultures, rules, and organizational structures all contribute to the technical pressures in cybersecurity. Organizational culture determines the perception of the value of security, how risk tolerance is shaped, and resource allocation. According to Khadka et al. (2025), punitive reactions to errors, excessively complicated procedures, or ambiguous accountability structures are some examples of organizational cultures that may inadvertently create obstacles to secure practices. Workplace cultures, rules, and organizational structures become stressors because they increase cognitive load, compress decision time, and create fear of blame, which forces cybersecurity professionals to operate under chronic uncertainty and moral tension (Khadka et al., 2025). For example, in a punitive culture, an analyst who mistakenly escalates a false positive is publicly criticized, so the next time a borderline alert appears, the analyst delays escalation to avoid humiliation; the delay enables attacker dwell time to increase, and the analyst experiences sustained anxiety, hypervigilance, and self-protective decision-making rather than mission-focused judgment. In an environment with excessively complicated procedures, an incident responder must complete multiple approvals and forms to isolate a compromised endpoint, so containment is slowed by bureaucracy, while leadership still demands immediate resolution, the responder experiences time pressure, frustration, and decision fatigue as procedural friction conflicts with operational urgency. In an ambiguous accountability structure, a cloud misconfiguration is discovered, but it is unclear whether Security, DevOps, or the vendor owns remediation; while teams debate responsibility, the vulnerability remains exposed, and the security lead absorbs blame from executives without having authority to act, creating role conflict, perceived helplessness, and burnout risk.

Frameworks for compliance are a common cause of cultural conflict. Although regulatory compliance can set baseline security requirements, if it is used as a checklist exercise disconnected from operational reality, it may also divert resources away from true risk reduction and toward documentation (Busetti et al., 2025). Research shows that compliance activities are more closely aligned with effective threat mitigation when reframed as a continuous organizational learning process (Busetti et al., 2025 CISA, 2023).

Compliance frameworks can generate cultural conflict when they become disconnected from operational reality, such as enforcing a uniform encryption or logging requirement without funding the engineering work to implement it, requiring quarterly access recertifications that consume analyst time while privileged access risks remain unaddressed, or mandating annual policy refresh cycles that produce new paperwork but do not change insecure workflows (Busetti et al., 2025). Compliance aligns more closely with real threat mitigation when it is treated as continuous learning, such as using risk-based scoping to focus control testing on crown-jewel systems, turning audit findings into prioritized remediation backlogs with owners and completion evidence, and integrating compliance checks into automated pipelines so misconfigurations are prevented and detected continuously rather than documented after the fact (Busetti et al., 2025 Cybersecurity and Infrastructure Security Agency, 2023).

Another important cultural element that affects stress levels in cybersecurity teams is a lack of clear communication and role clarity. According to Van der Kleij et al. (2017), establishing decision-making authority, having a common language across technical and non-technical stakeholders, and utilizing well-practiced crisis communication techniques are all crucial. Without these, incident responders deal with contradictory instructions, redundant work, and delayed reactions, all of which increase the strain on their bodies and minds.

A growing cultural focus is on workforce sustainability. According to Nobles (2022), burnout among cybersecurity workers is predicted by a persistent workload, insufficient recuperation time, and a lack of psychological safety. Interventions include providing employees with access to mental health resources, scheduling time for skill development and reflection, and intentional workload planning by alternating between high-intensity and low-intensity roles. Long-term retention and psychological safety are enhanced by leadership actions that normalize disclosing errors and promote asking for assistance.

## Understanding stress, fatigue, and burnout through theoretical frameworks

Cybersecurity is a high-reliability occupation in which human performance is continuously tested by time pressure, ambiguity, and sustained cognitive load, and the resulting strain is not incidental but structurally produced by the work system: analysts, engineers, and leaders operate amid high alert volume, incomplete information, adversarial deception, and competing priorities that compress decision windows and elevate the cost of error, even though attention, working memory, and executive control are finite and recovery opportunities are often insufficient. When stress and fatigue accumulate without adequate recovery, teams experience predictable declines in vigilance, judgment, and adaptive capacity. These conditions increase missed signals, mis-triage, delayed escalation, overreliance on early hypotheses, reduced collaboration, higher turnover, recurring failures, and the loss of institutional knowledge that reinforces understaffing and chronic urgency. To move beyond anecdotal explanations and reactive wellness responses, this section introduces theoretical frameworks that explain how workplace conditions translate into measurable human performance outcomes by treating stress, fatigue, and burnout as system-level phenomena rather than individual deficiencies; it applies fatigue science to circadian disruption and sleep-related cognitive impairment, occupational stress models to demand-control and effort-reward dynamics, and burnout constructs to exhaustion, cynicism, and reduced efficacy, thereby identifying actionable leverage points such as workload shaping, decision-rights design, alert-quality management, and protected recovery.

## Occupational stress models

Understanding burnout and sustained fatigue in cybersecurity work benefits from anchoring analysis in well-established occupational stress frameworks and fatigue science. The Job Demand–Control model and the Effort–Reward Imbalance model explain how chronic strain emerges when workload intensity is high, autonomy is constrained, and recognition or compensation does not match effort. Fatigue science then clarifies why performance degrades under sustained sleep restriction, circadian disruption, and irregular shift patterns, producing predictable declines in vigilance, working memory, and decision quality that can elevate operational risk. While stress is difficult to eliminate in cybersecurity environments, it is imperative that cyber operators and leaders understand how stress and fatigue develop, how they manifest in performance, and how they can be managed to protect decision quality, team resilience, and mission outcomes.

## Job Demand–Control model

Karasek's **Job Demand–Control (JDC)** model is one of the most well-known models in occupational health psychology (Karasek, 1979 Karasek & Theorell, 1990). Stress is most likely to happen when people have limited control over how they complete their work and are subjected to high job demands, including multitasking, large workloads, and time-sensitive decision-making. Decision latitude, or the capacity to choose one's own work pace, priorities, and techniques, is reflected in job control (Karasek, 1979 Karasek & Theorell, 1990).

This friction is noticeable in cybersecurity settings, especially SOCs. Analysts regularly deal with emergencies, including ransomware attacks or virus outbreaks, that call for a quick response. However, they are frequently unable to take significant action without permission due to organizational hierarchy or compliance constraints. Performance is weakened, and this mismatch between pressing expectations and restricted autonomy raises stress levels. According to the JDC model, stress can be decreased, and more productive performance can be supported, by increasing decision flexibility through pre-approved response playbooks or the appearance of authority to escalate actions.

## Effort–Reward Imbalance model

By highlighting equity in the workplace, Siegrist's **Effort–Reward Imbalance** (**ERI**) model provides a contrasting viewpoint (Siegrist, 1996; Siegrist, 2002). According to the model, when employees' emotional, cognitive, and temporal efforts are not adequately rewarded, chronic stress results. In addition to compensation, these benefits include respect, acknowledgment, and chances for professional growth (Siegrist, 1996; Siegrist, 2002).

Analysts in the cybersecurity field frequently put in long hours, remain on call on the weekends, and focus intently on challenging issues. The risk of burnout rises, and motivation falls when these sacrifices are not rewarded with opportunities for growth or recognition. According to the ERI model, companies may retain qualified workers and maintain morale in complex cybersecurity tasks by striking a balance between high effort and meaningful rewards, whether monetary or symbolic. Under the Effort–Reward Imbalance model, organizations can balance high-effort cybersecurity work by providing market-aligned rewards such as on-call stipends and incident-response differential pay, recovery-based rewards such as guaranteed comp time and enforced rest periods after major incidents, and symbolic-status rewards such as formal recognition that directly influences performance evaluations and promotion decisions.

## Fatigue science

Fatigue science explains how sleep loss, circadian misalignment, and prolonged cognitive effort degrade human performance through measurable changes in attention, working memory, reaction time, and executive control. Fatigue is not simply "feeling tired"; it is a physiological and neurocognitive state in which vigilance declines, error rates increase, and judgment becomes less reliable, particularly under monotony or sustained monitoring conditions. Circadian rhythm theory further clarifies that performance fluctuates throughout the day, with predictable troughs in alertness during overnight hours and mid-afternoon, and that shift work, late-night incident response, and rotating on-call schedules can chronically disrupt sleep timing and recovery. Because fatigue accumulates, short-term "push through" strategies can compound deficits that impair learning, emotional regulation, and risk perception, increasing susceptibility to irritability, disengagement, and burnout over time.

In cybersecurity, fatigue science applies directly because many roles demand continuous vigilance, rapid interpretation of ambiguous signals, and high-stakes decisions under uncertainty, often during irregular hours. A fatigued security operations analyst is more likely to miss weak indicators, misclassify alerts, or anchor on an early hypothesis, while a fatigued incident responder may accept incomplete containment actions, overlook lateral movement, or delay escalation to avoid additional workload. Fatigue also amplifies automation bias, increasing overreliance on tool outputs when independent verification is needed, and it reduces cross-team coordination quality by weakening communication clarity and increasing conflict. Practical implications follow: organizations can reduce fatigue-related risk by stabilizing on-call rotations, limiting consecutive night shifts, protecting recovery time after major incidents, reducing alert noise through detection maintenance, and pre-negotiating decision rights so critical actions are not debated when cognitive capacity is impaired.

## Circadian rhythms

Circadian rhythms are innate, endogenous mechanisms that govern the sleep-wake cycle, recurring approximately every 24 hours. These rhythms affect alertness, cognitive performance, reaction speeds, and mood. They are especially pertinent in cybersecurity settings characterized by continuous operations, such as SOCs, cyber defense facilities, and threat intelligence divisions.

Misalignment of work schedules with circadian cycles, particularly during nocturnal shifts, leads to diminished cognitive function, especially in jobs that require prolonged concentration or swift decision-making. An analyst assigned to the 2:00 a.m. to 8:00 a.m. shift may encounter diminished response times to warnings, decreased precision in log analysis, and challenges in correlating different danger indications. Chronic circadian misalignment leads to accumulated fatigue that may persist after the restoration of regular rhythms.

Addressing circadian disruption requires the implementation of strategies to manage tiredness risk. Implementing a forward rotation of shifts (morning → afternoon → night), restricting consecutive night shifts, and permitting extended recovery intervals between rotations can enhance cognitive performance. Integrating brief, regulated naps during circadian troughs and employing lighting techniques to mimic daylight can enhance attentiveness.

## Sleep deprivation effects

The consequences of sleep deprivation, both total and partial, are extensively studied in cognitive science. Moderate sleep deprivation can hinder decision-making, attention, and working memory to a level akin to alcohol intoxication. For cybersecurity analysts, whose responsibilities demand heightened alertness and swift analysis of intricate datasets, such deficits can yield immediate operational repercussions.

Acute sleep deprivation, shown by the loss of a whole night's sleep in response to a zero-day exploit, can lead to acute cognitive impairment. Chronic partial sleep deprivation, characterized by routinely obtaining fewer than six hours of sleep due to irregular shifts, results in cumulative consequences that are more challenging to identify yet equally detrimental. Operational risk in cybersecurity arises when exhausted analysts may fail to detect minor intrusion indications, misidentify threats, or make erroneous escalation choices.

Fatigue research emphasizes the necessity for organizational measures to prevent fatigue-related errors. Automated escalation systems that redistribute workload during peak fatigue periods, policies mandating rest after prolonged incidents, and cross-training to ensure incident coverage without excessive dependence on specific individuals can mitigate fatigue risk while preserving operational readiness.

## Burnout constructs

The **Maslach Burnout Inventory** (**MBI**) provides the most widely recognized framework for understanding burnout, characterizing it through three dimensions: emotional exhaustion, cynicism, and reduced personal accomplishment.

- **Emotional exhaustion**: This refers to the state of being emotionally overextended and devoid of emotional energy. In cybersecurity, emotional exhaustion often arises from prolonged exposure to high-alert situations, continuous incident escalations, and relentless crisis management without sufficient rest. For instance, an analyst who has overseen consecutive ransomware events over several weeks may encounter challenges with concentration, increased irritation, and diminished motivation.
- **Cynicism** (**depersonalization**): This entails cultivating a detached or adverse disposition towards work, coworkers, or clientele. In SOCs, cynicism may manifest as pessimism regarding new detection initiatives, diminished empathy for end users, or a contemptuous stance toward company security rules. For example, after several months of high-severity incidents and repeated leadership promises that "a new detection platform will fix the problem," a cybersecurity analyst begins dismissing proposals for new detection rules as "another pointless dashboard," responds to user-reported phishing with curt messages such as "read the policy," and openly mocks security procedures in meetings, treating them as performative rather than protective. Cynicism, initially a coping strategy for emotional detachment, can undermine teamwork and diminish the efficacy of security operations.
- **Diminished personal accomplishment** (**inefficacy**): This refers to the perception of decreased competence and achievement in the workplace. In cybersecurity, it may arise when analysts consistently observe adversaries circumventing barriers or when organizational limitations hinder the execution of essential security protocols. Ultimately, this feeling of futility may result in disengagement, withdrawal, and attrition.

Burnout never arises from a singular incident; instead, it accumulates over months or years of persistent stress without sufficient recuperation. Mitigating burnout necessitates comprehensive interventions, such as workload redistribution, formal acknowledgment programs, chances for skill enhancement, and leadership behaviors that promote help-seeking and error reporting.

## Integrative perspective

Although each paradigm presents distinct perspectives, their integrated use yields a thorough comprehension of stress, fatigue, and burnout in cybersecurity operations. The JDC model elucidates how elevated demands, coupled with minimal control, exacerbate strain. The ERI model underscores the discouraging effects of imbalanced effort and reward. Fatigue science delineates the physiological and cognitive deterioration linked to inadequate rest. The MBI encapsulates the psychological repercussions of sustained strain.

These frameworks converge around several key strategic imperatives for enterprises:

- Augment autonomy in cybersecurity positions by empowering analysts with decision-making ability commensurate with their experience
- Correlate rewards with effort to enhance motivation and acknowledge contributions during high-intensity operating phases
- Develop shift schedules that correspond with circadian principles and minimize exposure to peak fatigue intervals
- Observe burnout indications and implement early interventions to prevent adverse effects on operational performance
- Encourage psychological safety to ensure that employees can disclose exhaustion, errors, or systemic issues without fear of retaliation

Cybersecurity workers face a unique array of occupational stresses that, if left unaddressed, may lead to diminished performance, health issues, and increased employee turnover. By incorporating occupational stress models, fatigue research, and burnout constructs into policy, training, and leadership practices, businesses may establish cybersecurity environments that support both the performance and well-being of their cybersecurity professionals. By doing so, they safeguard their digital assets and maintain the human capital crucial for enduring security resilience. Burnout, fatigue science, and occupational stress models provide organizations with validated frameworks to assess and measure human performance risk by translating subjective strain into observable indicators and metrics, such as sleep-related impairment, workload-demand imbalance, perceived control and reward deficits, and burnout dimensions that can be monitored to guide targeted interventions.

# Assessment and measurement

Assessment and measurement are significant in cybersecurity because burnout and fatigue are operational risks that erode vigilance, judgment, and coordination well before failure becomes evident in incident outcomes. Without measurement, organizations typically rely on anecdotes, crisis signals, or turnover as delayed indicators, which leads to reactive interventions that arrive after performance has already eroded. By establishing systematic assessment of workload, alert volume and quality, on-call burden, recovery time, perceived control, and burnout dimensions, leaders can detect emerging strain patterns, identify the specific drivers (for example, chronic overtime versus role ambiguity versus tool noise), and target mitigations with precision rather than generalized wellness messaging. Measurement also enables accountability and continuous improvement: interventions such as detection tuning, staffing adjustments, rotation redesign, and decision-rights clarification can be evaluated against baseline metrics (for example, time-to-triage, after-hours hours, false-positive rates, and self-reported exhaustion), ensuring that human performance protection becomes a managed component of security resilience rather than an informal aspiration.

## Psychometric instrument for stress and burnout

A psychometric instrument for stress and burnout is a validated, questionnaire-based measurement tool that quantifies latent psychological constructs such as perceived stress, emotional exhaustion, cynicism, and reduced professional efficacy using standardized items and scoring methods, thereby producing reliable, comparable results across individuals, teams, and time periods. This matters because stress and burnout are frequently underreported, normalized, or misattributed to individual weakness, and cybersecurity environments often conceal early warning signs until errors, attrition, or incident failures emerge. For cybersecurity professionals, psychometric instruments are especially relevant because human performance directly shapes detection, response, and risk decision-making; when fatigue and burnout rise, vigilance, triage quality, collaboration, and retention predictably decline. By establishing baselines, identifying role- or team-level hotspots (for example, on-call coverage or high-noise monitoring), and evaluating whether interventions such as rotation redesign, alert reduction, decision-rights clarification, and recovery protections are working, psychometric measurement applies the same operational discipline used for technical metrics to the human system that enables cybersecurity resilience.

## Maslach Burnout Inventory (MBI)

The **Maslach Burnout Inventory** (**MBI**) is a prominent instrument for assessing occupational burnout. Burnout, as defined by Maslach and Jackson (1981), is a multidimensional syndrome comprising three elements: **emotional exhaustion** (**EE**), **depersonalization** (**DP**), and **reduced personal accomplishment** (**PA**). EE signifies a state of emotional depletion; DP denotes a distant or cynical perspective toward one's work; and RPA indicates a diminishment in perceived competence and achievement.

The MBI has been utilized in various sectors, including healthcare, education, and technology. In high-pressure technological settings, higher EE and DP scores have been associated with reduced collaboration and increased interpersonal conflict. The MBI's proprietary nature and reliance on self-reporting, despite its excellent validation, may limit accessibility and introduce bias. Notwithstanding these constraints, it remains a fundamental component of burnout evaluation when used alongside supplementary metrics (Maslach & Leiter, 2016b).

## Perceived Stress Scale (PSS)

The **PSS**, developed by Cohen et al. (1983), measures the degree to which individuals perceive circumstances as stressful, focusing on feelings of unpredictability, uncontrollability, and overwhelm over the preceding month. It offers a comprehensive assessment of felt stress, rather than focusing on specific incidents. In workplace studies, the PSS has been linked to turnover intentions, decreased job satisfaction, and absenteeism. In cybersecurity and IT operations, higher PSS scores are associated with higher error rates under high-volume workloads. The PSS is most useful when combined with physiological and operational indicators, even though it captures subjective stress perception. Here is a scenario and an example: in a security operations center, PSS scores spike during a month of high alert volume, and the same team experiences more mis-triaged tickets and delayed escalations, while several analysts report an intent to leave or take more sick days. The PSS becomes more actionable when paired with operational and physiological signals, such as linking higher scores to increased on-call pages, growing alert backlog, and reduced sleep or heart rate variability, which then guides targeted fixes such as detection tuning and rotation redesign.

# Physiological and behavioral metrics

Physiological and behavioral metrics are objective indicators that quantify stress and fatigue by measuring how the body and work patterns respond to sustained demands. Physiological metrics capture biological strain and recovery, such as sleep duration and quality, resting heart rate, and heart rate variability. Behavioral metrics capture observable performance and workload signals, such as on-call paging frequency, after-hours work, alert backlog growth, and increased rework or triage errors. These measures are important because self-reports can be delayed, minimized, or normalized in high-pressure cultures, whereas objective indicators can surface early risk before burnout becomes visible through turnover or incidents. In cybersecurity, physiological and behavioral metrics are relevant because cybersecurity defensive performance depends on sustained vigilance and rapid judgment, so monitoring these metrics could help leaders identify overloaded roles and evaluate whether mitigations such as alert reduction, personnel and work rotation redesign, or recovery protections are working.

## Heart Rate Variability (HRV)

**HRV** quantifies the temporal variation between consecutive heartbeats, indicating the equilibrium of the autonomic nervous system. Elevated HRV typically signifies adaptability and resilience, whereas diminished HRV correlates with stress, exhaustion, and impaired recovery capability (Shaffer & Ginsberg, 2017).

In operational settings, reductions in HRV have been observed during critical occurrences, prolonged work shifts, and jobs with elevated cognitive demands. Cybersecurity analysts exhibit notable reductions in heart rate variability during real-time event response, which correlates with increased self-reported stress levels. HRV can be persistently tracked by wearable devices, facilitating non-invasive, real-time evaluation; nevertheless, interpretation must consider lifestyle variables such as caffeine consumption and physical activity.

## Organizational data sources

Organizational data sources are important for cybersecurity because they provide the operational evidence needed to manage human performance, a core dependency for detection, response, and risk decision-making. Metrics such as alert volume and false-positive rates, ticket backlog, time-to-acknowledge, incident surge frequency, on-call paging intensity, after-hours work, and change-failure rates indicate when the security system is overloading its people, increasing error likelihood, slowing containment, and elevating exposure. When paired with staffing, turnover, and absenteeism data, these sources identify where fatigue, stress, and burnout are being generated by workflow design, tooling noise, or coverage gaps rather than individual weakness. This enables leaders to target risk-reducing interventions such as detection maintenance, automation of low-value work, rotation redesign, and recovery protections, and then verify whether those changes actually reduce workload pressure and strengthen operational resilience.

## Shift logs and overtime records

Work schedules, overtime records, and on-call duty logs are especially consequential in cybersecurity because defensive performance depends on sustained vigilance, rapid interpretation of ambiguous signals, and high-stakes decisions that degrade predictably under fatigue. Prolonged shifts, recurrent overtime, inconsistent hours, and clustered night pages increase sleep restriction and circadian disruption, which elevates the probability of mis-triage, delayed escalation, incomplete containment, and configuration mistakes during incident response and change windows. Evidence from safety-critical sectors shows that successive night shifts and heavy overtime are associated with higher burnout and increased error rates (Caruso, 2014). The same mechanisms apply when security teams must sustain alert monitoring, coordinate cross-functional responses, and maintain precision under time pressure. By routinely analyzing scheduling data, cybersecurity leaders can detect early overload signals such as increasing after-hours hours, repeated consecutive on-call days, prolonged incident resolution durations, and rising page-to-action ratios, then implement risk-reducing adjustments such as limiting consecutive night coverage, enforcing recovery time after SEV1 events, rebalancing on-call across functions, tuning alerting to reduce non-actionable pages, and adding surge staffing for peak threat periods; these changes can be validated by measurable improvements in paging frequency, overtime hours, time-to-acknowledge, and time-to-containment while sustaining analyst retention and decision quality.

## Incident response metrics

In cybersecurity and other high-pressure contexts, metrics such as **Mean Time to Detect (MTTD)**, **Mean Time to Contain (MTTC)**, and incident frequency function as performance indicators and indirect measurements of stress. Extended detection or containment durations, coupled with increased incident frequency, may lead to fatigue and emotional exhaustion among responders. Organizational trends suggest that teams managing prolonged, high-severity situations often exhibit simultaneous reductions in recovery indicators, such as HRV, and increases in reported stress levels. Monitoring these variables enables organizations to identify patterns of burnout risk and take action before a decline in performance and well-being occurs.

# Integration and practical implications

No solitary statistic adequately encapsulates the intricacies of work stress and burnout. A multi-modal assessment paradigm that incorporates psychometric, physiological, and organizational data offers the most dependable results:

- Psychometric instruments such as the MBI and PSS quantify subjective experiences
- Physiological measures, including HRV and EEG, provide objective, real-time indicators
- Organizational data sources disclose systemic factors contributing to stress

When evaluated collectively, these metrics enable organizations to differentiate between acute stress surges and persistent burnout threats. A combination of increased overtime hours, decreased HRV, and increased PSS scores strongly indicates the need for intervention. In contrast, steady physiological signs under heavy workloads may indicate good resilience techniques.

An effective evaluation of stress and burnout requires a multifaceted approach. Organizations can identify early warning indicators and formulate focused solutions by integrating psychometric self-reports, physiological monitoring, and organizational workload data. This comprehensive technique improves employee well-being while maintaining operational effectiveness in high-pressure settings. Organizational data sources do more than quantify workload; they reveal the organizational-level drivers of stress, fatigue, and burnout, such as staffing models, on-call design, alert governance, decision rights, and process friction, that ultimately determine cybersecurity performance and resilience.

# Organizational-level contributors to stress, fatigue, and burnout

Organizational structures, regulations, and workplace cultures significantly impact the well-being of cybersecurity workers. Unrealistic **service-level agreements** (**SLAs**) and persistent understaffing in SOCs lead to ongoing overload, while inflexible job titles restrict the utilization of skills and flexibility. The weariness of rotating or on-call employees is exacerbated by poor shift scheduling, which often includes inadequate recovery time (Lallie et al., 2020).

By inundating analysts with duplicate or unnecessary information, system design elements such as disjointed monitoring tools and inadequate SIEM integration exacerbate alert fatigue (Nobles, 2022). A lack of realistic threat simulations and incident response playbooks compromises readiness and increases the stress of crisis decision-making (Ahmed et al., 2021).

Inadequate leadership and culture also increase risk. A lack of supportive leadership creates a low psychosocial safety atmosphere, harsh punishment for errors, and poor communication channels, which lowers trust and resilience (Shoss et al., 2021). Furthermore, a lack of official methods for acknowledging efforts can demotivate employees, and rigid work schedules can lead to work-life conflict (Alshaikh, 2020; Khan et al., 2021). The collective ability to effectively address cybersecurity stress is undermined by dysfunctional team dynamics, which are typified by competition rather than collaboration (Lallie et al., 2020).

*Table 7.1* provides a list of some common organizational and individual-level factors associated with fatigue, stress, and burnout. Although this list is not exhaustive, these factors plays a critical role in highlighting the persistent human performance challenges in cybersecurity – in some cases, issues that managers often overlook or are ill-equipped to address.

| **Cause** | **Individual-Level Factors** | **Organizational-Level Factors** | **Source** |
|---|---|---|---|
| High Job Demands / Workload | Perfectionism; overcommitment; difficulty prioritizing; low stress resilience | Chronic understaffing in Security Operations Centers (SOCs); excessive ticket queues; unrealistic SLAs | Khan et al., Computers & Security (2021) |

| | | | |
|---|---|---|---|
| Lack of Job Control / Role Fit | Limited decision-making autonomy; misalignment between skills and assigned security tasks | Rigid job roles; lack of task variation; mismatch between analyst capabilities and assigned threat domains | Pahwa & Dissanayake, Journal of Cybersecurity (2022) |
| Shift Work / Irregular Hours | Disrupted circadian rhythms; chronic sleep deprivation from 24/7 SOC coverage | Rotating shifts; insufficient recovery time between shifts; unpredictable on-call requirements | Lallie et al., Forensic Science International: Digital Investigation (2020) |
| Poor Tool Usability / Cognitive Load | Mental fatigue from juggling multiple tools; frustration from complex alert triage | Fragmented monitoring platforms; high false-positive rates; poor SIEM integration | Nobles, Holistica Journal of Business and Public Administration (2022) |
| High-Stakes Decision-Making Under Pressure | Anxiety when responding to critical incidents; limited coping strategies for crisis events | Lack of rehearsed incident response playbooks; insufficient threat simulation exercises | Ahmed et al., IEEE Access (2021) |
| Leadership and Support Structures | Reluctance to seek assistance; low trust in management | Absence of supportive leadership; punitive culture around mistakes; poor communication channels | Shoss et al., Journal of Occupational Health Psychology (2021) |

| | | | |
|---|---|---|---|
| Work–Life Conflict | Inability to disconnect from alerts after work; poor personal time management | Expectation for off-hours availability; inadequate flexible work arrangements | Alshaikh, Computers & Security (2020) |
| Effort–Reward Imbalance / Recognition Gaps | Sensitivity to lack of recognition; reduced motivation | Minimal acknowledgment of contributions; inequitable promotion or bonus practices | Khan et al., Computers & Security (2021) |
| Poor Psychosocial Safety Climate | Mistrust in leadership commitment to well-being | Lack of mental health programs tailored to cybersecurity; absence of stress management policies | Shoss et al., Journal of Occupational Health Psychology (2021) |
| Interpersonal Conflict / Team Dynamics | Difficulty resolving disagreements with peers; low tolerance for criticism | Dysfunctional SOC team culture; competitive rather than collaborative environments | Lallie et al., Forensic Science International: Digital Investigation (2020) |

*Table 7.1: Organizational- and individual-level factors of stress, fatigue, and burnout*

Stress, burnout, and security fatigue continue to pose significant dangers to the efficacy of cybersecurity operations. Despite their well-documented effects, these challenges are often neglected, resulting in minimal engagement of human factors practitioners in developing effective mitigation methods. While security weariness is not a novel phenomenon, the escalating intricacy of cybersecurity has generated several manifestations of fatigue, complicating the resolution of the issue. Stress and burnout are particularly detrimental at the executive level, resulting in shorter tenures for senior security leaders.

Numerous businesses resort to technology-driven solutions to address threats, thereby increasing system complexity and introducing new vulnerabilities, a situation commonly referred to as *complexity debt*. This overlooks the human aspect, wherein performance deterioration directly undermines cyber protection. Human factors professionals can significantly contribute by finding friction points that burden operators, devising treatments to enhance resilience, and addressing the cognitive, physiological, and physical demands imposed on cybersecurity staff. Considering that adversaries frequently target human vulnerabilities, it is imperative to prioritize human performance. Inadequate research and the absence of human factors tactics may result in a significant deficiency in an organization's cybersecurity posture.

## Individual-level factors of stress, fatigue, and burnout

Individual characteristics, coping mechanisms, and role-specific difficulties are frequently associated with stress and burnout in cybersecurity workers. Reduced stress resilience results from the intersection of high occupational expectations with traits such as perfectionism, overcommitment, and difficulty setting priorities (Khan et al., 2021). Stress can be exacerbated when analysts are given duties that are not in line with their skills, which can lead to dissatisfaction and disengagement due to limited job control or poor role alignment.

Chronic sleep deprivation and cognitive fatigue are caused by disruptions to the circadian rhythm resulting from irregular shift work and round-the-clock operational coverage (Lallie et al., 2020). Because analysts must contend with fragmented platforms and high false-positive rates, poor tool usability leads to a prolonged cognitive burden (Nobles, 2022). Furthermore, analysts who lack efficient coping strategies or previous simulation practice may experience increased anxiety due to the strain of making important decisions (Ahmed et al., 2021).

Psychosocial and interpersonal factors are also important. While unresolved team conflicts can undermine morale and cooperation, a lack of trust in leadership may deter people from seeking help (Lallie et al., 2020 Shoss et al., 2021). Emotional weariness results from ongoing work-life conflict caused by an inability to manage personal time or unplug from alerts. Lastly, perceived disparities in work and reward, including little acknowledgment or unfair possibilities for promotion, lower motivation and increase the likelihood of burnout (Khan et al., 2021).

Coping mechanisms and resilience are crucial for mitigating the likelihood of burnout and minimizing the effects of work-related stress. People are better equipped to handle high-pressure situations if they have or learn adaptive coping methods, such as problem-focused solutions, mindfulness, and reframing approaches. According to research, resilience is not just an innate quality. It can also be developed through focused instruction and organizational support initiatives that enhance psychological fortitude and facilitate recovery from adversity. Resilience training helps workers maintain their performance under ongoing stress, thereby reducing their vulnerability to fatigue and burnout in occupations such as cybersecurity, where the demands of relentless attention to detail and high-stakes decision-making are prevalent.

Personality factors and the integration of work and life further influence vulnerability to burnout. While conscientiousness and openness to new experiences tend to act as a buffer against unfavorable outcomes, traits such as perfectionism, high neuroticism, and low emotional stability are substantially linked to an increased risk of fatigue and disengagement (Ajayi & Udeh, 2024). At the same time, maintaining psychological well-being requires efficient management of work-life boundaries. Role conflict is less likely to occur, and balance is more likely to be maintained by workers who successfully integrate their personal and professional duties or set clear limits. On the other hand, fuzzy boundaries, which are typical in flexible and remote work environments, can worsen stress and reduce chances for recovery. Therefore, it is crucial to implement organizational policies that promote boundary management and facilitate personal recovery to prevent the gradual decline from stress to burnout (Reeves et al., 2024).

## Prevention and intervention strategies

Without a doubt, stress, fatigue, and burnout can counter the best cybersecurity defenses; organizations should work to reduce and prevent them. Intervention and prevention of stress and fatigue are critical for mitigating burnout. Burnout is an occupational phenomenon that requires extensive recovery time (2-4 months) of being unplugged from work-related activities to recover fully. Failing to address burnout can lead to serious health problems. Therefore, the best way to avoid it is to practice stress prevention and intervention, as well as strategies for fatigue and other factors that lead to burnout.

*Table 7.2* lists strategic initiatives to combat burnout; although this list is not exhaustive, it provides managers, practitioners, and scholars with some insights into where to begin addressing burnout:

| Strategic Initiative | Description | References |
|---|---|---|
| Workplace Flexibility | Promoting flexible work arrangements, including remote work, adjustable hours, and boundaries, supports work-life balance and reduces stress. | Ajayi&Udeh(2024); Huarng (2001); Nepal et al. (2024); Reeves et al. (2024) |

| | | |
|---|---|---|
| Leadership and Recognition | Encouraging transformational leadership, personalized recognition initiatives, and appreciation programs that boost morale, satisfaction, and engagement. | Ajayi&Udeh(2024); Nepal et al. (2024); Huarng (2001) |
| Supportive Culture | Fostering an inclusive and collaborative environment with mentorship, team-building activities, and open communication to address emotional exhaustion and build mutual support among employees. | Reevesetal.(2021); Ajayi & Udeh (2024); Nepal et al. (2024); Huarng (2001) |
| Cognitive Load Management | Reducing cognitive demands by aligning complex tasks with low-stress periods, simplifying workflows, and addressing decision fatigue through intuitive design and optimized processes. | Reeves et al. (2021); Pham et al. (2019); Nepal et al. (2024) |
| Training and Development | Implementing tailored training programs, onboarding resilience strategies, and job-specific interventions to build skills and prepare employees for cybersecurity's psychological demands. | Huarng (2001); Reeves et al. (2021); Nepal et al. (2024) |
| Monitoring and Assessment | Regularly evaluate well-being using structured tools, such as the CyFa framework, to identify sources of fatigue and implement targeted interventions that address systemic and individual stressors. | Pittasetal.(2024); Ajayi & Udeh (2024); Nepal et al. (2024) |
| Workload Management | Utilizing dynamic prioritization frameworks, proactive workload assessments, and effective project management practices to balance tasks and minimize stress. | Nepal et al. (2024); Huarng (2001) |
| Mental Health Resources | Providing access to counseling, mindfulness programs, wellness technologies, and resilience training to address stress and promote well-being. | Ajayi&Udeh(2024); Nepal et al. (2024); Reeves et al. (2024) |

| | | |
|---|---|---|
| Policy and Systemic Changes | Developing policies that address systemic stressors, such as excessive workloads and role ambiguity, while safeguarding employee privacy and embedding burnout prevention in organizational practices. | Pittas et al. (2024); Reeves et al. (2024); Nepal et al. (2024) |
| Diversity and Inclusion | Promoting gender diversity, equitable treatment, and measures to eliminate cultural barriers, creating a supportive environment for underrepresented groups. | Reeves et al. (2024); Pittas et al. (2024) |
| Technology Integration | Leveraging apps and tools to monitor stress and wellness, designing human-centered systems to enhance engagement, and simplifying security requirements to align with employee capabilities. | Ajayi&Udeh(2024); Pham et al. (2019); Reeves et al. (2021) |
| Sleep Quality Improvements | Addressing poor sleep through manageable shift schedules, breaks, and work-life integration strategies to mitigate emotional exhaustion and improve recovery. | Reeves et al. (2024) |

*Table 7.2: Mitigation strategies to combat burnout (Source: Nobles, 2025)*

A coordinated set of organizational interventions (such as those listed in *Table 7.2*) can reduce burnout risk in cybersecurity by strengthening resilience, protecting workforce well-being, and increasing operational capacity under complex and persistent threat conditions; representative strategies include lowering alert noise through continuous detection tuning, redesigning on-call and staffing models to ensure predictable coverage and protected recovery time, and clarifying decision rights and escalation paths so responders can act quickly without unnecessary procedural friction.

- **Workplace flexibility**: Workplace flexibility represents a strategic intervention to mitigate occupational stress by promoting remote work, adjustable schedules, and clear work-life boundaries. Flexible arrangements empower employees to balance professional and personal responsibilities, which reduces strain and enhances productivity. Studies demonstrate that flexible work environments not only minimize burnout risks but also improve long-term retention by fostering autonomy and satisfaction (Ajayi & Udeh, 2024 Nepal et al., 2024 Reeves et al., 2024). Particularly in high-demand fields such as cybersecurity, flexibility can alleviate the cognitive and emotional toll of prolonged, high-stakes engagements.

- **Leadership and recognition**: Transformational leadership and recognition initiatives are vital in promoting psychological well-being and organizational resilience. Leaders who demonstrate empathy, provide constructive feedback, and recognize individual contributions foster higher morale and employee engagement. Recognition programs, whether personalized acknowledgments or structured appreciation systems, bolster intrinsic motivation and cultivate a sense of belonging. The literature underscores that strong leadership and authentic recognition act as buffers against stress-induced disengagement (Ajayi & Udeh, 2024 Nepal et al., 2024).
- **Supportive culture**: A supportive workplace culture is foundational to sustaining employee well-being. Inclusive and collaborative environments foster open communication, mentorship, and mutual support, which mitigate emotional exhaustion. Team-building and cross-functional collaboration encourage collective resilience and reduce feelings of isolation often associated with demanding work environments. Research confirms that such cultures strengthen organizational cohesion and provide protective factors against stress-related attrition (Reeves et al., 2021 Ajayi & Udeh, 2024 Nepal et al., 2024).
- **Cognitive load management**: Cognitive load management addresses the risks of decision fatigue and performance decline. Aligning demanding tasks with periods of lower stress, simplifying workflows, and applying intuitive system designs can significantly reduce employee strain. Optimized processes not only streamline task execution but also enhance mental clarity, decreasing errors in high-pressure contexts such as cybersecurity operations. By prioritizing cognitive ergonomics, organizations safeguard against employee exhaustion and errors (Reeves et al., 2021 Pham et al., 2019 Nepal et al., 2024).
- **Training and development**: Ongoing training and professional development act as preventive strategies against stress and burnout by equipping employees with both technical and psychological resilience skills. Tailored programs, onboarding strategies, and job-specific interventions provide employees with confidence and preparedness to face dynamic work environments. For example, organizations can create an employee resource group to address burnout in cybersecurity and help workers understand fatigue science and how to leverage mitigative strategies to combat burnout. Another example is conducting an annual assessment to measure stress, fatigue, and burnout in cybersecurity and identify progress in reducing organizational stress. Evidence highlights that investment in development contributes to long-term adaptability and reduces stress associated with skill mismatches or insufficient preparation (Reeves et al., 2021 Nepal et al., 2024).

- **Monitoring and assessment**: Systematic monitoring of employee well-being is crucial to proactively identifying and addressing stressors. Frameworks such as **CyFa** offer structured evaluation of cognitive and emotional fatigue, enabling early intervention before stress escalates to burnout. Regular assessments allow organizations to target systemic stressors, refine interventions, and personalize strategies for individuals. Such approaches are consistent with evidence-based recommendations for stress management in high-demand professions (Ajayi & Udeh, 2024 Nepal et al., 2024).
- **Workload management**: Balancing workloads through dynamic prioritization and project management frameworks prevents chronic stress accumulation. Overburdened employees are more susceptible to fatigue and diminished performance, particularly when deadlines are misaligned with available resources. Workload assessments provide insights into task allocation and ensure equitable distribution of responsibilities, which fosters productivity while reducing occupational strain (Nepal et al., 2024).
- **Mental health resources**: Providing accessible mental health resources remains a critical initiative for organizational well-being. Counseling services, mindfulness programs, wellness technologies, and resilience training offer direct mechanisms for stress reduction. Research indicates that employees who have access to such resources report lower rates of burnout and higher levels of satisfaction and retention (Ajayi & Udeh, 2024 Nepal et al., 2024 Reeves et al., 2024). Importantly, organizations that normalize mental health support reduce stigma and create safer environments for employee engagement.
- **Policy and systemic changes**: Addressing stress requires systemic interventions beyond individual coping strategies. Policies that limit excessive workloads, clarify role expectations, and safeguard employee privacy are essential for creating sustainable working conditions. Embedding burnout prevention into organizational policies ensures long-term cultural change and reinforces a proactive stance toward well-being (Nepal et al., 2024 Reeves et al., 2024).
- **Diversity and inclusion**: Diversity and inclusion initiatives enhance employee well-being by creating equitable and supportive environments. Addressing systemic inequities and promoting gender diversity reduces barriers that exacerbate stress for underrepresented groups. Inclusive practices contribute to fairness, psychological safety, and stronger collective resilience (Reeves et al., 2024).
- **Technology integration**: Human-centered technology integration is an effective strategy for aligning systems with employee capabilities. Applications that monitor wellness, tools designed to minimize friction, and streamlined security practices reduce stress caused by technical complexity. When aligned with cognitive and

ergonomic principles, technology serves as a facilitator rather than a burden, enhancing both engagement and performance (Ajayi & Udeh, 2024 Pham et al., 2019 Reeves et al., 2021).

- **Sleep quality improvements**: Sleep quality remains a critical determinant of employee resilience and recovery. Poor sleep is strongly linked to emotional exhaustion, diminished focus, and an increased risk of burnout. Interventions such as manageable shift schedules, structured breaks, and strategies for integrating work and personal life are essential to improving recovery cycles. Research emphasizes that addressing sleep-related challenges directly enhances cognitive performance and psychological health (Reeves et al., 2024).

## Interventions in system design

Human-centered interface design can reduce stress and exhaustion in high-demand operations by making the next correct action easier to identify, faster to execute, and harder to perform incorrectly (Norman & Draper, 1986 Endsley, 2020). In practice, this means simplifying screens to what operators need at that moment, using consistent labels and severity definitions, reducing unnecessary clicks, and adding safeguards such as confirmations for high-impact actions and simple rollback paths for reversible actions (Norman & Draper, 1986). Usability testing should be embedded throughout development so the system reflects real workflows and supports situation awareness under time pressure rather than forcing operators to mentally assemble context across multiple tools (Endsley, 2020).

A practical example is improving the security operations center phishing triage. If analysts currently move across multiple tabs to decide whether to escalate, redesign the workflow into a single triage view that presents essential context in one place: sender reputation, user impact, similar prior cases, indicators of compromise, and a recommended next step with a brief rationale. Provide one-click actions for common responses such as quarantining the message, blocking the sender, and opening a ticket, adding a short confirmation step for irreversible actions and include a time-limited undo option for reversible containment actions (Norman & Draper, 1986). Then run a short usability test with five to eight analysts using realistic scenarios, measure time to decision, false escalations, and perceived workload, and iterate until the workflow is consistently faster and less error-prone (Endsley, 2020).

Automation should reduce repetitive work while preserving human accountability for the final decision. For example, the system can automatically de-duplicate alerts and enrich them with domain age, authentication results, and threat intelligence matches, while requiring the analyst to confirm escalation and record the reasoning in a few structured fields to support clean shift handoffs. This approach is especially important because fatigue can degrade vigilance and judgment in cybersecurity work (Nobles, 2022). The result is a workflow that is easier to operate under time pressure, easier to recover from when errors occur, and more resilient during sustained operational demand.

# Best practices and lessons learned

To successfully lessen alert fatigue and analyst burnout, human factors interventions must encompass both system design and organizational policy, as demonstrated by the experiences of the case studies. Here are a few best practices you can adopt:

- Reducing alert fatigue and analyst burnout requires a holistic approach that addresses both system design and organizational policy. The case studies demonstrate that technical fixes alone are insufficient; sustainable improvement emerges when human factors principles guide how tools, workflows, and expectations are structured. When organizations treat analyst well-being as a core performance variable rather than an afterthought, they create environments where accuracy, vigilance, and resilience can be maintained over time.
- One best practice is the continuous monitoring of analyst workloads. By tracking operational tempo, high-risk missions, and the effects of organizational or technical changes, leaders can identify when cognitive strain is accumulating. This enables timely interventions such as rest cycles, workload redistribution, or resilience training, all of which help preserve operator judgment and mission effectiveness. Similarly, circadian-friendly scheduling plays a critical role in long-duration monitoring environments. Aligning shifts with natural biological rhythms reduces fatigue, supports sustained attention, and improves detection accuracy.
- Another important lesson is the value of assessing human performance metrics. Regularly collecting physiological, cognitive, and subjective workload data allows organizations to detect early signs of exhaustion and adjust processes before errors occur. This proactive approach is strengthened when multidisciplinary expertise is integrated into decision-making. Collaboration among leaders, human factors specialists, and cybersecurity engineers ensures that interventions address both technical demands and human limitations.
- Ultimately, prioritizing analyst well-being is essential. When organizations view human health and system efficiency as mutually reinforcing goals, they create security operations centers capable of long-term, high-quality performance. This mindset not only reduces burnout but also enhances the overall resilience and reliability of the cybersecurity mission.

These case studies collectively demonstrate that improving SOC performance necessitates a comprehensive, human-centered strategy that combines supporting organizational structures with ergonomic interfaces. This alignment strengthens defenses against changing threats by enhancing not only technical performance metrics but also the resilience and well-being of cybersecurity staff.

# Summary

In this chapter, we discussed that stress, fatigue, and burnout in cybersecurity are not merely individual well-being concerns; they are operational risk factors that directly weaken decision quality, elevate error likelihood, accelerate attrition, and reduce overall defensive effectiveness. The chapter provided insights into interpreting human performance degradation as a latent hazard within sociotechnical systems, and into viewing durable mitigation as an organizational resilience imperative rather than a reactive wellness initiative.

The chapter's learning outcomes centered on applying a human-centered, evidence-driven approach to cybersecurity management. Key topics included identifying primary drivers of burnout (technical demand, cognitive load, physiological strain, and culture), implementing practical mitigations (proactive monitoring, workflow and organizational restructuring, resilience and recovery practices, and alert-fatigue reduction through automation and improved design), and integrating human factors engineering as a strategic enabler that reframes "human error" as an opportunity to improve through intentionally designing for people.

The next chapter examines cyberpsychology in cybersecurity by analyzing how cognition, emotion, and behavior in digital contexts shape security outcomes and how these insights complement human factors to strengthen the psychological viability of cybersecurity by understanding how digitalization influences behavior.

# References


- Ajayi, F. A., & Udeh, C. A. (2024). Review of crew resilience and mental health practices in the marine industry: Pathways to improvement. *Magna Scientia Advanced Biology and Pharmacy*, *11*(2), 033-049.
- Albayrak, Z. S., Vaz, A., Bordes, J., Ünlü, S., Sep, M. S., Vinkers, C. H., ... & Yapici-Eser, H. (2024). Translational models of stress and resilience: An applied neuroscience methodology review. *Neuroscience Applied*, *3*, 104064.
- Alshaikh, M. (2020). Developing cybersecurity culture to influence employee behavior: A practice perspective. *Computers & Security, 98*, Article 102003. `https://doi.org/10.1016/j.cose.2020.102003`

- Arora, S., & Hastings, J. D. (2024). A survey-based quantitative analysis of stress factors and their impacts among cybersecurity professionals. *arXiv Preprint.* https://arxiv.org/abs/2409.12047
- Bussetti, S., & Scanni, F. M. (2025). Evaluating cybersecurity strategies in the energy sector. Evidence from Italy. *Rivista di Digital Politics,* (1), 165-194.
- Caruso, C. C. (2014). Negative impacts of shiftwork and long work hours. *Rehabilitation Nursing, 39*(1), 16–25. https://doi.org/10.1002/rnj.107
- Casper, A., & Sonnentag, S. (2020). Feeling exhausted or vigorous in anticipation of high workload? The role of worry and planning during the evening. *Journal of Occupational and Organizational Psychology, 93*(1), 215-242.
- Choo, K.-K. R. (2011). The cyber threat landscape: Challenges and future research directions. *Computers & Security, 30*(8), 719–731. https://doi.org/10.1016/j.cose.2011.08.004
- Cohen, S., Kamarck, T., & Mermelstein, R. (1983). A global measure of perceived stress. *Journal of Health and Social Behavior, 24*(4), 385–396. https://doi.org/10.2307/2136404
- Cybersecurity and Infrastructure Security Agency (CISA). (2024, January 17). CISA releases 2023 Year in Review showcasing efforts to protect critical infrastructure. *CISA.gov.* https://www.cisa.gov/news-events/news/cisa-releases-2023-year-review-showcasing-efforts-protect-critical-infrastructure
- Dykstra, J., & Paul, C. (2018). Cyber Operations Stress Survey (COSS): Studying fatigue, frustration, and cognitive workload in cybersecurity operations. Proceedings of the 11th USENIX Workshop on Cyber Security Experimentation and Test (CSET). USENIX Association.
- Endsley, M. R. (2020). The divergence of objective and subjective situation awareness: A meta-analysis. *Journal of cognitive engineering and decision making, 14*(1), 34-53.
- Gupta, V., Rangarajan, A., & Nobles, C. (2024). Burnout in the cybersecurity profession: A scoping review. In *Proceedings of the 2024 Midwest Association for Information Systems Conference.* https://aisel.aisnet.org/mwais2024/20/
- Huarng, A. S. (2001). Burnout Syndrome among Information System Professionals. *Inf. Syst. Manag., 18*(2), 1-6.
- Karasek Jr, R. A. (1979). Job demands, job decision latitude, and mental strain: Implications for job redesign. *Administrative Science Quarterly,* 285-308.

- Karasek, R. (1990). Stress, productivity, and the reconstruction of working life. *Health Work.*
- Kearney, P., Abdelsamea, M., Schmoor, X., Shah, F., & Vickers, I. (2023). *Combating alert fatigue in the Security Operations Centre.* SSRN. `https://doi.org/10.2139/ssrn.4633965`
- Khadka, K., Ullah, A. B., & Martinez Marroquin, E. (2026). Unmasking persuasion in phishing: a content analysis of principles of persuasion in emails and subject lines. *Information & Computer Security, 34*(1), 104-121.
- Khan, N., J. Houghton, R., & Sharples, S. (2022). Understanding factors that influence unintentional insider threat: A framework to counteract unintentional risks. *Cognition, Technology & Work, 24*(3), 393-421.
- Lallie, H. S., Debattista, K., & Bal, J. (2020). A review of attack graph and attack tree visual syntax in cybersecurity. *Computer Science Review, 35*, 100219.
- Leso, V., Fontana, L., Caturano, A., Vetrani, I., Fedele, M., & Iavicoli, I. (2021). Impact of Shift Work and Long Working Hours on Worker Cognitive Functions: Current Evidence and Future Research Needs. *International journal of environmental research and public health, 18*(12), 6540. `https://doi.org/10.3390/ijerph18126540`
- Mahboubi, A., Luong, K., Aboutorab, H., Bui, H. T., Jarrad, G., Bahutair, M., ... & Gately, H. (2024). Evolving techniques in cyber threat hunting: A systematic review. *Journal of Network and Computer Applications, 232*, 104004.
- Maslach, C., & Jackson, S. E. (1981). The measurement of experienced burnout. *Journal of Occupational Behavior, 2*(2), 99–113. `https://doi.org/10.1002/job.4030020205`
- Maslach, C., & Leiter, M. P. (2016a). Understanding the burnout experience: Recent research and its implications for psychiatry. *World Psychiatry, 15*(2), 103–111. `https://doi.org/10.1002/wps.20311`
- Maslach, C., & Leiter, M. P. (2016b). Burnout. In *Stress: Concepts, cognition, emotion, and behavior* (pp. 351-357). Academic Press.
- National Academies of Sciences, Engineering, and Medicine (NASEM). (2025). *Impact of Burnout on the STEMM Workforce: Proceedings of a Workshop.*
- Nepal, S., et al. (2024). Burnout in Cybersecurity Incident Responders: Exploring the Factors that Light the Fire [Article 27]. *Proceedings of the ACM on Human–Computer Interaction, 8*(CSCW1), Article 27. `https://doi.org/10.1145/3637304`

- Nobles, C. (2022). Stress, burnout, and security fatigue in cybersecurity: A human factors problem. *Holistica Journal of Business and Public Administration, 13*(1), 49–72. https://doi.org/10.2478/hjbpa-2022-0003
- Nobles, C. (2025, March). Exploring Mitigative Strategies to Prevent Burnout in Cybersecurity. In *Proceedings of the 19th International Conference on Cyber Warfare and Security*.
- Norman, D.A., & Draper, S.W. (Eds.). (1986). *User Centered System Design: New Perspectives on Human-computer Interaction* (1st ed.). CRC Press.
- Nwobodo, E. P., Strukcinskiene, B., Razbadauskas, A., Grigoliene, R., & Agostinis-Sobrinho, C. (2023, October). Stress management in healthcare organizations: the Nigerian context. In *Healthcare* (Vol. 11, No. 21, p. 2815). MDPI.
- Patterson, C. M., Nurse, J. R., & Franqueira, V. N. (2023). Learning from cyber security incidents: A systematic review and future research agenda. *Computers & Security, 132*, 103309.
- Pham, H., Brennan, L., Parker, L., Phan-Le, N. T., Ulhaq, I., Nkhoma, M., Nguyen, M. N., & colleagues. (2019). Enhancing cyber security behavior: An internal social marketing approach. *Information and Computer Security, 28*(2), 133–159. https://doi.org/10.1108/ICS-01-2019-0023
- Pittas, D., Delfabbro, P., & Reeves, A. (2024). How to De-CyFa the actor-observer bias in cybersecurity fatigue: Building the CyFa measure of attribution styles and mitigation strategies. *Computers & Security*, 104179.
- Rajivan, P., & Cooke, N. J. (2018). Information-pooling bias in collaborative security incident correlation analysis. *Human Factors, 60*(5), 626-639.
- Rangarajan, A., Nobles, C., Dykstra, J., Cunningham, M., Robinson, N., Hollis, T., & Gulotta, C. (2025, June). A roadmap to address burnout in the cybersecurity profession: Outcomes from a multifaceted workshop. In *International Conference on Human-Computer Interaction* (pp. 125–140). Cham, Switzerland: Springer Nature.
- Reeves, A., Delfabbro, P., & Calic, D. (2021). Encouraging employee engagement with cybersecurity: How to tackle cyber fatigue. *SAGE open, 11*(1), 21582440211000049.
- Reeves, A., Painson, M., & Buavicius, M. (2024). The sleepless sentinel: Factors that predict burnout and sleep quality in cybersecurity professionals. *Information & Computer Security, 32*(4), 477–491. https://doi.org/10.1108/ICS-11-2023-0222
- Santos, B., Costa, R. L. C., & Santos, L. (2024, August). Cybersecurity in Industry 5.0: open challenges and future directions. In *2024, the 21st Annual International Conference on Privacy, Security and Trust (PST)* (pp. 1-6). IEEE.

- Shaffer, F., & Ginsberg, J. P. (2017). An overview of heart rate variability metrics and norms. *Frontiers in Public Health, 5*, Article 258. `https://doi.org/10.3389/fpubh.2017.00258`
- Shoss, M. K., Horan, K. A., DiStaso, M., LeNoble, C. A., & Naranjo, A. (2021). The conflicting impact of COVID-19's health and economic crises on helping. *Group & Organization Management, 46*(1), 3-37.
- Siegrist, J. (1996). Adverse health effects of high-effort/low-reward conditions. *Journal of Occupational Health Psychology, 1*(1), 27.
- Siegrist, J. (2002). Effort-reward imbalance at work and health. In *Historical and current perspectives on stress and health* (pp. 261–291). Emerald Group Publishing Limited.
- Singh, T., Johnson, A. C., D'Arcy, J., & Harms, P. D. (2023). Stress in the cybersecurity profession: A systematic review of related literature and opportunities for future research. *Organizational Cybersecurity Journal: Practice, Process and People, 3*(2), 100–126. `https://doi.org/10.1108/OCJ-06-2022-0012`
- Tariq, R. A., Vashisht, R., Sinha, A., & Scherbak, Y. (2025). Medication Dispensing Errors and Prevention. StatPearls. Treasure Island (FL): StatPearls Publishing Copyright© 2025.
- Van der Kleij, R., Kleinhuis, G., & Young, H. (2017). *Computer security incident response team effectiveness: A needs assessment. Frontiers in Psychology, 8*, 2179.

# 8

# Cyberpsychology in Cybersecurity

Without a doubt, cyberpsychology is an emerging discipline. The study of the relationship between human behavior, cognition, and digital settings is known as **cyberpsychology**. Cyberpsychology, as defined by Ancis (2020), combines technological studies and psychological concepts to examine how digital systems impact human perception, identity, and decision-making. This integration encompasses digital trust, social influence, memory, and attention. Cyberpsychology is important in cybersecurity because it explains how human cognition, emotion, motivation, and social influence shape behavior in digital environments, including how attackers successfully exploit people through manipulation and deception. It shows how and why security controls fail in practice when they create excessive friction, overload attention, misalign with workflows, or trigger predictable decision biases, thereby producing workarounds and preventable errors. Cyberpsychology, therefore, enables evidence-based interventions that redesign systems, communications, and organizational culture so that secure behavior becomes more intuitive, sustainable, and resilient under real-world operational pressure. This suggests that cybersecurity vulnerabilities cannot be assessed solely by technical protection; human proclivities, biases, and behavioral patterns must also be considered.

This chapter aims to establish cyberpsychology as a fundamental component of cybersecurity resilience. Previous research indicates that psychological concepts apply to societal, corporate, and individual contexts (Endsley, 2021 Montañez et al., 2020 Washo & Moon, 2021). The chapter provides practical guidance on creating interventions that minimize human errors, mitigate insider risks, and prevent widespread manipulation by integrating cognitive, emotional, and social elements.

In this chapter, we will discuss the following key topics:

- Relevance of cyberpsychology in cybersecurity
- Foundations of cyberpsychology
- Cognitive and behavioral mechanisms of cyber risk
- Human-centered design, behavior, psychological impacts

# Relevance of cyberpsychology to cybersecurity

To preserve cybersecurity, human behavior, thought, and psychology are just as crucial as technological solutions. According to Montañez et al. (2020), adversaries successfully conduct phishing and social engineering attacks by exploiting human heuristics such as urgency, authority, and familiarity. Hijji et al. (2021) found that fear and uncertainty heightened the effectiveness of malevolent advertisements during the COVID-19 pandemic, indicating that psychological exploitation increases with societal pressure. These results demonstrate that human cognition has security flaws in addition to those in technology and software.

Cybersecurity techniques can anticipate manipulation attempts and enhance resilience against adversary exploitation by understanding the psychological factors that influence user behavior. This kind of understanding requires a disciplined, evidence-driven approach that treats security behavior as an outcome of cognition, emotion, motivation, social influence, and environmental design within a sociotechnical system. In practice, this is accomplished through a sequence of activities that (1) specify the behavior, (2) measure what drives it, (3) identify failure pathways, and (4) redesign the decision environment to reduce exploitability. Consequently, cyberpsychology provides a crucial perspective for developing security measures that safeguard against both technological invasions and mental manipulation. A clear understanding of how people think during security-relevant tasks is essential, which brings us to the core relationship between cognitive processes and defense performance.

## Cognitive processes and defense performance

In cybersecurity operations, cognitive elements, including situational awareness, memory, and attention, affect defensive performance. Situational awareness, as defined by Endsley (2021), refers to the ability to recognize important cues, understand their meaning, and predict potential outcomes. Cognitive load and attentional tunneling can compromise situational awareness in high-stakes settings, such as security operations centers, making it more challenging to identify threats and respond promptly. For example, an analyst overwhelmed by simultaneous alerts may fixate on a single log anomaly and overlook a correlated privilege escalation event elsewhere in the environment. This breakdown cascades across levels: the task suffers because critical cues are missed, the system becomes slower and less accurate in detecting intrusions, and the organization faces increased risk exposure as adversaries gain time and space to advance their attack. This evidence suggests that human cognitive limitations constrain even the most skilled analysts.

The requirement to design systems that adhere to cognitive principles is underscored by the fact that defensive performance can be compromised by overload from excessive alarms or poorly designed interfaces. Imagine a security operations center where an analyst monitors multiple dashboards that generate dozens of alerts per minute during a suspected intrusion. As the volume of low-value notifications increases, the analyst becomes cognitively overloaded and may overlook a subtle indicator of lateral movement hidden among the noise. This affects the task by fragmenting attention and reducing triage accuracy, the system by slowing detection and increasing false negatives, and the organization by giving adversaries more time to escalate privileges, exfiltrate data, or disrupt operations. Incorporating psychological concepts into the design of security systems improves operator precision and efficiency when time is critical.

## Multi-level scope of cyberpsychology in cybersecurity

In cybersecurity, cyberpsychology is applicable at the individual, corporate, and societal levels. The adoption of secure practices is influenced by individual-level characteristics, such as self-efficacy, weariness, and risk perception (Alsharida et al., 2023). Collective resilience at the organizational level is influenced by factors such as communication, security culture, and the leadership environment (Nifakos et al., 2021). Disinformation and rumor cascades are psychological attack vectors that erode stability and trust at the societal level (Washo & Moon, 2021). At the individual level, cyberpsychology helps organizations strengthen secure behavior by addressing self-efficacy, fatigue, and risk perception. Examples include role-based phishing simulations, fatigue-aware warning design, and MFA prompts built to reduce habituation. At the corporate level, cyberpsychology improves security culture and team resilience through leadership communication, psychological safety, and human-centered workflow design. Examples include non-punitive near-miss reporting, structured incident-response communication, and SOC practices that reduce alert fatigue and burnout. At the societal level, cyberpsychology supports defenses against disinformation and rumor cascades that undermine trust and stability. Examples include prebunking campaigns, crisis communication frameworks, and media literacy programs that reduce susceptibility to manipulation.

This tiered structure illustrates how cyberpsychology encompasses not only user behavior but also larger organizational and cultural contexts. Therefore, defensive strategies must be adjusted to account for psychological aspects at all three levels. A comprehensive approach that unites corporate, social, and human resilience against cyber threats is made possible by acknowledging this scope.

## Research gaps and the need for integration

Even with improvements in understanding cyberpsychology and its relevance to cybersecurity, a substantial gap persists in integrating cyberpsychology into cybersecurity planning. Behavioral science is not widely incorporated into system design and governance, and many methods remain technology-centric (Khadka et al., 2025). Most cybersecurity training programs focus more on awareness campaigns than on evidence-based instructional designs aligned with cognitive-behavioral principles (Prümmer et al., 2024). These discrepancies reveal that the approaches organizations typically use and those found to be effective in research, such as scenario-based learning and workload-aware design, are not aligned. This underuse of psychological insights makes systems more susceptible to human-centered attacks and reduces their long-term resilience. Cyberpsychology must be integrated into every stage of the security lifecycle, from design to training and policy, to close this gap between research and practice.

# Foundations of cyberpsychology

Modern cyberpsychology is grounded in the historical evolution of psychology in relation to technological interactions. With technological innovation, psychological research grew to encompass online identity, digital trust, and social behavior in networked contexts (Ancis, 2020). These advancements demonstrate that cyberpsychology developed as an extension of applied psychology in response to technological change rather than emerging independently. Psychological concepts that were previously researched in physical task contexts (like aviation or industrial operations) became as relevant in cyberspace as systems grew more intricate and interconnected. Cyberpsychology is thus a logical extension of human factors research into the digital age, given an awareness of the historical trajectory of psychology and technology interaction. Building on this foundation, the next section examines the key psychological principles most relevant to cybersecurity, with emphasis on how cognition, emotion, motivation, and social influence shape security behavior and vulnerability.

## Key psychological principles relevant to cybersecurity

Fundamental psychological concepts such as **motivation**, **perception**, **cognition**, and **decision-making** directly affect cybersecurity vulnerabilities and behaviors. Perception and cognition influence how people pay attention to, decipher, and react to security cues. According to studies on attention, security operators often experience attentional narrowing when working in high-alert situations, which makes it more challenging to spot subtle irregularities (Endsley, 2021). For example, during an active ransomware incident, a SOC analyst may focus intensely on containment alerts from one critical server cluster and overlook a low-volume but anomalous outbound connection from a secondary system; that missed signal can represent lateral movement or data staging that enables the adversary to persist despite initial containment.

Studies reveal that users often underestimate cyber risk and prioritize convenience when choosing a password or authentication method, highlighting the importance of heuristics and biases in decision-making (Vance et al., 2018).

The success or failure of training interventions can also be explained by behavioral science and motivation. Protection Motivation Theory, for example, links self-efficacy, perceived severity, and efficacy to adherence to security practices (Boss et al., 2015). Training succeeds when it changes motivation, not only awareness. Protection Motivation Theory explains this clearly: employees are more likely to follow security practices when they view threats as serious and relevant, believe the recommended action works, and feel confident they can perform it correctly (Boss et al., 2015). For example, phishing training that combines realistic risk examples, a simple reporting protocol, and short practice simulations with feedback typically outperforms one-time awareness modules because it strengthens perceived severity, response efficacy, and self-efficacy at the same time. These guidelines illustrate how fundamental psychological processes impact cybersecurity. Low motivation, poor risk assessment, and attentional errors are not isolated user shortcomings but rather recurring patterns in cognition and behavior. Understanding these concepts makes cyberpsychology crucial to comprehending why security measures work or do not work for people.

## Human factors engineering, ergonomics, and cyberpsychology

Human factors engineering, ergonomics, and cyberpsychology are closely linked fields because they all focus on designing systems that account for human capabilities and limitations. Optimizing human-system interaction to improve performance, safety, and well-being has long been a focus of human factors research (Salvendy, 2012). Initially developed to increase comfort and reduce physical strain, ergonomic design concepts have expanded into cognitive ergonomics to address information processing and mental stress (Wilson, 2014). For example, a security operations center may go beyond an ergonomic workstation setup with adjustable chairs, proper monitor height, and good lighting by also redesigning the work for mental demands. This could include ranking alerts by risk, simplifying dashboards to reduce clutter, and providing decision-support prompts to analysts during serious incidents. This shift not only reduces physical strain but also improves information processing, lowers cognitive overload, and helps analysts sustain judgment quality during prolonged monitoring periods. The mismatch between human capabilities and system design in cybersecurity often manifests as noncompliance, workarounds, and security fatigue (Nifakos et al., 2021). For example, during a live incident, a SOC requires analysts to manually reauthenticate across multiple tools before isolating a compromised endpoint. Under pressure, analysts start reusing shared admin sessions and delaying ticket documentation to move faster, leading to policy noncompliance, unsafe workarounds, and escalating security fatigue.

Building on this progression, the next section examines frameworks commonly applied in cyberpsychology to systematically analyze digital behavior, cognitive workload, motivation, trust, and decision-making under cyber conditions. These frameworks translate the field's core premise into practical models that explain why users act as they do in virtual environments and how security systems can be designed to better align with human psychological realities.

## Frameworks and theories commonly applied in cyberpsychology

To describe and forecast human behavior in digital and security environments, cyberpsychology relies on well-established theoretical frameworks. A concept closely related to security training and interface design is **Cognitive Load Theory** (Sweller et al., 2011), which describes how high mental demands can impair learning and decision-making. Frameworks for assessing the usability, trust, and cognitive burden of digital systems are offered by human–computer interaction (HCI) models (Sharp et al., 2019). Furthermore, the protection motivation theory (Boss et al., 2015) and the technology acceptance model (Davis, 1989) are widely used to forecast the adoption of security practices and adherence to corporate policy.

**Protection Motivation Theory** explains why people decide to take protective action when they believe they face a meaningful threat. In cybersecurity, this means an employee is more likely to use multifactor authentication, avoid phishing links, or follow security procedures when they believe the cyber threat is serious, feel personally vulnerable, believe the protective action will be effective, and feel capable of carrying it out. From a cyberpsychology perspective, the model is especially useful because it focuses on how people think, feel, and respond to perceived digital risk, including fear, motivation, confidence, and behavioral intention in online environments.

The **Technology Acceptance Model** explains why people accept or reject a technology system. In cybersecurity, the model suggests that employees are more likely to adopt secure technologies, such as password managers, endpoint protection tools, secure portals, or reporting systems, when they see them as useful and easy to use. In cyberpsychology, this model helps explain the human side of technology behavior by showing how perceptions, attitudes, and user experience shape security compliance. If a security tool feels confusing, frustrating, or disruptive, users may avoid it even when it is technically effective.

Together, these models are highly relevant to both cybersecurity and cyberpsychology because they connect security behavior with human perception and decision-making. Protection Motivation Theory helps explain why individuals feel motivated to protect themselves from cyber threats, while the Technology Acceptance Model helps explain whether they will actually use the tools and systems designed to support secure behavior. Used together, they provide a stronger understanding of why people either comply with or resist cybersecurity practices in real-world organizational settings.

Cognitive Load Theory explains that excessive mental demand degrades security decisions; for example, during a phishing simulation, reducing clutter and simplifying warning text improves detection accuracy. HCI frameworks evaluate usability, trust, and workload; for example, a SOC dashboard redesign that prioritizes critical alerts can reduce analyst fatigue and missed threats. Protection Motivation Theory and the Technology Acceptance Model explain why users adopt security behaviors; for example, MFA adoption increases when users perceive threats as serious, perceive controls as effective, and perceive the authentication process as easy to use.

These frameworks offer structured methods for evaluating how individuals respond to security measures, interpret information, and adopt or reject technology. Crucially, by offering quantifiable dimensions and theoretical underpinnings, they enable scholars and practitioners to transcend anecdotal observations. Using these frameworks helps position cyberpsychology as an increasingly theoretically sound and continually developing field that enables methodical investigation and supports evidence-based cybersecurity interventions. Together, these frameworks can establish a practical foundation for examining how core cognitive processes in cybersecurity shape attention, judgment, and secure behavior under operational pressure.

# Cognitive processes in cybersecurity

Cognitive processes are central to cybersecurity because detection, interpretation, and response all depend on human attention, memory, and judgment under uncertainty and time pressure. From a human factors perspective, many security failures arise not from lack of effort but from poor alignment between cognitive capabilities and system design, including overload, unclear interfaces, and workflow friction. Integrating cognitive principles into cybersecurity design therefore strengthens performance, reduces the likelihood of errors, and enhances resilience across both individual operators and socio-technical systems.

## Attention and vigilance

In security operations, constant monitoring is a sustained attention demand that gradually degrades performance, leading to a decline in vigilance, missed detections, and erroneous dismissals. Vigilance is described as "effortful, stressful work" by human factors research, with performance deficits beginning to appear within minutes and worsening over the course of a watch period (Warm et al., 2008). During a prolonged incident response engagement, a cloud security engineer continuously reviews IAM policy changes and access logs across multiple accounts to prevent privilege abuse. After several hours of sustained monitoring, subtle anomalies, such as a rare cross-account role assumption from an unusual region, are missed as vigilance declines. The delay allows the attacker to maintain persistence and expand access before containment actions are triggered.

Laboratory vigilance paradigms that evaluate lapses and response-time variability and offer transferable measures for operational contexts include the **Psychomotor Vigilance Task** and the **Detection Response Task** (Biondi, Gamble, & Strayer, 2024). Laboratory vigilance paradigms are controlled research methods used to assess sustained attention, or a person's ability to remain alert and focused over time, particularly during repetitive or monotonous tasks. Two widely used examples are the **Psychomotor Vigilance Task** and the **Detection Response Task**. The **Psychomotor Vigilance Task** measures behavioral alertness by requiring an individual to respond as quickly as possible to a visual stimulus, making it useful for examining the effects of fatigue, sleep loss, and reduced attention. **The Detection Response Task**, by contrast, measures attentional capacity and cognitive workload by requiring an individual to detect and respond to intermittent signals while simultaneously performing another task. Together, these paradigms provide researchers with reliable methods for studying attention, fatigue, and performance in both laboratory and applied operational settings.

Network defense monitoring is now more accurately modeled by cyber-specific vigilance tasks (e.g., continuously scanning SIEM dashboards for low-frequency anomalies hidden in high-volume alerts, monitoring identity and access logs for unusual privilege escalation or cross-account role assumptions, and correlating endpoint, DNS, and network telemetry over extended periods to detect stealthy lateral movement), which show quantifiable declines in performance over time, including reduced hit rates for true threats, longer detection and triage latency, increased false negatives, and greater decision inconsistency as event streams lengthen, signal rarity increases, and adversary behaviors become more evasive (Guidetti et al., 2023). The factors that accelerate vigilance loss, low base rates, high information density, frequent non-actionable signals, and intermittent critical targets are closely mapped to **security operations center (SOC)** procedures. Multiple Resource Theory also predicts performance costs when finite attention pools are saturated by concurrent visual, auditory, and cognitive channels, increasing the risk of attentional tunneling and inattentional blindness (Sharpe, 2025). In cybersecurity, Multiple Resource Theory arises when defenders must process too many channels at once, leading to missed critical signals. For example, a SOC analyst watches multiple visual dashboards while handling auditory incident-bridge updates and composing cognitive triage decisions, then overlooks a subtle lateral-movement alert because attention narrows to ransomware containment. In another case, a cloud responder tracks console alerts, chat escalations, and ticket workflows simultaneously, leading to inattentional blindness to a brief anomalous cross-account role assumption that appears in audit logs. A key control for human-centered cybersecurity is to design SOC consoles and alert mechanisms with human attention in mind. This results in fewer, clearer, and better-prioritized signals.

A domain-specific sign of alertness loss caused by excessive low-value warnings is **alert fatigue**. SOC alert fatigue can be mitigated through automation, augmentation, and process redesign (e.g., AI-assisted triage and prioritizing), according to recent peer-reviewed research. Exaggerated alarm volumes and low signal-to-noise ratios desensitize analysts and invite them to overlook important occurrences, according to empirical and review research in cybersecurity (Ban, 2021 Zaid et al., 2024). Alert orchestration must combine algorithmic screening with transparent justifications and robust feedback loops. These elements help maintain attention, calibrate trust, and prevent complacency. Without intentional human-factors safeguards, increased automation can exacerbate the "out-of-the-loop" issue and further erode vigilance. To adjust thresholds and keep analysts vigilant, SOC directors should establish quantifiable alert budgets, use progressive summarization, and solicit post-event feedback.

## Decision-making under stress

Decision-making under stress in cybersecurity is a critical area of study, particularly within cyberpsychology, which explores the psychological factors shaping how individuals perceive and respond to cyber threats. Stress can significantly affect cognitive processes, leading to cognitive bias and emotional responses, which in turn influence the effectiveness of decision-making. Let's look at how these psychological dimensions shape responses to cybersecurity threats.

**Cognitive biases** play a significant role in decision-making under stress because stressful conditions often reduce attentional control, constrain working memory, and limit cognitive flexibility. When individuals are under pressure, they are more likely to rely on mental shortcuts rather than careful, analytical reasoning, which increases the likelihood of biased judgment. For example, confirmation bias may cause a person to focus on information that supports an initial belief, while availability bias may lead recent or emotionally charged events to seem more likely than they truly are. Stress can also intensify anchoring, overconfidence, and threat-based interpretations, especially in environments marked by time pressure, uncertainty, and high consequences. As a result, decisions made under stress may become narrower, less adaptive, and more susceptible to error. In contexts such as cybersecurity, healthcare, and emergency response, recognizing how cognitive biases influence stressed decision-making is essential for enhancing judgment quality and reducing operational risk.

Cyber operations impose sustained attentional demands as analysts triage alarms, dashboards, and logs, creating conditions that are ripe for cognitive overload, where task demands outstrip processing capacity and performance deteriorates (Clark & Mayer, 2016). Overloads fragment attention, degrade situational awareness, and increase the likelihood of missed cues or misclassification of severity, effects that become pronounced during high-pressure incident response (Al-Hashem & Satti, 2023 McCarthy et al., 2022). Stress magnifies these vulnerabilities and is associated with elevated false negative rates, response delays, and reliance on ad hoc strategies, consistent with the Yerkes–Dodson law, which describes the relationship between arousal and performance (Lindstrom et al., 2021).

**Emotional responses** play a vital role in decision-making under coercion, especially in situations such as manipulation or social engineering that require a decision under time pressure. Stress can broaden emotions such as fear, anxiety, and urgency, influencing how individuals react to perceived threats. Under stress, individuals can resort to fight-or-flight responses, which complicates their ability to analyze threats rationally (Singh, 2025). For example, a cybersecurity analyst facing an imminent threat may be overwhelmed and not thoroughly investigate an irregularity that requires careful consideration. As emotions cloud judgment, the likelihood of errors increases, underscoring the importance of emotional regulatory strategies in high-stress scenarios.

The implications of these psychological aspects for threat response strategies are profound. Understanding the interaction between cognitive bias and emotional responses can lead to more effective training and simulations for cybersecurity personnel. By creating environments that simulate high-stress situations, organizations can enhance their ability to adapt. Additionally, the application of psychological research techniques, such as stress-inducing training and management, can mitigate adverse impacts on decision-making (Al-Hashem & Saidi, 2023 Singh, 2025).

The integration of cyberpsychology principles in training and cybersecurity protocols is essential. Understanding cognitive bias and emotional responses can significantly enhance decision-making under stress, leading to more effective threat response strategies. As organizations continually face the evolution of cybersecurity, a comprehensive understanding of the human element becomes imperative to promote resilience and effectiveness in cyber defense.

## Heuristics

**Heuristics** are cognitively economical rules of thumb that simplify decision making by focusing attention on a limited set of cues to produce sufficiently accurate judgments under uncertainty and time pressure (Tversky & Kahneman, 1974 Gigerenzer et al., 1999). Heuristics can be powerful accelerants for cybersecurity decision-making when uncertainty is high and time is limited, provided that cue sets are deliberately designed, clearly scoped, and regularly revalidated. A cue set is deliberately designed by starting with a single decision-use case, selecting a small set of empirically useful cues, assigning explicit weights, and defining action thresholds. A cue set is clearly scoped by documenting where it is valid (environment, threat type, user role, data quality conditions), where it is not valid, and when mandatory human escalation overrides the rule. A cue set is regularly revalidated by tracking outcomes, measuring error patterns, testing attacker adaptation, and recalibrating weights and thresholds on a fixed cadence or after major incidents.

For example, a cybersecurity team may develop a weighted cue set to determine when workforce cloud login activity warrants stepped-up authentication or temporary account lockout. In this approach, suspicious indicators are assigned risk values based on their relative significance, such as impossible travel (+3), new device (+2), unusual network or proxy use (+2), first-time country (+2), and repeated MFA failures (+3). Impossible travel refers to login attempts from geographically distant locations within a time frame that would be infeasible for the same user, while repeated MFA failures may indicate attempted unauthorized access. The model is deliberately scoped to workforce cloud logins and excludes approved VPN routes and privileged accounts that require human review. To maintain validity, the cue set is re-evaluated monthly using standard security metrics, including true and false positive rates, missed compromises, time to containment, and attacker drift, with weights adjusted as adversarial patterns change. This approach is consistent with research on fast-and-frugal decision rules, which indicates that in noisy and data-sparse environments, simple models based on a small number of diagnostically useful cues can outperform more complex analytic approaches.

Operational studies in security operations centers support this view by demonstrating that shared mental models, structured decision points, and standardized cues enhance detection, deception, and incident response, whereas ambiguous workflows lead to delays and errors (Reeves et al., 2023). At the human level, heuristics enable rapid filtering of signals and swift action. However, they can also skew judgment. The availability heuristic can inflate the perceived likelihood of well-publicized threats, representativeness can privilege look-alike features over diagnostic evidence, such as domain provenance and authentication results, and anchoring can lock investigations into early labels that resist revision as new facts emerge (Tversky & Kahneman, 1974). The availability heuristic refers to how people judge a threat as more likely when examples come to mind quickly (for example, recent, vivid, or highly publicized incidents), even though base-rate or case-specific evidence does not support that judgment. For example, in cybersecurity, a team may overprioritize a widely reported ransomware pattern simply because it is memorable, while underweighting quieter but more diagnostic indicators in this case.

Repetition introduces additional risk because homogeneous warnings can lead to habituation, which necessitates varied, context-aware prompts that maintain salience and relevance (Kirwan et al., 2020).

Because users have limited cognitive bandwidth, security controls should default to safe settings and minimize workflow friction, so attention is conserved for genuinely high-risk decisions rather than routine tasks (Beautement et al., 2009). In practice, organizations should maintain curated catalogs of sanctioned heuristics with provenance and validity scope, embed feedback loops that measure performance and retire fragile cues, and schedule periodic red-team challenges to check for drift into bias (Schaltegger et al., 2024 Reeves et al., 2023). A human-centered security posture leverages these principles to create a day-to-day advantage by highlighting diagnostic signals at the moment of choice, requiring explicit checks for alternative explanations within case workflows, and positioning users as capable partners whose bounded rationality can be harnessed into timely, accurate defensive actions (Zimmermann et al., 2024). Because secure decisions depend on what users notice, retain, and interpret under operational pressure, the next section examines memory, information processing, and human factors in cybersecurity as the cognitive foundation of resilient defensive performance.

# Memory, information processing, and human factors in cybersecurity

Memory and information processing constitute foundational mechanisms in cyberpsychology, exerting a direct influence on user behavior, threat detection, and organizational security performance. Effective cyber defense requires interfaces and training regimes that align with human cognitive capacities, minimize extraneous cognitive load, and support accurate recall and calibrated judgment under stress. A synthesis of the literature on memory, information processing, and situational awareness indicates that security outcomes improve when systems respect cognitive constraints and when training cultivates robust, retrieval-ready knowledge structures alongside decision strategies that function reliably in high-tempo environments. To ground these findings, the next section examines memory and information processing as the cognitive basis for accurate detection, sound judgment, and timely response in cybersecurity contexts.

## Memory and information processing

**Memory** supports the execution of routine security practices, including recognizing trustworthy sites, recalling authentication procedures, and adhering to incident playbooks, yet remains vulnerable to omissions and distortions that can lead to insecure actions. Omissions and distortions that can lead to insecure actions mean that users may either forget critical security information or remember it inaccurately, resulting in missed safeguards, incorrect decisions, and increased exposure to cyber risk. Research describing the role of prior experience in shaping present threat perceptions highlights that modeling the relationship between stored knowledge and current appraisal can enhance the prediction of user decisions and enable more targeted interventions (Al-Hashem & Saidi, 2023). For example, an employee who has previously encountered multiple phishing emails that used urgent invoice language may appraise a new "payment overdue" message as high risk and report it quickly, whereas an employee with no similar prior exposure may treat the same message as routine and click the link. Modeling these experience-based appraisal differences allows security teams to predict who is more likely to misclassify threats and deliver targeted interventions, such as scenario-specific simulations and just-in-time warning prompts.

**Information processing** refers to the encoding, evaluation, and response to security-relevant cues and varies across individuals in ways that correlate with threat discernment and compliance. Examples of security-relevant cues include mismatched sender domains, unusual login locations or times, repeated multifactor authentication prompts, unexpected attachment types, certificate warnings, abnormal privilege-escalation requests, unfamiliar payment-change instructions, and discrepancies between displayed URLs and actual link destinations. Empirical evidence links stronger cognitive skills to more consistent detection of phishing and anomalous content, as well as to safer practices, suggesting that awareness programs should target skill development rather than solely rule memorization (Moustafa et al., 2021). For instance, security warnings function optimally when designed to match user encoding and retrieval processes; framing, timing, and habit scaffolding can reduce cognitive load and promote automatic, correct responses, thereby increasing the likelihood that alerts translate into effective action (Weickert et al., 2023). Collectively, these findings suggest that memory cues, recognition-based controls, and processing-aware messages improve both the accuracy and consistency of security behavior.

Memory retrieval is especially vulnerable under pressure because working memory can become overloaded, well-rehearsed procedures may become harder to access, and even familiar cues may be misread or overlooked. One way to reduce this problem is to use structured decision frameworks that guide people through a clear sequence of thinking steps. A well-known example is the observe-orient-decide-act, or OODA, cycle, which helps individuals first notice what is happening, then interpret its meaning in context, decide on a course of action, and finally act on that decision. In high-tempo environments, repeated pattern-recognition practice and procedural schemas such as OODA can enhance prioritization, stabilize judgment, and strengthen resilience by making the decision process more explicit and reducing demands on limited cognitive resources.

## Situational awareness

**Situational awareness** in cybersecurity encompasses the perception of environmental elements, comprehension of their meaning, and projection of future system states, serving as a prerequisite for timely detection and coordinated response (Endsley, 1995). Examples of environmental elements in cybersecurity include unusual outbound traffic patterns, spikes in failed authentication attempts, new privileged account creation, endpoint process anomalies, unexpected firewall rule changes, DNS query irregularities, threat intelligence indicators, and concurrent alerts across identity, network, and cloud platforms. Training approaches that stimulate focused engagement and provide immediate feedback, such as gamified and neuroergonomic methods, have been shown to improve attentional focus and diagnostic acuity, thereby strengthening situational awareness in complex cyber defense contexts (Ask et al., 2023).

Gamified methods and neuro design can enhance situational awareness in cybersecurity by helping people notice threats, understand what they mean, and respond appropriately. Gamified methods use features such as points, levels, timed challenges, and feedback to make security training more engaging and to reinforce secure decision-making. Neuro design, or neuro-ergonomic design, refers to designing systems around how the human brain processes attention, memory, fatigue, and mental workload. In cybersecurity, this includes simplified dashboards, prioritized alerts, fatigue-aware scheduling, and checklist-based support during stressful incidents. As data volume and speed increase, machine learning can further support situational awareness by identifying unusual patterns, ranking the most important alerts, and helping analysts focus on the signals that matter most. In cyberpsychology, these approaches are valuable because they examine how users perceive risk, sustain attention, and make decisions under pressure in digital environments. They also help researchers and practitioners understand how cognitive and emotional processes influence secure behavior, threat recognition, and human interaction with cybersecurity systems.

Surveys of cyber situational awareness systems emphasize that technical capability alone is insufficient; genuine gains depend on user understanding, workflow integration, and transparent human-system coordination that enable operators to interpret and trust system outputs (Alavizadeh et al., 2022). Psychological literacy among practitioners further influences outcomes by shaping beliefs, affect, and social influences that govern adherence and vigilance, indicating that capability development must address cognitive, socio-behavioral, as well as technical factors (Debb, 2021 Hadlington & Ryding, 2025 Taylor & Whitty, 2024).

## Design and training implications

Interface design should employ progressive disclosure and principled signal prioritization, suppress low-value noise, and make high-risk cues salient through grouping, ranking, and consistent mappings. Memory-centered interaction can be supported through checklists, just-in-time prompts, and recognition-based inputs that reduce recall requirements and increase adherence to correct sequences. Explanations should be tailored to user roles and decisions, prioritizing concise, action-relevant rationales over opaque technical details to foster appropriate trust.

Stress-aware design should minimize interaction cost by simplifying flows, improving perceptual clarity, and enabling recovery from slips. Accessibility and inclusion demand multimodal presentation, plain language, and compatibility with assistive technologies to ensure that security-critical information is perceivable and actionable by diverse users. Training should privilege retrieval strength via spaced practice and scenario-based exercises that replicate time pressure and ambiguity, thereby consolidating protocols in long-term memory and enhancing recall during incidents (Morris et al., 2022). Organizational programs should build psychological literacy, normalize use of playbooks and handoffs that externalize memory and reduce working-memory load, and integrate human-in-the-loop analytics that present anomalies with clear verification and escalation pathways, ensuring that automation augments rather than overwhelms human judgment (Abuabid, 2025 Alavizadeh et al., 2022).

Cybersecurity effectiveness depends on respecting and leveraging human cognitive realities. Memory and information processing shape whether users notice, comprehend, and act on security cues, while situational awareness structures perception, interpretation, and anticipation in volatile environments. Attention limits and stress underscore the need for interfaces and workflows that manage cognitive load, scaffold accurate recall, and facilitate informed decision-making. A coherent strategy that integrates memory-centered interaction, decision-ready explanations, inclusive presentation, retrieval-oriented training, psychologically informed culture, and human-in-the-loop analytics offers a viable path to stronger user behavior, faster and more accurate threat detection, and greater organizational resilience across an evolving digital landscape.

# Impact of stress, anxiety, and user motivation on cyber hygiene and behavior change

The interaction between emotional and behavioral factors in IT security is a fundamental area of study that highlights the complexities of user interactions with digital technology. Psychological elements such as stress and anxiety have been shown to significantly influence the way individuals engage with safety protocols, often affecting their decision-making processes. A qualitative examination of the emotional landscape surrounding IT security reveals that high levels of stress and anxiety can impair cognitive functioning, leading individuals to dismiss the risks associated with their online behaviors (Al-Hashem & Saidi, 2023). This reduced perception of risk often results in riskier online habits, ultimately increasing users' vulnerability to cyber threats.

The following section examines how emotional states, motivational drivers, and cognitive biases jointly shape cybersecurity behavior, with direct implications for risk perception, cyber hygiene, and compliance in both individual and organizational contexts. By analyzing stress, anxiety, convenience trade-offs, false security beliefs, and organizational emotional climate, this discussion clarifies why effective cybersecurity strategies must integrate psychological design principles alongside technical controls and policy mandates.

The following behaviors and biases are listed below:

- Both chronic and acute stress can negatively impact an individual's attention and judgment, which are critical components in assessing IT and cybersecurity risks. For example, users experiencing heightened anxiety may engage in avoidance behaviors, such as neglecting security updates or ignoring alerts, thereby exacerbating their exposure to potential cyberattacks (Fatima et al., 2024). These emotional responses are not merely byproducts of user experience; they significantly dictate individuals' willingness and ability to engage meaningfully with cybersecurity measures. Therefore, understanding these psychological dynamics is vital for developing effective cybersecurity education and intervention strategies.
- Motivation plays a crucial role in determining user behavior toward cybersecurity practices. The interaction between intrinsic motivations (e.g., a desire for personal security) and extrinsic motivators (e.g., compliance with organizational policies or fear of consequences) shapes how users adopt secure online behaviors. When individuals feel empowered and view cybersecurity as personally relevant, they are more likely to engage in proactive behaviors. However, when overwhelmed by stress or feelings of inadequacy about their technical competence, users may disengage from recommended practices, illustrating a clear link between emotional states and adherence to cybersecurity protocols (Al-Hashem & Saidi, 2023).
- Risk perception, especially when filtered through emotional states like anxiety, presents further challenges in encouraging safe cybersecurity behaviors. Some individuals may overestimate the risks associated with basic online activities, while others may become desensitized to significant threats, adopting a casual or dismissive approach to cybersecurity. This duality creates challenges for educators and policymakers, who must strike a balance between conveying urgency and avoiding paralyzing fear. Targeted awareness campaigns that account for users' emotional states can promote informed decision-making over reactive or reckless behavior (Fatima et al., 2024).
- User motivation and risk perception are often closely intertwined with emotional factors, revealing how psychological states can either mitigate or exacerbate cybersecurity risks. Convenience often takes precedence over secure practices. Users may prioritize ease of access over adherence to protocols. Ayanbode et al. (2024) note that when faced with the choice between convenience and security, users frequently opt for the former, especially when time-saving benefits are apparent. This tendency is further amplified by psychological phenomena such as "fear of missing out," which encourages impulsive engagement with online platforms without thoroughly assessing associated risks.

Perceived risk is shaped not only by objective probability but also by emotional responses and cognitive biases. Individuals often underestimate cybersecurity threats when they perceive themselves to be in a safe environment, which can lead to relaxed vigilance and poor security habits. For example, an employee working from a trusted home network assumes the environment is safe and disables multifactor authentication prompts to reduce friction. Days later, the employee enters credentials into a spoofed single sign-on page, resulting in account compromise. Nassir et al. (2024) highlight how this misalignment between real threats and perceived safety contributes to the persistence of internal vulnerabilities, in which trusted users, either inadvertently or deliberately, compromise security. Such findings emphasize the need for education programs that recalibrate user perceptions and reinforce realistic threat assessments.

- The emotional climate within organizations plays a substantial role in shaping users' cybersecurity behavior. Stress and anxiety can surface when users face complex protocols or fear consequences following security violations. These emotional barriers often result in disengagement or resistance. Conversely, fostering positive emotions, such as a sense of empowerment gained through training, can enhance users' commitment to secure practices. Singh (2025) underscores that organizations promoting a supportive, non-punitive culture tend to see greater motivation and adherence to cybersecurity protocols. Building on this foundation, emotionally intelligent awareness strategies can be used to translate motivation into sustained, secure behavior by aligning security messaging, training design, and reinforcement practices with users' emotional and cognitive realities.

## Emotionally intelligent awareness strategies

To effectively improve cybersecurity behaviors, awareness campaigns must resonate emotionally with users. Messaging should emphasize not only the technical aspects but also the personal and collective benefits of safe practices. Communications tailored to users' emotional and experiential realities can create stronger motivation for behavior change. By integrating emotional intelligence into training and communication, organizations can foster deeper engagement and encourage long-term behavioral transformation.

Sustained cybersecurity performance depends not only on technical controls, but also on the ability to change human behavior under real operational constraints. In practice, that change is often impeded by psychological barriers such as threat normalization, low self-efficacy, decision fatigue, and resistance to effortful new routines. Cognitive bias and behavioral gaps further weaken adherence by distorting risk judgments and creating inconsistencies between what users know and what users actually do in high-pressure moments. Overcoming this behavioral inertia, therefore, requires cybersecurity strategies that combine clear behavioral design, emotionally intelligent reinforcement, and low-friction safeguards that make secure action the default rather than the exception. The following barriers and behaviors are listed below:

- **Psychological barriers to behavior change**: Human psychology has a significant impact on attitudes toward cybersecurity. One major obstacle is the widespread stress and anxiety associated with navigating digital threats. Users often experience cognitive overload from constant exposure to cybersecurity messages, which can lead to feelings of helplessness and disengagement (Nygren et al., 2023). Cybersecurity messages that often cause cognitive overload include multi-paragraph phishing alerts filled with technical jargon and unclear action steps, repeated high-urgency pop-ups that do not distinguish low-risk from high-risk events, and incident notifications listing many indicators without prioritization or role-specific guidance. This emotional fatigue can lead to desensitization, where users begin to disregard phishing warnings or data breach alerts as background noise rather than taking them seriously (Enders & Kreutzer, 2022).
- **Cognitive bias and behavioral gaps**: Risk perception is often distorted by misplaced confidence or lack of awareness. Research shows that while many users acknowledge common risks, such as using weak passwords, only a small proportion take action to mitigate them. For example, Chadwick et al. (2023) found that although two-thirds of users understood the risks of weak passwords, only a minority actually used stronger alternatives. This disconnect highlights the need for educational strategies that bridge the gap between awareness and action, as well as psychological alertness
- **Overcoming behavioral inertia**: Changing habitual behavior requires more than awareness; it demands sustained support. Users often remain anchored in familiar routines, making it challenging to adopt new cybersecurity practices (Peters et al., 2022). While behavioral nudges and reminders can be effective, their impact may diminish over time without consistent reinforcement (Sharma et al., 2024). Long-term behavior change must be supported by a strategic framework that reinforces new habits while accounting for emotional resistance.

## Human factors in security system design

Across the contemporary digital landscape, security systems serve a fundamental role in safeguarding sensitive information against a wide array of threats. Despite this centrality, usability challenges frequently hinder their adoption and effective use. Such challenges often take the form of convoluted authentication workflows, extended and perplexing protocols, and unintuitive interfaces. These barriers generate friction during user interactions and foster resistance to protective measures. Studies emphasize the necessity of balancing rigorous information security requirements with a satisfactory user experience (Groen et al., 2023).

## Usability challenges in security systems

A persistent difficulty arises from the interaction between security robustness and application complexity. Many security measures, such as multi-factor authentication and stringent password rules, are perceived as obstacles rather than protective controls, encouraging workarounds and policy circumvention. Typical behaviors include weak passwords, easily guessable credentials, and credential reuse across platforms, all of which degrade organizational security posture (Albarrak, 2024). The gap between technical requirements and practical user capabilities remains a critical concern for system designers and policy makers.

Let's look at some of the usability challenges in security systems:

- A high cognitive load imposed by complicated requirements substantially contributes to usability failures. Ambiguous navigation, inadequate guidance, and inconsistent interface cues can elevate frustration and confusion, increasing the likelihood of errors and diminishing engagement with protective measures. Evidence indicates that perceived task complexity prompts disengagement, thereby enlarging vulnerability surfaces within security architectures (Kang et al., 2022).
- Traditional, reactive paradigms emphasize breach prevention without equal attention to seamless interaction. Examples of traditional reactive paradigms include annual one-size-fits-all awareness training deployed only after major incidents, blanket password rotation mandates applied uniformly across all roles regardless of risk exposure, organization-wide lockouts and access restrictions triggered after breaches without workflow-specific exception design, generic phishing simulations that penalize users but provide minimal role-based coaching, and security policy rollouts that prioritize strict compliance enforcement while deferring usability testing until after adoption problems emerge. Uniform controls applied to heterogeneous user groups neglect variation in roles, contexts, and technical competencies. A cyber-related example is enforcing the same strict multifactor reauthentication interval for all users, including privileged administrators, faculty, finance staff, and help-desk personnel, despite major differences in risk exposure, workflow demands, and technical proficiency. Such undifferentiated models risk alienating segments of the intended user base. Re-examining underlying design philosophies is therefore warranted, as prioritizing security over usability can ultimately undermine overall effectiveness.

## Human-centered design as a strategic response

**Human-centered design** (**HCD**) offers a path toward solutions that are simultaneously secure and intuitive. Active engagement of representative users during research, prototyping, and validation enables alignment between behavioral patterns, preferences, and pain points on one hand, and control strength on the other. The integration of human–computer interaction principles supports adaptive interfaces, context-aware authentication, and simplified workflows that sustain compliance while maintaining rigorous standards (Groen et al., 2023).

Usability considerations extend beyond individual interactions to organization-wide compliance. When personnel experience security protocols as overly restrictive, adherence declines and residual risk increases. Empirical findings indicate that programs prioritizing user experience within security architectures achieve higher compliance and fewer violations, demonstrating that adoption depends on both control strength and perceived ease of use (Jones & Smith, 2024).

## Design principles and practical recommendations

Translating human-centered cybersecurity theory into practice requires design principles that are technically rigorous, behaviorally realistic, and operationally sustainable across diverse user populations. The following recommendations outline how participatory design, cognitive clarity, behavioral science, adaptive authentication, and continuous feedback can work together to strengthen security outcomes while reducing friction, errors, and disengagement. Below are some design recommendations:

- **Participatory and iterative methods:** Continuous involvement of representative users throughout discovery, prototyping, and evaluation yields solutions that satisfy strict requirements while reflecting practical expectations and capabilities (Almeida, 2025).
- **Intuitive interfaces and clear signaling:** Direct navigation, reduced cognitive load, accessible language, and explicit step-by-step cues decrease errors and increase task completion. Educational scaffolding tailored to distinct user segments strengthens a security-conscious culture (O'Malley, 2025).
- **Behaviorally informed mechanisms:** Incorporation of psychological and social insights supports motivational elements, such as positive reinforcement and judicious gamification, that encourage secure behavior without undue mental burden (Karwowski et al., 2025 Sachs, 2025).
- **Context-aware and risk-adaptive authentication:** Adaptive policies that modulate requirements based on device trust, network context, behavioral baselines, and transaction risk reduce friction during low-risk access while preserving stringent

verification for high-risk events. Risk-based step-up authentication exemplifies this approach (Almazrouei et al., 2025).

- **Continuous feedback and system learning:** Embedded feedback channels enable the reporting of friction points and comprehension gaps, allowing for rapid iteration. Non-intrusive threat alerts and change notifications sustain awareness without overwhelming attention resources.

Effective security depends not only on cryptographic strength and policy rigor but also on sustained, organization-wide engagement. Human-centered design, behaviorally informed controls, and risk-adaptive orchestration collectively bridge the long-standing divide between protection and practicality. By institutionalizing these principles, organizations can enhance compliance, reduce error rates, and bolster resilience in an increasingly digital environment.

# The psychological profiles and traits of cyber offenders

As indicated by Gaia et al. (2021), psychological profiles of cyber offenders frequently reveal dark personality traits that shape criminal behavior. **Machiavellianism**, **narcissism**, and **psychopathy** appear as salient indicators of cyber-offending tendencies. Such traits manifest not only in interpersonal contexts but also in the strategic planning and execution of attacks, where deception, exploitation, and betrayal are instrumentalized to achieve criminal objectives.

As discussed by Gaia et al. (2021), Machiavellianism is characterized by manipulativeness, moral disengagement, and a focus on self-interest, enabling deception without remorse. Offenders exhibiting Machiavellianism tend to design attacks that leverage betrayal and calculated exploitation to maximize gains.

According to Hani et al. (2024), narcissism is marked by grandiosity, entitlement, and a pronounced need for admiration, which complicate the motivational landscape of cyber offenders. Elevated narcissism can motivate offending to assert superiority and enhance self-image, with recognition and status within illicit communities pursued as ends in themselves.

Hani et al. (2024) further note that psychopathy, defined by callousness, impulsivity, and shallow affect, supports engagement in harm with minimal concern for consequences. Emotional detachment fosters calculated decision-making and a failure to appreciate victims' psychological harm, thereby reinforcing deviant patterns.

## Manipulation and social engineering tactics

Kumaran (2025) emphasizes that manipulation tactics used by cyber offenders frequently emerge from dark-trait constellations, especially within social engineering. Techniques such as phishing, pretexting, and baiting exploit knowledge of human cognition and emotion, capitalizing on trust, fear, and naivety to induce disclosure of sensitive information or unwitting participation in harmful acts. Psychological profiling of high-profile cases further supports preventive strategies that address both technical and human factors (Kumaran, 2025).

- Drawing on Cialdini (2009) and Cristescu et al. (2022), social-engineering efficacy is rooted in the systematic exploitation of cognitive biases and affective triggers. Authority bias and social proof can increase compliance with persuasive lures by making malicious requests appear legitimate and socially validated. Trait-linked susceptibilities also shape risk, as Siddiqi et al. (2022) found that high agreeableness may increase compliance with flattering or prosocial appeals, whereas high neuroticism may heighten anxiety and impulsive responses to threat cues. Hare (1999) explains that offenders high in Machiavellianism or psychopathy often display cognitive empathy with deficient emotional empathy, enabling precise manipulation without remorse.
- Monteiro et al. (2020) describe overconfidence as a dynamic that affects both offenders and victims. Overconfidence can lead to risky decisions by offenders and inflate victims' perceived ability to judge the legitimacy of messages, thereby facilitating successful impersonation. Note that cognitive dissonance facilitates the rationalization of harmful actions as necessary or justified retaliation, thereby reducing guilt and sustaining repeated offending, as Gaia et al. (2020) observe.

## Organizational and community implications

As argued by Gaia et al. (2020, 2021), the interaction of dark traits, manipulation tactics, and cognitive vulnerabilities has consequences that extend beyond immediate losses. Attacks erode end-users' trust, elevate collective anxiety, and normalize defensive skepticism in digital interactions. A nuanced understanding enables the development of controls, training, and incident-response procedures that preempt psychological exploitation.

## Human-centered countermeasures

Groen et al. (2023) and Siddiqi et al. (2022) support integrating psychological insight with technical control. Effective mitigation can be organized into four mutually reinforcing lines of effort:

- **Targeted awareness and inoculation:** As recommended by Cristescu et al. (2022), training should expose users to realistic lures and explain specific biases being exploited to improve detection and resistance

- **Adaptive verification:** In line with human-centered design principles, using context-aware prompts and progressive disclosure should reduce unnecessary friction while preserving scrutiny for high-risk actions (Groen et al., 2023)
- **Message hygiene and friction design:** Consistent warning cues, clear affordances, and mandatory pauses for high-impact actions counter urgency-driven impulsivity (Cialdini, 2009)
- **Behavioral analytics:** Monitoring for anomalous interaction patterns, combined with user-reported signals, surfaces persuasion-driven compromise at earlier stages (Monteiro et al., 2020)

Building on Gaia et al. (2021) and Hani et al. (2024), dark personality traits such as Machiavellianism, narcissism, and psychopathy interact with social engineering tactics and cognitive biases to enable cyber offending. A synthesis of psychological profiling, bias-aware education, and human-centered security design strengthens organizational resilience by addressing technical and behavioral vectors simultaneously.

# Social and societal dimensions of cyber conflict

Cyber conflict is fundamentally a cyberpsychological phenomenon as much as a technical one, because outcomes are shaped by perception, cognition, emotion, identity, and social influence in digital environments. Adversaries exploit these psychological and collective mechanisms to manipulate behavior, degrade trust, intensify polarization, and destabilize institutional legitimacy at scale. From this perspective, cyberpsychology provides the analytic lens needed to explain how influence operations, disinformation cascades, and digitally mediated group dynamics become instruments of conflict. The following section examines the social and societal dimensions of cyber conflict through this cyberpsychological framework.

## Cyberbullying, harassment, and online aggression

As established by Kowalski, Giumetti, Schroeder, and Lattanner (2014), cyberbullying constitutes a pervasive public health problem that is associated with depression, anxiety, and somatic complaints comparable in magnitude to traditional bullying. Empirical evidence suggests that the affordances of digital platforms intensify aggression through anonymity, asynchronicity, and the invisibility of audiences, collectively diminishing social accountability and heightening disinhibition (Suler, 2004). These affordances increase the likelihood of persistent harassment, pile-ons, and reputational damage that extend beyond school or workplace boundaries (Kowalski et al., 2014). For example, a university student is targeted in a private class group chat after a minor disagreement, when anonymous accounts begin posting edited screenshots and insults late at night and then encourage others to repost the content across public social platforms. Because messages are asynchronous and widely visible, harassment continues beyond campus hours, rapidly escalating into a coordinated pile-on that damages the student's reputation and social relationships. Over several weeks, the student develops anxiety, depressed mood, sleep disruption, and stress-related headaches, illustrating how digital affordances can intensify aggression and produce mental-health effects comparable to severe in-person bullying.

As argued by Jane (2014), technology-facilitated abuse frequently targets women and marginalized groups and operates through coordinated harassment, doxxing, and threats that aim to silence participation. This pattern aligns with broader findings that online aggression scales rapidly through networked amplification and that harmful content can be strategically weaponized to intimidate and exclude. Meta-analytic and longitudinal studies further suggest bidirectional associations between perpetration and victimization, with exposure to online aggression predicting later offending and vice versa (Kowalski et al., 2014). These dynamics underscore the need for interventions that combine platform governance, evidence-based digital citizenship curricula, and accessible reporting and support mechanisms.

## Groupthink, conformity, and herd behavior in digital communities

As demonstrated by Muchnik, Aral, and Taylor (2013), even minimal social cues such as prior upvotes or downvotes create durable herding effects that skew collective judgments on large platforms. Experimental manipulation of initial ratings produced substantial cascades that inflated subsequent evaluations in a path-dependent manner, highlighting how early signals shape emergent consensus. Complementing this effect, Centola (2010) showed that the structure of social networks influences behavioral diffusion, with clustered networks promoting more reliable adoption of health behaviors than random networks, thereby illustrating how community topology governs conformity dynamics. For example, in a university cybersecurity awareness campaign, students are encouraged to enable multifactor authentication and report phishing messages. When adoption begins inside tightly connected peer cohorts, such as residence halls, student organizations, or cohort-based classes, repeated reinforcement from multiple trusted peers leads to faster and more durable uptake than in loosely connected, random communication networks. This pattern illustrates Centola's finding that a clustered network topology strengthens conformity dynamics and improves the reliability of diffusion for protective behaviors.

As theorized by Postmes et al. (1998), the Social Identity model of Deindividuation Effects (SIDE) explains how salient group identities and anonymity can amplify norm conformity online, even in the absence of face-to-face cues. When identity cues are group-level rather than individual, conformity to perceived in-group norms increases, which can facilitate both prosocial coordination and toxic mobbing. At the population scale, Del Vicario et al. (2016) documented homophilous polarization and echo-chamber formation on social platforms, demonstrating that ideologically congruent communities preferentially consume and endorse consistent narratives while ignoring corrective information. For example, during a major ransomware incident affecting public services, a community forum can first enable prosocial coordination by rapidly sharing verified outage updates and recovery resources, but the same network can quickly shift into toxic mobbing when influential accounts promote an unverified accusation against a specific employee or group. As ideologically aligned users repeatedly circulate the same claim within their own clusters, corrective evidence from official incident reports receives little engagement and is dismissed as untrustworthy. This illustrates homophilous polarization and echo-chamber dynamics, where narrative consistency inside identity-aligned communities outcompetes factual correction at the population scale. Together, these findings suggest that seemingly weak signals and platform architecture have a powerful influence on opinion cascades, groupthink, and herd behavior.

## Cognitive warfare, disinformation, and manipulation of collective psychology

As shown by Vosoughi, Roy, and Aral (2018), false news spreads farther, faster, and more widely than trustworthy news on X (formerly Twitter), particularly for political content, due in part to its novelty and emotional content, which increase the likelihood of retweets. Cognitive and motivational mechanisms facilitate this spread. Pennycook and Rand (2019) found that susceptibility to misinformation is strongly associated with reduced analytic reasoning rather than partisanship per se, implying that accuracy prompts and reasoning supports can mitigate belief in falsehoods. Extending the literature on post-truth dynamics, Lewandowsky, Ecker, and Cook (2017) outlined mechanisms by which misinformation endures, including familiarity, source confusion, and motivated cognition, and proposed corrective strategies such as providing coherent alternative explanations and emphasizing accuracy over the repetition of myths.

As an upstream defense, Roozenbeek and van der Linden (2019) provided evidence that "psychological inoculation" through interactive simulations of manipulation techniques builds attitudinal resistance to misinformation by pre-exposing users to weakened examples of common tactics. At the ecosystem level, Guess, Nagler, and Tucker (2019) and Guess, Nyhan, and Reifler (2020) demonstrated that exposure to misinformation on social media is highly concentrated among small subsets of users and domains, suggesting that targeted interventions, such as friction, downranking, and source-level interventions, may yield outsized benefits. Collectively, this research describes a cognitive-warfare environment in which attention, affect, and identity are strategically leveraged to manipulate collective psychology, and in which prebunking, timely debunking, and platform design reforms constitute complementary defenses.

## Psychological resilience of societies against large-scale cyber threats

As articulated by Norris et al. (2008), community resilience emerges from a network of adaptive capacities that include social capital, economic development, information and communication, and community competence. These capacities buffer stressors and facilitate rapid recovery following disruptions. In the cyber context, Linkov and Kott (2019) argued that resilience requires a shift from purely preventive security to a portfolio that also emphasizes robust detection, graceful degradation, and rapid reconstitution of essential functions. This orientation reframes societal preparedness as the ability to absorb, adapt, and recover from cyber shocks, rather than eliminating all failures.

As evidenced by Roozenbeek and van der Linden (2019), psychological inoculation enhances cognitive resilience by strengthening recognition of manipulative tactics before exposure during crises. Patel et al. (2017) further demonstrated that community resilience benefits from trusted risk communication, participatory planning, and inclusive governance structures that cultivate self-efficacy and collective efficacy. Translating these insights to cyber emergencies implies investing in cross-sector exercises, redundancy for critical services, transparent and timely communication during incidents, and public-facing prebunking campaigns that reduce panic and rumor contagion. Integrating social-psychological interventions with technical incident response fosters societal resilience by aligning human behavior, institutional trust, and infrastructural robustness.

Online aggression harms mental health and civic participation, group-level dynamics amplify conformity and herd behavior, and adversarial actors exploit cognitive mechanisms to orchestrate large-scale manipulation. Durable societal protection requires a dual strategy that couples technical safeguards with social-psychological capacities, including inoculation against manipulation, trustworthy communication, and community competence. Advancing this agenda entails rigorous evaluation of platform architectures, targeted public health–style interventions, and institutional designs that can absorb and adapt to cyber disruptions while sustaining democratic deliberation.

# Emerging areas of cyberpsychology in cybersecurity

Emerging areas of cyberpsychology in cybersecurity are increasingly defined by the interaction of human cognition, behavior, and machine intelligence in high-stakes digital environments. Key frontiers include AI and automation, human-AI teaming in cyber defense, the psychological implications of quantum and post-quantum security transitions, behavioral biometrics in authentication, and predictive insider-threat modeling using psychometric and behavioral data. Collectively, these domains shift the field from static user-awareness paradigms toward dynamic, data-informed models of trust, decision-making, identity, and risk. Examining these areas is essential for designing cybersecurity systems that remain technically robust while also psychologically valid, ethically governed, and behaviorally resilient.

# AI and automation

As demonstrated by Lee and See (2004), the appropriate reliance on automation depends on calibrated trust, which reflects an agent's perceived competence, predictability, and transparency. Miscalibration yields misuse or disuse in complex settings. Human–automation research and meta-analyses converge on the conclusion that design features, performance history, and task context jointly shape trust formation and reliance behavior, making measurement and tuning of trust central to deployment in high-stakes cyber operations (Hancock et al., 2011 Schaefer et al., 2016).

As shown by Miller (2019), the quality of explanations influences user mental models and downstream decisions. Explanations that align with social-science principles promote a better understanding and more discerning acceptance of automated recommendations. For example, a fraud-detection system that simply displays "High Risk: Block Transaction" often leads analysts either to over-trust or dismiss the recommendation because the reasoning is opaque. If the same system provides a concise, behaviorally grounded explanation, such as "Risk elevated due to first-time device, unusual geolocation, and mismatch with normal transaction timing; confidence 0.82; recommended action: step-up verification," analysts form a more accurate mental model of what the model is detecting and make more discerning decisions about when to accept, question, or override the recommendation.

In applied security analytics, local post-hoc methods such as **Local Interpretable Model-Agnostic Explanations (LIME)** help analysts interpret why a machine learning model flagged a specific event by showing which features contributed most to that outcome. This makes it possible to examine individual alerts more carefully without reducing the predictive strength of the underlying model, thereby supporting cognitive delegation while maintaining human oversight (Miller, 2019 Ribeiro et al., 2016).

For example, if a security model flags a login attempt as suspicious, LIME can show that the alert was primarily influenced by factors such as an unfamiliar device, repeated failed login attempts, and access from an unusual geographic location. By revealing the reasons behind the alert, LIME helps the analyst judge whether the event reflects a genuine threat or a false positive, allowing the model to assist decision-making without replacing human review.

# Human–AI teaming in cyber defense

As reviewed by Endsley (2017), effective human–autonomy system teaming requires maintaining situation awareness, transparent role allocation, and authority boundaries to avoid out-of-the-loop performance decrements under dynamic workload. Evidence from human–autonomy team research indicates that teaming benefits depend on transparency and coordination mechanisms that surface system intent, uncertainties, and action affordances during time-pressured defense tasks (Lyons et al., 2021 O'Neill et al., 2020).

As demonstrated by Ben-Asher and colleagues, cognitive models of cyber defenders can capture recognition–primed decision processes and inform the division of labor between analytic agents and human analysts. Teaming architectures that leverage cognitively plausible agents to triage events and propose options have shown promise for improving detection and response while preserving human judgment on ambiguous cases (Ben-Asher et al., 2015 Veksler et al., 2020).

## Psychological implications of quantum and post-quantum security

As argued by Mosca (2018), the prospect of cryptographically relevant quantum computing creates a transition risk, in which organizations must plan for adversaries who can now harvest encrypted data and subsequently decrypt it, necessitating a timely migration to post-quantum cryptography. From a psychological perspective, classic risk-perception research suggests that abstract, delayed, and unfamiliar hazards elicit less concern than vivid and proximate threats, which can delay organizational action even when the objective risk is high (Slovic, 1987). Together, these findings suggest that effective migration requires not only technical roadmaps but also communication strategies that counteract present bias and unfamiliarity by concretizing timelines and consequences for stakeholders.

## Behavioral biometrics in authentication

As documented by Teh et al. (2013), keystroke dynamics offer a mature behavioral biometric modality, whose unobtrusiveness enables continuous or step-up verification with a modest user burden. Foundational demonstrations of behavioral signals include mouse-movement re-authentication, which models individual motor patterns to detect impostors during sessions. Subsequent work generalizes this approach to multimodal continuous authentication, fusing keystroke and pointer dynamics to sustain security with minimal interruption (Mondal & Bours, 2017 Pusara & Brodley, 2004). The psychological advantage arises from leveraging habitual motor signatures that are hard to consciously spoof, although deployment must address intra-user variability, accessibility, and privacy of behavioral traces.

## Predictive models of insider threats using psychometric and behavioral data

As shown by Greitzer and colleagues, integrative models that combine cyber telemetry with psychosocial indicators can identify precursors of insider risk and support prioritization for human review. Empirical work demonstrates that linguistic markers, performance anomalies, and psychosocial stressors can be combined into risk scores, provided that governance and validation safeguards are in place to guard against false positives and unfair profiling (Greitzer et al., 2013 Greitzer et al., 2019). Complementary surveys map insider-threat taxonomies and datasets, supporting reproducible evaluation of machine-learning approaches that incorporate human factors alongside technical behavior. This literature suggests that predictive systems are most effective when embedded in organizational processes that include confidential support pathways, just culture principles, and strict data minimization policies (Al-Mhiqani et al., 2020 Homoliak et al., 2019).

Across these emerging areas, converging evidence indicates that cybersecurity outcomes depend on human cognition and organizational context as much as on algorithmic performance. Trust-aware automation design, principled explainability, and well-structured human–AI teaming can enhance detection and response without eroding oversight. Communication strategies informed by risk-perception science can accelerate post-quantum transitions. Behavioral biometrics can enhance authentication with minimal visible friction if evaluated for stability and fairness. Insider-risk prediction is feasible when psychosocial and behavioral signals are integrated under rigorous governance. Together, these lines of research outline a human-centered agenda for resilient cyber defense.

# Summary

Cyberpsychology has become essential for explaining cybersecurity outcomes through four interconnected dimensions: cognition, behavior, organizational dynamics, and societal psychology. This synthesis shows that resilience depends on human-centered design, realistic workflows, just culture leadership, and trustworthy practices that align security with how people think and act under pressure. Progress requires interdisciplinary integration of psychology, human factors engineering, and cybersecurity to link mechanisms to measurable outcomes and strengthen evidence-based governance. The next phase of the field should prioritize stronger methods, shared taxonomies and data standards, and practical translation into design, procurement, training, and policy. Overall, cyberpsychology enables a shift from tool-centric security to evidence-based socio-technical systems that improve resilience, equity, and trust.

To operationalize these insights, the next chapter, **Human Factors Analysis and Classification System (HFACS)**, provides a structured framework for identifying where and why human-related failures emerge in cybersecurity incidents.

# References


- Abuabid, A. A. (2025). A data-driven approach to cybersecurity situational awareness: Insights from machine learning. *Journal of Innovative Digital Transformation.* https://www.emerald.com/insight/content/doi/10.1108/JIDT-03-2025-0013/full/html
- Ahmad, A., Maynard, S. B., Park, S., & Park, H. (2021). How can organizations develop situation awareness for incident response? *Computers & Security*, 102, 102153.
- Ahmad, H., Ullah, F., & Jafri, R. (2025). A survey on immersive cyber situational awareness systems. *Journal of Cybersecurity and Privacy*, 5(2), 33.
- Al-Haija, Q. A. (2024). Human factors in cyber defense. In *The Art of Cyber Defense* (pp. 260–270). CRC Press.
- Alavizadeh, H., Jang-Jaccard, J., Enoch, S. Y., Al-Sahaf, H., Welch, I., Camtepe, S. A., & Kim, D. D. (2022). A survey on cyber situation-awareness systems: Framework, techniques, and insights. *ACM Computing Surveys*, 55(5), 1–37.
- Albarrak, A. M. (2024). Integration of cybersecurity, usability, and human-computer interaction for securing energy management systems. *Sustainability*, 16(18).
- Al-Hashem, N., & Saidi, A. (2023). The psychological aspect of cybersecurity: Understanding cyber threat perception and decision-making. *International Journal of Applied Machine Learning and Computational Intelligence*, 13(8), 11-22. https://student.wp.odu.edu/ihenr002/wp-content/uploads/sites/35258/2024/04/ThePsychologicalAspectofCybersecurity.pdf
- Almazrouei, S. R., Camelia, F., Leal, R., Ferris, T. L., Kaya, G. K., & Chatzimichailidou, M. (2025). Human factors integration in complex systems: Awareness, challenges, and strategies. *Ergonomics*, 1–21. https://www.tandfonline.com/doi/abs/10.1080/00140139.2025.2536543
- Almeida, J. P. C. D. (2025). Human-centered design integration on product development. https://recipp.ipp.pt/entities/publication/8776b6a6-c750-47a1-aad6-6abe189b84f2
- Al-Mhiqani, M. N., Ismail, M., Ab Manan, J. L., Anbar, M., & Al-Sarem, M. (2020). A review of insider threat detection: Classification, machine learning techniques, datasets, open challenges, and recommendations. *Applied Sciences*, 10(15), 5208. (MDPI)

- Alsharida, R. A., Al-Rimy, B. A. S., Al-Emran, M., & Zainal, A. (2023). A systematic review of multi-perspectives on human cybersecurity behavior. *Technology in Society*, 73, 102258.
- Ancis, J. R. (2020). The age of cyberpsychology: An overview. Technology, Mind, and Behavior, 1(1). `https://tmb.apaopen.org/pub/2yn6jhyv/release/1`
- Ask, T. F. (2024). Neuroergonomic approaches to understanding and improving communication of recognized cyber threat situations. `https://ntnuopen.ntnu.no/ntnu-xmlui/handle/11250/3136538`
- Ask, T. F., Knox, B. J., Lugo, R. G., Helgetun, I., & Sütterlin, S. (2023). Neurophysiological and emotional influences on team communication and metacognitive cyber situational awareness during a cyber engineering exercise. Frontiers in Human Neuroscience, 16, 1092056. `https://www.frontiersin.org/articles/10.3389/fnhum.2022.1092056/full`
- Ask, T. F., Knox, B. J., Lugo, R. G., Hoffmann, L., & Sütterlin, S. (2023, June). Gamification as a neuroergonomic approach to improving interpersonal situational awareness in cyber defense. *In Frontiers in Education* (Vol. 8, p. 988043). Frontiers Media S.A.
- Ask, T. F., Knox, B. J., Lugo, R. G., Hoffmann, L., & Sütterlin, S. (2023, June). Gamification as a neuroergonomic approach to improving interpersonal situational awareness in cyber defense. *In Frontiers in Education* (Vol. 8, p. 988043). Frontiers Media SA.
- Ask, T. F., Knox, B. J., Lugo, R. G., Hoffmann, L., Sütterlin, S., & Ask, T. F. (2021). A gamification approach to improving interpersonal situational awareness in cyber defense. *PsyArXiv*, 2021, 2-18. `https://osf.io/preprints/psyarxiv/c95kw/download/`
- Ayanbode, N., Abieba, O. A., Chukwurah, N., Ajayi, O. O., & Ifesinachi, A. (2024). Human factors in fintech cybersecurity: Addressing insider threats and behavioral risks. *Journal of Cybersecurity in FinTech*, 14(2), 34–49.
- Baddeley, A. (2012). Working memory: Theories, models, and controversies. *Annual Review of Psychology*, 63(1), 1–29.
- Bakshy, E., Messing, S., & Adamic, L. A. (2015). Exposure to ideologically diverse news and opinion on Facebook. Science, 348(6239), 1130–1132. `https://doi.org/10.1126/science.aaa1160`

- Ban, T., Samuel, N., Takahashi, T., & Inoue, D. (2021, August). Combat security alert fatigue with AI-assisted techniques. In Proceedings of the 14th Cyber Security Experimentation and Test Workshop (pp. 9–16).
- Ben-Asher, N., Oltramari, A., Erbacher, R. F., & Gonzalez, C. (2015). Ontology-based adaptive systems of cyber defense. In Proceedings of STIDS (pp. 1–8). (CEUR-WS)
- Biondi, F. N. (2024). Adopting stimulus detection tasks for cognitive workload assessment: Some considerations. Human Factors, 66(12), 2561–2568.
- Bone, J. (2024). Cognition in Cybersecurity Situational Awareness. Cognitive risk institute, 1(1), 10-13140. `https://www.researchgate.net/profile/James-Bone-6/publication/379076804_Cognition_in_Cybersecurity_Situational_Awareness/links/65f9c7f7a4857c796260cdd7/Cognition-in-Cybersecurity-Situational-Awareness.pdf`
- Bone, J. (2024). Cognition in cybersecurity situational awareness. Cognitive Risk Institute, 1(1), 10-13140.
- Boss, S. R., Galletta, D. F., Lowry, P. B., Moody, G. D., and Polak, P. (2015). What do systems users have to fear? Using fear appeals to engender threats and fear that motivate protective security behaviors. MIS Quarterly, 39(4), 837-864.
- Centola, D. (2010). The spread of behavior in an online social network experiment. Science, 329(5996), 1194–1197. `https://doi.org/10.1126/science.1185231`
- Chadwick, S., Montague, A., & Patel, R. (2023). User password behavior and cybersecurity risks. Cybersecurity Journal, 8(1), 55–70.
- Cialdini, R. B. (2009). Influence: Science and practice (5th ed.). Pearson.
- Cowan, N. (2001). The magical number 4 in short-term memory: A reconsideration of mental storage capacity. Behavioral and Brain Sciences, 24(1), 87–114.
- Cristescu, I., Ciupercă, E. M., & Cîrnu, C. E. (2022). Exploiting personality traits in social engineering attacks. Romanian Journal of Information Technology & Automatic Control, 32(1). `https://rria.ici.ro/documents/89/art._Cristescu_Ciuperc%C4%83_C%C3%AErnu.pdf`
- Davis, F. D. (1989). Perceived usefulness, perceived ease of use, and user acceptance of information technology. MIS Quarterly, 13(3), 319–340.
- Debb, S. M. (2021). Keeping the human in the loop: Awareness and recognition of cybersecurity within cyberpsychology. Cyberpsychology, Behavior, and Social Networking, 24(9), 581–583.

- Del Vicario, M., Bessi, A., Zollo, F., Petroni, F., Scala, A., Caldarelli, G., ... Quattrociocchi, W. (2016). The spreading of misinformation online. Proceedings of the National Academy of Sciences, 113(3), 554–559. https://doi.org/10.1073/pnas.1517441113
- Dupont, B., Shearing, C., Bernier, M., and Leukfeldt, R. (2023). The tensions of cyber-resilience: From sensemaking to practice. Computers & Security, 132, 103372.
- Enders, A., & Kreutzer, K. (2022). Risk fatigue in the digital age: Why users ignore cyber alerts. Information Security Review, 7(3), 210–223.
- Endsley, M. R. (1995). Toward a theory of situation awareness in dynamic systems. Human Factors, 37(1), 32–64.
- Endsley, M. R. (2017). From here to autonomy: Lessons learned from human–automation research for human–autonomy teams. Human Factors, 59(1), 5–27.
- Endsley, M. R. (2021). Situational awareness. Handbook of Human Factors and Ergonomics, 434–455.
- Fatima, F., Hyatt, J. C., Rehman, S. U., De La Cruz, E., Nadella, G. S., & Meduri, K. (2024). Resilience and risk management in cybersecurity: A grounded theory study of emotional, psychological, and organizational dynamics. Journal of Economy and Technology, 2, 247–257.
- Franke, U. (2014). Cyber situational awareness: A systematic review of the literature. Computers & Security, 46, 18–31. (ScienceDirect)
- Gaia, J., Ramamurthy, B., Sanders, G., Sanders, S., Upadhyaya, S., Wang, X., & Yoo, C. (2020). Psychological profiling of hacking potential. https://scholarspace.manoa.hawaii.edu/bitstream/10125/64014/1/0220.pdf
- Gaia, J., Sanders, G., Sanders, S., Upadhyaya, S., Wang, X., & Woo, C. (2021). Dark traits and hacking potential. Journal of Organizational Psychology, 21(3). https://par.nsf.gov/servlets/purl/10335905
- Gigerenzer, G., Todd, P. M., & ABC Research Group. (2000). *Simple heuristics that make us smart.* Oxford University Press.
- Greitzer, F. L., Carroll, T. E., & Roberts, J. C. (2019). Design and implementation of a comprehensive insider threat framework. Procedia Computer Science, 152, 47–54. (ScienceDirect)
- Greitzer, F. L., Kangas, L. J., Noonan, C. F., Brown, C. R., & Ferryman, T. (2013). Psychosocial modeling of insider threat risk based on behavioral and word-use analysis. e-Service Journal, 9(1), 106–138. (ResearchGate)
- Groen, E. C., Feth, D., Polst, S., Tolsdorf, J., Wiefling, S., Iacono, L. L., & Schmitt, H. (2023). Achieving usable security and privacy through human-centered design. In

Human factors in privacy research (pp. 83–113). Springer. https://library.oapen.org/bitstream/handle/20.500.12657/76226/1/978-3-031-28643-8.pdf#page=90

- Guidetti, O. A., Harris, C., Devine, A., & Strickland, L. (2023). The Western Australian Cyber Defense Task: A modern vigilance task for network defense. Frontiers in Psychology, 14, 1270970 (PMC).
- Guess, A., Nagler, J., & Tucker, J. (2019). Less than one percent of Twitter users produce 80 percent of fake news exposure. Science Advances, 5(1), eaau4586. https://doi.org/10.1126/sciadv.aau4586
- Guess, A. M., Nyhan, B., & Reifler, J. (2020). Exposure to untrustworthy websites in the 2016 U.S. election. *Proceedings of the National Academy of Sciences*, 117(27), 16819–16824.
- Hadlington, L., & Ryding, C. (2025). Human factors and cybersecurity: The psychology of online safety and security. Taylor & Francis.
- Hancock, P. A., Billings, D. R., Schaefer, K. E., et al. (2011). A meta-analysis of factors affecting trust in human–robot interaction. Human Factors, 53(5), 517–527. (PubMed)
- Hani, U., Sohaib, O., Khan, K., Aleidi, A., & Islam, N. (2024). Psychological profiling of hackers via machine learning toward sustainable cybersecurity. *Frontiers in Computer Science*, 6, 1381351. https://www.frontiersin.org/articles/10.3389/fcomp.2024.1381351/full
- Hare, R. D. (1999). Without Conscience: The Disturbing World of the Psychopaths Among Us. Guilford Press.
- Hijji, M., Qureshi, B., & Zaman, F. (2021). A multivocal literature review on growing social engineering during the COVID-19 pandemic. *IEEE Access*, 9, 155013–155038. https://doi.org/10.1109/ACCESS.2021.3127172
- Homoliak, I., Toffalini, F., Guarnizo, J. D., Elovici, Y., & Ochoa, M. (2019). The insider threat survey: Definitions, taxonomies, modeling, and countermeasures. *ACM Computing Surveys*, 52(6), Article 112. (arXiv)
- Jane, E. A. (2014). "Back to the kitchen, cunt": Speaking the unspeakable about online misogyny. *Continuum*, 28(4), 558–570. https://doi.org/10.1080/10304312.2014.924479
- Jensen, R., Li, X., & Mahoney, J. (2022). Effective cybersecurity training: A role-specific approach. *Journal of Cyber Education*, 4(2), 19–34.
- Jones, A., & Smith, B. (2024). Usability-centric security governance and organizational compliance outcomes. *Journal of Information Security Management*, 12(3), 145–168.

- Kang, R., Dabbish, L., Fruchter, N., & Kiesler, S. (2022). My data just goes everywhere: Understanding the cognitive burden of security tasks. *Proceedings of the ACM on Human-Computer Interaction*, 6(CSCW2), 1–27.
- Karwowski, W., Salvendy, G., Endsley, M., Rouse, W., Salmon, P., Stanney, K., ... Stanton, N. (2025). Grand challenges for human factors and ergonomics. *Theoretical Issues in Ergonomics Science*, 26(4), 361–456. https://www.tandfonline.com/doi/abs/10.1080/1463922X.2024.2431336
- Khadka, K., & Ullah, A. B. (2025). Human factors in cybersecurity: An interdisciplinary review and framework proposal. *International Journal of Information Security*, 24(3), 1–13.
- Kowalski, R. M., Giumetti, G. W., Schroeder, A. N., & Lattanner, M. R. (2014). Bullying in the digital age: A critical review and meta-analysis of cyberbullying research among youth. *Psychological Bulletin*, 140(4), 1073–1137. https://doi.org/10.1037/a0035618
- Kumaran, D. N. (2025). Psychological profiling of cybercriminals in high-profile cases: A digital forensic approach.
- Lee, J. D., & See, K. A. (2004). Trust in automation: Designing for appropriate reliance. *Human Factors*, 46(1), 50–80. (PubMed)
- Leichtmann, B., Verma, S., & Benlian, A. (2023). Effects of explainable artificial intelligence on trust and human–AI interaction. *Computers in Human Behavior*, 141, 107626. (ScienceDirect)
- Lewandowsky, S., Ecker, U. K. H., & Cook, J. (2017). Beyond misinformation: Understanding and coping with the "post-truth" era. *Journal of Applied Research in Memory and Cognition*, 6(4), 353–369.
- Linkov, I., & Kott, A. (2019). Fundamental concepts of cyber resilience: Introduction and overview. Springer Series in Reliability Engineering, 1–25. https://doi.org/10.1007/978-3-319-77492-3_1
- Lyons, J. B., Wynne, K. T., Mahoney, S., & Capiola, A. (2021). Human–autonomy teaming: Definitions, debates, and directions. *Frontiers in Psychology*, 12, 589585. (PMC)
- Miller, T. (2019). Explanation in artificial intelligence: Insights from the social sciences. *Artificial Intelligence*, 267, 1–38. (ScienceDirect)
- Mondal, S., & Bours, P. (2017). A study on continuous authentication using a combination of keystroke and mouse biometrics. *Neurocomputing*, 230, 1–22. (ACM Digital Library)
- Monteiro, J. A. L. G., Ramamurthy, B., Sanders, G. L., Sanders, S., Upadhyaya, S., Wang, X., & Yoo, C. (2020). Psychological profiling of hacking potential.

- Mosca, M. (2018). Cybersecurity in an era with quantum computers: Will we be ready? *IEEE Security & Privacy*, 16(5), 38–41. (ACM Digital Library)
- Moustafa, A. A., Bello, A., & Maurushat, A. (2021). The role of user behaviour in improving cyber security management. *Frontiers in Psychology*, 12, 561011.
- Muchnik, L., Aral, S., & Taylor, S. J. (2013). Social influence bias: A randomized experiment. *Science*, 341(6146), 647–651.
- Nassir, N. F. M., Rauf, U. F. A., Zainol, Z., & Ghani, K. A. (2024). Revealing the multi-perspective factors behind insider threats in cybersecurity.
- Nifakos, S., Chandramouli, K., Nikolaou, C. K., Papachristou, P., Koch, S., Panaousis, E., & Bonacina, S. (2021). Influence of human factors on cybersecurity within healthcare organisations: A systematic review. *Sensors*, 21(15), 5119.
- Norris, F. H., Stevens, S. P., Pfefferbaum, B., Wyche, K. F., & Pfefferbaum, R. L. (2008). Community resilience as a metaphor, theory, set of capacities, and strategy for disaster readiness. *American Journal of Community Psychology*, 41(1–2), 127–150. https://doi.org/10.1007/s10464-007-9156-6
- O'Malley, M. T. (2025). Supporting the Navy through model-based systems engineering: The development of a human factors and ergonomics framework for unmanned surface vehicles (Master's thesis, Purdue University).
- O'Neill, T. A., McNeese, N. J., Barron, A. G., & Schelble, B. G. (2020). Human–autonomy teaming: A review and analysis of the empirical literature. *Frontiers in Psychology*, 11, 2212. (PMC)
- Pennycook, G., & Rand, D. G. (2019). Lazy, not biased: Susceptibility to partisan fake news is better explained by lack of reasoning than by motivated reasoning. *Cognition*, 188, 39–50.
- Postmes, T., Spears, R., & Lea, M. (1998). Breaching or building social boundaries? SIDE effects of computer-mediated communication. *Communication Research*, 25(6), 689–715. https://doi.org/10.1177/009365098025006006
- Prümmer, J., van Steen, T., & van den Berg, B. (2024). A systematic review of current cybersecurity training methods. *Computers & Security*, 136, 103585.
- Pusara, M., & Brodley, C. E. (2004). User re-authentication via mouse movements. In Proceedings of the 2004 ACM Workshop on Visualization and Data Mining for Computer Security (pp. 1–8).
- Raywood-Burke, G. (2023). Cognitive load and subjective time pressure: How contextual factors impact the quality of cybersecurity decision making (Doctoral dissertation, Cardiff University). https://orca.cardiff.ac.uk/id/eprint/169273/

- Reeves, A., et al. (2023). Understanding decision making in security operations and the barriers to cyber deception. *Frontiers in Psychology*, 14, 1165705.
- Ribeiro, M. T., Singh, S., & Guestrin, C. (2016). "Why should I trust you?" Explaining the predictions of any classifier. In Proceedings of KDD 2016 (pp. 1135–1144).
- Roozenbeek, J., & van der Linden, S. (2019). Fake news game confers psychological resistance against online misinformation. *Palgrave Communications*, 5(65), 1–10. `https://doi.org/10.1057/s41599-019-0279-9`
- Sachs, D. S. (2025). Behavioral insights in cybersecurity: A guide to digital human factors. CRC Press.
- Salvendy, G. (Ed.). (2012). Handbook of human factors and ergonomics. John Wiley & Sons.
- Sandoval Rodríguez-Bermejo, D., Maestre Vidal, J., & Estévez Tapiador, J. (2021, August). Stress as an adversarial factor for cyber decision making. In Proceedings of the 16th *International Conference on Availability, Reliability and Security* (pp. 1–10). `https://dl.acm.org/doi/abs/10.1145/3465481.3470047`
- Schaefer, K. E., Chen, J. Y., Szalma, J. L., & Hancock, P. A. (2016). A meta-analysis of factors influencing the development of trust in automation. *Human Factors*, 58(3), 377–411.
- Sharpe, B. T. (2025). The sustained attention paradox: A critical commentary and synthesis. *Psychological* Review (advance online).
- Sharp, H., Preece, J., & Rogers, Y. (2019). Interaction design: Beyond human–computer interaction (5th ed.). Wiley.
- Siddiqi, M. A., Pak, W., & Siddiqi, M. A. (2022). A study on the psychology of social engineering-based cyberattacks and existing countermeasures. *Applied Sciences*, 12(12), 6042.
- Singh, T. (2025). Psychology and its impact on cybersecurity. In Cybersecurity, Psychology and People Hacking (pp. 29–41). Cham: Springer Nature Switzerland.
- Suler, J. (2004). The online disinhibition effect. *CyberPsychology & Behavior*, 7(3), 321–326.
- Sweller, J. (2011). Cognitive load theory. In Psychology of Learning and Motivation (Vol. 55, pp. 37–76). Academic Press.
- Tariq, S., Baruwal Chhetri, M., Nepal, S., & Paris, C. (2025). Alert fatigue in security operations centers: Research challenges and opportunities. *ACM Computing Surveys*, 57(9), 1-38.

- Taylor, J., & Whitty, M. (2024). An exploration of the awareness and attitudes of psychology students regarding their psychological literacy for working in the cybersecurity industry. *Psychology Learning & Teaching*, 23(2), 298–314.
- Teh, P. S., Zhang, N., Teoh, A. B. J., & Chen, K. (2013). A survey of keystroke dynamics biometrics. *Scientific World Journal*, 2013, 408280. (PubMed)
- Veksler, V. D., Buchler, N., Bickel, J., & Martin, J. M. (2020). Cognitive models in cybersecurity: Learning from expert hackers. *Frontiers in Psychology*, 11, 1490. (PMC)
- Warm, J. S., Parasuraman, R., & Matthews, G. (2008). Vigilance requires hard mental work and is stressful. *Human Factors*, 50(3), 433–441. (SAGE Journals)
- Washo, A. H. (2021). An interdisciplinary view of social engineering: A call to action for research. Computers in Human Behavior Reports, 4, 100126.
- Weickert, T. D., Joinson, A., & Craggs, B. (2023). Is cybersecurity research missing a trick? Integrating insights from the psychology of habit into research and practice. *Computers & Security*, 128, 103130.
- Wickens, C. D., Hollands, J. G., Banbury, S., & Parasuraman, R. (2013). Engineering psychology and human performance (4th ed.). Psychology Press.
- Wilson, J. R. (2014). Fundamentals of systems ergonomics/human factors. *Applied Ergonomics*, 45(1), 5–13.
- Woods, N., & Siponen, M. (2024). How memory anxiety can influence password security behavior. *Computers & Security*, 137, 103589. (ScienceDirect)
- Zaid, T., Alenezi, M., Jaradat, R., & Alshamrani, A. (2024). Emerging trends in cybersecurity: A holistic view on challenges and solutions. *IEEE Access*, 12, 10412–10445. (PMC)
- Zimmermann, V., et al. (2022). Hybrid password meters for more secure passwords: A comprehensive study of password meters including nudges and guidance. *Behaviour & Information Technology*, 41(14), 3044–3068. (Strathprints)

# Get this book's PDF version and more

Scan the QR code (or go to `packtpub.com/unlock`). Search for this book by name, confirm the edition, and then follow the steps on the page.

UNLOCK NOW

*Note: Keep your invoice handy. Purchases made directly from Packt don't require an invoice.*

# 9

# Benefits of Human Factors Analysis and Classification System in Cybersecurity

Human-factors breakdowns are a significant contributor to adverse cybersecurity outcomes across sectors, frequently precipitating incidents, attacks, breaches, and errors. Human factors breakdowns are failures in the interaction among people, technology, tasks, and organizational processes that increase the risk of cybersecurity errors, incidents, and breaches. This concept emphasizes that many cybersecurity failures are not solely technical problems or individual mistakes but result from poorly aligned system conditions that shape human performance. One example is a phishing attack in which an employee clicks a malicious link while under time pressure and cognitive overload. Another example is cloud misconfiguration in which an administrator accidentally exposes data because security settings are confusing or difficult to navigate. In both cases, the breakdown reflects human-system design and organizational conditions, not only personal error.

To address this challenge, the **Human Factors Analysis and Classification System** (**HFACS**), grounded in Reason's barrier-based "*Swiss-cheese*" model of organizational accidents, offers a rigorous multi-level taxonomy for converting narrative incident accounts into analyzable causal structures. Reason's **Swiss-cheese model** of organizational accidents is shown in *Figure 9.1*:

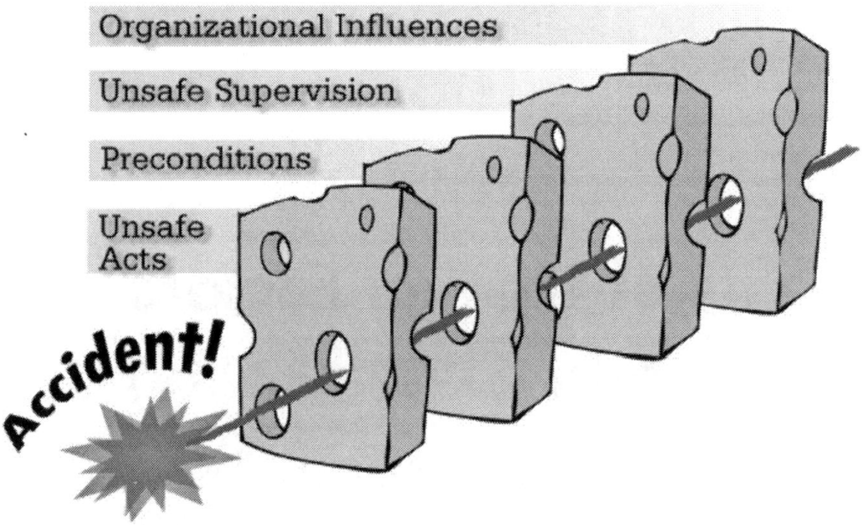


*Figure 9.1: Swiss-cheese model (Source: https://hfacs-healthcare.com/the-hfacs-framework/)*

This model promotes a systems perspective, viewing human error not as the root cause but as a symptom of deeper organizational conditions. Within this framework, organizations implement multiple defensive barriers across technology, procedures, supervision, and governance. These barriers are structured in a sequential manner, with higher-level influences shaping lower-level behaviors. Failures at any level create vulnerabilities, either active, occurring close to the event, or latent, stemming from distant conditions that can align across layers to produce adverse outcomes. The Swiss Cheese model is applicable to cybersecurity by providing a methodology to understand how latent and active failures lead to catastrophic events in cybersecurity. A latent failure is a hidden system weakness, such as poor design, weak policy, or inadequate training, that creates conditions for error. An active failure is the immediate human error or unsafe action, such as clicking a malicious link or misconfiguring a system, that directly contributes to an incident. The Swiss Cheese model will be explained in more depth in the chapter.

This chapter provides a comprehensive review for applying HFACS to cybersecurity operations, including its definition, scope, origin, and theoretical foundations. It details the system's four-level structure and introduces an expanded, domain-specific treatment of layers and associated nanocodes tailored to digital environments such as **security operations centers (SOCs)**, **identity and access management (IAM)**, software delivery pipelines, cloud and **operational technology (OT)** systems, and higher-education enterprises. The application of HFACS enables consistent post-incident analysis, cross-case trend discovery, and targeted, system-level interventions, emphasizing prevention and a just culture over blame.

By the end of this chapter, readers will be able to explain how HFACS strengthens cybersecurity by providing a structured, evidence-based framework for identifying, classifying, and mitigating human, supervisory, and organizational contributors to cyber incidents. In this chapter, we will cover the following topics:

- What is HFACS?
- The need for HFACS in cybersecurity
- HFACS theoretical foundations
- Error science
- Enabling a blame-free culture
- HFACS and risk management
- Structure of HFACS: four cascading levels
- Need for a modified HFACS-Cyber framework

# What is HFACS?

HFACS is a human factors framework used to analyze how multiple layers of failure contribute to accidents by exploring the adverse outcomes. HFACS is a hierarchical, evidence-oriented taxonomy that classifies contributory factors to adverse events across four cascading levels:

- Unsafe Acts (Example: An employee clicks a phishing link)
- Preconditions for Unsafe Acts (Example: The employee is fatigued and managing too many tasks)
- Supervisory Factors (Example: The team did not receive updated phishing training)
- Organizational Influences (Example: Leadership underfunded security awareness and staffing)

The HFACS preserves causal coherence by requiring analysts to connect what a person directly did at the time of the incident to the immediate conditions that influenced that action, and then to the relevant supervisory and organizational drivers, rather than skipping levels and making unsupported causal claims. This structured analytic discipline converts complex incident narratives into consistent, comparable data, which helps identify latent conditions, recurring control weaknesses, and patterns of systemic drift over time (Larouzee & Le Coze, 2020 Perneger, 2005 Reason, 1990 Wiegmann & Shappell, 2022). For example, in a phishing-related credential compromise, the analyst would not stop at the employee clicking the malicious link. Using HFACS, the analysis would trace that action to immediate conditions such as cognitive overload and email ambiguity, then to supervisory factors such as outdated awareness training, and finally to organizational influences such as understaffing and weak investment in secure communication tools. This produces a more accurate explanation of the breach and a stronger basis for prevention.

Contemporary applications in cybersecurity extend the same logic to digital operations with high cognitive load, complex interfaces, and distributed authority structures (Wiegmann & Shappell, 2022). Codified subcategories at the "sharp end," including skill-based errors, decision errors, perceptual errors, and procedural or exceptional violations, are analytically linked to preconditions such as fatigue and interface affordances, to supervisory practices such as planning assumptions and oversight bandwidth, and to organizational determinants such as resource allocation, climate, and process design. This principle protects explanatory integrity, supports inter-rater reliability, and reduces hindsight bias by binding each inference to contemporaneous artifacts such as change records, staffing rosters, and interface captures (Wiegmann & Shappell, 2022).

# The need for HFACS in cybersecurity

HFACS is needed in cybersecurity because incidents are rarely caused by a single user mistake or technical failure. It provides a structured way to examine what a person did during an incident, the immediate conditions that shaped that action, and the supervisory and organizational factors that made the event more likely. This prevents oversimplified explanations, reduces blame-focused analysis, and helps organizations identify deeper systemic weaknesses that repeatedly contribute to breaches. By organizing incident data in a consistent way, HFACS also makes it easier to compare cases, detect patterns, and design stronger prevention strategies across people, processes, and technology. Additionally, HFACS can be used to prevent further incidents by assessing the data and mitigating weaknesses in the defensive layers.

# HFACS theoretical foundations

Safety-science syntheses further differentiate active failures at the operational "sharp end" from latent conditions embedded within supervision and organizational structures at the "blunt end" (Larouzee & Le Coze, 2020 Perneger, 2005), a distinction that contemporary expositions of the HFACS reinforce in favor of organizational learning over individual fault (Wiegmann & Shappell, 2022). Defensive layers include technology configurations, procedural controls, training and staffing arrangements, supervisory oversight, and organizational governance.

Building on this architecture, HFACS translates the conceptual account into a practicable, evidence-driven taxonomy that preserves causal adjacency across four levels: (a) Unsafe Acts, (b) Preconditions for Unsafe Acts, (c) Supervisory Factors, and (d) Organizational Influences (Wiegmann & Shappell, 2022). Adjacency requires disciplined tracing from observed actions to immediately adjacent preconditions, and then to supervisory and organizational contributors, without speculative tier-jumping directly from frontline behavior to board-level causation (Larouzee & Le Coze, 2020 Perneger, 2005).

Critiques of the Swiss-Model caution that frameworks such as HFACS should not be used as if they can identify one clear and final cause of an incident (Larouzee & Le Coze, 2020 Perneger, 2005). Instead, HFACS is better understood as an inquiry scaffold, or a structured way to guide analysis across different parts of a system. Think of it as an investigative process to uncover fundamental causes of a significant data breach or cyber attack at different levels in the organization. This is important in cybersecurity because incidents rarely result from a single error. More often, they emerge from a combination of technical, human, supervisory, and organizational factors that interact over time. When used in this way, HFACS helps analysts ask better questions, look beyond blame, and identify patterns of weakness across the system. This leads to stronger root-cause analysis and more effective corrective actions. In cybersecurity, the Swiss Cheese Model is especially useful because it shows how breaches can occur when multiple layers of defense fail at the same time. Rather than blaming one user mistake or one failed control, the model encourages analysts to examine how factors such as workload pressure, misaligned workflows, weak supervision, policy drift, and under-resourced security controls combine to create a path to harm. This systems-based view is highly relevant in cybersecurity settings, where alert saturation, configuration debt, unclear shared-responsibility models, and release schedules that move faster than risk checks can increase the chance that several defenses will fail together rather than separately (Wiegmann & Shappell, 2022 Larouzee & Le Coze, 2020 Perneger, 2005). A socio-technical interpretation extends the barrier model by recognizing joint causation across people, processes, technologies, and organizational contexts. Under this lens, Unsafe Acts frequently reflect reasonable local adaptations to workload and tooling constraints; Preconditions often encode cognitive load, handoff frictions, and interface affordances. Supervisory Factors capture planning assumptions, exception management, and oversight bandwidth. Organizational Influences capture resourcing, climate, and governance patterns (Wiegmann & Shappell, 2022). The HFACS linkage of each stratum to concrete evidence converts narrative incident accounts into analyzable structures that expose patterns of latent conditions and inform system-level interventions (Perneger, 2005).

Applying HFACS in cybersecurity requires a practical approach that focuses on what should be measured, how evidence should be analyzed, and how lessons learned should be used to strengthen the system (Larouzee & Le Coze, 2020 Perneger, 2005 Wiegmann & Shappell, 2022). First, analysis should extend beyond technical controls alone and also examine human and organizational factors, such as workload, usability, training, communication handoffs, and governance. Second, investigators should trace incidents step by step across system levels rather than jumping too quickly to high-level conclusions, making sure to show how unsafe actions connect to preconditions, supervisory issues, and organizational influences. Third, HFACS should support continuous learning by turning recurring patterns into corrective action, such as redesigning controls, updating runbooks, adjusting staffing, strengthening incentives, and improving vendor oversight. In this way, HFACS becomes not just a classification tool, but a structured method for understanding and reducing cybersecurity risk.

In summary, Reason's barrier theory supplies the causal architecture for understanding organizational accidents (Reason, 1990), and the Human Factors Analysis and Classification System supplies the operational discipline for evidentiary analysis and prevention (Wiegmann & Shappell, 2022). Together, these perspectives elevate analysis from person-centric error narratives to socio-technical causation (Larouzee & Le Coze, 2020 Perneger, 2005), preserve rigor through causal adjacency, and enable prevention by revealing modifiable latent conditions across supervision and organizational governance. In cybersecurity, this error-science foundation is especially important because incidents that appear to result from isolated user actions often emerge from deeper interactions among workload, tool design, supervisory practices, and organizational controls.

## Error science

Error science is the systematic, interdisciplinary study of human, organizational, and system errors, focusing on their causes, patterns, and prevention mechanisms (Reason, 1990; Dekker, 2014 Hollnagel, 2017). It seeks to explain why errors occur, how they propagate through complex sociotechnical systems, and how their consequences can be mitigated or eliminated through design, training, and policy interventions (Reason, 1990; Hollnagel, 2017). By integrating multiple disciplines, error science provides a structured framework to shift attention from individual blame to systemic understanding, thereby supporting proactive strategies to enhance safety and performance.

Error science examines human error as a predictable and analyzable phenomenon rather than a random or purely individual failure (Reason, 1990 Dekker, 2014). The field integrates human factors engineering, cognitive psychology, systems engineering, safety science, and organizational behavior to develop evidence-based models for identifying and managing error pathways (Reason, 1990; Hollnagel, 2017). Some examples of evidence-based models mitigating error pathways include the HFACS, which classifies contributing factors across human, supervisory, and organizational levels; the Swiss Cheese Model, which explains how harm occurs when multiple defenses fail in alignment; and the **Systems-theoretic accident model and processes / systems-theoretic process analysis (STAMP/STPA)**, which examines failures in control and feedback within complex systems. Other examples include the **functional resonance analysis method (FRAM)**, which analyzes how normal work variability can combine into failure, and Bayesian network models, which estimate the probability of error pathways and incident outcomes. In cybersecurity, these models help identify and manage pathways such as cloud misconfiguration, delayed escalation, and access-control failure. Central to this approach is the recognition of systemic causation and the importance of latent conditions that shape the environment in which active errors occur. This perspective underscores error management strategies rather than punitive measures, thereby encouraging organizational learning and resilience (Dekker, 2014 Hollnagel, 2017).

Human error is defined as unintended actions or decisions that deviate from expected performance or procedures, and is commonly categorized into slips, lapses, mistakes, and violations (Dekker, 2014 Reason, 1990). Latent conditions refer to system-level weaknesses, such as poor procedures, inadequate supervision, or flawed interfaces, that create fertile conditions for active errors (Reason, 1990). Error management emphasizes detection, containment, and organizational learning, recognizing that not all errors can be prevented. This aligns with resilience-oriented approaches (Dekker, 2014 Hollnagel, 2017). Systemic causation captures the emergence of errors from the interaction of technology, processes, environments, and human cognition, consistent with systems and resilience perspectives (Hollnagel, 2017 Reason, 1990).

A foundational influence on error science is the Swiss Cheese Model, which conceptualizes accidents or incidents as the alignment of multiple latent and active failures across defensive layers (Reason, 1990). This model shifts the analytic focus from individual culpability to systemic vulnerability, emphasizing that errors are symptoms of deeper system flaws rather than isolated acts. This conceptual shift has informed modern safety and reliability engineering practices across numerous high-risk domains. A cybersecurity example is a ransomware incident through remote access. An attacker gains access by reusing a password on a remote desktop service. The breach is not caused by a single failure. It occurs because multiple defenses fail in alignment, such as weak password practices, no multi-factor authentication, delayed patching, limited network segmentation, and inadequate monitoring. In Swiss Cheese terms, the ransomware attack succeeds because the gaps in several layers line up at the same time.

## Applications across domains

Applications of error science span multiple critical industries and contexts. In aviation and aerospace, error science informs accident investigation and pilot training programs (Shappell & Wiegmann, 2017). In healthcare, it supports patient safety initiatives and medication error reduction strategies (Reason, 1990 Hollnagel, 2017). Within the nuclear power sector and other high-reliability operations, it provides tools for preventing cascading system failures (Hollnagel, 2017). Cybersecurity incident analysis increasingly draws upon error science to understand how human errors intersect with technical vulnerabilities (Dekker, 2014 Hollnagel,

2017), while manufacturing and transportation systems apply error science to enhance reliability and operational safety (Reason, 1990).

Within cybersecurity, error science provides a structured analytical lens for understanding how human behaviors, such as misconfigurations, phishing susceptibility, and policy violations, intersect with technical vulnerabilities (Dekker, 2014 Hollnagel, 2017 Shappell & Wiegmann, 2017). Applying error taxonomies allows analysts to identify error-prone scenarios and design proactive mitigations that enhance organizational resilience. By framing cybersecurity incidents as systemic failures rather than individual lapses, error science supports more effective defense strategies, risk management, and the integration of human factors into technical and procedural security architectures.

## Methodological tools

A variety of methodological tools help translate error science principles into practical ways of studying, classifying, and reducing failure in complex systems. One of the most widely used is the HFACS, which provides a structured taxonomy for examining how unsafe actions, preconditions, supervisory issues, and organizational influences contribute to incidents (Shappell & Wiegmann, 2017). In practice, HFACS helps investigators move beyond blaming a single individual by showing how errors often emerge from interacting conditions across multiple levels of the system. In cybersecurity, for example, HFACS can help analysts examine not only a mistaken click or misconfiguration, but also the surrounding factors such as alert fatigue, inadequate training, weak supervision, or policy gaps that made the error more likely.

Other tools complement this systems-based approach. **Failure mode and effects analysis (FMEA)** is used to identify where a process, technology, or workflow might fail and to prioritize those risks before harm occurs (Reason, 1990). This makes it especially useful for prospective risk management, such as evaluating vulnerabilities in authentication workflows, incident response procedures, or cloud access controls. Root cause analysis is more retrospective and is used after an event to trace how an incident occurred and to uncover deeper latent conditions rather than stopping at the most visible error (Reason, 1990). Event and resilience analyses extend this perspective by examining how systems respond under stress, variability, and disruption, with attention not only to failure but also to adaptation and recovery (Hollnagel, 2017). Collectively, these tools support both backward-looking learning from incidents and forward-looking efforts to strengthen system design, decision-making, and organizational resilience. It is important to highlight that while this chapter focuses on HFACS, there are other tools, such as root cause analysis and FMEA, that are just as helpful. However, HFACS provides a means of thoroughly examining latent and active failures across the organization to prevent future incidents and attacks and to strengthen the organization's cybersecurity defense posture.

The strategic goal of error science is not to eliminate error entirely, a fundamentally infeasible objective, but to understand, predict, and manage it effectively (Reason, 1990 Dekker, 2014 Hollnagel, 2017). This involves designing resilient systems that anticipate and absorb human variability, building feedback loops for learning from incidents and near misses, and enhancing human performance through training, automation support, and cognitive engineering. Such a framework creates robust socio-technical systems capable of sustaining performance under dynamic and uncertain conditions.

# Enabling a blame-free culture

The concept of blame in cybersecurity constitutes a critical and often contentious domain with substantial implications for an organization's overall security posture. Although assigning accountability remains necessary for governance and compliance, a punitive blame culture is widely regarded as detrimental to effective security management. Emphasizing culpability over causation narrows organizational attention to isolated missteps and obscures the complex socio-technical conditions that enable incidents.

A blame-focused internal culture actively harms security outcomes in several ways. Fear of punishment discourages prompt reporting of mistakes, such as clicking a phishing link, thereby delaying detection and containment, and increasing the severity and cost of breaches. Fixation on the individual who erred diverts inquiry from systemic contributors, including inadequate training, ambiguous or conflicting policies, technical vulnerabilities, and flawed security architectures. When prevention yields to punishment, organizational learning stalls. Diminished psychological safety further suppresses the surfacing of weak signals and constructive suggestions, as personnel seek to avoid reputational harm or perceived incompetence rather than engage in candid disclosure.

A **blame-free** or **Just Culture** offers a constructive alternative, drawing on practices from high-reliability sectors such as aviation and healthcare. The central aim following an incident is rigorous learning: understanding why the failure occurred and implementing design, process, and policy changes that reduce the likelihood and impact of recurrence. A Just Culture distinguishes human error, an inevitable byproduct of complex work, from malicious, reckless, or intentionally non-compliant behavior that warrants disciplinary response. Within this framework, employees are not penalized for honest mistakes, while organizational leadership retains accountability for providing usable systems, adequate training, clear procedures, and resources that enable secure performance. A concise cybersecurity example of Just Culture is a cloud administrator who accidentally exposes a storage bucket during a rushed deployment. Instead of only blaming the administrator, the organization examines the full context, including workload, interface complexity, weak peer review, and change-control gaps. The response addresses accountability appropriately while also fixing system issues. The positive outcomes are earlier incident reporting, stronger root-cause analysis, better control redesign, and fewer repeat errors. This strengthens both security and organizational trust.

HFACS enables and supports a blame-free culture by providing a structured, evidence-based taxonomy that distinguishes unsafe acts from their preconditions, unsafe supervision, and organizational influences. By mapping errors to latent conditions and supervisory or organizational drivers, HFACS redirects attention from individual culpability to systemic causation, thereby reducing scapegoating and promoting learning. HFACS strengthens post-incident analysis through consistent coding, increases inter-rater reliability in investigations, and translates findings into actionable organizational interventions, such as procedure redesign, interface improvements, staffing adjustments, and targeted training. Alignment between HFACS and Just Culture principles fosters transparent reporting, disciplined root-cause analysis, and leadership accountability for system design, collectively enhancing resilience and continuous improvement (Reason, 1990 Shappell & Wiegmann, 2017).

Beyond internal governance, blame intersects with strategy in the external domain of the nation-state and transnational cyber conflict. Attribution remains technically and analytically challenging given the limitations of digital forensics and the ease with which adversaries can obfuscate origins or plant deceptive indicators. Public assignment of blame thus functions as a geopolitical act as much as a technical conclusion, employed to deter adversaries, justify responses, or meet broader political objectives even when evidentiary details cannot be fully disclosed. Concurrently, accountability expectations within interconnected supply chains have intensified, with organizations and governments pressing vendors and contractors to meet verifiable cybersecurity standards to maintain baseline resilience across shared ecosystems.

Collectively, these considerations indicate that effective cybersecurity governance requires movement from punitive reflexes toward systemic learning, discriminating accountability, and transparent responsibility across internal operations, strategic communications, and supply chain relationships. Such an approach enhances resilience by encouraging timely reporting, enabling root-cause remediation, and aligning leadership accountability with the socio-technical realities that shape secure performance.

# HFACS and risk management

The HFACS provides a comprehensive framework for identifying, categorizing, and analyzing human and organizational contributors to adverse events across high-risk domains. By imposing a disciplined taxonomy that spans organizational influences, unsafe supervision, preconditions for unsafe acts, and the unsafe acts themselves, HFACS aligns incident investigation with system-level learning rather than post hoc attribution. Cross-domain utility appears in aviation, healthcare, mining, construction, maritime operations, warehousing, and related sectors, where consistent causal coding yields comparable datasets and translational insights that inform control redesign and policy refinement (Aji & Susilowati, 2024 Batalden & Sydnes, 2013 Wiegmann & Shappell, 2000 Zhang et al., 2020). This same value is increasingly relevant in cybersecurity, where incidents are often analyzed through fragmented technical logs or case-specific narratives that limit cross-case learning. Applying consistent causal coding in cybersecurity can help organizations systematically compare phishing events, misconfigurations, insider actions, access control failures, and response breakdowns across units and sectors, thereby revealing recurring human, supervisory, and organizational contributors that can inform stronger control design, governance, and resilience policy.

A principal contribution of HFACS lies in systematically identifying contributing factors beyond proximate operator actions. For example, if a CISO approves an accelerated system rollout without sufficient security testing and the organization later experiences a breach, HFACS does not stop at the CISO's decision. It extends the analysis to preconditions such as incomplete risk information and time pressure, supervisory factors such as weak challenge processes or limited cross-team review, and organizational influences such as incentive structures that prioritize speed to deployment over security assurance. This approach produces a more accurate explanation of the incident and supports stronger corrective action at the system level. A layered architecture brings latent organizational conditions and supervisory practices into view, showing how they shape frontline performance and enabling interventions that address deeper sources of risk. Evidence from mining indicates that preconditions for unsafe acts and unsafe supervision frequently dominate accident pathways, directing attention to targeted mitigations at those levels rather than solely to worker behavior (Helvida et al., 2022 Moosavi & Kamyab, 2022). In long-term care and healthcare, adapted HFACS variants highlight system design weaknesses and planning gaps, informing risk management plans that strengthen safety controls and reduce the recurrence of adverse events (McGrane et al., 2023).

HFACS also supports prioritization and quantification when integrated with analytical methods such as Bayesian networks, multi-criteria decision analysis, and simulation. HFACS becomes more useful for prioritization when combined with quantitative methods. Bayesian networks estimate how factors across HFACS levels influence incident risk. **Multi-criteria decision analysis (MCDA)** helps compare corrective actions using criteria such as risk reduction, cost, and feasibility. Simulation tests how changes in staffing, workload, policies, or controls may affect outcomes before implementation. Together, these methods help organizations move from causal classification to evidence-based decision-making. In cybersecurity, HFACS integrated with decision-analysis tools can identify high-leverage contributors to incidents such as cloud misconfigurations, privileged access misuse, or delayed incident escalation, thereby guiding targeted process redesign, supervision enhancements, and control investments. When HFACS-coded incident data are combined with Bayesian models, organizations can estimate which causal pathways, such as configuration complexity, time pressure, weak change oversight, or inadequate staffing, most strongly predict breach likelihood or severity, which supports focused prevention strategies and more effective allocation of security resources.

HFACS also enhances cybersecurity risk management through cross-context adaptability. In cloud and hybrid environments, systematic HFACS coding improves root-cause clarity by linking exposed storage, identity misconfigurations, or segmentation failures to human, supervisory, and organizational conditions rather than treating them as isolated technical mistakes. In security operations centers and infrastructure teams, HFACS helps analysts trace how alert overload, unclear escalation protocols, and policy drift propagate to frontline response errors, thereby strengthening the evidentiary basis for risk modeling and control redesign. In this way, HFACS supports more proactive and system-level prevention strategies across diverse cybersecurity settings.

Beyond retrospective analysis, HFACS contributes to proactive prevention and learning cultures by structuring near-miss reporting, thematic synthesis, and feedback loops that inform design and supervision. Occupational health and safety studies using HFACS link richer narratives and consistent coding to improvements in safety climate, supervisory oversight, and the evidentiary basis for risk controls across hospitals, healthcare, and mines (Afshari et al., 2019 Hizriansyah & Maretalinia, 2025 Verma & Chaudhari, 2017). These practices align with Just Culture principles, reinforcing psychological safety and encouraging timely disclosure of weak signals that precede harm.

Economic decision-making and risk financing also benefit from HFACS-enabled insight. In cybersecurity, HFACS can be used to link human, supervisory, and organizational contributors to measurable loss patterns, such as cloud misconfiguration exposure, delayed incident escalation, privileged access misuse, and change-management failures. This allows organizations and insurers to develop more precise cyber risk models, align premiums and coverage conditions with demonstrated control maturity, and connect investments in training, staffing, workflow redesign, and governance to measurable reductions in breach likelihood and severity. In this way, HFACS outputs become organizational levers that influence both cybersecurity performance and financial outcomes.

Recent methodological advances further extend HFACS utility in cybersecurity through analytics and visualization of risk pathways. For example, association-rule mining can reveal recurring combinations of contributors, such as alert overload plus unclear escalation thresholds plus understaffed shifts, that precede delayed response events. Network analysis can map how organizational influences, supervisory gaps, and frontline conditions interact across incident types, helping analysts identify both direct and indirect contributors to compromise. Multi-criteria decision models can then prioritize interventions by weighing expected risk reduction, implementation cost, operational feasibility, and time to impact.

Together, these approaches strengthen the evidentiary basis for cyber risk management by moving from isolated incident narratives to analyzable patterns of socio-technical failure.

These approaches support holistic intervention portfolios that address systemic couplings rather than isolated nodes of failure.

In conclusion, HFACS advances risk management by furnishing a layered causal architecture, enabling prioritization through quantitative integration, demonstrating adaptability across sectors, fostering learning cultures that act on near-miss intelligence, informing economic optimization, and revealing risk networks that guide systemic interventions. When embedded in governance and resilience programs, HFACS facilitates sustained improvement from the individual task level to deep organizational processes, enhancing the reliability and safety of complex operations (Aji & Susilowati, 2024 Batalden & Sydnes, 2013 Khanal et al., 2024 Souza & Russomano, 2017 Wiegmann & Shappell, 2000 Zhang et al., 2020).

# Capitalizing on prevention

The aviation, healthcare, nuclear power, and space exploration domains use HFACS to prevent deadly and costly accidents. HFACS is not meant to be punitive or to identify end-users for punishment; instead, it is designed to prevent major cybersecurity incidents. The cybersecurity sector should take heed and use HFACS to prevent costly and operationally crippling catastrophes. For example, an organization can analyze its data and reports to identify troubled areas, areas lacking sufficient security controls, or high-risk operations, and engineer solutions to prevent active and latent failures from aligning. This is depicted in the Swiss-cheese model in the next section.

A preventive approach allows organizations to develop nanocodes under the modified HFACS based on native operations, cybersecurity strategy, and risk appetite. It is important to note that organizations should modify the HFACS taxonomy to meet their specific needs. Trying to apply the taxonomy as is might not yield the desired results. Tailoring HFACS is not easy and will require considerable effort; however, once it is modified and applied, the organization will have a mechanism in place to thoroughly investigate and prevent incidents from occurring. This process is continuous and requires constant application as processes, people, technologies, and organizational and system factors are continually evolving.

One salient objective is to create nanocodes and align them with the different levels and categories of the HFACS model. Each nanocode should reflect the organization's environment. Failure to assess the nanocodes and tailor them specifically could prevent organizations from preemptively breaking the chain of events that result in catastrophes, which we will now discuss.

## Structure of HFACS: four cascading levels

The HFACS was originally developed by behavioral scientists within the United States Navy to address growing concerns about human performance shortfalls in aviation operations (Shappell & Wiegmann, 2003). To systematically evaluate how performance decrements contribute to accidents, its creators drew upon scientifically grounded investigation theory, most notably Reason's *Swiss-cheese model in Figure 9.1.* This model promotes a systems perspective, viewing human error not as the root cause but as a symptom of deeper organizational conditions. Within this framework, organizations implement multiple defensive barriers across technology, procedures, supervision, and governance. These barriers are structured in a sequential manner, with higher-level influences shaping lower-level behaviors. Failures at any level create vulnerabilities, either active, occurring close to the event, or latent, stemming from distant conditions that can align across layers to produce adverse outcomes.

The following cybersecurity scenario enhances understanding of the Swiss-cheese model by illustrating a **phishing-based ransomware attack** in a healthcare organization. A staff member receives an email that appears to be a legitimate invoice from a known vendor. The employee opens the attachment, malware executes, credentials are captured, and the attacker later moves through the network and deploys ransomware. The breach is severe, but it is not caused by one action alone. It occurs because multiple defensive layers each had a weakness, and those weaknesses aligned. The HFACS framework helps analysts examine an incident across multiple levels of the system rather than attributing failure to a single mistake. In the phishing example below, each layer shows how frontline actions, immediate conditions, supervisory practices, and organizational decisions combined to create a path to compromise. The layers below are the HFACS model's actual layers.

- **Unsafe Acts (frontline actions)**: This is the action closest to the incident. In this case, the employee clicks the phishing email attachment and enables content in the file. That action is visible and immediate but is only one part of the failure path.
- **Preconditions for Unsafe Acts:** These are the conditions that made the unsafe act more likely. The employee may have been fatigued, under time pressure, and processing a high volume of messages. The phishing email may also have looked highly credible, making it difficult to detect. These human and task conditions created the opportunity for error.
- **Unsafe Supervision**: Supervisory and management practices that failed to protect frontline staff. For example, the team may not have received recent phishing simulations or updated security awareness training. Supervisors may also have

normalized excessive workload, reducing employees' ability to carefully review suspicious emails.

- **Organizational Influences**: Leadership may have underinvested in email filtering, endpoint protection, staffing, and cyber training. The organization may also have lacked strong policies for patching, segmentation, and incident response readiness. These strategic decisions created latent weaknesses that remained hidden until the attack occurred.

In Swiss Cheese terms, the ransomware incident happened because the "holes" in each layer aligned. The model shows why cybersecurity events should be analyzed as **system failures across multiple barriers**, rather than as a single user mistake.

HFACS operationalizes this theory by defining four analytically adjacent levels, each with standardized definitions, exemplars, and coding rules that support inter-rater reliability and cross-case trend analysis. This structured approach shifts the focus from individual blame to identifying modifiable barrier degradations, thereby enhancing organizational learning and prevention (Shappell & Wiegmann, 2003 Wiegmann & Shappell, 2022).

HFACS offers organizations a powerful framework for understanding and mitigating the systemic breakdowns that contribute to accidents and safety incidents. Rather than focusing solely on individual errors, HFACS enables a comprehensive analysis of the entire system, identifying latent conditions, organizational influences, and recurring patterns in human performance that lead to unsafe outcomes. By examining historical data, organizations can proactively uncover trends and vulnerabilities, allowing for targeted, data-driven interventions that enhance safety and reduce incident rates. *Figure 9.2* breaks down the key components of this framework:

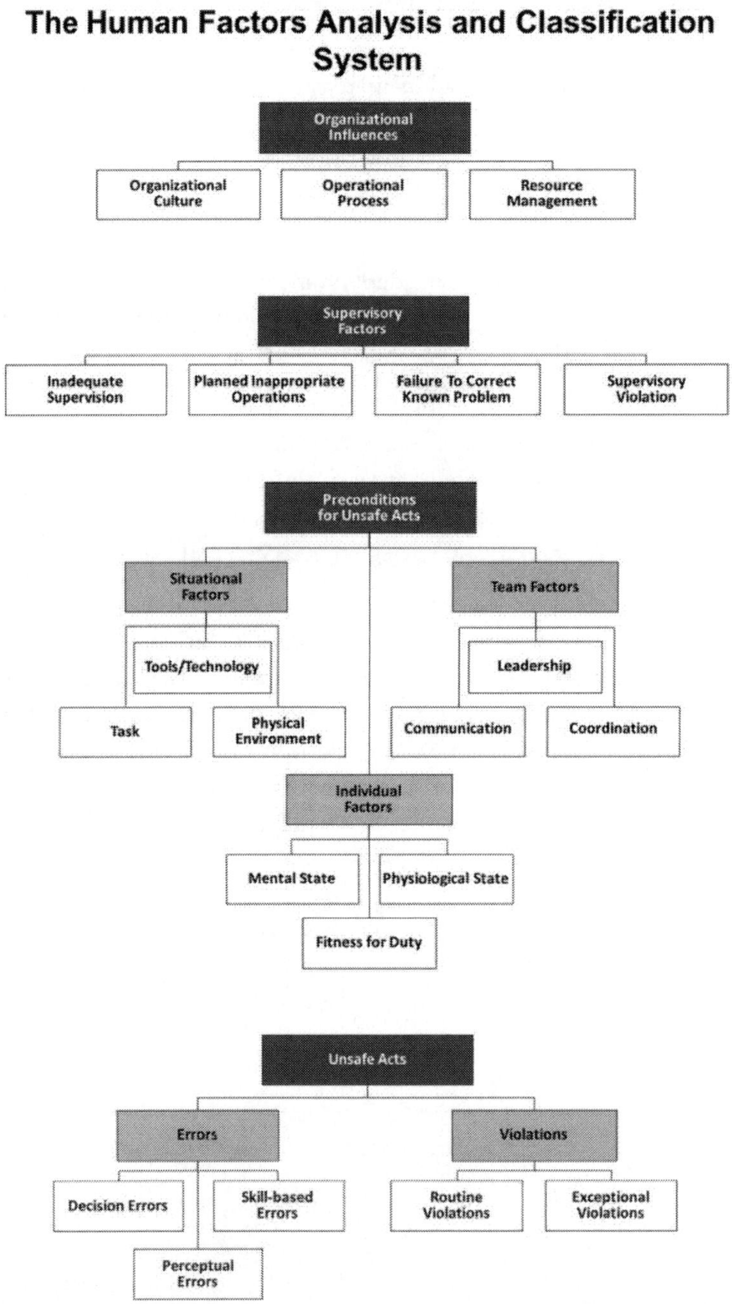


*Figure 9.2. The Human Factors Analysis and Classification System (Source: https://hfacs-healthcare.com/the-hfacs-framework/)*

HFACS breaks down complex events into structured categories, helping analysts trace unsafe acts back to their psychological origins or organizational deficiencies. This structured approach is equally valuable in cybersecurity because it improves the quality of incident investigations and supports the development of more robust, searchable security event databases. When organizations classify incidents consistently across unsafe acts, preconditions, supervisory factors, and organizational influences, they can compare cases over time and identify recurring risk patterns that would otherwise remain hidden in isolated technical reports. This makes it easier to prioritize corrective actions based on evidence rather than anecdote.

For example, a large healthcare system could apply HFACS to phishing incidents, cloud misconfigurations, and delayed-escalation events across its hospitals. After coding incidents over a year, the organization might find that a high proportion of serious events involve routine violations, such as repeated bypassing of change-control steps, the use of shared privileged accounts, or informal workarounds during high-workload periods. By identifying this trend, leadership could target interventions such as workflow redesign, stronger supervisory review, safer system defaults, and clearer accountability practices. Over time, this HFACS-informed approach would help reduce repeat incidents, strengthen organizational learning, and improve overall cyber resilience.

Ultimately, HFACS empowers organizations to shift from reactive responses to proactive safety management, fostering a culture of continuous improvement and resilience in high-risk environments. Organizations can leverage HFACS to prevent cybersecurity incidents, attacks, and breaches by analyzing its data and developing mitigative strategies to break the chain of events that lead to catastrophic cyber events.

Let's now look at this system in detail.

## Level 1: Unsafe acts

Level 1, **Unsafe Acts**, encompasses frontline behaviors observed at the operational point of performance.

- **Decision errors** involve rule-based or knowledge-based misjudgments during configuration approvals, access exceptions, or incident triage. Typical examples include approval of an insecure security group based on an incorrect rule interpretation and authorization of an emergency entitlement without adequate risk appraisal.
- **Skill-based errors** involve slips and lapses during routine tasks such as firewall edits, identity entitlement changes, or command-line operations conducted under distraction.

- **Perceptual errors** arise from misperceiving alert salience or misunderstanding console affordances under high cognitive load, often during alert surges or live incident response.
- **Violations** represent departures from established procedures, either routine or exceptional, such as bypassing multi-factor authentication during an outage or implementing a change outside approved windows. Classification at this level requires concrete artifacts, for example, timestamped change records, terminal histories, and console captures, to distinguish errors from violations and to separate rule-based decisions from skill-based slips.

It is important to highlight the difference between routine and exceptional violations through a cybersecurity lens. In cybersecurity, routine violations are repeated workarounds that become normalized, such as administrators regularly sharing privileged accounts or skipping formal change approvals to move faster. Exceptional violations are rare, crisis-driven departures from policy, such as temporarily bypassing multi-factor authentication during a major outage to restore critical access. The distinction matters because routine violations signal control drift and cultural weakness, while exceptional violations reflect high-pressure decision-making during abnormal events.

## Level 2: Preconditions for unsafe acts

Level 2, **Preconditions for Unsafe Acts**, captures local conditions that shape performance at the point of work

- **Individual factors**: Adverse mental states include fatigue, cognitive tunneling, and stress during surge windows created by patch cycles, seasonal onboarding, or incident backlogs. Adverse physiological states include extended shifts, circadian disruption, and illness, all of which degrade attention and memory.
- **Situational factors**: The technological and physical environment includes console complexity, confusing defaults, fragmented telemetry, poor display ergonomics, and workspace constraints that induce error through excessive context switching or low visual salience. Personnel factors include mismatches between skill and tool demands, tenure and training gaps for newly assigned staff, and workload misallocation that concentrates high-risk tasks on a small set of engineers.
- **Team factors**: Team dynamics and communication factors include handoff ambiguity, breakdowns in shared mental models, and coordination lags across security, operations, and development groups. Evidence for preconditions arises from schedules, on-call logs, training matrices, tool inventories, handoff transcripts, and usability findings, thereby enabling targeted interventions such as staffing buffers, revised runbooks, and user-interface redesign.

## Level 3: Supervisory factors

Level 3, **Supervisory Factors**, addresses managerial practices that configure frontline conditions.

- **Inadequate supervision** appears in insufficient code-review standards, limited runbook rehearsal for high-risk tasks, and weak oversight of privileged access
- **Planned inappropriate operations** include release cadences that preclude risk gates, maintenance windows that overlap with peak business activity, and staffing ratios that do not support safe execution
- **Failure to correct known problems** includes the accumulation of security exceptions, deferred certificate rotation, and unresolved audit findings that remain open across multiple quarters
- **Supervisory violations** involve explicit or implicit pressure to circumvent change control to meet deadlines or service-level targets
  Documentary evidence includes standard operating procedures, change-advisory minutes, exception registers, audit trackers, and staffing plans, allowing linkage from supervisory patterns to corrective actions such as revised approval workflows, rehearsal requirements, and service-level incentives aligned with safety

## Level 4: Organizational influences

Level 4, **Organizational culture**, covers portfolio-level determinants that shape supervisory practice and local work

- **Resource management** concerns under-investment in training, usability, and operability; inadequate budgets for security automation and human-centered design; and insufficient time allocation for reliability work
- **Organizational climate** reflects just-culture norms, clarity of risk appetite, and the presence of symbolic compliance that substitutes paperwork for meaningful control effectiveness
- **Organizational process** includes siloed ownership across security, IT, and compliance; fragmented vendor governance that obscures third-party risk; and immature learning loops that fail to translate incident insights into durable design changes.

Evidence includes budget records, organizational policies, vendor contracts, governance charters, and metrics from corrective-action programs. Interventions at this level involve strategic investment decisions, explicit risk appetite statements, integrated ownership models, and governance architectures that connect incident learning to enterprise planning and vendor management.

## Purpose of nanocodes and their use in HFACS

Nanocodes in the HFACS are highly granular sub-categories nested under the standard HFACS taxonomy (e.g., Unsafe Acts, Preconditions for Unsafe Acts, Supervisory Factors, Organizational Influences). Their purpose is to define each category with precise, observable descriptors so that investigators can code incident data consistently at a fine level of detail.

The organization and supervision nanocodes sections help analysts move beyond frontline errors by identifying the management and institutional conditions that shape cybersecurity performance. The nanocodes below are examples of how they are applied to sections. Organization nanocodes capture higher-level influences such as resource allocation, operational tempo, training, policy, and culture, while supervision nanocodes focus on leadership oversight, planning, accountability, and supervisory compliance. In cybersecurity, these categories are useful for explaining why incidents recur, for example, when understaffing, weak governance, unclear priorities, or poor supervisory enforcement create conditions that increase misconfigurations, delayed escalations, and policy violations.

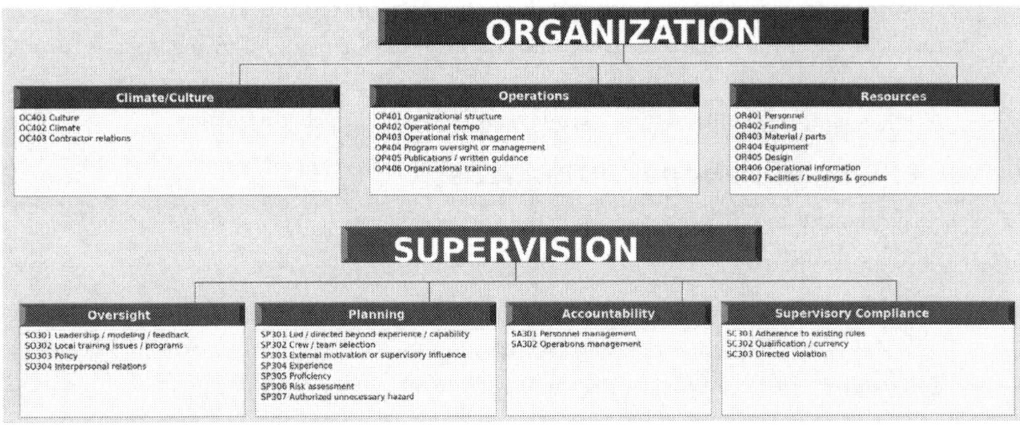


*Figure 9.3: Examples of NASA nanocodes at the organizational and supervision levels (Source: NASA, 2023)*

> **Note**
>
> A high-resolution version of this image is available in the Graphic Bundle. You can access the graphics here: `https://packt.link/gbp/9781806118335`.

The precondition nanocodes section helps analysts identify the immediate human, environmental, and task conditions that make cybersecurity errors more likely. These nanocodes capture factors such as cognitive overload, fatigue, complacency, communication breakdowns, interface complexity, and information quality, which often shape performance before an incident occurs. In cybersecurity, precondition nanocodes are useful for explaining why actions such as missed alerts, misconfigurations, or delayed responses happen because they reveal the operational conditions that influence decision-making and execution.

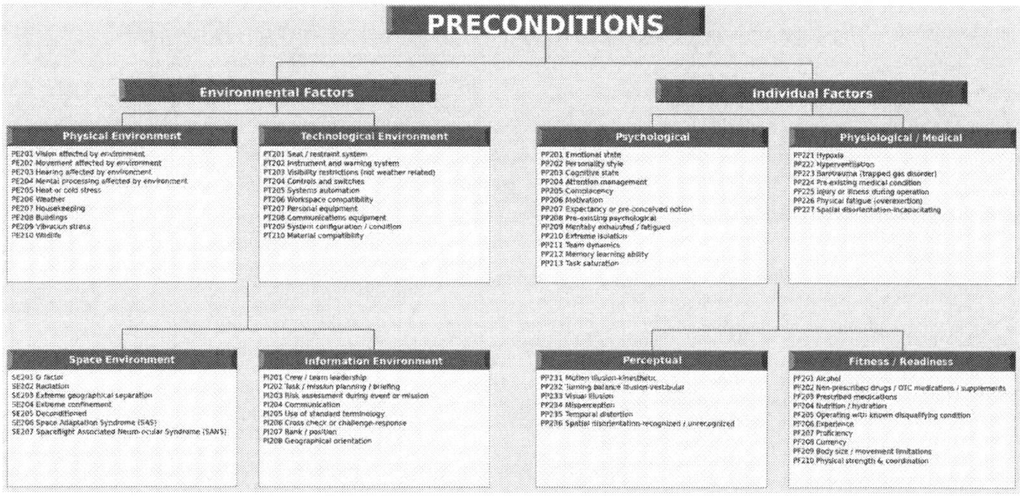


*Figure 9.4: Examples of NASA nanocodes at the precondition level (Source: NASA, 2023)*

> **Note**
>
> A high-resolution version of this image is available in the Graphic Bundle. You can access the graphics here: `https://packt.link/gbp/9781806118335`.

The ACT nanocodes section helps analysts classify the specific actions taken at the point of the cybersecurity incident, such as incorrect action, omitted action, misperception, or violation of procedure. These nanocodes provide a consistent way to document what happened at the frontline level without stopping the analysis there. In cybersecurity, ACT nanocodes are useful for coding events such as clicking a malicious link, applying the wrong configuration, failing to escalate an alert, or bypassing a required control, which then supports deeper analysis across preconditions, supervision, and organizational influences.

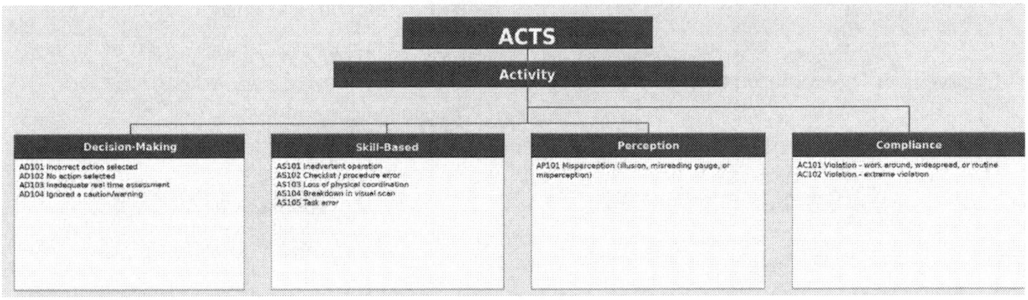


*Figure 9.5: Examples of NASA nanocodes at the unsafe acts level (Source: NASA, 2023)*

> **Note**
>
> A high-resolution version of this image is available in the Graphic Bundle. You can access the graphics here: `https://packt.link/gbp/9781806118335`.

Nanocodes serve as a critical mechanism for operationalizing HFACS by translating broad categorical frameworks into precise, behaviorally anchored labels. Functionally, nanocodes refine higher-level HFACS categories into specific, observable actions and errors; for example, within the "Skill-Based Errors" category, nanocodes might indicate "omitted checklist step," "mis-sequenced action," or "inadequate instrument cross-check." Structurally, this system is organized hierarchically, beginning with the HFACS level, followed by category, sometimes subcategory, and ultimately the nanocode, which provides the most granular point of analysis.

In application, these nanocodes are used during event investigations to tag causal and contributory factors with a high degree of specificity, enhancing inter-rater reliability, enabling richer trend analyses, and guiding targeted interventions. This methodological precision yields multiple benefits, including improved data quality for understanding the epidemiology of human error, strengthened benchmarking across organizational units or temporal spans, and direct support for interventions such as training, procedural redesign, supervisory adjustments, and policy refinements.

The following are a few examples:

- **Unsafe Acts → Errors → Skill-Based**: "attention fixation," "checklist step omitted," "habit intrusion"
- **Preconditions → Environmental Factors → Technological**: "interface affordance mismatch," "alert salience insufficient"
- **Supervision → Inadequate Supervision**: "training currency not maintained," "tasking beyond qualification"
- **Organization → Resource Management**: "staffing below minimum," "competing production pressure"

In short, nanocodes are the fine-grained vocabulary that makes HFACS analytically actionable, turning broad human-factors concepts into specific, codable phenomena that support robust learning and prevention. Without a doubt, the cybersecurity domain would need to modify the existing HFACS model to fit and apply to cybersecurity operations. *Figure 9.6* presents an example of agency nanocodes organized as a frequency chart. The colors distinguish broad HFACS-related categories, and the numbers at the ends of the bars show how often each nanocode appeared in the coded cases. In other words, the number is the frequency count for that specific nanocode. A higher number means that issue appeared more often across the incidents or events being analyzed, which suggests it may be a recurring weakness or pattern within the organization.

The color scheme appears to group the nanocodes by higher-level analytic domains. For example, the darker purple codes near the top reflect organizational-level influences, such as operational information, equipment, funding, training, program oversight, and operations tempo. The bright pink and magenta sections represent supervisory and precondition-related factors, including rule enforcement, supervisory pressure, proficiency, training issues, personnel management, fatigue, distraction, complacency, and communication or planning problems. The lighter pink and related tones continue this focus on human, environmental, and performance-shaping conditions, such as memory limits, motivation, workspace incompatibility, visibility restrictions, and environmental effects. The blue codes at the bottom represent unsafe acts or performance-level errors, including misperception, breakdowns in visual scan, overcontrol or undercontrol, inadvertent operation, inadequate real-time assessment, incorrect action execution, and actions taken too soon. Thus, the colors help readers quickly distinguish whether a code belongs primarily to organizational influences, supervisory issues, preconditions, or unsafe acts.

The alphanumeric structure of each nanocode also serves an important purpose. The letters indicate the general category or domain, while the numbers identify the specific coded issue within that category. For instance, codes such as OR, OP, OC, and SV point to broader organizational or supervisory domains, while PP, PC, PT, and PE appear to identify preconditions or performance-shaping factors, and AD, AS, AP, and AV refer to action-level errors or unsafe acts. This structure allows analysts to code incidents consistently and also makes it easier to aggregate findings across many cases. For example, if AD005 Inadequate Real-Time Assessment appears 39 times, that immediately signals a recurring action-level problem that may require targeted intervention.

The frequencies shown in the figure help the organization identify which issues are most common. For example, AD005 Inadequate Real-Time Assessment has a frequency of 39, PT010 Fuels or Materials has 33, PC004 Miscommunication has 32, and OP006 Organizational Training has 30. These higher-frequency nanocodes suggest areas where the organization may need to focus attention because they recur more often than others. By contrast, nanocodes with frequencies of 1 or 2 may still matter, but they appear less often and may represent more isolated or contextual issues.

Most importantly, organizations should develop nanocodes that fit their own environment rather than simply adopting another agency's list without modification. Nanocodes are most useful when they reflect the actual language, workflows, hazards, technologies, and recurring failure patterns of the organization using them. For example, a cybersecurity organization would likely need nanocodes that differ from those used by NASA or another operational agency. Instead of codes such as fuels or materials, the organization might create nanocodes for alert fatigue, phishing susceptibility, MFA failure handling, cloud misconfiguration, privilege escalation gaps, incomplete log visibility, weak incident escalation, policy drift, vendor dependency, or patching delay. These codes should still align to the broader HFACS structure, but the labels and definitions should be tailored to the organization's own mission and risk profile.

A practical way for organizations to develop their own nanocodes is to begin with the major HFACS levels and then create narrower subcodes based on actual incident reports, after-action reviews, audit findings, and expert input from personnel across technical, supervisory, and leadership roles. After initial development, the codes should be tested on real cases to see whether analysts can apply them consistently. Over time, the organization can refine the codebook by merging vague codes, clarifying definitions, adding missing categories, and retiring codes that do not provide analytic value. In this way, nanocodes become a living organizational taxonomy that supports pattern recognition, root-cause analysis, and more targeted corrective action.

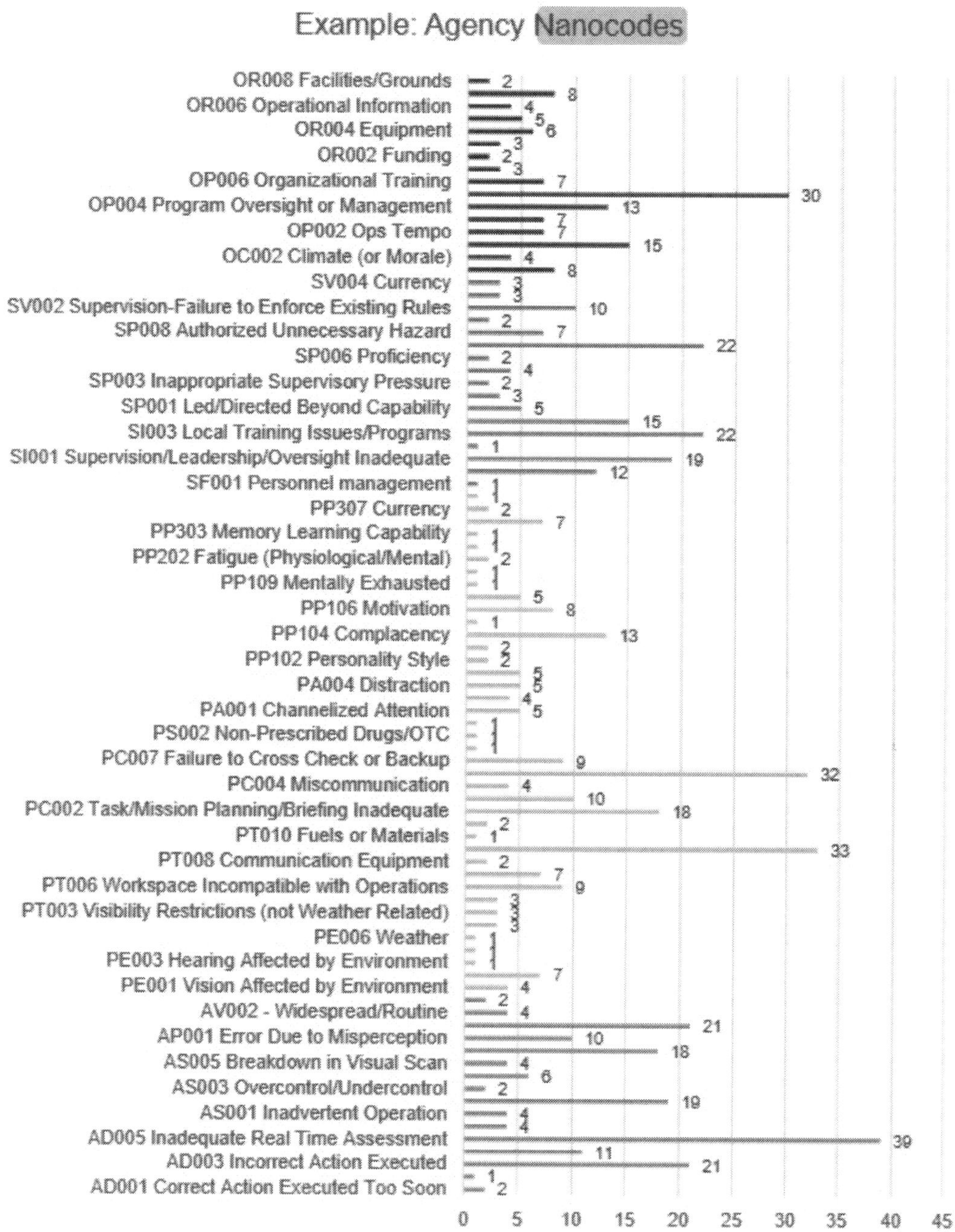


*Figure 9.6: Example of NASA nanocodes(Source: NASA, 2023)*

## Need for a modified HFACS-Cyber framework

Organizations need a structured human-factors methodology, such as a modified HFACS-Cyber framework, to systematically examine how unsafe acts, preconditions, supervisory factors, and organizational influences combine to produce cyber incidents. This is necessary because many cybersecurity investigations still focus too narrowly on technical artifacts or frontline mistakes, which can obscure the human, supervisory, and organizational conditions that repeatedly produce risk. A modified HFACS-Cyber program provides a consistent method for coding incidents using cyber-relevant categories such as alert overload, configuration complexity, policy drift, access-control workarounds, and governance gaps. In cybersecurity, this approach is essential because it improves analytic consistency, strengthens cross-incident comparison, supports more reliable risk databases, and helps organizations prioritize corrective actions that address systemic causes rather than isolated symptoms. This section explores the applications of a modified HFACS-Cyber framework to provide organizations with a scientifically based approach to identify cyber incidents and attacks, foundational causes, and methods for preventing catastrophic incidents and attacks in the future.

## Continuous application to near misses and assessments

Beyond sharpening post-incident learning, a continuously applied modified HFACS supports a proactive risk posture for near-misses (for example, change-related exceptions and pipeline rollbacks) and routine assessments (for example, red-team findings and phishing exercises). Although HFACS originated as an accident-investigation framework, evidence from cloud-centric adaptations demonstrates that iterative coding of day-to-day signals surfaces high-friction pathways before those pathways culminate in a breach. Repeated, like-for-like coding turns scattered lessons into leading indicators that guide system and policy redesign, converting episodic insights into a durable prevention cadence.

Across multiple high-risk domains, including aviation, rail, maritime, healthcare, mining, oil and gas, and unmanned aerial systems, researchers and practitioners have modified HFACS to fit the specific operational, technical, and organizational realities of their environments. Cybersecurity is now following the same path by adapting HFACS to analyze issues such as cloud misconfigurations, human error, supervisory gaps, and policy-driven risk in digital systems.

## Alignment with behavioral cybersecurity strategy

Continuous HFACS coding aligns with a behavioral cybersecurity strategy that couples measurement with a closed-loop improvement process. Behavioral science cautions that awareness campaigns alone rarely change behavior at scale. A superior sequence prioritizes adaptation of systems and processes first (sensible defaults, friction-reducing nudges, automation, and guardrails), followed by role-specific training and targeted behavior-change campaigns, all wrapped in feedback mechanisms that measure effectiveness and unintended effects such as "shadow security." Modified HFACS taxonomies map directly onto this sequence: codes identify where to simplify workflows, where to embed just-in-time cues, and where knowledge or motivation deficits persist. Interventions are thus ordered from design to education to communication, rather than defaulting reflexively to training.

## Explicit treatment of human performance degraders

A further strength of HFACS for cyber leadership is explicit treatment of human performance degraders, such as fatigue, overload, and burnout, as preconditions that propagate to unsafe acts. Security fatigue and chronic workload correlate with policy workarounds and configuration errors. Coding those factors in HFACS ensures representation on the risk register with accountable ownership and mitigation plans, rather than dismissal as individual failings. Behavioral guidance also warns that stacking initiatives without guardrails can induce additional fatigue; therefore, strain metrics and recovery practices must be integrated into the improvement loop to avoid risk migration.

## Governance integration and investment discipline

HFACS provides a common language that integrates with governance artifacts such as risk registers, control libraries, and audit evidence. Code heatmaps distinguish problems that demand process re-engineering (for example, OP1 Process Uncodified, OP2 Process Impractical) from problems that require supervisory redesign or usability enhancements to tooling. This decomposition supports rational capital allocation, defensible prioritization, and evidence of continuous enhancement during audits. Establishing a formal human-factors program to run, interpret, and act on HFACS analyses closes a persistent blind spot in many enterprises, where technology spending overwhelms attention to human performance engineering and ad-hoc practices persist.

## Minimal viable implementation playbook

A modified HFACS-Cyber framework can be most effective when it is implemented as a disciplined operational practice rather than a one-time analytic exercise. A minimal viable implementation playbook provides organizations with a practical starting point for building a consistent evidence base, translating findings into targeted interventions, and embedding human-factors insights into governance and continuous risk management. This approach helps ensure that incident learning is systematic, measurable, and directly tied to prevention. Below are some straightforward points for establishing a minimal viable playbook:

1. Define a minimal set of domain-specific nanocodes tailored to the environment (for example, CI/CD approvals, infrastructure-as-code guardrails, identity policy variants, and exception management)

2. Apply the codes consistently across incidents, near-misses, and routine assessments to build a comparable evidence base.
3. Quarterly, translate the top organizational and supervisory findings into an engineered behavioral strategy: redesign affordances and defaults, add nudges and just-in-time prompts, deploy role-specific training, run a concise communications campaign, and instrument feedback for both effectiveness and unintended effects.
4. Track strain and fatigue alongside traditional performance indicators to prevent risk reintroduction through initiative overload.
5. Feed results into governance artifacts to sustain accountability and demonstrate risk reduction over time.

## Outcomes that matter for leadership

Without a doubt, HFACS can assist with transforming a cybersecurity program from a reactive, person-centric view of error to a system-centric model in which leaders remove structural drivers of noncompliance, monitor fatigue explicitly, and demonstrate measurable reductions in misconfigurations and other human-enabled events. Cumulative experience from cloud-focused HFACS applications and behavioral cybersecurity practice indicates three durable benefits:

- Reduced subjectivity in causal analysis
- Elevation of prevention over post hoc remediation
- Enhanced durability of security enhancements through closed-loop learning

In short, a modified HFACS provides leaders with metrics that matter, a prioritized backlog of systemic fixes, and a repeatable cadence for demonstrating risk reduction over time.

## Weaknesses in HFACS

HFACS is a widely utilized framework for retrospective analysis of human errors following incidents. However, recent scholarly discourse points out inherent weaknesses that limit its evidential robustness and practical applicability. One primary limitation is the lack of built-in mechanisms for quantitative risk assessment and prioritization within HFACS. This deficiency has prompted researchers to integrate HFACS with methodologies such as FMEA to introduce scoring and ranking capabilities to support decision-making. Without this amalgamation, HFACS predominantly serves a descriptive function and fails to gauge the relative severity, probability, or detectability of different failure modes.

Moreover, various studies have noted a tendency within HFACS to disproportionately focus on immediate actions occurring at or near the incident site, while neglecting broader organizational and external influences. This bias has been particularly highlighted in research within the rail and offshore transport domains, prompting calls for explicit expansions of HFACS to encompass regulatory, political, and societal factors as external layers of causality.

The credibility of HFACS is further challenged by concerns regarding the reliability of inter-rater agreement, particularly when analysts encode information from incomplete narratives or summaries. This issue poses a threat to the reproducibility of findings across contexts unless rigorous coder training, decision protocols, and adjudication mechanisms are implemented.

HFACS, as a taxonomy-based system, provides limited support for modeling the dynamic, multilevel transmission of latent organizational deficiencies to frontline behaviors. To bridge this representational gap, scholars advocate combining HFACS with structural or cognitive modeling techniques, such as structural equation modeling, path analysis, and network methodologies, to make intermediary pathways and interaction effects explicit. Additionally, the direct transfer of HFACS across sectors has revealed discrepancies in constructs and terminology, necessitating sector-specific adaptations to maintain construct validity and diagnostic accuracy.

Another critical constraint of HFACS is its retrospective nature, which hampers proactive risk management unless its outcomes are explicitly linked to leading indicators and prospective monitoring tools. Evidence from high-reliability sectors suggests integrating HFACS findings with safety climate assessments, workload data, staffing metrics, and control health indicators to enhance the predictive and preventive value of the analysis. In practical applications, there is a tendency to overweight human and immediate supervisory error categories while underweighting upstream managerial and organizational contributions, thereby diverting attention from systemic redesign efforts.

The inferential fidelity of HFACS is heavily dependent on data quality and analytical expertise. Inadequate, inconsistent, or heterogeneous incident records can diminish the granularity and accuracy of categorization assignments, potentially biasing aggregated learning or trend analyses. Even with comprehensive documentation, expert judgment plays a central role in category selection and boundary delineation within HFACS, introducing variability across investigators in the absence of calibration and adjudication procedures. Moreover, HFACS has limited capacity to represent technical design flaws or environmental conditions, underscoring the need for complementary utilization of system-theoretic or engineering-focused models to maintain a comprehensive system-level perspective.

## Challenges of implementing HFACS in cybersecurity

Integrating the HFACS into cybersecurity requires targeted adaptation to domain-specific phenomena. Initially developed for aviation and subsequently applied in other safety-critical domains dominated by physical processes, HFACS must be reconstructed to account for intangible cyber threat vectors and socio-cognitive dynamics, including insider threats, social engineering, and policy nonadherence. Cyber contexts demand categories that capture behaviors such as employees' unfamiliarity with organizational policies, ambiguous procedural guidance, and interface-induced slips and lapses, which broaden the scope of "unsafe acts" beyond physical operator errors (Zeng et al., 2022). Accordingly, HFACS layers and subcategories require cyber-specific definitions and exemplars that connect human actions to organizational influences and technical failure modes in digital ecosystems.

The intrinsic complexity of cybersecurity as a sociotechnical enterprise presents further challenges. Cyber failures frequently emerge from nonlinear interactions among human operators, automation pipelines, software-defined infrastructures, and institutional processes rather than from isolated human missteps. This interactional complexity complicates the reliable assignment of causal codes and demands HFACS extensions capable of representing dependencies across organizational policies, security operations workflows, and adaptive adversary behaviors (Jaboski & Jaboski, 2021 Zeng et al., 2022). Without such extensions, analyses risk overemphasizing proximal human actions while underrepresenting latent systemic contributors distributed across technology stacks and governance structures.

A robust HFACS application depends on high-quality incident data that delineate human contributions and contextual conditions with sufficient granularity. In cybersecurity, incident reporting that captures human factors is often sparse, inconsistent, or intentionally limited due to confidentiality, privacy constraints, and legal exposure. The result is an incomplete evidentiary basis for fine-grained coding across HFACS layers. Moreover, adversary-induced behaviors, such as social engineering, hinge on subtle cognitive and socio-behavioral cues that are rarely captured in operational logs or post-incident summaries, further degrading data quality for human-centric analysis (Alzubaidi et al., 2023 Salahdine & Kaabouch, 2019). Addressing these deficits requires standardized, privacy-aware human-factors fields in incident reporting, along with methods to augment sparse data using validated analytic and learning techniques.

Alignment between HFACS and automated cybersecurity tooling introduces additional integration hurdles. Contemporary defenses rely extensively on intrusion detection systems, threat intelligence pipelines, and machine learning classifiers that may serve as opaque decision elements, limiting traceability from machine outputs to human-interpretable causes. To ensure that HFACS insights inform alert triage, playbook design, and control selection, organizations must advance explainable, interpretable analytics that enable human analysts to connect algorithmic detections to HFACS-relevant precursors and organizational drivers. Achieving this alignment requires governance for model transparency, human-AI teaming practices, and feedback loops that translate HFACS findings into feature engineering, rule refinement, and interface adjustments (Salahdine & Kaabouch, 2019 Zhang et al., 2021).

Organizational culture and policy enforcement materially shape the distribution of unsafe acts and preconditions in cyber operations. Unsafe behaviors often reflect insufficient policy clarity, irregular training cadence, or cultural norms that discourage timely reporting and peer escalation. Embedding HFACS thus necessitates assessments that make organizational influences explicit, including leadership priorities, workload and staffing, and the usability of security tooling. Such visibility can face resistance rooted in privacy concerns, measurement fatigue, and perceived surveillance, which must be addressed through Just Culture principles, transparent metrics governance, and participatory design of monitoring practices (Jaboski & Jaboski, 2021 Zeng et al., 2022).

The pace and adaptability of cyber threats make taxonomy maintenance a moving target. Static HFACS codebooks can lag novel attack patterns, emergent socio-technical workflows, and evolving user-adversary interactions. Sustained relevance requires periodic codebook updates, versioned nanocodes, and mechanisms for rapidly incorporating new human-error modes associated with sophisticated phishing, identity abuse, and software supply-chain compromises. Continuous learning pipelines that link incident response retrospectives to taxonomy curation are therefore essential (Nguyen & Reddi, 2021 Shaukat et al., 2019).

Finally, effective use of HFACS in cybersecurity depends on integration with broader risk and resilience frameworks. While HFACS excels at structured causal analysis of human and organizational contributors, resilience goals demand coupling those insights with enterprise risk registers, business impact analyses, and recovery planning. Embedding HFACS outputs into scenario-based exercises, control rationales, and metrics for adaptive capacity can align micro-level human-error findings with macro-level continuity and safety objectives in complex industrial and critical-infrastructure settings (Rahim et al., 2024). Such coupling supports prioritization of systemic interventions over isolated corrective actions and advances organization-wide learning.

In summary, the integration of HFACS into cybersecurity faces challenges related to domain-specific adaptation, representation of sociotechnical complexity, incident-data scarcity and variability, coordination with opaque automated defenses, cultural and policy frictions, rapid threat evolution, and alignment with enterprise resilience and risk management. Addressing these challenges requires cyber-tailored taxonomies, improved data practices, explainable analytics, culture-aware implementation, agile codebook governance, and explicit linkage to resilience frameworks to realize HFACS's full value in cyber contexts.

## Summary

HFACS-Cyber offers a holistic approach to cybersecurity by helping organizations examine how human behavior, technology design, supervisory practices, and organizational conditions interact to produce risk. Rather than isolating incidents as technical failures or individual mistakes, the framework supports a system-level understanding of cyber events across unsafe acts, preconditions, supervision, and organizational influences. This enables cybersecurity programs to benefit more comprehensively from stronger investigations, clearer cross-incident comparisons, more reliable risk data, and better-targeted interventions in training, workflow design, governance, and control engineering. In this way, HFACS-Cyber strengthens cybersecurity not only at the incident-response level, but across the broader enterprise risk, resilience, and prevention ecosystem.

With this human-factors foundation established, the next chapter examines identification and technology strategies that organizations can use to detect, manage, and reduce human-centered cybersecurity risks in operational environments.

## References


- Aas,A.L.,Theophilus,S.C.,&Gong,Y.(2008; 2017; 2025). HFACS for oil and gas (offshore/pipelines). (onepetro.org)
- Afshari, D., Jafarzadeh, Z., Mosavianasl, Z., & Jahani, F. (2019). Identification and evaluation of human errors using human factor analysis and classification system based on fuzzy hierarchy theory: A case study in the cement industry. Occupational Medicine. https://doi.org/10.18502/tkj.v11i1.1777
- Aji, D. B., & Susilowati, I. (2024). Analysis of light vehicle accident data at PT Z period 2018–2022 using human factor analysis and classification system–mining industry framework. Journal of Social Science. https://doi.org/10.46799/jss.v5i4.891
- Alharasees, O., Al-Rabeei, S., & Kale, U. (2022). Human factors analysis and classification system–AHP drone model assessment. https://doi.org/10.35116/aa.2022.0030
- Alzubaidi, L., Bai, J., Al-Sabaawi, A., Santamara, J., Albahri, A. S., Al-dabbagh, B. S. N., Fadhel, M. A., Manoufali, M., Zhang, J., AlTimemy, A. H., Duan, Y., Abdullah, A., Farhan, L., Lu, Y., Gupta, A., Albu, F., Abbosh, A., & Gu, Y. (2023). A survey on deep learning tools dealing with data scarcity: Definitions, challenges, solutions, tips, and applications. Springer Science+Business Media. https://doi.org/10.1186/s40537-023-00727-2

- Antoro, D. W. B. E., & Priadi, A. A. (2019). Ship accident prevention under organizational influences on ship operation by using gap analysis. Knowledge E. https://doi.org/10.18502/kss.v3i23.5140
- Batalden, B., & Sydnes, A. K. (2013). Maritime safety and the ISM Code: A study of investigated casualties and incidents. Springer Science+Business Media. https://doi.org/10.1007/s13437-013-0051-8
- Dekker, S. (2014). *The field guide to understanding 'human error'*. Ashgate.
- ElBardissi, A., et al. (2007). Application of HFACS to operating room medical errors. *Annals of Thoracic Surgery.*
- FAA. Human Factors Analysis and Classification System—Maintenance Extension (HFACS-ME). (Aviation maintenance). (Federal Aviation Administration).
- FRA. (2005). Human Factors Root Cause Analysis... using HFACS-RR. (Federal Railroad Administration)
- Helvida, A., Haznadarević, L., Vranješ, B., Bijelić, B., & Stojiljković, E. (2022). A methodological approach for analysis of human errors in the production system. University of Pisa. https://doi.org/10.22190/fuwlep2202063h
- Hizriansyah, H., & Maretalinia, M. (2025). Human error and near misses in hospital occupational safety: A root cause analysis using the HFACS framework. *Open Access Health Scientific Journal.* https://doi.org/10.55700/oahsj.v6i2.95
- Hollnagel, E. (2017). *Safety-II in practice: Developing the resilience potentials.* Routledge.
- Hsu, H., Hwang, M., & Tsou, P. (2023). Applications of BWM and GRA for evaluating the risk of picking and material-handling accidents in warehouse facilities. *Applied Sciences.* https://doi.org/10.3390/app13031263
- Jaboski, M., & Jaboski, A. (2021). Shaping the safety culture of high-reliability organizations through digital transformation. MDPI.
- Jalali, M., et al. (2023). Application of HFACS in healthcare (review). (pmc.ncbi.nlm.nih.gov)
- Jing, M., Zhang, G., Yang, D., & Qin, H. (2024). Research on risk identification of coal mine ventilation systems based on HFACS and Apriori algorithm. *Advances in Civil Engineering.*
- Kaptan, M., et al. (2021). Evolution of HFACS in marine accident analysis; plus HFACS-MA exemplars. ScienceDirect.

- Khanal, A., Chaudhary, N. K., Pandey, B., & Thapa, B. S. (2024). Review of hydrogen-related accidents: Root causes, mitigation strategies, and recommendations for secure utilization. IOP Publishing.
- Li, W., & Harris, D. (2007). A systems approach to training aeronautical decision making: From identifying training needs to verifying training solutions. Cambridge University Press.
- Lenné,M.,Patterson,J.,&Shappell,S.(2012); Patterson, J., & Shappell, S. (2010). HFACS-MI in mining (ScienceDirect).
- Ma, Q., & Wang, G. (2022). Aircraft insurance costs management for sustainable general aviation: Insights from general aviation enterprises in China. *Transportation Research Record.*
- Manjunath, S., & Bharath, A. A. (2023). Improving the process of accident analysis using human factor analysis and classification system (HFACS) framework in construction. *International Journal of Scientific Research in Engineering and Management.*
- Mazaheri, A., Montewka, J., Nisula, J., & Kujala, P. (2015). Usability of accident and incident reports for evidence-based risk modeling: A case study on ship grounding reports. Elsevier BV.
- McGrane, N., Dunbar, P., & Keyes, L. M. (2023). Contributing factors to adverse events in long-term care facilities in Ireland: A content analysis. Elsevier BV. `https://doi.org/10.1016/j.jamda.2023.11.015`
- Moosavi, S. A., & Kamyab, S. (2022). Risk safety assessment of human factors using analytical hierarchy process approach. Hamadan University of Medical Sciences. `https://doi.org/10.52547/johe.9.2.111`
- National Aeronautics and Space Administration. (2023). *NASA-HDBK-8709.25: Human factors handbook (*version 1.4): Procedural guidance and tools [NASA technical handbook].
- Nguyen, T. T., & Reddi, V. J. (2021). Deep reinforcement learning for cyber security. IEEE. `https://doi.org/10.1109/tnnls.2021.3121870`
- Niu, L., Zhao, J., & Yang, J. (2023). Risk assessment of unsafe acts in coal mine gas explosion accidents based on HFACS-GE and Bayesian networks. *Processes.* `https://doi.org/10.3390/pr11020554`
- Nobles, C. (2022). Investigating cloud computing misconfiguration errors using HFACS. (Cybersecurity/cloud)
- Rahim, M. F. H. M., Reniers, G., Yang, M., & Bajpai, S. (2024). Risk assessment methods for process safety, process security, and resilience in the chemical process industry: A

thorough literature review. Elsevier BV. https://doi.org/10.1016/j.jlp.2024.105274

- Reason, J. (1990). *Human error.* Cambridge University Press.
- Reinach, S., & Viale, A. (2006). Application of a human error framework to conduct train accident/incident investigations (HFACS-RR). (ScienceDirect)
- Salahdine, F., & Kaabouch, N. (2019). Social engineering attacks: A survey. MDPI. https://doi.org/10.3390/fi11040089
- Shappell, S., & Wiegmann, D. (2000). *The Human Factors Analysis and Classification System: HFACS* (aviation baseline). (ROSA P)
- Shappell, S. A., & Wiegmann, D. A. (2017). *A human error approach to aviation accident analysis: The Human Factors Analysis and Classification System.* Routledge.
- Shaukat, K., Luo, S., Varadharajan, V., Hameed, I. A., & Xu, M. (2019). A survey on machine learning techniques for cyber security in the last decade. IEEE. https://doi.org/10.1109/access.2020.3041951
- Souza, M. R. C., & Russomano, T. (2017). Experiência na utilização do modelo HFACS na estruturação de mapas causais de eventos adversos. EDIPUCRS. https://doi.org/10.15448/2179-703x.2017.1.27186
- UAV applications of HFACS: Risk early-warning and predictive uses (onlinelibrary.wiley.com)
- Verma, S., & Chaudhari, S. (2017). Safety of workers in Indian mines: Study, analysis, and prediction. Elsevier BV. https://doi.org/10.1016/j.shaw.2017.01.001
- Wiegmann, D. A., & Shappell, S. A. (2000). A human error analysis of commercial aviation accidents using the Human Factors Analysis and Classification System (HFACS). https://doi.org/10.1037/e420582004-001
- Zeng, M., Dian, C., & Wei, Y. (2022). Risk assessment of insider threats based on IHFACS-BN. MDPI. https://doi.org/10.3390/su15010491
- Zhang, X., Chen, W., Xi, Y., Hu, S., & Tang, L. (2020). Dynamics simulation of the risk coupling effect between maritime pilotage human factors under the HFACS framework. *Journal of Marine Science and Engineering.* https://doi.org/10.3390/jmse8020144
- Zhang, Z., Hamadi, H. A., Damiani, E., Yeun, C. Y., & Taher, F. (2021). Explainable artificial intelligence applications in cyber security: State-of-the-art in research. IEEE. https://doi.org/10.1109/access.2022.3204051

## Get this book's PDF version and more

Scan the QR code (or go to `packtpub.com/unlock`). Search for this book by name, confirm the edition, and then follow the steps on the page.

UNLOCK NOW

*Note: Keep your invoice handy. Purchases made directly from Packt don't require an invoice.*

# 10

# Identification and Technology Strategies of Human Factors in Cybersecurity

Recognizing human factors in cybersecurity requires moving from examining implemented controls to analyzing security in practice, acknowledging that breaches and near misses often arise from foreseeable interactions among individuals, processes, and technology under time constraints, uncertainty, and conflicting objectives. This entails systematically delineating the influence of cognitive demands, usability limitations, role clarity, training sufficiency, organizational norms, and incentive frameworks on security decision-making and behavior throughout the enterprise. Techniques such as human-system interaction mapping, task analysis, and cognitive workload analysis systematically identify sources of friction, ambiguity, and overload in actual workflows, encompassing authentication, access provisioning, monitoring and triage, change management, and incident response. Behavioral risk identification enhances this research by identifying patterns of workaround adoption, noncompliance, or hazardous shortcuts that emerge when security standards clash with operational realities. Collectively, these methodologies provide a practical basis for understanding human performance variability and for delineating adverse situations.

Technological solutions for incorporating **human factors engineering** (**HFE**) convert these diagnostic insights into design and governance measures that alleviate cognitive load while preserving security effectiveness. Alert enrichment, workflow automation, and decision-support systems can expedite time-to-action and reduce reliance on memory, while adaptive security interfaces can customize prompts, friction, and guidance based on user role, risk context, and job importance. Technical solutions are most efficacious when integrated into a strategic roadmap that organizes enhancements across the dimensions of personnel, processes, and platforms, aligns role-specific access and operational protocols with actual tasks, and delineates quantifiable outcomes (such as diminished tool transitions, expedited containment, reduced rework rates, and enhanced policy compliance). A comprehensive HFE roadmap integrates human-system interaction mapping, task and workload analysis, and behavioral risk identification with technology strategies, including automation to reduce cognitive load and adapt interfaces, to achieve sustainable improvements in performance, safety, and cyber resilience.

This chapter will cover the following topics:

- Identifying human factors in cybersecurity environments
- Technology strategies for integrating HFE
- Strategic implementation roadmap

# Identifying human factors in cybersecurity environments

Understanding human factors in cybersecurity environments involves mapping human-system interactions to reveal friction points and interface challenges. Task and cognitive workload analysis then highlights moments of overload or complexity that can impair judgment and defensive performance. Behavioral risk identification further uncovers patterns of shortcuts, noncompliance, and habitual errors that signal deeper socio-technical vulnerabilities.

## Human-system interaction mapping

The crucial first step in applying HFE principles to cybersecurity involves a comprehensive mapping of all human-system interactions across the organizational ecosystem. The mapping must go beyond asset and control inventories to document end-to-end workflows that include authentication, access provisioning and deprovisioning, firewall and router configuration, threat detection and hunting, and formal incident reporting and response. Human-system interaction mapping is a structured method for visualizing how people, technologies, processes, and decisions interact across a workflow. In practice, teams identify key actors, tasks, tools, data handoffs, and decision points, then map where friction, delay, cognitive overload, or error risk is most likely to occur. The map is then used to redesign interfaces, roles, and process steps so the system better aligns with human strengths and limitations. When executed well, it turns abstract user experience concerns into actionable design and governance changes that enhance performance, safety, and resilience.

Here is a short example: a healthcare organization finds that suspicious-account alerts are detected quickly, but containment (account lock, token revocation, and conditional access changes) is consistently delayed on night shifts. Leaders initially attribute the issue to analyst performance. Human-system interaction mapping shows a different cause. Analysts must pivot across multiple dashboards to confirm identity context, then request containment actions they do not have privileges to perform. Escalations to IAM follow inconsistent paging norms, and the ticketing form requires redundant data entry. The map also reveals an ambiguous decision threshold: analysts hesitate to disable clinician accounts because procedures do not clearly balance security action with patient-care risk. Based on the map, the organization (1) enriches SIEM alerts with identity context and direct links to the correct IAM actions, (2) creates a pre-approved "clinical safe containment" playbook with explicit decision criteria, (3) grants SOC leads limited containment privileges after hours, and (4) simplifies escalation and ticketing. Containment times drop, workarounds decrease, and night-shift decision fatigue is reduced.

The analytical objective extends to modeling cognitive and physical demands at each touchpoint, from the workload imposed on a security operations center analyst parsing dense visualizations to the memory burden on a general employee manipulating complex password rules. Human factors research demonstrates that accurate characterization of task demands, representations, and constraints is foundational for anticipating error modalities and performance breakdowns in complex socio-technical systems (Norman, 2013; Stanton et al., 2013). For example, a concise illustration of this would be a secure code review embedded within a DevSecOps pipeline. Teams often assume that the task is simply to clear static analysis findings before merge, but the real demands include time pressure, noisy tool output, unclear risk labels, and fragmented context across pull requests, scanners, and ticketing systems. This creates predictable errors, such as dismissing exploitable findings as false positives or prioritizing low-impact issues over critical ones. Human factors-informed redesign, such as clearer severity representations, context-linked findings, and decision checklists at merge gates, reduces these errors and strengthens release security.

Upon completion of the interaction map, the resulting blueprint enables the identification of human vulnerabilities embedded within routine and high-stakes security work. Analysis can reveal design/cognition misalignments, such as excessive reliance on working memory in multi-step phishing response checklists, ambiguous or poorly grouped interface elements in access management consoles, or unnecessary navigation depth during privilege changes. Empirical studies in usable security and organizational behavior indicate that such misalignments elevate the likelihood of slips, mistakes, and violations, whereas interfaces that reduce cognitive load and support recognition over recall increase compliance and reduce workarounds (Beautement et al., 2009; Kirlappos and Sasse, 2012). The map, therefore, functions as an evidence-based diagnostic, allowing prioritization of the most consequential touchpoints for redesigning.

Carefully mapping how people interact with security tools gives teams real evidence of where to reduce friction, so the safest choice is also the easiest. From there, teams can redesign workflows with practical guardrails, reveal information only when needed, build interfaces that help people recover from mistakes, and use visuals that are faster and easier to read under pressure. When these human-centered design choices are built into cybersecurity systems, organizations often see better user decisions, fewer policy violations, and stronger overall security outcomes. In that way, the interaction map becomes a practical playbook that helps human factors experts, security teams, and leaders turn broad policy goals into everyday designs people can actually use correctly.

## Task and cognitive workload analysis

Task analysis examines the specific cognitive, perceptual, and motor requirements associated with every security-related activity, providing a detailed breakdown of what the human is actually asked to do. For end users, this might involve dissecting the steps required for a seemingly simple action, such as **multi-factor authentication (MFA)**. While mandatory for security, the task of retrieving a code from a separate device, remembering a biometric gesture, or navigating complex single-sign-on interfaces introduces numerous cognitive frictions throughout the day. Across time, these frequent small interruptions may add to user frustration and can nudge people toward insecure shortcuts. For highly technical staff, such as security analysts working in **security operations centers (SOCs)**, task analysis reveals the critical issues of alert fatigue and chronic cognitive overload. These professionals must rapidly process and triage thousands of alerts daily, a task environment that inherently leads to vigilance decrement and a high probability of missing legitimate threats buried within the noise. Identifying points where cognitive load is high for end users and experts alike can provide useful diagnostic insights to prioritize and scope targeted human factors interventions.

This analysis must explicitly address the widespread issue of fatigue and stress across all user groups, recognizing that cybersecurity professionals, information technologists, and even non-technical employees are becoming chronically fatigued and stressed by the ever-increasing demands of the cybersecurity landscape. For example, a company layers on MFA checks, phishing drills, security popups, and recurring policy confirmations. Security analysts become overloaded with alerts, IT teams are swamped with access issues, and non-technical employees are constantly interrupted. As fatigue rises, people miss signals, rush decisions, and click through controls without thinking. A human factors approach would streamline low-value demands, focus attention on high-risk moments, and balance workload so that secure actions remain practical day to day. Completing work-related cybersecurity tasks, such as the preceding example, can quickly diminish one's cognitive abilities.

Cognitive workload analysis moves beyond simply charting steps to measuring the mental effort required, often using metrics such as response time, error rate, and subjective feedback scores to quantify the burden. For example, a security team evaluated its phishing-report triage process by measuring analyst response time to each case, classification error rate, and a weekly self-reported mental effort score. The data showed that when analysts had to switch across multiple tools and interpret inconsistent alert labels, response times increased, error rates rose, and perceived effort scores climbed. This made the cognitive burden visible and helped the team justify a redesign of the triage interface and workflow. For a typical employee, the constant barrage of phishing simulations, password rotation reminders, and compliance training contributes to a generalized "security fatigue" that dulls their responsiveness. For technical teams, burnout and high turnover are direct results of poorly designed systems that generate excessive false positives and require repetitive manual work. When organizations clearly measure the sources of stress in their workflows, they can focus on applying human factors engineering to drive improvements, such as refining interfaces, automating repetitive work, and simplifying high-friction steps, which helps redesign human-system interactions to strengthen security resilience while also supporting employee well-being.

## How to do task analysis in cybersecurity

The following steps outline a practical process for conducting task analysis in a cybersecurity workflow:

1. **Pick one bounded scenario.** Choose a concrete workflow with a clear start and end (for example, "triage a phishing report," "investigate a high-severity SIEM alert," or "contain a compromised account"). Define the success criteria (containment within X minutes; correct severity classification; complete documentation).
2. **Identify roles and boundaries.** List everyone who touches the work (SOC analyst, IAM engineer, system owner, and service desk) and where handoffs occur. Capture constraints such as change windows, privilege limitations, approval requirements, and on-call rules.
3. **Map the workflow as performed.** Observe the task in real time and collect artifacts (tickets, runbooks, chat transcripts, and dashboards). Break the work into steps: triggers → data gathering → decision points → actions → documentation → closure. Record tools used at each step, inputs/outputs, and where people switch systems.
4. **Locate failure and delay points.** Mark steps with frequent rework, ambiguity, waiting, or workarounds (for example, "must request IAM to revoke tokens," "severity labels unclear," or "duplicate data entry"). Deliver a task map that shows where performance degrades and why.

## How to do cognitive workload analysis

The following steps outline a practical process for conducting cognitive workload analysis:

1. **Annotate the task map with workload drivers.** For each step, identify what makes it mentally demanding: time pressure, alert volume, uncertainty, interruptions, context switching, memory demands, and high-stakes judgment.
2. **Measure workload using three complementary sources**:
    - **Subjective**: A brief post-task survey (for example, NASA-TLX) to capture perceived mental demand, time pressure, effort, and frustration
    - **Behavioral**: Time-to-decision, errors, rework, missed escalations, and documentation quality
    - **Operational telemetry**: Alert queue depth, false-positive rate, number of tool pivots, number of handoffs, paging frequency, and after-hours volume
3. **Diagnose where overload changes outcomes.** Identify steps where workload correlates with mistakes or delays (for example, missed indicators after multiple tool switches; incorrect severity under time pressure; delayed containment due to handoffs).
4. **Design and validate fixes.** Prioritize interventions that reduce avoidable load: alert enrichment, fewer tool pivots, clearer thresholds, checklists at decision points, better handoff protocols, calibrated automation, and staffing/on-call adjustments. Re-measure the same metrics after changes to confirm that workload and performance improved.

## An example of task and cognitive workload analysis

At 2:15 a.m., the SOC receives an "Impossible travel" alert for a faculty member's account, followed by multiple failed MFA prompts and a successful sign-in from an unfamiliar location. The account has access to email and shared drives.

### Task analysis example

The following example illustrates how task analysis can be applied to a cybersecurity workflow, showing how the work unfolds step by step in a real operational scenario:

1. **Trigger and intake**:
    a. Alert arrives in SIEM and creates a ticket.
    b. Analyst confirms severity criteria (privileged account, sensitive data, active session, etc.).

2. **Rapid scoping (establish what is true)**:
    a. Check identity provider logs: sign-in location, device, client app, MFA events, and conditional access results.
    b. Check email activity: suspicious inbox rules, forwarding, and OAuth grants.
    c. Check endpoint context: known device versus unknown device, EDR detections, and VPN usage.
3. **Decision point – compromise likelihood**:
    a. Determine whether this is a travel/VPN false positive, MFA fatigue attack, password spray, or true credential theft.
    b. Decide whether to contain immediately or continue evidence gathering for a few minutes.
4. **Containment actions (stop ongoing access)**:
    a. Revoke sessions and refresh tokens.
    b. Force password reset and require MFA re-registration.
    c. Temporarily block sign-in or require step-up authentication.
    d. If privileged, disable the account and rotate credentials/keys.
5. **Eradication and hardening**:
    a. Remove malicious mailbox rules and forwarding.
    b. Review OAuth consents and remove suspicious app grants.
    c. Validate conditional access policies (device compliance, geo-fencing, and risk-based sign-in).
6. **Recovery and communication**:
    a. Coordinate with the help desk to verify user identity and restore access safely.
    b. Notify user and relevant stakeholders, document actions, and update the incident timeline.
7. **Closure and learning**:
    a. Post-incident review: how long to contain, what steps created the delay, and what evidence was missing.

The primary deliverable is a workflow map that explicitly represents the end-to-end identity-compromise process, specifying the roles involved (for example, the SOC analyst, IAM engineer, messaging administrator, and help desk), the tool touchpoints that mediate critical actions and evidence collection (such as the identity provider console, SIEM, email administration platform, and endpoint detection and response tools), and the operational handoffs that govern execution authority and timing (including who is authorized to revoke sessions and tokens, who can remove malicious mailbox rules, and who can initiate or validate multifactor authentication re-registration).

## Cognitive workload analysis example

The following example highlights how cognitive workload analysis can be used to identify points in the workflow where mental load increases and to understand the factors that contribute to these spikes. The following are the key high-load points in the workflow:

1. **Ambiguous alert context**:
    - "Impossible travel" is often noisy. The analyst must decide quickly whether it is real.
    - *Workload driver*: Uncertainty + time pressure.
2. **Tool switching and fragmented evidence**:
    - The analyst pivots among SIEM, IdP logs, email admin, and EDR.
    - *Workload driver*: Context switching + working memory demands.
3. **High-stakes decision threshold**:
    - Disabling an active user can disrupt operations; delaying can allow data theft.
    - *Workload driver*: Risk trade-offs + fear of business impact.
4. **Privilege-dependent delays**:
    - The analyst lacks permission to revoke tokens or remove mailbox rules and must escalate.
    - *Workload driver*: Handoff latency + coordination burden.

## How you measure workload (practical metrics)

**Workload** in an identity-compromise response can be operationalized through a set of complementary behavioral, process, and subjective indicators that collectively capture time pressure, cognitive switching costs, and error-related rework. Key temporal measures include **time-to-contain**, defined as the elapsed minutes from initial alert receipt to verified session and token revocation, and **decision latency**, defined as the interval between the analyst's first review of corroborating evidence and the formal containment decision. Workflow complexity can be quantified using tool pivots, measured as the number of distinct security and administrative consoles accessed prior to containment, which serves as a proxy for context switching and information fragmentation. Quality and reliability of performance can be assessed through rework rate, operationalized as the proportion of cases reopened due to missed compromise artifacts such as malicious mailbox rules or unauthorized OAuth grants. In addition, queue pressure, measured as the number of concurrent alerts assigned or active during the event window, provides an ecologically valid indicator of competing demands on attention and prioritization. Finally, subjective workload should be captured using a brief post-incident administration of the **NASA Task Load Index** (**NASA-TLX**), which enables analysts to report perceived mental demand, temporal demand, effort, and frustration, thereby triangulating objective performance metrics with the operator's experienced cognitive burden.

Workload during identity-compromise response can be reduced, and operational outcomes enhanced, by redesigning the sociotechnical system to decrease uncertainty, minimize context switching, and standardize high-stakes decisions. **Alert enrichment** is a foundational intervention because it front-loads critical context, such as user role, recent MFA history, device posture, and direct links to the relevant identity provider log views, thereby reducing time spent searching across tools and reconstructing situational awareness. In parallel, a **containment-first playbook** with explicit decision criteria (for example, a predefined risk score threshold that triggers immediate token revocation) constrains ambiguity and accelerates decisive action under time pressure. **Role-based access tuning** further reduces handoff latency by granting SOC leads narrowly scoped after-hours permissions for session and token revocation, which is often the most time-critical containment step. Where feasible, **one-click response actions** can operationalize this playbook through automated sequences (for example, revoke sessions, force password reset, and temporarily block sign-in), improving consistency and reducing execution burden. Finally, **standardized decision aids**, such as brief checklists for "credential theft suspected," help prevent omission errors by prompting analysts to complete commonly missed steps, including mailbox-rule review and removal of unauthorized OAuth grants. Collectively, these changes shift the response from ad hoc, memory-dependent work toward cognitively compatible workflows that support faster containment, fewer oversights, and more reliable performance.

# Behavioral risk identification

Organizations must fundamentally analyze behavioral patterns to identify risks tied to human decision-making, which remains a primary vector for successful cyberattacks. Modern security perimeters are defined not only by firewalls, but also by the daily actions of employees, vendors, and contractors. In this context, **user and entity behavior analytics** (**UEBA**) should be understood as an enabling mechanism within a human-factors strategy, not as a substitute for human-centered risk analysis. UEBA provides structured visibility into behavior so that analysts can interpret intent, context, and operational meaning more effectively.

To operationalize this perspective, security teams use UEBA to continuously evaluate large datasets, including system logins, network activity, access to sensitive databases, and application usage, in order to establish a statistical baseline of normal behavior for each user and entity. Meaningful risk identification occurs when behavior deviates substantially from the baseline, such as a developer accessing financial records without role-based justification or a routine user initiating a large-scale data transfer during unusual hours. This approach allows security leaders to move beyond static, rule-based alerts and prioritize threats that signal high-risk shifts in human operational patterns.

Here is a short example: at 2:17 a.m., UEBA generates a high-severity alert for a software developer account. The alert is triggered by three correlated deviations from that user's baseline: an off-hours login from a new device, first-time access to the finance database, and an unusually large export of records to a cloud storage application the user has never used.

The analyst's next step is triage and contextual validation. They first verify whether the activity can be explained by a legitimate business need by checking the user's role, active tickets, and change calendar. They then contact the user's manager and the user through a secondary channel to confirm whether the session is authorized. Because the behavior remains unexplained, the analyst escalates to incident response, temporarily suspends the account, blocks the destination for data transfers, and preserves logs for forensic review. This sequence shows that UEBA does not replace human judgment; it focuses analysts' attention on high-risk behavioral change so that a human decision can determine intent and response.

To effectively translate observed behavioral anomalies into actionable mitigation strategies, security leaders must classify these actions using a structured error taxonomy. The **Human Factors Analysis and Classification System** (**HFACS**) is a comprehensive framework for identifying, analyzing, and classifying human factors that contribute to accidents and adverse incidents. It is gaining some initial traction in cybersecurity. The HFACS, which originated in high-reliability fields such as aviation safety, provides the necessary structure to classify human-initiated incidents into distinct categories: (a) errors (honest mistakes or failures of skill), (b) lapses (failures of memory or attention), or (c) violations (deliberate, though often well-intentioned, disregard for policy). This classification is important because it dictates the correct remedial response. For example, a "skill-based error" suggests a need for better system design or training, whereas a "routine violation" indicates a flawed policy or organizational pressure (such as an impossible deadline) that compels the user to bypass controls to complete their job. To ensure accurate diagnosis and effective remediation, many leading organizations are now prioritizing the hiring of human factors specialists and organizational psychologists (this is predominantly observed in some European organizations and not so much in the U.S.). These professionals are instrumental in applying the HFACS framework, translating technical data into meaningful insights about cognitive load, system design, and policy effectiveness.

The application of a systematic framework such as HFACS shifts the security function from a reactive, punitive role to a proactive, diagnostic one. By systematically classifying all security incidents and near-misses against a common taxonomy, organizations can aggregate data to identify the actual root causes of human risk, which often reside not with the individual user, but in latent organizational failures. If analysis reveals a high prevalence of "lapses," the focus shifts to simplifying authentication processes and reducing cognitive and procedural friction in everyday work. If it reveals "organizational violations," senior leadership must address cultural issues or unsustainable workloads. In practice, this often means streamlining authentication flows, reducing the number of repetitive prompts, enabling low-friction phishing-resistant MFA, and aligning session timeouts with actual task patterns. Teams should also test revised workflows with end users to confirm that security steps are understandable, timely, and minimally disruptive. The objective is to enhance secure behavior by design, not to demand perfect vigilance under poor usability conditions.

If analysis instead reveals organizational violations, the response must move beyond individual accountability and address systemic drivers. Senior leadership should examine whether performance targets, staffing levels, or turnaround expectations are implicitly rewarding policy bypass. That review should be followed by concrete structural changes, such as recalibrating deadlines, clarifying non-negotiable control points, and holding managers accountable for compliance climate within their units. In this case, risk treatment is primarily cultural and operational: the organization must remove the conditions that normalize unsafe workarounds.

This expertise is crucial for addressing cultural issues, unsustainable workloads, and policy friction identified by error taxonomies such as HFACS. This data-driven approach moves security away from the ineffective cycle of punishing individuals and toward continuous process improvement, allowing the institution to design controls, policies, and interfaces that are inherently more resilient to human factors.

# Technology strategies to enable HFE integration

Technology strategies that enable HFE integration include automation and cognitive load reduction, in which repetitive cybersecurity tasks are automated so personnel can focus on higher-order judgment and anomaly interpretation. In this approach, automation should be designed to support human oversight by presenting concise, decision-relevant context rather than producing excessive low-value alerts. Adaptive security interfaces then personalize workflows, prompts, and risk cues based on user role, task criticality, and demonstrated proficiency, which encourages secure behavior without introducing unnecessary friction. At the same time, behavior monitoring and feedback loops should transform interaction data into actionable insight, enabling teams to detect recurring lapses, policy friction points, and emerging workload stressors before they escalate into incidents. When implemented together, these elements create a socio-technical security environment in which technology enhances human performance, reinforces resilient decision-making, and supports continuous organizational learning.

## Automation and cognitive load reduction

Automation technologies such as **security orchestration, automation, and response (SOAR)** platforms can reduce cognitive load by automating routine security tasks, allowing analysts to focus on higher-order decision-making. Automation also reduces human variability, a leading contributor to misconfigurations and delays in incident response.

In cybersecurity, automation refers to the implementation of automated procedures and systems that perform operations with minimal human intervention. This strategy offers various benefits from a human factors perspective, primarily by reducing cognitive load and improving operational effectiveness. High data volumes and time-sensitive threats are standard features of cybersecurity systems that can be too much for human operators to handle. By handling routine monitoring, threat identification, and initial response steps, automation reduces this difficulty. This enables human analysts to focus on solving complicated problems and making strategic decisions. The ideas of cognitive ergonomics, which emphasize optimizing human performance through careful task design and workload allocation, are consistent with this division of labor.

Notwithstanding these advantages, automaticity presents several difficulties that need to be viewed from a human factors perspective. The possible decline in situational awareness among cybersecurity experts is a significant worry. Human operators' capacity to comprehend the broader context of security issues may be diminished when autonomous systems remove them from the decision-making process. Their ability to successfully intervene during system breakdowns or when confronted with new dangers may be hampered by this detachment. Automation bias, or the tendency to place too much faith in automated results, can also lead to serious mistakes. When automated systems generate false positives or negatives, this is especially troublesome because human operators might not challenge or confirm the system's findings.

The decline of human abilities is another problem linked to automaticity. Cybersecurity experts may become less adept at manual methods and analytical reasoning as automated technologies progressively replace routine tasks. When manual intervention is necessary, such as during system outages or complex attacks that evade automated detection, this loss of experience can be harmful. Additionally, openness and accountability may be hampered by the opacity of many automated systems, sometimes referred to as the "black box" problem. It is hard to verify results, fix mistakes, or have confidence in the system's reliability when operators do not understand how automated systems make decisions.

Human factors engineering promotes human-centered automation as a solution to these issues. This method highlights the importance of keeping people "in the loop" or "on the loop," ensuring that operators remain aware of and in control of automated processes. For example, in a SOC, AI can triage alerts and recommend severity, but analysts review the evidence and make final response decisions. This keeps humans in the loop while training reinforces model interpretation, confidence limits, and false-positive detection. In enterprise email security, automation can quarantine suspicious messages, but authorized users and analysts can override with documented justification. This keeps humans in the loop and supports training on when overrides are valid and where automated detection can fail. Training curricula must be created to maintain essential competencies and promote comprehension of the reasoning behind and constraints of automated systems.

The ultimate objective is to strike the right balance between leveraging automation to enhance performance and preserving the cognitive, perceptual, and decision-making capabilities essential for effective cybersecurity operations. Adaptive security interfaces operationalize this balance by aligning security friction, prompts, and controls with real-time user context and risk, ensuring that automation augments human capability rather than diminishing it.

## Adaptive security interfaces

Adaptive user interfaces that adjust based on user role, context, and behavior can significantly reduce the likelihood of errors. Adaptive security interfaces are security controls that adjust in real time based on user context and risk. They adjust prompts, authentication steps, and warnings based on factors such as device, location, behavior, and task sensitivity. The aim is to reduce friction in low-risk situations and apply stronger controls in high-risk situations. This human-centered design supports clearer decisions, better compliance, and fewer unsafe workarounds.

For example, presenting simplified dashboards to end users while offering advanced configurations to administrators aligns interface complexity with user capabilities. In cybersecurity, adaptive interfaces are designed to respond quickly to contextual shifts, attack scenarios, and user behavior, thereby improving system resilience and usability. These interfaces customize user experiences and security responses by utilizing behavioral analytics, AI, and real-time feedback mechanisms. Adaptive interfaces, unlike static systems, continually change in response to user interactions and environmental inputs, enabling more efficient threat mitigation and decision support. Adaptive cybersecurity systems are most effective when they are intentionally designed around human behavior rather than imposed as purely technical controls (Khadka and Ullah, 2025). Consider a practical scenario in a healthcare network: a nurse attempts to access a patient record from a familiar workstation during a normal shift, and the system allows streamlined access with minimal interruption; later, that same account is used to request bulk exports from an unfamiliar device at an unusual hour, triggering step-up authentication, a contextual warning, and analyst review. In this design, the system does not treat every interaction with equal friction, and it does not assume that users will always act with perfect consistency under pressure. Instead, it aligns security responses with role, context, workload, and risk, which reduces unsafe workarounds during routine care while strengthening controls when behavior shifts become meaningful. This is precisely how human-centric design reduces vulnerability exposure and increases compliance: it makes secure behavior feasible in daily operations and automatically enables proportionate intervention when risk escalates.

The creation and improvement of adaptive cybersecurity interfaces heavily rely on HFE. HFE works to ensure that interfaces are user-friendly, reduce cognitive load, and facilitate sound decision-making under pressure by drawing on concepts from behavioral science, ergonomics, and cognitive psychology. Nobles et al. (2025) describe Human Factors Engineering-as-a-Service (HFEaaS) as a practical way to "bake in" human factors work as an ongoing service, rather than treating usability and workflow design as a one-time project. The core idea is that adaptive security only works well when it is continuously tuned to how people actually operate. That means routinely collecting feedback from real incidents and daily operations (for example, alert handling time, false positives, time-to-contain, number of tool pivots, escalation delays, rework from missed steps, and user friction reports), then using that data to adjust policies, playbooks, and interface cues. Instead of guessing where the pain points are, the model creates a repeatable loop: measure what users struggle with, fix the highest-impact issues, deploy changes, and validate that the change reduced errors and response time. This approach emphasizes aligning human capabilities and limitations with system functionality to reduce error rates and boost user confidence. Given that human error is still a major contributor to security breaches, incorporating HFE into cybersecurity design is not just a technical improvement but also a strategic necessity.

In practice, HFEaaS delivers three concrete capabilities. First, **iterative feedback loops** turn operational metrics and frontline feedback into a prioritized backlog of "human performance fixes" (for example, simplifying an access approval flow or reducing noisy alerts). Second, **tailored interface design** ensures that what the SOC sees, what IT administrators see, and what end users see is purpose-built for their tasks and risk context, with clear decision thresholds, minimal steps, and embedded guidance that reduces memory reliance. Third, **usability audits** function as structured checks on whether security tools and workflows are causing unnecessary friction, confusion, or workarounds, and they produce specific remediations (for example, alert enrichment standards, consistent labeling, one-click containment actions, or clearer "why you are blocked" messages). The practical payoff is fewer low-value interruptions, faster and more consistent response actions, higher compliance because workflows are easier to follow, and better overall resilience during high-pressure events.

Real-world applications of adaptive cybersecurity interfaces illustrate HFE integration by dynamically calibrating security friction and decision support to the user's context and risk. For example, Microsoft Entra Conditional Access, Google Workspace Context-Aware Access, Okta Adaptive MFA, and Microsoft's Report Phishing interface can each be described as adaptive cybersecurity interfaces because they modify the user's security experience based on situational signals rather than applying uniform controls. **Microsoft Entra Conditional Access** is adaptive because it conditionally permits, restricts, or requires step-up authentication based on evaluated context such as sign-in risk, device compliance, location, and application sensitivity, thereby calibrating friction to observed risk. **Google Workspace Context-Aware Access** is adaptive because it gates access to organizational resources using contextual attributes such as user identity, device posture, and network or location signals, enabling differentiated access decisions that change as conditions change. **Okta Adaptive MFA** is adaptive because it varies authentication requirements through policy rules that incorporate contextual and risk indicators, strengthening verification when anomalies are detected while reducing unnecessary prompts in low-risk sessions. **Microsoft's Report Phishing interface** is adaptive in a user-centered sense because it embeds reporting directly within the email client at the moment of user judgment, reducing the cognitive and procedural effort required to escalate suspected threats and enabling faster organizational response through streamlined, context-bound user action.

Adaptive alert systems can suppress duplicate low-value notifications and escalate only behaviorally significant anomalies, such as privilege misuse combined with unusual data movement, which helps teams focus on true operational risk. For example, a low-value notification is a **single failed login alert for a non-privileged user**, which often reflects benign causes such as mistyped passwords, expired credentials, cached logins, or VPN issues. These alerts exist because detection rules are frequently configured for high sensitivity to avoid missing early compromise signals, but they become low-value when they are surfaced as standalone interrupts without correlation or actionable context. Customized training programs can then tailor each role with scenario-based exercises, such as phishing triage for help desk staff, insider risk escalation for SOC analysts, and decision-making under time pressure for incident commanders, thereby strengthening both performance and resilience during real events.

Collectively, this pattern of alert noise, low-value notifications, context fragmentation, and role-specific decision demands demonstrates why cybersecurity frameworks should incorporate HFE to redesign interfaces, escalation criteria, and workflows so that users can act decisively with less cognitive load and fewer errors.

## Behavior monitoring and feedback loops

Embedding behavioral analytics into security systems represents a crucial shift from perimeter defense to human-centric security. This approach utilizes UEBA to establish a comprehensive baseline of expected user activity, monitoring everything from login times and data access patterns to typing speed and mouse movements. When a user deviates significantly from their established profile (for example, attempting to access sensitive data outside regular working hours or downloading a large volume of files), the system flags the activity as an anomaly that may signal a compromised account or careless user behavior. This process effectively transforms security from a static set of rules into a dynamic, learning system capable of detecting subtle, context-aware threats that rigid firewall rules would typically miss, thereby acting as an early warning system for organizational risk.

The actual value of behavioral monitoring lies in real-time feedback loops that guide user behavior toward secure practices without resorting to punitive measures. Drawing heavily on principles from behavioral economics, these mechanisms employ "nudges" (subtle, low-friction prompts that guide users toward the optimal choice). For example, rather than blocking a user trying to upload a file to an unapproved cloud service, a prompt might appear asking, "Are you sure? Please confirm this file does not contain sensitive client data," while simultaneously presenting the pre-approved, secure sharing service as the default, easy-to-select alternative. Real-world applications have shown that these "just-in-time" or "context-aware" warnings are far more effective than mandatory annual training because they interrupt risky behavior at the moment of decision, thereby creating teachable moments and reducing the cognitive load on the user (Eze, 2025).

By prioritizing prompts and non-punitive nudges over immediate disciplinary action, organizations cultivate a security culture based on collaboration rather than fear. This strategy addresses the well-documented problem of "security fatigue," in which users become overwhelmed and begin to ignore security protocols. When users feel the security system is helping them, rather than constantly punishing them, they are more likely to internalize secure habits. This positive feedback mechanism encourages users to become active participants in the defense process, leading to sustained behavioral change and measurable reductions in internal security incidents, particularly those stemming from preventable causes such as weak passwords or phishing attempts. Ultimately, this human-computer interaction approach converts the traditionally weakest link in the security chain (the user) into one of its most vigilant defenders.

## Strategic implementation roadmap

Strategic implementation begins with a rigorous baseline assessment of the cybersecurity ecosystem, emphasizing human interaction points across workflows, organizational culture regarding security behaviors, and the effectiveness of existing training programs. Evidence collection should include structured surveys to quantify attitudes and behaviors, semi-structured interviews to surface contextual nuances, and retrospective reviews of incident and near-miss data to identify recurrent human-system failure modes. Resulting findings should produce a risk-ranked map of socio-technical pain points, gap analyses against policy and control expectations, and priority hypotheses for intervention. Following baseline development, framework selection and customization should align with the organizational context. Frameworks such as HFACS or the Swiss cheese model (this model indicates that incidents happen when multiple defenses each have gaps, and those gaps align, allowing a threat to pass through all layers) can be adapted to cybersecurity by defining explicit categories and subcategories, such as policy misalignments, supervision gaps, and operator errors, and by augmenting them with domain-specific nanocodes that enable consistent, high-granularity classification and longitudinal comparison.

A critical element of this strategic roadmap involves deliberate partnerships with human factors and psychology professionals. These partnerships enable organizations to focus on systematically reducing human friction within cybersecurity ecosystems. By embedding subject-matter expertise early in the architecture and design phases, organizations can ensure that technical controls, workflows, and security policies align with cognitive and behavioral realities. Human factors specialists provide actionable insights on user interaction, workload balance, and error precursors. At the same time, psychology professionals contribute a deeper understanding of behavioral motivators, stress responses, and decision-making under pressure. These perspectives help principal architects design secure systems that are not only technically sound but also optimized for how humans actually behave in operational contexts.

However, the current shortage of human factors and psychology professionals has significantly impeded the field's ability to mitigate human-induced cybersecurity errors. Many organizations rely heavily on technical solutions without integrating behavioral science expertise, resulting in systems that are secure on paper but fragile in practice. This gap contributes to persistent issues such as poor security culture, misaligned policy implementation, insecure workarounds, and operational fatigue, all of which elevate organizational risk. The lack of specialized professionals has also delayed the identification of root causes in incident analyses, often leading to superficial remediation rather than systemic correction.

To address this deficit, strategic implementation must begin with securing human factors expertise as a foundational capability rather than a supplemental resource. Establishing formal roles for human factors engineers and psychologists within cybersecurity programs ensures that behavioral risk considerations are integrated from initial planning through to execution and evaluation. These experts should work directly with principal system architects, security engineers, and governance teams to embed principles of usability, cognitive ergonomics, and behavioral design into the technological stack.

Technology integration should operationalize the selected human-factors framework by enabling targeted capabilities across the security stack. Priority capabilities include automation tools that reduce error-prone manual steps, behavioral analytics platforms that detect risky interaction patterns and measure the effects of interventions, and user-interface adaptations that minimize cognitive load and promote secure defaults. Integration activities should align with existing architectures for identity, endpoints, networks, and the cloud, using reference integrations, data schemas, and event-taxonomy harmonization to ensure interoperability and observability. Governance requirements should shape design choices for data protection, privacy, and auditability. At the same time, success criteria should be anchored in leading and lagging indicators such as time to detect human-factor precursors, reductions in policy-exception rates, improvements in task success underload, and increases in secure-behavior adherence.

Continuous improvement processes should institutionalize human-factors integration as an iterative quality system rather than a one-time deployment. Monitoring programs should pair incident and near-miss analysis with ongoing measurement of training efficacy, simulation outcomes, and behavioral telemetry to detect drift and emerging risks. Feedback loops should connect analytic findings to governance and strategy through cadence-based reviews, codebook refinements for HFACS or Swiss cheese adaptations, targeted redesign of workflows and interfaces, and role-specific training updates. Organizational learning should be reinforced through cross-functional councils that track corrective action completion, validate sustained effects, and recalibrate priorities based on evolving threat landscapes and capacity constraints, thereby maintaining alignment among human capabilities, control design, and mission objectives.

Ultimately, the strategic imperative is clear: cybersecurity resilience requires deliberate, sustained integration of human factors and behavioral science expertise. This integration transforms security architectures from rigid technical systems into adaptive socio-technical ecosystems designed to support human operators, reduce cognitive strain, and mitigate human-induced risk.

## Organizational and cultural considerations

Organizational and cultural considerations in cybersecurity must begin with workforce empowerment, ensuring that personnel have decision-making authority, role-relevant training, and psychologically safe channels to report risks without fear of reprisal. Policy and regulation alignment should translate external requirements into clear, usable internal procedures so compliance expectations are operationally realistic rather than administratively symbolic. Common barriers and challenges include resistance to change, fragmented governance, alert fatigue, and misaligned incentives that reward speed or output over secure behavior. Sustainable progress requires leadership commitment, workforce empowerment, and policy and regulation alignment.

## Sustainable progress requires leadership commitment

Without a doubt, it takes a clear, consistent commitment from leadership to integrate HFE into cybersecurity. Leaders need to see human factors as a strategic asset essential to organizational resilience and to enabling enterprise risk management, not a side issue or a training afterthought. Developing a security culture that prioritizes usability, human performance, and adaptive system design requires a change in mentality. HFE concepts must be actively promoted by leadership in workforce development, budgeting, and cybersecurity planning. Visible executive backing for HFE initiatives promotes cross-functional collaboration among technical teams, human factors experts, and end users, and signals the organization's relevance.

Organizations should incorporate human factors indicators into their risk management frameworks and performance dashboards to institutionalize HFE within cybersecurity governance. Metrics on alert fatigue levels, interface usability scores, user error rates, and training efficacy are examples of these indicators. We have found that incorporating HFE into governance frameworks promotes ongoing development and enables proactive detection of human-system vulnerabilities. Organizations can more accurately evaluate how human-centered design affects threat detection, incident response, and overall system resilience by coordinating HFE metrics with cybersecurity key performance indicators. As part of the cybersecurity strategy, this integration ensures that human factors are not only recognized but also actively measured and managed.

## Workforce empowerment

Workforce empowerment is a critical element in cultivating a resilient security culture. When employees perceive themselves not merely as subjects of policy but as active participants in organizational defense, their engagement with security protocols becomes more consistent and intrinsically motivated. HFE approaches reinforce this engagement through participatory design, integrating user perspectives into the development of security tools and procedures. This ensures that system interfaces, workflows, and policies reflect the lived realities of those who interact with them daily. Research demonstrates that user-centered security design leads to greater adherence and lower error rates because users are more likely to internalize procedures they helped shape (Norman, 2013).

Participatory strategies also help build a shared sense of responsibility and trust between employees and security leadership. By incorporating end users into decision-making processes, organizations can surface latent usability issues, reduce friction in security workflows, and foster mutual accountability. This alignment between system requirements and user capabilities minimizes cognitive and procedural barriers that often result in noncompliance or workarounds. Empirical findings indicate that employees who are engaged in security-related discussions and decisions demonstrate greater policy adherence and are more likely to detect and report security incidents (Kirlappos and Sasse, 2012). Such involvement transforms security from a top-down directive into a shared organizational value.

Finally, empowerment strategies create a positive feedback loop in which trust, compliance, and usability reinforce one another. When users trust the system and the organization, they are more inclined to follow protocols and contribute to collective security goals. In turn, systems designed with user input are more usable, reducing error rates and enhancing organizational resilience. This aligns with human factors principles that emphasize designing for human strengths rather than treating human behavior as a liability. Studies have shown that security cultures built on empowerment, rather than enforcement alone, produce more sustainable security behaviors and higher overall security performance (Beautement et al., 2009). By embedding HFE principles into security governance, organizations can strengthen both individual responsibility and systemic defense.

## Policy and regulation alignment

Policy and regulatory alignment represent a foundational pillar for embedding HFE principles into organizational security governance. Modern regulatory frameworks increasingly recognize that human behavior is integral to the effectiveness of security controls. Instead of viewing individuals as passive compliance agents, contemporary approaches stress the importance of designing systems and policies that account for human capabilities and limitations. Regulatory bodies have progressively integrated human factors considerations into their guidance, acknowledging that policies built without attention to usability or user experience are less likely to achieve their intended security outcomes. This evolution reflects a shift from a purely technical compliance model toward one that recognizes the socio-technical nature of cybersecurity governance (National Institute of Standards and Technology, 2022).

Embedding human-centered design principles directly into policy frameworks ensures that security requirements align with operational realities and user needs. Standards such as **national institute of standards and technology (NIST)** guidelines and **international organization for standardization (ISO)** usability standard ISO 9241-210 provide structured methodologies for integrating usability, accessibility, and cognitive ergonomics into security practices. For example, NIST emphasizes the need to consider human-system interaction in risk management and control design to reduce operational error and enhance resilience (NIST SP 800-53). Similarly, ISO 9241-210 advocates participatory design and iterative evaluation processes, ensuring that security controls are not only technically sound but also cognitively compatible with the workforce. This alignment reduces the likelihood of noncompliance caused by overly complex procedures and fosters sustainable security behaviors across organizational levels.

Regulatory alignment with human factors principles further supports accountability, auditability, and organizational resilience. Policies anchored in recognized standards facilitate clearer governance structures, improve implementation consistency across departments, and simplify external audits. More importantly, they make compliance more achievable and less burdensome for end users, which strengthens both adherence and trust. Studies in cybersecurity governance indicate that organizations integrating human-centered frameworks experience lower error rates, more consistent compliance, and improved incident response performance (Maalem Lahcen et al., 2020). By embedding usability standards and human factors considerations into regulatory and policy structures, organizations can align security governance with human performance realities, thereby enhancing both security effectiveness and organizational adaptability.

## Barriers and challenges

Adaptive integration of HFE into cybersecurity is impeded by entrenched organizational assumptions that privilege technical controls over socio-technical design. Resistance to change persists when security governance fails to account for cognitive workload, task fit, and usability constraints, leading to policies that are formally adequate but operationally brittle. Policy adherence depends heavily on whether employees perceive controls as clear, fair, and workable, not merely on whether policies exist (Sommestad et al., 2014). For example, when a file-sharing policy is complex and poorly explained, staff often bypass it to meet deadlines. When leaders clarify purpose, reduce friction, and enforce rules consistently, adoption increases. Culture and leadership advocacy, therefore, function as primary drivers of compliance, not secondary factors.

Embedding participatory design into security planning addresses this barrier by aligning control requirements with work as done rather than merely work as imagined, thereby increasing perceived efficacy and ownership. Given the relative novelty of HFE applications in cybersecurity, capability gaps frequently emerge. Building internal expertise through targeted hiring, cross-training with usability and human factors specialists, and structured partnerships with academic units and professional bodies, including the Human Factors and Ergonomics Society.

Measurement complexity constitutes a second-order challenge that directly influences adaptability. Human behavior exhibits situational variability and path dependence, rendering purely technical metrics insufficient for governance decisions. Robust evaluation, therefore, requires a mixed-methods approach that combines sensitive quantitative indicators of behavior and knowledge with qualitative assessments of context, workflow friction, and mental models. Validated instruments from the human aspects of information security literature demonstrate that multidimensional constructs such as awareness, intent, and routine practice can be reliably measured, but only when embedded in iterative assessment cycles and linked to design interventions and leadership messaging (Parsons et al., 2017). Integrating such measures with incident and process data enables attribution of improvements to specific HFE interventions, reduces uncertainty about return on investment, and supports continuous adaptation. Collectively, leadership-driven culture change, capability development through multidisciplinary collaboration, and rigorous socio-technical measurement frameworks provide a coherent strategy for overcoming resistance, addressing expertise gaps, and managing the inherent complexity of evaluating human-centered security performance (Maalem Lahcen et al., 2020; Parsons et al., 2017; Sommestad et al., 2014).

## Summary

In conclusion, effective human factors-centered cybersecurity requires structured planning, strategic alignment, and sustained organizational commitment. Integrating human factors frameworks with technical infrastructure and governance enables organizations to manage the interaction between human behavior and security outcomes, shifting practice from reactive awareness efforts to proactive risk anticipation, adaptive system design, and durable behavior change. This integration strengthens resilience, reduces error-prone actions, and aligns workforce performance with cybersecurity strategy. Looking ahead, the growing influence of generative AI, quantum-resistant architectures, and autonomous defense systems will intensify the need for rigorous HFE, with future work emphasizing predictive behavioral modeling, AI-supported decision augmentation, and scaled HFACS-based behavioral analytics.

The next chapter translates these principles into an implementation path for operationalizing human factors across cybersecurity programs.

## References


- Beautement, A., Sasse, M. A., and Wonham, M. (2009). *The compliance budget: managing security behaviour in organisations.* In Proceedings of the 2008 New Security Paradigms Workshop (pp. 47–58). DOI 10.1145/1595676.1595684.
- Eze, F. C. (2025). *Human factors in cybersecurity: Novel approaches for improving users' behavior and decision making in cybersecurity context.* International Nexus Multidisciplinary Research Journal, 1(2), 192–207. `https://inmrj.org/index.php/nexus/article/view/34` (`inmrj.org`)
- Greitzer, F. L., and Frincke, D. A. (2010). *Combining traditional cyber security audit data with psychosocial data: Towards predictive modeling for insider threat mitigation.* Insider Threats in Cyber Security, 85–113. DOI 10.1007/978-1-4419-7133-3_5

- International Organization for Standardization. (2019). *ISO 9241-210: Ergonomics of human-system interaction — Human-centered design for interactive systems.* ISO.
- Khadka, K., and Ullah, A. B. (2025). *Human factors in cybersecurity: An interdisciplinary review and framework proposal.* International Journal of Information Security, 24(3), 1–13. `https://doi.org/10.1007/s10207-025-01032-0`
- Kirlappos, I., and Sasse, M. A. (2012). *Security education against phishing: A modest proposal for a major rethink.* IEEE Security & Privacy, 10(2), 24–32.
- Maalem Lahcen, R. A., Caulkins, B., Mohapatra, R., and Kumar, M. (2020). *Review and insight on the behavioral aspects of cybersecurity.* Cybersecurity, *3*(1), 10.
- National Institute of Standards and Technology. (2022). *Security and Privacy Controls for Information Systems and Organizations (SP 800-53 Rev. 5).* NIST.
- Nobles, C., and Robinson, N. (2024). *The benefits of human factors engineering in cybersecurity.* Cybersecurity Risk Management: Enhancing Leadership and Expertise, 53.
- Nobles, C., Rangarajan, A., and Burrell, D. (2025). *Human Factors Engineering-as-a-Service in Cybersecurity.* In *Handbook of Research on Cybersecurity Risk in Contemporary Business Systems* (pp. 280–298). IGI Global. `https://doi.org/10.4018/979-8-3693-6437-6.ch014`
- Norman, D. A. (2013). *The design of everyday things.* Basic Books.
- Parsons, K., Calic, D., Pattinson, M., Butavicius, M., McCormac, A., and Zwaans, T. (2017). *The human aspects of information security questionnaire (HAIS-Q): two further validation studies.* Computers & Security, 66, 40–51.
- Sommestad, T., Hallberg, J., Lundholm, K., and Bengtsson, J. (2014). *Variables influencing information security policy compliance: A systematic review of quantitative studies.* Information Management & Computer Security, 22(1), 42-75.
- Stanton, N. A., Salmon, P. M., Rafferty, L. A., Walker, G. H., Baber, C., and Jenkins, D. P. (2013). *Human Factors Methods: A Practical Guide for Engineering and Design.* CRC Press.
- Verizon. (2025). *Data Breach Investigations Report.* Verizon Communications.
- Wang, Y., Hu, R., Lin, S., Schultz, M., and Delahaye, D. (2021). *The impact of automation on air traffic controllers' behaviors.* Aerospace, 8(9), 260. `https://doi.org/10.3390/aerospace8090260`
- Wiegmann, D. A., and Shappell, S. A. (2017). *A Human Error Approach to Aviation Accident Analysis: The Human Factors Analysis and Classification System.* Routledge.

# Get this book's PDF version and more

Scan the QR code (or go to `packtpub.com/unlock`). Search for this book by name, confirm the edition, and then follow the steps on the page.

UNLOCK NOW

*Note: Keep your invoice handy. Purchases made directly from Packt don't require an invoice.*

# 11

# Implementation Path for Human Factors in Cybersecurity

This final chapter bridges theory and execution by transforming the psychological, cultural, and technical principles discussed throughout the book into a structured roadmap for cybersecurity leaders, managers, and practitioners. For example, by including concepts such as mental workloads into technical and architectural design, organizations will see a reduction in burnout, stress, and missed detections. By following this framework, organizations can design teams, tools, and workflows that reflect real human capabilities—building stronger, smarter, and more resilient security operations.

In this chapter, we will cover how to implement a human-centered mindset at all levels in the organization, how to assess the environment for human factor readiness, how to design tools and applications for human performance, and how to build a culture for psychological safety and resilience for cybersecurity teams. We will also cover which continuous learning mechanisms are important, how to measure success and build feedback loops, and how to implement those changes into policies and processes.

In this chapter, we will cover the following topics:

- Human-centered mindset
- Assessing the current environment
- Designing for human performance
- Psychological safety and resilience: a cultural shift
- Continuous learning and improvement
- Measurement, metrics, and feedback

- Policy and process in human factors
- Sustainability in change: leadership and vision

## Human-centered mindset

There are many places one could start when implementing all the concepts in this book, but the best way to start is to shift our mindset. Creating a full human-centered approach to cybersecurity includes reframing how we view cybersecurity as both a discipline and a program. As a discipline, cybersecurity is a comprehensive practice protecting digital systems, networks, and data from destruction, manipulation, and modification. Cybersecurity as a program is about multiple teams and skills that form a cohesive group, including security operations, engineering, architecture, and design.

Everything from the technology we use to the automation that extends our human capability is meant to complement our work, not replace it. Having a strong cybersecurity mindset encourages people to make the best decisions possible in any defensive system. However, that mindset needs to shift to align with organizational strategy, culture, and system design.

To start, consider the humans who utilize cybersecurity tools, the operators and engineers who protect our organizations. A human-centered mindset wants to understand how those workflows, dashboards, and automation all work to support perception, memory limitations, and decision-making. Every optimization for teams should move to reduce unnecessary complexity and cognitive load on operators and engineers. Mistakes or poor decision-making are not a failure, but an opportunity to create learning signals and understand the root of the problem. Why was a detection missed? Was it because there are 15 individual dashboards with separate logins and 4 hops between each one to access them? Is it possible that someone was unable to find one of the systems or log in because of the complex nature of the environment? This is not human error; it is an opportunity to redesign systems to support our operators.

Consider how psychology plays into security design. When thinking about a problem facing a cybersecurity team, consider attention, fatigue, bias, and stress responses when developing playbooks, systems, and policies. Automation and AI are critical elements to supporting humans, but leverage human judgment instead of overly relying on that automation to make decisions. It's all about the balance between using AI where it makes sense, but preserving human oversight, innovation, and creativity where it counts. When teams work together, they continue to encourage cross-role and cross-team communication between analysts, engineers, and leadership to maintain a common mental model. Above all else, the mission and impact on the organization rule over competing priorities. When all else fails, lead with empathy and trust.

An example of integrating cross-role and cross-team communication in the real world is the integration of a **detection engineering** (**DE**) team in conjunction with a **security operations center (SOC)**. The SOC identifies potential alerts and issues, and feeds the information to the DE team, who then create rules and blocking to reduce the number of alerts that make it to the SOC. It becomes a cohesive feedback loop between teams that ultimately improves the security and reduces risk. This is just one example of how cyber teams can complement each other with different skill sets and continue to grow and mature their practices together.

# Assessing the current environment

Now that your mindset has shifted and is ready for more input, let's focus on assessing the current cybersecurity program and team. Whether the team is large or small, teams should come together to understand their current baseline. Even if the technical controls and cyber practices are at a mature level, teams may be missing visibility into how individuals interact with those systems and tools. Assessing the current state is more than looking at an inventory; it's about identifying where human performance supports cybersecurity outcomes. However, to take in that full picture, teams should establish a realistic view of what cognitive workloads look like for security analysts, how teams communicate, and the overall usability of tools and applications in day-to-day operations.

Starting with awareness and culture with the cybersecurity leadership team, how do they understand human factors concepts? Even with a mindset shift, how many leaders are aware of human factors principles across engineering, design, and psychology? Consider looking at where errors are discussed, false negatives are evaluated, or where teams may suppress failures or missed detections. A good place to start is looking at **root cause analyses** (**RCAs**) after incidents or outages with an objective mindset. Was the team honest? Did the team openly discuss where processes or tools failed and could be improved?

If a team is not honest about potential impacts or mistakes, it will lead to a continued lack of awareness, and real improvements will not be discussed or implemented. If the team does not feel psychologically safe to share their opinions openly and freely, teams may experience the same issues time and again, never getting to the root of the problems. Fostering a safe space for open discussion allows for faster identification of the root problem, as well as a reduction in repeat occurrences of similar issues.

Next, investigate where mental workloads, cognitive demands, alert volume, and context switching may be an issue. Are teams showing signs of alert or security fatigue? Are team shift rotations working well and supporting team members who may support the third shift consistently? Once leaders can evaluate areas where cognitive overload may exist, it's time to evaluate which tools could be prioritized for evaluation and investigation. Look for areas where excessive alerts are clogging up queues, interfaces are poorly designed, or prioritization is not clearly defined. Usability reviews can be an effective measurement tool to understand dashboards, ticketing tools, and workflows, as well as where automation is leveraged.

Three things that leaders should walk away with from this stage are as follows:

- A human factor readiness review across culture, business workflows, and design aspects
- A prioritized list of where intervention makes the most sense (tools, processes, culture, etc.)
- A baseline measurement across fatigue indicators and error trends to start

These examples provide a few easy ways that leaders can start to implement human factor engineering principles into their security operations teams. Everyone needs a starting point; even though it may feel overwhelming to integrate all of the suggestions, teams have to start somewhere. By adding thoughtful questions and analysis of current programs, leaders can start to identify the best starting places to integrate human factors across cybersecurity programs. Once a baseline assessment and review are done, leaders can start to understand how applications and tools can be developed or utilized more effectively for how humans interact with tools.

# Designing for human performance

Humans are complex, but technology grows at such a fast pace that we must adapt and overcome new interfaces, applications, and especially the use of **artificial intelligence** (**AI**). Emerging technology changes the way we make decisions, interact, and, ultimately, how efficiently we use said technology. The better we design our new applications and systems, the easier it is for humans to adapt and leverage new technology faster.

Now that the assessment is complete, your mindset is in the right place. Let's take a deep dive into how designing tools, applications, and systems can influence operations positively. Designing for human performance is not just about the tools; it's about optimizing cognitive, physical, and emotional aspects of work so that analysts and engineers can operate well under pressure. The goal is to ease the burdens of repetition, allowing for innovation and creativity to take the seat, so that humans can perform at their best and build better systems. The aim for integrating human factors is to help analysts and engineers succeed in their work and build the processes, tools, and systems to support that.

Human-centered security design begins with simplifying decision paths. Teams should remove unnecessary steps, redundant clicks, excessive dashboards, and context switching that do not directly support operational or decision-making tasks. By streamlining workflows and reducing friction, organizations can improve decision speed, decrease cognitive strain, and lower the likelihood of human error.

Effective human factors design requires intentional visual structure within applications and tools. Dashboards and alerts should present a clear hierarchy of importance using contrast, grouping, spacing, and consistency. Colors must reinforce meaning and align with alert criticality and vulnerability prioritization. When visual cues are standardized and purposeful, analysts can triage faster and maintain situational awareness while under pressure.

Human performance degrades under sustained cognitive load, so systems should be designed to protect attention as a finite resource. Analysts are constantly reviewing multiple tools, alerts, dashboards, emails, and open source intelligence. Treating mental workload as an operational risk results in more resilient teams, better judgment and decision-making, and more sustainable security operations.

Finally, cybersecurity leaders can focus on integrating usability testing into all aspects of the program. For example, in a SecOps team, consider including end users in tool evaluations and even designing new process workflows. Use their expertise to decide what tool decisions matter the most; maybe the best option is not to replace a tool, but to configure a current tool in a new way. Even using short iterative feedback loops (think in hours, not days) can help reveal how a tool is intended to be used versus the actual implementation. Environmental factors are just as important as software decisions; consider how *human-in-the-loop* testing can identify communication breakdowns. And finally, consider scheduling shift rotations to balance lower cognitive tasks with higher awareness tasks such as alert monitoring during peak hours. Using all of these options for designing around human limits will not only improve performance and efficiency but also provide a safe environment for analysts and engineers to learn, fail, and continuously improve.

# Psychological safety and resilience: a cultural shift

Mindset shifted. Check. Assessment complete. Check. Human performance considerations. Check. Now, onto building a culture that supports and even encourages psychological safety and resilience across the organization. Even the best-designed tools and processes will fail without a culture that embraces them and sees the value. Human-centered cybersecurity truly depends on how we as humans treat each other in high-stress situations. How we communicate, recover, and learn from mistakes all have impacts, whether positive or negative, on how operators and engineers thrive under pressure. The following items are truly meant to help organizations and teams have honest conversations about what's working, what's not, and how to iterate and improve on that over time. A human-centered cybersecurity program will not be built in a day, but taking steps to identify and implement these strategies will yield great returns in the short and long term.

As a first example, if a cybersecurity team has been constantly discouraged from sharing real-time data or mistakes, the mindset will be harder to shift. If previous employees were fired for sharing a mistake in a detection model or a missed detection, psychological safety will be harder to achieve. Another example is if a security engineer raised a flag early in the design process that users would have trouble interacting with a system, but they were told to continue developing anyway, they may struggle to believe that leadership really wants to implement change. Psychological safety is earned, just like respect and trust in any other field.

First, cybersecurity leaders can encourage and normalize individuals to speak up and question the known. One of the great detriments to any program is someone saying, "*This is how we've always done it.*" There may be times when either budget or resources will not allow for massive change, but it doesn't have to happen all at once. Encourage analysts and engineers to report anomalies, share near-misses, and speak up about risks or mistakes without fear of blame. For example, bring small groups of analysts into a room regularly for stand-up meetings, and suggest open discussions on what works and what doesn't. Leadership should lead by example, providing examples of their own mistakes to their teams, showing them that vulnerability and openness will provide mechanisms for improving their own skills and decision-making.

Focus on a learning environment that provides structured learning reviews after an incident, hone in on the process design, understand situational context, and what led to decisions. Each of these aspects will allow teams to reflect on how processes and decisions can be improved over time, and it starts with adoption by leadership. Leaders should be encouraged to speak up about uncertainty, share reasoning and any logic behind decisions, and ask for help when things go wrong.

Second, leverage short daily syncs to cover priorities and surface possible friction between teams. Standups need not be longer than five to seven minutes (depending on the size of the team), but provide a positive touchpoint for connection, interaction, and sharing of information. Leaders can also understand and recognize human limitations; this includes cognitive workloads and how shift work can impact someone's emotional and physical well-being. Provide access to stress management resources and encourage team members to speak up about burnout before it has a negative impact on the individual or the team. For example, at nine o'clock, the team can get together Monday through Friday for regular operational tasks, but an early Friday morning could be set aside to provide open communication using anonymous platforms. Tools such as Mural can be used for team members to provide feedback about possible friction topics, such as whether another team is blocking work or has closed an operational ticket without explanation or resolution.

And finally, encourage teams to cross-train or allow role-swapping (when possible), to strengthen both flexibility in skills, identify potential gaps in tooling or communication, and build relationships between teams. Leaders must create a culture that includes both safety and resilience, removing reactive or ineffective communications, which will allow teams to feel trusted and supported to adapt to strenuous situations. To build a strong and resilient culture, leaders must start with communication and collaboration but ultimately move into mechanisms that embrace continuous improvement across teams.

## Continuous learning and improvement

Human-centered cybersecurity is all about iterative learning and continuous feedback loops, because implementing these strategies will take place over time, versus attempting to do all of these steps at once. Technology is moving far faster than in previous years, but our analysts and engineers can, too. Traditional training mechanisms no longer serve a fast-paced cybersecurity team or adaptive thinking mindset. Building a continuous learning program starts with removing compliance and checklists and focusing more on decision-making, teamwork, and situational awareness skills. Training should be based on job role, duties, and contextual situations related to the individual. For example, a SecOps team wouldn't necessarily be trained on how to prevent phishing attacks, because their role is focused on what happens when someone clicks on a malicious link.

Learning should include building metacognitive skills as well, such as recognizing bias, fatigue, and attention drift. For example, attention drift can happen when someone is looking at the same screen of alerts or notifications for hours. The most up-to-date statistics from 2025 found that the attention span on one screen is anywhere from 45 to 90 seconds, down from previous numbers in 2024. Those numbers alone indicate that attention drift happens within minutes, not hours. Analysts and engineers who stare at the same repetitive screens may miss alerts or detections because of the ability to focus on one screen.

Understanding psychological terms can help individuals prevent burnout, address stress before it impacts operations, and, ultimately, reflect on what tools and techniques work better for them as individuals, rather than attempting to mirror what other colleagues are doing. Each person thinks differently, operates uniquely, and should be encouraged to find the techniques that work best for them. For example, a security analyst may be able to switch context easily for hours without losing attention or detail. But another analyst may require brain breaks every 30 minutes, whether that's standing and stretching, or taking a break from the queue for 2 to 3 minutes to check email or other communication channels. Understanding what works for the individual allows full focus and attention on their role.

There are multiple training formats that organizations can consider outside of the annual training or week-long training sessions:

- **Microlearning and reinforcement**: 5–10 minutes more frequently
- **Simulated attack labs**: Identify and address stress

- **After-action reviews (AARs)**: Lesson feedback loop
- **Adaptive learning platforms**: Take feedback and tailor training difficulty

To implement microlearning and reinforcement, cyber leaders can host weekly *Lunch and Learn* or stand-up meetings on Mondays to cover one topic. For example, on a Monday morning, teams could cover *Psychological Safety* awareness or *Mental Workloads*. In simulated attack labs, individuals will be prompted in a cyber scenario to identify where stress or burnout may occur. For example, cyber engineers must watch a demonstration of SOC analysts working through a variety of tools and decide which cognitive function is most associated with the task.

For AARs, cyber leaders should not just request the document, but schedule meetings with the teams and address any challenges with the issue. For example, if there was a data exfiltration incident, cyber leaders could encourage an open forum about what went well, what did not, and what could be improved next time. Cyber leaders should open the discussion with their own observations on what they could have done better, to encourage a safe environment for feedback. For adaptive learning platforms, using the same cybersecurity training year after year is ineffective. Adapt learning mechanisms for cognitive function, latest emerging trends, and to provide multiple mechanisms for education: questions and answers, opening widgets for more information, and engagement with the learning platform.

Learning, training, and education are not built equally. We all have different modes and mechanisms for retaining information, so consider that what might work for one may not work for all. The recommendation is to try a few different options and evaluate how teams learn. Did the information become actionable and measurable, and ultimately, was the team upskilled and performing at a higher level? To build measurable outcomes, the next section will guide leadership on how to evaluate and understand what training works, what doesn't, and how to keep iterating with new processes and techniques.

# Measurement, metrics, and feedback

Human-centered cybersecurity can only succeed when progress is measured in a quantifiable way. This is the reason why some human factors programs do not succeed; it can be difficult to effectively measure how people and systems interact, not just how many tickets an analyst closes in a day. The goal is to identify and capture aspects of performance quality, cognitive health, and adaptability without reducing humans to simple statistics. One important metric is decision quality: how well analysts and engineers make the right decisions when it comes to true positives, false positives, and identifying anomalies. Another metric that can be measured over time is workload balance: how well teams balance ticket queues, project deadlines, and overall context switching when working on multiple tasks.

Qualitative measurements have value: combine operational metrics with surveys, interviews, and behavioral observations. Numbers are helpful to understand trends, but narratives explain *why* they occur. It becomes easier to track patterns, understand operational limitations, and even identify early signals of fatigue. Using qualitative analysis can identify where communication breakdowns occur, how cognitive load impacts outcomes and risk, and, ultimately, improve risk reduction and resiliency effectiveness. Using the combination of quantitative and qualitative data can help to establish feedback loops, whether in retrospectives or quarterly reviews. Use these times to discuss patterns to drive continuous improvement, versus focusing on tickets closed, number of commits, or time to remediation.

There are several ways to accomplish the longitudinal perspective on metrics:

- Rate of incident escalation accuracy
- Reported fatigue levels via short pulse surveys
- Percentage of reclassified or reopened tickets due to incomplete data
- Cross-team response (time between detection and response)
- Retention of procedures and bias mitigation strategies
- Utilize dashboards that display human-centered KPIs alongside technical metrics

Utilizing these mechanisms will help to build a mature and robust human factors cybersecurity program. But only focusing on metrics and measurements will not be the entire solution; organizations must also consider how they frame cybersecurity expectations. Without a robust and clear cybersecurity policy and process that includes human factors initiatives, teams may not feel that these new mechanisms are necessary or required.

# Policy and process in human factors

For human factors to become ingrained in your cybersecurity program, it must be built into the organization's governance, policies, processes, and operating procedures. Embedding human-centered thinking will ensure that it lives past individual initiatives and long into building consistency, accountability, and effectiveness across the organization. This integration transforms human factors from a one-time task into a long-standing philosophy and cultural shift for cybersecurity professionals. At the core of adding human factors into cybersecurity policies, each aspect of the organizational structure should be reviewed. This includes everything from the top-level security policy to architectural reviews, and even within the **incident response (IR)** playbooks. Usability, workload management, and quality of communication should all be considered in technical documentation and the policies that align with organizational strategy.

Here are a few examples of how to align human-centered cybersecurity practices into procedural documentation or playbooks. The **national institute of standards and technology (NIST) cybersecurity framework (CSF)** is a document to help organizations manage and reduce cybersecurity risks. Implement *Human-System Interaction* under both the *Identify* and

*Respond* aspects of the framework to understand where miscommunication or cross-team collaboration is required. A number of security operations teams leverage the MITRE ATT&CK framework for mapping attack techniques to vulnerabilities. Instead of using the framework and technical controls alone, incorporate decision context and response coordination as part of the evaluation criteria when looking at alerts or vulnerabilities. Documentation and frameworks should not be static documents, but a dynamic and 360-degree view of the cybersecurity program, able to adapt and build additional capabilities that support a human-centered approach.

A few more areas to consider when building a human-centered governance approach are as follows:

- In post-incident reviews or retrospectives, encourage human error analysis and build a shared knowledge base across teams
- Provide recurring opportunities to surface friction points (whether anonymous or in leadership forums)
- Include a human factors liaison or representative between cybersecurity teams in technical, architectural, or design reviews

To encourage human error analysis, cyber leaders should offer their own perspective on how they may have made mistakes or could have come to different decisions. Providing a top-down approach to honesty will offer a safe environment for engineers and analysts to share their own perspectives. Using this information, processes and documentation can be updated to account for the latest feedback. An *open-door policy* extends to both open forums with technical teams, as well as opportunities for teams to provide feedback anonymously. A great example is using a tool such as Mural to allow engineers in a meeting to provide anonymous feedback, then allow for leadership to discuss with teams openly. A human factors liaison could be someone with both technical and human factors expertise to lead discussions, offer fresh perspectives, and provide a psychologically safe space for individuals to share feedback.

Now that an organization has rewritten and embraced new policies that consider the **human factors engineering** (**HFE**) components, teams should move into what the future looks like. Policies, a new framework, and fresh mindsets are all a great starting place, but leadership and the vision of an organization must align around those new strategies. Without a top-down or leadership-first attitude, teams may struggle not just to utilize those new processes and mindsets, but may not be encouraged to do so, either.

# Sustainability in change: leadership and vision

Leadership has a critical role in the implementation and success of a human-centered cybersecurity program. Embedding human factors into cybersecurity and technology initiatives is not a single task, but an ongoing commitment to reducing risk and supporting the humans that protect our organizations. Leaders must leverage deliberate reinforcement, provide a clear vision, and champion human-centered thinking as an operational advantage. When leaders demonstrate curiosity and innovative thinking using human factors in decisions, analysts and engineers can start to adopt that type of critical thinking. Human factors can be included in mission statements, onboarding and training, as well as operational procedures.

A dedicated human factors role is not an immediate priority; it may become a focus later as organizations begin to see the benefits of human-centered approaches in their cybersecurity programs. Most organizations can see the benefits by simply encouraging and leveraging human factors in their current teams, without requiring a full-time role to perform those duties. Leaders can recognize collaborative efforts, learning, and innovation to improve overall cybersecurity initiatives and reduce risk. Leaders can evangelize and share success stories of leveraging human factors principles in defensive roles. Discuss how human factors have prevented an incident, or even when design principles have reduced false positives and improved accuracy in results. Long-term success depends on leadership that views human factors as a discipline, one that will mature as quickly as technology.

# Summary

Cybersecurity is not simply about the technical controls, vulnerabilities, and risks that our organizations face; it is about the people: how they perceive risk, make decisions, and, ultimately, respond in highly complex situations. For far too long, our field has focused on the systems, applications, and dashboards that provide a picture of risk, instead of building better defenses around our human operators. This book has argued for a shift in that thinking, from control to collaboration, from compliance to understanding cognition.

Across each chapter, you see a familiar pattern: the limitations of our working memory, the importance of understanding human cognition, the cost of fatigue, and the power of trust. Each component of a human-centered cybersecurity program points toward a single truth: cybersecurity programs succeed when they account for how people actually operate, not just the tools they use and policies that are applied. Leveraging the human-centered security approach will take time; it cannot be accomplished by using a simple checklist. However, organizations that invest in usability, resiliency, and communication with the same rigor as they do in tooling and techniques will create adaptive and effective defense systems.

The future of cybersecurity belongs to the teams that can code, adapt, and, ultimately, understand and implement cognitive functions into their programs. It belongs to the leaders who see that every alert, notification, investigation, and tool is touched by human judgment and understanding. In the end, resilience is not about surviving a cyber threat; it is about designing systems, tools, and cultures that allow people to think clearly, act decisively, and recover stronger and faster. The future of cybersecurity is human.

## Get this book's PDF version and more

Scan the QR code (or go to `packtpub.com/unlock`). Search for this book by name, confirm the edition, and then follow the steps on the page.

UNLOCK NOW

*Note: Keep your invoice handy. Purchases made directly from Packt don't require an invoice.*

# 12

# Unlock Your Exclusive Benefits

Your copy of this book includes the following exclusive benefits:

**DRM-Free PDF Version**

Download DRM-free PDF and ePub copies of this book.

**7-Day Packt Library Access**

Get 7-day unlimited access to 8,000+ books and videos. No credit card required.

Available for first-time Packt+ trial users only.

**Next-Gen Reader Access**

Read this book on Packt Reader with progress sync, dark mode and note-taking.

Follow the guide below to unlock them. The process takes only a few minutes and needs to be completed once.

# Unlock this Book's Free Benefits in 3 Easy Steps

## Step 1

Keep your purchase invoice ready for *Step 3*. If you have a physical copy, scan it using your phone and save it as a PDF, JPG, or PNG.

For more help on finding your invoice, visit `https://www.packtpub.com/en-us/unlock?step=1`.

> Note
>
> **Note:** If you bought this book directly from Packt, no invoice is required. After *Step 2*, you can access your exclusive content right away.

## Step 2

Scan the QR code or go to `packtpub.com/unlock`.

On the page that opens (similar to *Figure 12.1* on desktop), search for this book by name and select the correct edition.

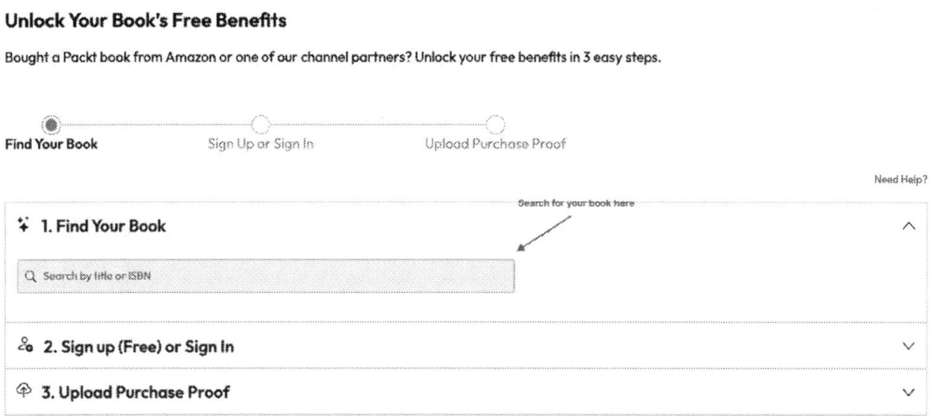


*Figure 12.1: Packt unlock landing page on desktop*

## Step 3

After selecting your book, sign in to your Packt account or create one for free. Then upload your invoice (PDF, PNG, or JPG, up to 10 MB). Follow the on-screen instructions to finish the process.

## Need Help

If you get stuck and need help, visit `https://www.packtpub.com/unlock-benefits/help` for a detailed FAQ on how to find your invoices and more. This QR code will take you to the help page.

> Note
>
> **Note**: If you are still facing issues, reach out to `customercare@packt.com`.

# Other Books You May Enjoy

If you enjoyed this book, you may be interested in these other books by Packt:

**Agentic AI for Offensive Cybersecurity**

Orhan Yildirim

ISBN: 9781806114474

- Understand agentic AI principles for offensive security
- Evaluate and select AI frameworks for security automation
- Build your first AI-driven recon workflow using n8n
- Automate attack surface discovery and port scanning with AI
- Design PCI segmentation testing workflows with n8n
- Build web app testing tools using MCP
- Automate exploitation, payload generation, and reporting
- Create threat intelligence agents that monitor CVE feeds

**The OSINT Handbook**

Dale Meredith

ISBN: 9781837638277

- Work with real-life examples of OSINT in action and discover best practices
- Automate OSINT collection and analysis
- Harness social media data for OSINT purposes
- Manage your digital footprint to reduce risk and maintain privacy
- Uncover and analyze hidden information within documents
- Implement an effective OSINT-driven threat intelligence program
- Leverage OSINT techniques to enhance organizational security

# Packt is searching for authors like you

If you're interested in becoming an author for Packt, please visit `authors.packtpub.com` and apply today. We have worked with thousands of developers and tech professionals, just like you, to help them share their insight with the global tech community. You can make a general application, apply for a specific hot topic that we are recruiting an author for, or submit your own idea.

# Share your thoughts

Now you've finished *Human Factors in Cybersecurity*, we'd love to hear your thoughts! Scan the QR code below to go straight to the Amazon review page for this book and share your feedback or leave a review on the site that you purchased it from.

*https://packt.link/r/1806118335*

Your review is important to us and the tech community and will help us make sure we're delivering excellent quality content.

# Index

# D



# E



# F

Made in United States
Orlando, FL
12 September 2026

87593305R00184